COMMENTARY

ON THE

HINDU SYSTEM OF MEDICINE.

COMMENTARY

ON THE

HINDU SYSTEM OF MEDICINE.

T.A. WISE, M. D.

GYAN

Published by

GYAN

Gyan Publishing House
5, Ansari Road
Daryaganj, New Delhi-110002
Phone: 011-47034999, 9811692060
E-mail: books@gyanbooks.com

Distribution Network
gyanbooks.com
India, USA, Canada, UK, Australia, France

ISBN : 978-81-212-9558-1 (PB)
First Published, 1845

2nd Impression 2023

Printed at: Gyan Press, Delhi.

COMMENTARY ON THE HINDU SYSTEM OF MEDICINE.

Author: T. A. WISE,

COMMENTARY

ON THE

HINDU SYSTEM OF MEDICINE.

BY

T. A. WISE, M. D.

MEMBER OF THE ROYAL COLLEGE OF SURGEONS, AND OF THE ROYAL MEDICAL AND CHIRURGICAL SOCIETY; CORRESPONDING MEMBER OF THE ZOOLOGICAL SOCIETY OF LONDON, AND OF THE PHILOMATIC SOCIETY OF PARIS.

BENGAL MEDICAL SERVICE.

1845.

CONTENTS.

BOOK III.

Therapeutics.

Page

BOOK IV.

Practice of Physic.

BOOK V.

Midwifery, and diseases of Women and Children.

PRELIMINARY REMARKS.

In every country individuals are to be found who occupy themselves in endeavours to discover the means of alleviating pain, and of curing diseases. In Europe especially, the different countries were so connected together as to enable the physician to profit by the discoveries of his neighbours, and the historian to trace the progress of the sciences among the various races of mankind from the Indus to the Atlantic, and from the time when medicine emerged from the obscurity of ancient fable to the present age. During this long period we know the individuals and the people who have added to our medical knowledge, and can prove that all these different systems have a common source; being originally derived from the family of Hippocrates. Those distinguished benefactors of mankind first explained the nature and treatment of diseases, and reduced to theory the various phenomena of the human body. The Grecian Philosophers were assisted by the Egyptian sages, who appear to have obtained much of their knowledge from some mysterious nation of the east. Egypt, after having had her institutions destroyed by the sword of the conqueror, became the seat of Grecian learning; which was afterwards transferred to the east, where under the fostering care of the Caliphs of Bagdad medicine was cultivated with diligence and success. It received still farther additions from the east; and thus improved it was conveyed by the Muhammadan conquerors into Spain. From thence it was communicated to other parts of Europe; where it has exercised the genius of many great men, with so much advantage to suffering humanity.

Among the sacred records of the Hindus there is a system of medicine, prepared at a very early period, that appears to form no part of the medical science, and is not supposed to have enlightened the other nations of the earth: a system for which the Hindus claim an antiquity far beyond the period to which the history of the heroic age is supposed to extend.

The following commentary is intended to describe the Hindu science of medicine. Insulated in their position, and residing in a rich and fruitful country, the Hindus appear to have been satisfied with the knowledge and power which they had acquired at a very early period, and affectionately attached to their own country, they retained for ages their own opinions and practices, amidst various revolutions. Their country was repeatedly overrun by the Muhammadans, who destroyed and persecuted them with the most relentless cruelty, without making any impression on their religious belief, or diminishing the respect and veneration which they bore to their sacred records. Freed for a time from their persecutors, their luxuriant country quickly resumed its former fruitfulness; and the intelligent and industrious inhabitants, under peaceful and sagacious princes, who promoted the happiness of their subjects rather than increased their own power by conquest, were soon restored to their former prosperity. The description of the medical profession by a people, so remarkable for the early period at which they reached an advanced state of power and learning, must be interesting, as it will enable us to trace the extent and modifications of civilization in a nation unconnected with any other, and instructive as pointing out the means by which such an advancement in the social state was accomplished.

In tracing the progress of Philosophy among such a people, it is necessary to observe, that human nature exhibits a general resemblance among all nations; while the absence of absolute identity, is accounted for by the influence of climate, habits, customs, and political state. Hence there exists a certain resemblance in the general speculations of different nations, which, however erroneous in many respects, must be acknowledged to have some foundation as regards the facts upon which they are based. This will be pointed out in the following work, and will be of use as defining, with more exactness, particular opinions. Doubtful facts in medicine may thus be illustrated and established, and distant analogies between tenets detected, which will corroborate the testimony of history, and lead us to compare those first principles, upon which systems are founded. With this intention I propose, in the following work, to follow the classification pursued by the Hindus, in some of their minor particulars, and shall add as much of their reasoning on facts, as will enable the reader to understand their system; but, in order that the value of these ancient records may be better appreciated, I have reduced the medical knowledge of the ancient Hindus to what I suppose to be, the order best adapted for exhibiting its real value.

In a second part, it is my intention to trace the decline of the medical profession in India, and the best means of removing the state of ignorance, which now prevails over the whole of Hindustán.

This work has grown upon me imperceptibly. Interested in the History of the medical science, for a number of years I had employed my leisure in noting the development of systems in different schools and nations, and was induced at an early period of my residence in Bengal, to examine the Hindu medical Shástras. I translated and compared what I considered the most valuable parts of different manuscripts, when I found that my materials had accumulated so much, that they were too bulky for my original purpose; it then occurred to me that the following commentary might be worthy of being published separately, as containing interesting information, which had not hitherto been placed before the public. An accomplished scholar had indeed given an interesting account of Hindu opinions regarding certain diseases;* a persevering traveller had afforded a sketch of certain opinions contained in the Hindu medical Shástras, as translated into the Tibetan language;† an antiquarian, and a distinguished physician had given some of their peculiar opinions, as found in the medical works of the south of India;‡ and an able lecturer had combined all this information with im-

* Professor Wilson, Tran. Med. and Phy. Society Calcutta, vol. 1, Oriental Magazine for March, 1823.

† Mr. A. Soma de Köros, Journal Asiatic Society, Calcutta; No. 37, January, 1835.

‡ Dr. Heyne's Tracts on India, and Ainslie's Materia Medica Indica, Lond.—Ed.

portant additions of his own ;* but a comprehensive view of their system of medicine, which it is the intention of the present work to supply, is still wanting to complete our information on the subject.

While other branches of Hindu philosophy have been made the frequent subject of discussion, and much that is curious and important has been discovered by European philosophers, it is remarkable into what neglect the medical Shástras have fallen ; from the contempt with which the conquerors of Hindustán regarded the scientific knowledge of the Hindus. This explains, why their system of medicine was despised, and their works neglected, and forgotten. When the English student directed his attention to the Sanskrit language, he seldom extended his examination to the medical Shástras, with which the bráhmans were rarely conversant; and when he did study the subject, it was in a cursory manner, and he in general was incompetent to judge of the real value of such professional works. Under such circumstances Sir William Jones asserts, "that there is no evidence that in any language of Asia there exists one original treatise on medicine considered as science." "Even Medicine and Surgery," says Mill, "to the cultivation of which so obvious and powerful an interest invites, have scarcely, beyond the degree of most uncultivated tribes, attracted the rude understandings of the Hindus."

The following Commentary on the most ancient records of the Hindu medicine will sufficiently refute such opinions ; and will at the same time prove, that these works contain much that is interesting and instructive.

Another cause, which produced the neglect of the Hindu Medical Science on the part of the Muhammadan conquerors of Hindustán, is that they were so prepossessed in favor of their own system of medicine, as to have little respect for that of a vanquished people. More lately, the diffusion of the European system of medicine operated as a discouragement to the study of the Sanskrit works ; and the prejudice against the national system grew stronger, as the ancient Medical Works became more inaccessible from their rarity, and imperfect copies were substituted, as the ignorance of

* Royle on the antiquity of Hindu medicine, 1838.

the people increased. The expense of drugs was also considerable, and the difficulty of procuring them genuine became greater, as they were less sought after and appreciated, which led to the introduction of inferior substitutes. Thus confidence in these medical prescriptions diminished still more; and the consequence of such neglect was, to increase the prejudice against the ancient science even among the Hindus, and to lead to the substitution of superstition and quackery. The system of Bhutaredya, which included the offering up of certain prayers and incantations, was introduced; as well as the worshipping of village gods, for the cure of diseases, as proper medical assistance became more difficult, to meet the pressing wants of the people. The native practice of medicine may now be said to be in this lamentable state of depression over all Hindustán; but, it was far otherwise, as cultivated by the ancient Hindus. A very few practitioners may still be found in the neighbourhood of cities, in the service of rich individuals in whose families the ancient treatises of their forefathers are studied, and transmitted from generation to generation. I have had the happiness of knowing such a family of hereditary physicians, rich, independent, and much respected.* Among such, the ancient Medical Works are so highly valued; that the influence of station, rank, and money, will often be ineffectually exerted in procuring these manuscripts. In some cases, it is even difficult to obtain permission to copy such works, at the owner's house; from a belief that all the good to be derived from their possession, which God had bestowed on the individual and his family, would vanish on the work being sold, or even the precepts communicated to unauthorized individuals.

The climate, and the materials of which these ancient Works are composed, render them very liable to be destroyed. Some are already lost, and the difficulty of procuring correct copies of the remainder, is yearly increasing. Under these circumstances, it is believed that the following Commentary will be considered interesting, as embody-

* After some enquiry I find there are not more than four or five persons, in this part of India, who are acquainted with the Hindu Medical Shástras.

ing all that is considered worthy of preservation in the ancient Hindu medical writings. These treatises appear to have been prepared at a very early date. In order to investigate this very important fact, it will be necessary to make a few remarks on the history, literature, chronology, and sciences of the Hindus; which are all so combined with each other, and interwoven with their theology, as to require elucidation, before the originality of their medical system can be proved, some of their theoritical notions understood, and the probable age determined, in which the medical writings were prepared.

1*st. History.* That portion of the Caucasian race of mankind, which inhabited the fertile plains south of the lofty range of mountains extending eastward from the Caspian Sea, and forming the northern boundary of modern Hindustán, was probably the original stock of the Hindu nation;—a nation which from the most ancient testimony, as well as from the character of its social institutions, is considered to have been coeval with the first formation of men into social communities. These early inhabitants of the world increased so rapidly in number and power, that at the æra of the building of Babel, they are described as "journeying from the East;" and, as resolving, on their arrival in the land of Shinar, to build "a city and tower, whose top may reach into heaven." From them, and from his great progenitor, Shem, Abraham probably obtained all the learning then known.

It was the knowledge acquired by the privileged class of bráhmans, and the habits of industry of the other classes, joined to their skill in adding to the comforts and elegancies of life, that explained the power and riches of these eastern nations at that remote period, and which caused them to be regarded as proverbially possessed of the "wisdom of the East," (1 Kings ch. iv., v. 30.) Little, however, was known of the Hindu nation previous to the conquest of Alexander. That great monarch carried his arms beyond the Indus; and one of his successors, Seleucus Nicator, advanced as far as the Ganges. It is interesting to note the language of the historian of the Macedonian hero. After his victory over Porus, Alexander, in his harangue to his troops, assures them, "that they were now going to enter those famous countries so abundant in riches, that even what they had found and seen in Persia would appear as nothing in comparison to them." (Quintus Curtius, lib. x., ch. 1.) Herodotus, Diodorus, and Arrian, describe the strength of the Hindu armies, the number of their war-chariots, the excellence of their arms and appointments, and the strength of their fortresses; and Strabo and Plutarch agree with them in asserting the high state of civilization to which India had then attained; and that it was full of large and rich cities, had roads with mile-stones, and inns for the accommodation of travellers, and carried on a considerable trade with their neighbours.

A people, who had distinguished themselves at such an early age, by their power and riches, as well as by their successful cultivation of the sciences, may be supposed to have studied with much care the means of succouring the wounded and maimed, of alleviating pain, and curing diseases. The Hindu history of medicine proves this to have been the case; for one of the fourteen *ratnas,* or precious objects, which their gods are believed to have produced by churning the ocean, was a learned physician. This proves of what importance they considered the healing art, and accords with the opinion of the best informed of the ancients. Arrian informs us, that, in the expedition of Alexander to India, "the Grecian physicians found no remedy against the bites of snakes; but the Indians cured those who happened to fall under that misfortune." "For this reason," Nearchus tells us, "Alexander, having all the most skilful Indians about his person, caused proclamation to be made throughout the camp, that whoever might be bitten by one of these snakes should forthwith repair to the royal pavilion to be cured. These physicians are also said to have made other cures; but, as the inhabitants have a very temperate climate, they are not subject to many varieties of disease. However, if any among them feel themselves much indisposed, they apply to their Sophists (bráhmans), who, by wonderful, and even more than human means, cure whatever will admit of it."*

2*d*. *Literature*. The Sanskrit language, so majestic, so richly reflected, and so ancient, is still viewed as the na-

* Arrian's Indian History, Edited by Mr. Brooke, Lond. 1729, vol. ii. ch. 15, p. 232.

tional language, not only from its being that in which the oldest works in Indian literature are composed, but also as it was at one time the language of a considerable part of India, especially of those regions near the Ganges, as the Province of Bahar, in which were laid the scenes of many of the most ancient Indian poems.

The early period at which Sanskrit was cultivated, and the success with which the study was attended, prove the great capacity of those who made it the object of pursuit. In some cases, it seems to have been blended with other languages, and in others it probably absorbed the dialects of the aborigines. Its analogy to the languages with which scholars are familiar, and its connection with the local religion, arts, and sciences, like those of Greece and Rome, render tbe study exceedingly interesting, and excite a desire to become acquainted with its literary remains, containing as they do memorials of an ancient theology, of poetry, science, and philosophy, which have exerted an influence over the most distinguished nations of antiquity, and to which even Europe is indebted for the rudiments of her learning.

3d. Chronology. The Hindus divide their Chronology into four ages (yugs). The three first were probably fanciful. During each of these ages, mankind was supposed to have lost a part equal to one fourth of truth and moral rectitude, until the last, or wicked age (kali yug), in which man becomes wholly depraved and sinful. It is probable that the second age (dwapar yug), is the renovated world, described by Moses, in which we find a chaos, or the wreck of a former world, upon the surface of which moved the Spirit of God. The *Swáyambhara*, Adimo, or Adom, was the man-woman of the Hindus; who was separated into a male and female, like our first parents, and became the first progenitors of mankind. By both accounts, the life of man extended to one thousand years ;* and the days of their gods were as a thousand years of mortals, to which St. Peter seems afterwards to allude.†

The Hindus pretend that the present age, or kali yug, began in the year B. C. 3101 ; or with the entrance of the sun into the sign *Áswin*, the first of the 27 *Nakshatras*, or man-

* Methusalem died at the age of nine hundred and sixty-nine years.

† See his Second General Epistle, ch. iii. v. 8.

sions of the fixed lunar zodiac. This is now considered to be merely an assumed era. According to Menu, Noah lived in the third or in the beginning of the fourth yuga, when the age of man was fixed at one hundred years. The long interval that intervened before oral traditions were recorded in written characters, and the advancement which such a step proved, accounts for the pride which marked these first efforts of genius; and the superiority which such a knowledge indicates, explains the authority which the Bráhmans usurped. As these sages were occupied in the investigation of the operations of nature, they soon acquired great authority from their being likewise employed in the service of the divinity, to whom they were regarded as allied in friendship, and from whom they were supposed to have derived their accurate knowledge. This is said to be so extensive that their geometry, arithmetic, and astronomy, "surpassed that of Ptolemy; their music that of Phythagoras; their mechanics that of Archimedes; their theology that of Plato; and their logic that of Aristotle." In proof of the early and high civilization of the Indians, Colonel Call, chief engineer at Madras, states as follows: "It may safely be pronounced that no part of the world has more marks of antiquity for arts, sciences, and civilization, than the peninsula of India, from the Ganges to Cape Comorin. I think the carvings on some of the Pagodas and Choultries, as well as the grandeur of the work, exceeds any thing executed now-a-days, not only for the delicacy of the chisel, but the expense of construction, considering, in many instances, to what distances the component parts were carried, and to what heights raised."*

Nor do the Hindus appear to have derived their knowledge from any of their neighbours. The Greeks were the only people from whom they could have borrowed their information; but, besides the distance, and the absence of frequent communication between the two countries, the Hindus were naturally so averse to travelling, and so little desirous of intercourse with foreigners, their having borrowed their literature seems to stand on an exceedingly slender basis.

4*th. Sciences.*—The knowledge the Hindus possessed of medicine, as well as of the other sciences, may, therefore,

* Philosophical Transactions, vol. lxii. p. 354.

be considered as forming a criterion by which we may judge of their pretensions to originality. The date of their astronomical tables cannot now be determined, but their accuracy is unquestionable. According to their astronomy the Zodiac was divided into twenty-seven constellations; the ecliptic into signs, degrees, and minutes; the planes of the sun and moon, the length of the solar year, the accelerated motion of the moon, the inequality of the precession of the equinoxes, &c. was probably obtained by the Europeans from the Hindus, and formed the foundation of the astronomical knowledge, which was improved and extended by the genius of the west.

The Hindu notions of Philosophy are likewise original, and as they explain some of their opinions regarding the physiology of the body, or microcosm, I shall add a few remarks on this curious subject. According to the Hindu philosophers space was first created by *Brahma*,* in which the five elements of the material world (ether, air, fire, water, and earth),† were confusedly mingled together. He separated them, and assigned to each its proper place, for the performance of its office. He first separated the subtile ether, which has the quality of conveying sound, from which was derived the pure and potent air, a vehicle of scents, and endowed it with the quality of touch and sound; from ether proceeded light or fire, making objects visible, dispelling gloom, and had the qualities of figure, touch, and sound. From light proceeded water, with the quality of touch, sound, colour, and taste; and from water was deposited earth, with the qualities of touch, sound, colour, taste, and smell. In each of the elements of organs was contained more or less of the qualities of happiness, action, and inertness. From *satwa-gun*, the first quality in space, arose the power of hearing, in which organ is contained much of the element of pure ether, and in this manner the perception of sound is conveyed to the soul by means of the mind; air, in like man-

* *Brahma* (ব্রহ্ম), the Great God; *Paramátmá* (পরমাত্মা), the Supreme Being; *Pradhána* (প্রধান), Nature; *I'shwara* (ঈশ্বর), the Supreme Ruler of the Universe.

† See page 30.

ner, conveys the sense of touch or feeling through the skin; fire, sight through the eye; water, taste through the tongue; and earth, smelling through the nose to the soul. The whole of these five elements, and their functions, give birth to the power of thought and decision. From the second, or active quality (*Raja-gun*) in space, arose speech; from the same quality in air, arose the power of the hands; in light, that of the feet; in water, that of generation; and, in matter, that of expulsion. The five senses, the five organs of action, the heart, which comprises sense and action with mind, are animated by the soul from the embryo state.

The soul desires knowledge, and, through the channel of the mind, acts on vision, and produces the perception of visible objects; through the ear, the perception of sound; through the skin, touch, &c. It invigorates the five active members, the five perceptive members, five elements, &c. It is pure, beholds everything as an indifferent spectator, while united with matter; in the same way as the eye is affected by light, the pot of water by the fire, iron by the magnet, fire by fuel, the shadow by the substance, the arrow by the string of the bow, so does the Divine particle act through the material organic world.

The soul, when it exists in the body, has the qualities of piety, morality, and justice,—of happiness and misery,—of continence and lust,—of anger, folly, arrogance, avarice, and ignorance,—of energy, breathing, dejections, will, and understanding,—of mental judgment, memory, knowledge, effort, and sensibility.

The combination of the soul and body gives rise to the different dispositions of persons, which are derived from *Prikriti*, or Nature.

1st. A happy disposition (*Satwa-gun*)* is said to be derived from *Vishnu*.† If, in excess, it affords light, and produces knowledge and happiness, the person avoids bad, and strives to perform good actions; he has patience; is a lover of truth, holiness, faith, knowledge, and understanding; has no bad desire; possesses a good memory; is charitable, just, firm,

* From *Satwa*, good, and *gun*, a quality.

† From *Vish*, to overspread.

and is devoid of anger; is contented, and without avarice: hence, when "*gyáni*" (from *gyán*, wisdom) appears at all the gates of the body, it indicates that *Satwa-gun* predominates within. When such a person dies, his soul is conveyed to the regions of those immaculate beings who are acquainted with the Most High. He becomes a Deva.

2d. An active disposition (*Raja-gun*)* proceeds from *Brahma*, and signifies desire, the love of gain, industry, and commencement of works: and produces unhappiness when in excess. Such a person is miserable, inquiet, unforgiving, and pervaricating. He has no mercy; is haughty, proud, lascivious, intemperate, passionate, changeable, and covetous. When a person with such a disposition dies, his soul re-animates another body of a different and inferior nature.

3d. When an inert or wicked disposition (*Tama-gun*)† is in excess, it proceeds from *Siva;* and is indicated by a want of energy and love of retirement, secrecy, and distraction of thought; he neither believes in God nor in another state of existence; he is a great sinner; is without understanding or knowledge, so as to be unable to take care of his wealth; and is sensual, slothful, procrastinating, and stupid. When such a person dies, his soul is conceived again in the womb of irrational animals.

Each of these dispositions confine the incorruptible spirit of the body. The *Satwa-gun*, being pure, clear, and free from defects, inspires the soul with sweet and pleasant consequences—the fruit of wisdom. The *Raja-gun* is of a passive nature, arising from the effects of worldly desire, and imprisons the soul with the sense of sloth, intoxication, and the feelings produced by action. The *Tama-gun*, being the offspring of ignorance, is the confounder of all the faculties of the mind. As one or other of these qualities predominates so will the character of the individual be formed.

The harmonious action of the five elements and their qualities constitutes health; and the increase or diminution of one or more of the humors, formed from the elements, produces disease. To reduce these humors when superabundant, and increase them when wanting, were the principles upon which

* From *Raja*, to desire, and *gun*, quality.

† From *Tama*, darkness, and *gun*, quality.

their system of cure was based. To accomplish these objects a strict regimen was enforced, and certain articles of food and particular medicines were prescribed to increase or diminish these elements according as they were supposed to have deviated from the healthy proportion.*

Another peculiarity of the Hindu belief is the supposed separation of the human race into four classes in order that they might be multiplied. Each of these classes has different qualities, distinctions, and occupations.

1st Class.—The Bráhmans, the emblems of wisdom, proceeded from Brahma's mouth; and their occupation is to pray, to read, and to instruct.

2nd Class.—The Khetriya, the emblem of strength, came from his arms; and they are destined to hold the land, to defend, and to govern.

3rd Class.—The Baishya (or epitome of nourishment) are sprung from Brahma's navel; and their province is to cultivate the land, to traffic; and, by these means to provide man, in the social state, with the necessaries of life.

4th Class.—The Sudra, the emblem of subjection, proceeded from Brahma's feet; and are intended to labour, to serve, to travel, &c.

As the Bráhmans were allowed to marry into the other classes, there were, at an early period, other distinctions to be made. The offspring of the Bráhman with the daughter of a Baishya, was called Ambasta, or, more commonly, Baidya; and it is stated in Menu, that their profession is Medicine.

The early age at which this division of the Hindu nation into castes took place, each of which was devoted to a particular branch of the useful or ornamental arts, rapidly accelerated the advancement of knowledge. It enabled this people to accumulate the experience of generations, and to acquire a

* "There is a class of physicians," according to Megasthenes, "among the Germanes (Bráhmans) who rely most on diet and regimen, and next on external applications, having a great distrust of the effects of more powerful modes of treatment. They are also said at that early period (about A. D. 300) to have employed charms in aid of their medicines." (Strabo, lib. xv.)

degree of expertness, and to develope an extent of ingenuity, that, even in the present advanced state of the arts in Europe, has scarcely been equalled. The distinctions of sects likewise enabled the nation to set apart the most distinguished class, in order that they might devote themselves to the acquisition of knowledge; and the Bráhmans thus became, like the Druids and Monks of Europe, at a much later period, the great improvers, and, by their skill and enterprise, taught the nation how much happiness and comfort might be extracted from the rich resources of nature. The knowledge of a remedy to assuage pain, or of a principle in the prevention or cure of a disease, was too important a discovery not to be recorded; and the physicians were so sensible of the vast importance of such knowledge, as to seek not only to retain them in their families but likewise to test their accuracy, and to modify and extend them according to their own experience.

The difficulties of the subject, and the importance of health, while these induced the Hindu sages to accumulate observations, must have proved to them the weakness of their unassisted faculties, and their ignorance of the operations of nature, which led them to call in the assistance of their gods either as practitioners, or as counsellors.*

The following are the names of Hindu gods, who were supposed to possess a knowledge of the medical profession.

Brahma, the creator, or creative principle.
Siva, the destroyer, or destroying principle.
Indra, the king of heaven.
Surya, the god of the sun.
Dhanwantari, the great physician, king of Benares.
Ashwinikumaras, the twin physicians of the gods.
Daka, the *Prajápati*.

Rishis—*Obree*.
,, *Baradása*.
,, *Parásara*.

* "This was more natural from their believing that sickness was a proof of guilt of the person in the present or in a former state of existence; so that even in the time of Alexander it was considered disgraceful for the holy sophists (bráhmans) to be sick; and they put an end to themselves when they fell into that calamity." (Strabo, lib. xv.)

No goddess of medicine is represented as having flourished until at a late period, when the small-pox made its appearance and committed great ravages in Hindustán.

Particular gods are supposed to superintend different parts of the body, and it is to them that prayers are offered up before operations are performed or medicines exhibited. The following are the chief of their gods:

Ungi, fire,	superintends the	tongue.
Báyu, air, ...	"	life.
Indra, firmament,....	"	strength.
Baruna, water, ...	"	understanding.
Surya, sun, ...	"	sight.
Chandra, moon, ...	"	understanding
Vishnu, preserver,....	"	courage.
Brahma, creator, ...	"	soul.
Samudra, ocean, ...	"	navel.
Dhruba, stars, ...	"	eyebrows.

These are the chief, although all the gods have particular duties assigned to them to answer particular ends, and are accordingly propitiated in their several characters.

These deities were supposed, at different periods, to have taken compassion on the sufferings of their weak and erring creatures on earth, and communicated to a few favored mortals, the means of preventing and curing diseases. The following are the principal medical works that were thus imparted to the Hindus:

1. The *Áyur Veda* is the most ancient system of medicine, and is of the highest authority. The age in which it was written is not known, and fragments only of the MS. are now procurable. From the terseness of the descriptions, there is said to have been considerable difficulty in understanding it, and many commentaries were written on the subject, and it is to them alone we have to refer. In the first part of the following work I have given an account of this curious *Veda*, which is said to have been prepared by *Brahma* in the *Satya Yug*.

2. The second work, called *Áyugranta*, is said to have been written by *Siva* in the *Tretá Yuga*. Part of this work is said to be recorded in some of the *Tantras*.

3. The nature of medicines and diseases is treated of in

some of the *Puránas,* particularly in the *Ugní Purán.* These works were prepared by *Deities* and *Rishis,* and some of them are still procurable.

4. We find the names of the following authors in the *Mahábhárata;** they are said to have flourished under *Yudhisthira,* in the beginning of the *Kali Yuga.*

Author's Name.	Name of the Work.	
	Found.	Supposed to be irrecoverable.
Atrya	Atri Sangitá	
Ugni Besa, Charaka	Charaka	
Bhíla		Bhila Tantra.
Jatukarna		Jutukarna Tantra.
Parásara		Parásara Sangitá.
Hárita	Hárita Sangitá	
Kárparí		Kárparí Tantra.
Dhanwantari, Sushruta	Sushruta	

These works are supposed to have been prepared by different *Munis,* on the plan in a great measure of the original *Áyur Veda.* The anatomical part appears to have been prepared from actual dissection. The following is a list of the principal medical works which are now found in Hindustán, after the great works of *Charaka* and *Sushruta.* They are arranged in the probable order in which they were prepared:—

Aupadhanaha, a system of Surgery.
Aurabhra, Do.
Bhila Tantra, a system of Medicine.
Jatukarna Sangitá, Do.
Parásara, Do.
Hárita, Do.
Bhágavata, Do.
Bháva-prakása, Do.
Todrananda, Do.
Chakradatta, Do.
Pracharrarantabali, Do.
Sarangadhara, Do.

* *Written, according to Bently, A. D.* 600?

Rájanirghanta, a system of Materia Medica.
Chakradatta, Do.
Drabyaguna, a commentary on the last work.
Mádhaba Nidána, a system of Nosology.
Bangaja Ratnábali, a system of Pharmacy.
Rasa Ratnákar, treats of metallic preparations.
Rasendrachintámani, Do.
Rasendrakalpadruma, Do.
Madhumati, a system of Medicine.*

The names of Dhanwantari, who is also called the King of Benares (Kásí Rájá) or Debadása, is found stated with those of Charaka and Sushruta in poems written in the time of Nala Rájá. These poems are allowed, from internal evidences, to be of great antiquity. In Charaka the names of the *Munís*† appear to have flourished before mythology was introduced into the Hindu system of religion; as these names have no connection with the names of their gods, who were afterwards most probably introduced by degrees, as the various objects and operations of nature were deified and named by their votaries. Professor Wilson supposed‡ "that from the Charaka and Sushruta being mentioned in the Puránas, the ninth or tenth century is the most modern limit of our conjecture; while the style of the authors, as well as their having become the heroes of fable, indicate a long anterior date. One commentary on the text of Sushruta, made by Ubhalta, a Cashmerian, is probably as old as the twelfth or thirteenth century, and his comment, it is known, was preceded by others." Dr. Royle, in his "Essay on the Antiquity of Indian Medical Science," has cited passages from the Latin translations of Avicenna, Rhazes, and Serapion, in which the Charaka is mentioned. Professor Wilson is of opinion, that the Arabians of the eighth century cultivated the Hindu Works on Medicine before those of the Greeks; and that the Charaka, the Sushruta, and the treatise called Nidána, &c., were translated and studied by the Arabians in the days of Harun and Mansur (A. D. 773), either from the

* See also Sir Whitelaw Ainslie's Materia Indica, vol. ii. p. 491.

† See Note on Mill's History of India, vol. ii. p. 232.

‡ See Sir W. Jones' preface; and Mountstuart Elphinstone's History of India, vol. i. p. 427 *et seq.*

originals, or more probably from translations made at a still earlier period into the language of Persia.*

Others suppose that the Vedas were compiled in the fourteenth century before Christ† (see Asiatic Researches, vol. viii. p. 489), and the *Áyar Veda* supplement added probably some centuries afterwards, about the time of Menu's code of laws (B. C. 900 ?).

This remarkable code appears to have been written at a time when the prejudices of caste, &c. did not exist; and when looking at the Sun or stroking a cow were sufficient to purify a person who had touched a human bone.

As the result of the above remarks it appears that at a very early age the Hindus had made much greater advances in civilization, and the arts and sciences than any other ancient people; and while the nations of the west have been slowly advancing in civilization during the last two thousand years, the Hindus, by the depressing influence of foreign subjugation, are at present in a lower social condition than they appear to have been in, three centuries before the Christian era. It was most probably at this early period that they studied the healing art with such success as to enable them to produce systematic works on medicine, derived from that source of knowledge which the prejudice of mankind is so much opposed to. Sushruta informs us that a learned physician must combine a knowledge of books, or theoretical knowledge with dissection of the human body, and practice. This explains why the ancient system of Hindu medicine was so complete in all its parts, and so permanent in its influence and warrants the inference that several centuries were required to form it.‡

In comparing these Medical Works, and compiling the

* See the Remarks by Professor Wilson on the Indian Physicians at the Court of Bagdad; by Rev. W. Cureton.—*Journal of the R. A. Society*, vol. vi. p. 105.

† Mr. Colebrooke arrived at this conclusion from a passage from the *Jyotish* of one of the *Vedas*, when the northern Solstitial point is reckoned to be in the middle of *Aslesha* and the southern at the beginning of *Sravishtha*, or *Dhanishtha*; and then declares what he had elsewhere shown that "such was the situation of those cardinal points in the Fourteenth Century before the Christian era."

‡ See Professor Wilson's Note on Mill's History of India, vol. ii. p. 232.

following Commentaries, I have rejected some portions as worthless, while I retained all such parts as appeared peculiar in theory, or important in practice. I have sometimes been obliged to restore passages altered by the carelessness or ignorance of compilers, or of commentators. It is probable other portions might have been omitted or enlarged with advantage; I believe, however, it will be found, that I have erred more frequently in the latter than in the former particular. For arriving at the true meaning of words and expressions, I have had the assistance of able Pandits, of these I must particularly mention the assistance I have derived from Abhaycharan Tarkapanchánan, now superintendent of the Bengálí department of the College of Muhammad Mohsem, Hoogly, and of Madhusudan Gupta, Lecturer of Anatomy to the Medical College, Calcutta, whose accurate knowledge of the medical shástras is combined with an extensive knowledge of the sciences of Europe.

To the general reader I beg leave to state, that I have embodied what I conceived to be important and curious in these most ancient records of medicine; and I trust that the publication will be of use in removing that blind reverence which an imperfect knowledge of the Medical Shástras is so liable to engender among the Native physicians, and which has operated most perniciously in retarding the advancement of knowledge; while at the same time it will assist in giving the proper degree of credit to the ancient Hindu philosophers. An examination of their works will convey an idea of the extent and accuracy of the knowledge of the ancient Hindus, and will enable the physician to compare it with that of Europe, amongst its ancient inhabitants, as well as the moderns. As utility is the principal object of this compilation, I have added such remarks, as appeared to me important in illustrating the history of certain diseases, such as syphilis, small-pox, &c.

The orthography and pronunciation of the Sanskrit proper names will be sufficiently correct if attention be paid to the following rules:—

1st. The consonants to be pronounced as in English,

2nd. The vowels as in the Italian language. The long vowels will be distinguished by the following marks:

á is to be sounded like a in papa.
a ... ay in say.
í ... ee in see.
o ... o in so.
u ... oo in too.

I regret to find many errors in the orthography of names, and in one or two places the opinions of the Moderns have been stated with those of the Ancients. These errors would not have occurred had I not been obliged, on account of ill health, to leave India; and had I not on my return to this country, been stationed at a distance from Calcutta, as the work passed through the press. I feel most grateful to those friends who kindly, and ably, assisted me in the emergency.

Dacca, 20th September, 1845.

A COMMENTARY ON THE HINDU SYSTEM OF MEDICINE.

—o—

BOOK I.

THIS BOOK WILL BE DEVOTED TO THE CONSIDERATION OF THE ORIGIN AND HISTORY OF MEDICINE; OF THE RANK OF PRACTITIONERS AND DUTIES OF TEACHERS; OF THE CHARACTER AND DUTIES OF PUPILS; OF THE DUTIES OF THE PHYSICIAN, ATTENDANTS, AND PATIENT; AND OF THE RECOMPENCE OF PRACTITIONERS.

CHAPTER I.

Origin and History of Medicine.

IN the sacred works of the Hindus it is recorded that the four immortal Védas *, named Rig, Yajur, Sáma, and Atharva were received from Bramhá, one having been produced from each of his four mouths. These works were the original code of divine legislation, and contained all the knowledge required by mankind during the Satya Yuga †, or the first age, during which man remained prosperous, virtuous, happy, and free from disease.

In the second age, or Treta Yuga, a third of mankind were reprobate; and disease appeared, life was curtailed, and memory impaired.

* From *ved*, to know. Besides the four Vedas, the Hindús have other sacred records; as the Shastres, or commentaries upon the Vedas, now the great rule of faith. Eighteen of the most celebrated Puranas were written by Vyása, the "compiler," an inspired Brahman, one of the seven immortal beings of the regal race of Púrú. He was aided by other celebrated Pandits such as Paila, Vaisam Payana, Jaymini, and Súmantú. Besides these, the Hindús have numerous other commentators of their sacred works.

† From *Satya*, truth and *Yuga*, age.

In the third age, or Dwâpara Yuga, half of the human race were depraved ; and during the Káli Yuga, the present age, the corruption of mankind was such as to cause a still farther curtailment of life, and embittered it by numerous diseases.

Bramha, however, had such compassion on man's weakness and suffering, that, he produced a second class of sacred books called Upavédas*, one of which named Ayur-veda, which was intended to teach the proper manner of living in this world, by preventing and curing diseases in the present state ; and while the individual thus enjoyed health he may perform the various purposes of this world, and thereby ensure his happiness and prosperity in another state.

Other Shastres say that this Ayur-veda was obtained from Siva. It is the sacred medical record of the Hindus ; and is of the highest antiquity, and authority. This work is said to have consisted of one thousand sections, of a hundred stanzas each, or a lack of verses (slokas). Bramha, pitying the weakness and suffering of mankind, and the impossibility of their learning so large a work, abridged it, and divided it into eight parts (tantra). Little of the original work has escaped the destructive ravages of time. Fragments only have been preserved, in the works of commentators ; but, as all their information on the science was derived from what was considered the full and true account of every branch of the healing art, we are enabled, through their works, to judge of the arrangement of the great original : these divisions are as follows :—

1*st.*—*Salya*, Surgery, included the mode of removing external substances accidently introduced into the body, as grass, wood, stones, iron, earth, bones, hair, and nails. Pus, which has not been evacuated, and also the means of removing the dead child from its mother ; of healing wounds inflicted by sharp instruments, as knives ; of applying bandages, and using surgical instruments, in the different operations ; of applying escharotics and fire ; and of the treatment of different kinds of inflammation, abscesses, and other surgical diseases.

2*nd.*—*Sálákya*, includes the description and the treatment of external and organic diseases of the eyes, ears, mouth, nose, and other diseases which are situated above the clavicles.

These two divisions constitute the surgical diseases of modern schools.

* Joined to, or appended to. A kind of supplementary Vida, said to be derived immediately from the Vedas. There are four of these, the first is called Ayur-veda ; *Ayus*, signifying the period of living; and *ved*, to know.

3rd.—*Káyachikitsá.* That is describes the diseases which affect the whole body; as fevers, dysentery (otesára), hematemisis (raktapeta), consumption (soshá), mania (unmada), epilesy (apasnara), Leprosy (kusta), diabetes, (bamutra), gonorrhæa (maha), and other diseases of the same kind.

This may be considered as constituting the practice of Physic.

4th.—*Bhutavidya,* or the means of restoring the deranged faculties of the mind, supposed to be produced by demoniacal possessions; as by the anger of the God's (*Devtas*), devils (*asurs*), or another kind of devils (*gandarba*), demigods or devils (*Jaksha*), giants resembling devils (*rakshas*), spirits of dead men (*petrigriha*), and other kinds of devils (*pihochas*).

These various demigods, when enraged, were supposed to enter into the person, and produce the various diseases of the mind; which could only be removed by prayers, medicines, ablutions, and offerings to the offended deity.

5th.—*Kaumárabhritya,* comprised the treatment of Infants, the effects of bad milk and improper diet; the nature of infant diseases, including those produced by the displeasure of certain demigods (*Graha*) *. In this division also was included the treatment of wet-nurses when their milk was bad.

6th.—*Agadatantra.* In this division the administration of antidotes for poisons was considered; as for preventing the effects and diseases produced by mineral, vegetable, and animal poisons; as the bites of dangerous serpents, insects, &c.

7th.—*Rasáyanatantra* treated of those medicines which cure diseases in general, and restore youth, beauty, and happiness. This division embraced chemistry, or more properly alchemy; as the chief end of the chemical combinations described in it are mostly metallurgic, and the intention was to discover the universal medicine, the panacea that would render health permanent and life perpetual. Such a medicine was supposed to preserve the energies of youth, strengthen memory, lengthen life, and prevent as well as cure diseases.

8th.—*Vájîkarana-tantra.* This division made known the best means of increasing the human race, by pointing out the mode by which tone was given to the weakened organs of generation, when the sensibility of these parts became diminished or deranged.

These remarks, on the division of this most ancient work, as given

* Many of the diseases of children are still supposed to be produced by the entrance of devils, into the child's body; which are expelled by particular prayers offered up to *Panchanana* (Siva.)

in Susruta, &c., are the only parts which have come down to us. They afford the most incontestable evidence of the Hindú Medical writings having been the result of observation and experience; although the authors assigned a divine origin to them, in order to increase the respect paid to the books, and to themselves. They thus seem to have arranged the diseases according to the frequency of the assistance required from the art, and in the order in which the knowledge of medicine naturally advanced.

The sacred *Ayur Veda* contained also a description of the structure of the human body obtained from dissection; an account of the causes and diseases to which it is subject, reduced to a systematic form; the enumeration of many useful remedies; and the precepts for preserving health, and curing diseases.

In some of the shastres (Charaka, Susruta) it is stated that Bramha first instructed *Dakhsa* the *Prajapatí*, the father of *Durga*, in the *Ayur Veda*, as he was an ocean of wisdom. He wrote a book named the *Chikitsa-Darshana*, and by him it was communi cated to the two *Ashwins*, or offspring of the Sun (Surja). Others say that Bramha gave the *Ayur Veda* to *Surja*, who like the Phœbus of the Greeks, was supposed to be the fountain of medical knowledge among the Hindus. The Ashwins became the medical attendants of the Gods, wrote works on medicine named *Chikitsa-ratnatantra*, and the *Bramhagya*. By their remarkable cures, the *Ashwins* became very celebrated. When the fifth head of Bramha was cut off by *Bayraba*, it was joined again by them, so great was their knowledge of Surgery. They also cured immediately the wounds in the battle between the Gods (*devtas*), and giants (*asura*). Indra had another opportunity of judging of their knowledge by their curing his paralytic arm. Many other remarkable cures were accomplished by the two Ashwins. On witnessing these effects Indra became desirous of examining the *Ayur-veda*, and he was taught by the Ashwins.

Some time after this, mankind, in consequence of their wickedness, became divided into sects, ignorant, restless, unhappy, and afflicted with numerous painful, and dangerous diseases; and as health is the origin of desire, virtue, holiness, riches, and external happiness, so disease diminishes strength, energy, faith, knowledge, holiness, and length of life. It also debilitates the senses, and defiles and destroys the soul.

The sacred Sages (Munis) were grieved at a spectacle so melancholy, and, in order to search for a remedy, *Bharadwaja*, *Atreya*, with numerous sages, met in the Himaleya Mountains.

According to Charaka their names were as follows:—

*Angira, Jamadagni, Vasishto, Kásyapo, Bhrigu, Atreya, Gautama, Sánkhya, Pulastya, Nárada, Osita, Agasta, Bamadeva, Markandeya, Aswanáyan Parikshi, Bhikshuratreya, Bharadwaja, Kapinjala, Viswamitra, Aswaranya, Bhargaba, Chyabana, Obhijit, Gargya, Sandilya, Kaundilya, Abarkshi, Devala, Galavo, Sankritya, Vaijavapi, Kusika, Vadarayana, Barisa,. Saraloma, Kapya, Katyayana, Kankayana, Kaikasaey, Dhauma, Marichi, Casyapo, Sarkarakshyo, Hiranyakshyo, Lokakshya, Paingi, Saunaka, Sakuneya, Maitreyao, Gautamayani** and others.

These holy sages were distressed at the sight of the weakness and sufferings of mankind, which had increased to such a degree, that they saw, with the eyes of their understandings, that the only method of removing such calamities was by the assistance of Indra.

These prophets resolved to send one of their number to the thousand eyed Indra in Heaven, to make known to him the condition of mankind. *Bharadwaja* agreed to go to Indra to acquire a knowledge of medicine. He went, and beheld him resplendant like fire, and by the following prayer propitiated his favor : Oh ! king of the Gods ! created for the salvation of mankind, I have been sent by the sages of the earth, to ask your assistance. Take pity on the weakness and infirmities of man, and teach us the*Ayurveda.* Indra was pleased to grant the prayer of the petitioner, and enlighten him in the precepts of the science of medicine ; as, from his acquirements, these alone were required to be imparted. These precepts embraced an enumeration of the causes, symptoms, and the properties of medicines for those in health, as well as in sickness.

With this knowledge of *Ayur-veda*, the sage returned, and related to the *Rishis* the principles which he had thus acquired. These consisted of :—

1. General character of every thing (Sámana.)
2. Classification (Visesa.)
3. Elements (Drabya.)
4. Qualities (Guna.)
5. Actions (Karma.)
6. Combinations (Sanjoga.)

By means of such a knowledge, the Rishis remained healthy, and happy. Among these *Atreya* imparted the knowledge which he had thus acquired to his pupils, for the good of mankind ; among these, the chief were *Agnibesa, Bhela, Jatukarna, Parasaro, Harita,* and *Kshyarapani.*

* I give these names, as their meaning is now unknown ; proving this work to have existed before the Hindú Pantheon was instituted, from which their proper names are now derived.

The understandings of these sages being opened, by the instruction they received, and they distinguished the peculiarities of diseases, the qualities of medicines, and gained much distinction by the cures they performed. They are said to have lived in health to a very old age. These sages wrote works called by their own names, as *Agnibesatantra*, *Bhelatantra*, *Jatukarnusanhíta*, *Purasárasanhíta*, *Haritasanhíta* and *Kshyarapanitantra*.

These works were read before the assembly of the sages (*Rishis*), who were so much pleased with their arrangement, and the instruction conveyed, that with a noise which reached to Heaven they resounded the praises of the authors. *Agnibesa* was declared to have produced the best practical work, and after it was corrected by *Charaka* it received his name. He therefore became the instructor of practitioners upon earth, as the *Prajapati* were in Heaven ; and this is the most ancient and the most celebrated Hindú Médical work.

As it is arranged in the form of dialogues between the master and his pupils, the plan is desultory ; for although it follows the division into eight parts of the Ayur Véda, the subjects discussed seem naturally to have arisen at the conferences, between the master and students. Thus, the 1st division contains the Materia Medica, the arrangement, and the uses of Medicines, the rank of practitioners, the origin of medicine, &c.

The following may be offered as an example of the manner in which philosophical subjects are treated in one of the chapters of Charaka. They are the questions asked by the pupil *Agnibesa,* which were answered by *Atreya* their teacher. "What is the soul? How is it produced? What is the cause of the formation of the body? Is the soul ignorant or wise? Is it eternal or destructable? What are the temperaments? What are the diseases? What are the proofs of the existance of the soul? Why do some pundits say that the soul is inert, independent, represses the passions (bhassi), omnipresent, and omnipotent? Why do they call the soul *ketragan,* or emanation of the deity? Why is it called witness of the actions of the body (*Sáki*)? If inert, why do we see its actions? If independent, why does it enter the body? When a represser of the passions (*bhassi*), why is it always desirous of enjoying the passions, and greaving over our misfortunes? If the soul is omnipresent, why does it not feel the pains of others? If omniscient why do we not see it in mountains, and hills, and other things? Does the soul exist before or after the formation of the body? If the soul is the science or witness, has it any other judge? How does it support the pains of disease? Do practitioners employ means to prevent disease, to cure them when present, and what is the treatment? What is the cause of pain in disease, and where is it situated? How many kinds of pains are there? How are the pains removed?"

The work of Charaka is of the highest rank; but from the author's want of exact anatomical and pathological knowledge, his manner of treating the subject, and arrangement of diseases it is often obscure, although his descriptions may be accurate. In this work simple medicines are described, as well as their combinations. These remedies increased in number, and became more extravagant in their combinations, in the theraputical department of more modern works.

In other works of authority, it is stated that when the Vedas were lost in the deluge they were recovered by the great serpent *Ananta**, upon the thousand head of which the world rests. At the churning of the ocean by the gods (*Devtas*), and demons (*Asuras*), the water of the ocean was converted into milk, and then into butter, from which precious gifts (*ratnas*) were derived. Among these was Dhanwantari, the physician, or holy sage, the possessor of the water of life (*Amrita*†) drank by the immortals.

Dhanwantari was instructed in the *Ayur Vēda* by Indra, and practised medicine with great success in Heaven, and became celebrated there: But witnessing the ignorance and misery of mankind, and the frequency and fatality of the diseases which afflicted them, he descended upon earth to cure their maladies, and to instruct them in the means of preventing, as well as of curing diseases. He became king of *Kasí*, or Benares, and acquired much celebrity by the cures which he performed. The divine sages, aware of his great knowledge, and witnessing the misery of mankind in consequence of their ignorance, resolved to petition Dhanwantari to assist them.

With this intention *Oupudhnuba, Baiturana, Aurabhra, Poushkalabata, Karabirja, Goupuraa, Rukeeta, Susruta,* were selected to visit *Devadasa* or *Dhanwantari*, king of Kasi, formerly the practitioner of Heaven. On their arrival at Benares, they found that Dhanwantari had retired to the Jungles. They followed him to his retirement, and as they approached him, after mutual salutations, they delivered the following address:—" Deign Sovereign Ruler, to bestow upon us the power of preventing and curing the many diseases under which mankind is suffering,—affecting their bodies (*Sarira*), tormenting their minds (*Manah*), and which, with the nu-

* A *devta* also *Vishnu;* which is to say the end, endless, eternal, boundless.

† *Amrita*, that which gives life.

merous accidental (*agunta*) and natural diseases (*swabhabika*), distress them so much that they seem to be without friends. Their seeming destitution grieves us much, and we pray that you will bestow upon us a work to instruct us in the cause, the nature, and the cure of diseases; for retaining health, and for promoting the welfare of the soul in another world. Like scholars, we come to receive this information from you." Dhanwantari answered, "Your wishes shall be granted." The sages then informed their preceptor that as they were all of the same sect; one of them should ask the questions, and write down the answers required, and the others observe the answers.

Susruta, son of *Visâmitra*, a contemporary of Rama, was chosen to be the person to be instructed in Medicine. Dhanwantari said that Ayur-véda is for the cure of diseases, and for the preservation of health. But it is too voluminous to be recollected by the present degenerate race of mankind; he therefore recommended Sursuta to abridge it, and to arrange it into parts, so as to be easily understood by every one who perused it with attention.

The work which Susruta prepared is still preserved, and after Charaka, it is the oldest book in Medicine which the Hindús possess, and is still of high authority. The manner in which it was produced is as follows:—

Dhanwantari asked his pupils, on what shall I first lecture? They answered, on Surgery; because formerly there were no diseases among the gods, and wounds were the first injuries which required treatment. Besides the practice of surgery is more respected, as affording immediate relief, and is connected with the practice of medicine; although the latter has no connexion with surgery. This was agreed to; and we find the explanation of the eight parts of Ayur-véda, in six Books of Susruta, as follows:—

1*st.*—Surgery (Sútra Sthána), in which is considered the origin of medicine; the rules for teaching, the duty of practitioners, the selection and uses of instruments and medicines, the influence of the weather on health, and the practice to be followed after surgical operations. Then follows the description of the diseases of the humours and surgical diseases; the restoration of defective ears and noses; and the removal of extraneous substances which have entered the body; the different stages of inflammation with their treatment, different forms of wounds and ulcers, and the regimen of patients labouring under surgical diseases. The description of good and bad diet; of prognosis; the kind of messengers to be employed by the sick; and of diseases,

* From Su, well and Sruta, Shastres.

produced by the deranged actions of the senses, and of incurable diseases. Then follows the preparations required for accompanying a rajah in war, the duty of the practitioners, the difference of climates, the different classes of medicines according to their sensible qualities, a description of the fluids, and of the different preparations, and articles of food. These subjects are treated of in forty-six chapters.

2nd.—Nosology (Nidána Sthána) the description and Diagnosis of diseases produced by vitiated humours, or derangements of blood, bile, wind, and phlegm. The symptoms and causes of Rheumatic diseases, of piles, stone, fistulo-in-ano, leprosy, diabetes, gonorrhœa, and ascitis ; the symptoms of unnatural presentations in midwifery, large internal abscesses, erysipelas, scrofula, hydrocele, venereal diseases, and diseases of the mouth. These subjects are considered in sixteen chapters.

3rd.—Anatomy (Saríra Sthána), or structure of the body. The description of the soul, and the elementary parts of the body ; of puberty ; of conception ; of the growth of the different parts of the body ; of bleeding ; of the treatment of pregnancy, and of infants. This division has ten chapters.

4th.—Therapia (Chikitsa Sthána), in which the exhibition of medicines, the history of inflammations, the treatment of fractures, rheumatic diseases, piles, stone, fistula-in-ano, leprosy, diabetes, and dropsy are given : the manner of extracting the child in unusual positions, the remedies for restoring health and strength, and for prolonging life ; the means of preventing diseases ; the use of clysters ; and of errhines, and the use of the smoke of different substances. These are considered in forty different chapters.

5th.—Toxocology (Kalpa Sthána). The means of distinguishing poisoned food, and descriptions of different mineral, vegetable, and animal poisons, with their antidotes is given under this head. This division is treated of in eight chapters.

6th.—The supplementary section (Locales Uttara Sthána) includes various local diseases ; as those of the eye, nose, ears, and head, with their treatment ; the symptoms and treatment of fever, and its varieties ; dysentery ; consumption ; *gulma ;* diseases of the heart ; jaundice ; discharges of blood, and fainting. This is followed by the treatment of intoxication, of cough, hiccough, asthma, hoarseness of voice, worms, sterterous vomiting, cholera, dispepsia, and disuria. It also treats of madness, epilepsy, apoplexy, the different tastes of substances with their effects ; the means of retaining health, and the different opinions of practitioners regarding the humours. These subjects are treated in sixty-six chapters.

It thus appears that the ancient commentators on the ayur-veda did not allow the prejudices that now exist against touching the dead Body, to interfere with that important and necessary branch of knowledge, which can alone be acquired by dissection.

The Charaka and Susruta are the ground work of the more recent medical systems; in which their authors have uniformly adhered to the classification, and general details of the originals. But these imitators being ignorant of anatomy, and the usual causes of diseases, are still more defective in their descriptions particularly when they did not follow the more ancient writers.

It was by means of the works of Charaka and Susruta that all the sages (Munis) are alleged to have been instructed in medicine; and the variety of opinion to be found in the treatises they afterwards wrote, was in consequence of the shortness of their compilations, their poetical form, and the great extent and difficulty of the subject. These Sages are said to have practised medicine as a means of accomplishing much good to mankind; and they became famous by the number of lives which they saved. Those who were taught by Charaka, became Physicians; and the followers of Susruta, Surgeons.

Charaka is superior to Susruta in the accuracy of his descriptions, in the classification of diseases, and in the plan of treatment which he recommends. While Susruta is principally celebrated for his anatomical descriptions, and judicious principles of surgery which his work contains.

To such authorities the Hindu practitioners invariably looked, to the entire neglect of that careful and continued examination of the progress of diseases, by which alone their true nature, and successful treatment are discovered. The works of these commentators embraced the whole system, and the erroneous principles upon which their theoretical speculations were built is not detected, in consequence of the contracted space occupied in their descriptions, which discard minute observations on disease, or specific details regarding the opinions of others.

The two following Medical works deserve to be mentioned here. *Babhata* compiled a treatise called *Ostongo-reedoya.* This was principally taken from Charaka and Susruta. The manner of treating the subject, and the arrangements are much the same. It is written in a clear style, and the author explains passages which were not before understood, in the original works.

About three hundred years ago, a compilation was made from all the most celebrated medical works, and called *Baboprukasa.* The author collected all that was most precious from the works left by other sages, and named the work after himself. By its clearness, and excellent arrangement this work explains the difficulties of the more ancient medical shastres, forgotten, and corrupted. This work was compiled for the use of practitioners, and is prefered by them, as it gives an admirable account of all the practical parts of the Hindu medical science.

CHAPTER II.

Rank of Practitioners, and Duties of Teachers.

In the Puránas it is stated that a young woman of the *Vaisya* caste, called *Ambá*, was serving as a menial to *Galaba*, the Muni. He was much pleased with her, and while blessing her, informed her, that she would have a beautiful and respected son. She told this to her parents, who asked the sage how that could be, as she was not married; and that the birth of a child would bring disgrace upon the whole family. The sage told them that it would be so; that the child should be called *Virabhadra* (very fortunate), that he would be much respected, and his profession would be that of medicine. This child was the first of the Vaidya, * or Medical caste.

His thirteen sons were taught by the sacred Sages the works they had written, and they became most learned pundits, and skilful physicians. It is from their descendants that the Hindu physicians are derived, and now form the caste of Vaidhyas. These physicians have free access to various shastres, or commentaries on the sacred writings. Brahmans learn the medical shastres for their advantage; Khetriyas for the benefit of their health, and Vaidyas for their subsistence. The two first castes are not allowed to receive any pecuniary recompense for their assistance to the sick.

Other castes may learn the medical works when they are honest, learned, and men of good descent. Even those of the degraded Sudra caste may be taught the Ayur-veda, under such circumstances.

Teacher. "The feet of the Teacher is the origin of all happiness, and, like a light in a dark room, he will illuminate the contracted, and dark mind of the pupil; or, as quicksilver, properly mixed with other metals and exposed to heat, will be changed to gold, so will the words that come out of his mouth be pure and valuable."

* Or one who understands *vidyá* (i. e.) the Ayur-ved, or Medical Shastre.

In the ancient works it is stated that the teachers of the medical profession were Rishis, or Ascetic sages. They conveyed their instruction in the form of lectures, which were delivered in open public places, at which many students attended. These sages travelled about with their pupils, curing diseases, so as to afford them the means of witnessing the effects of different manners and customs, and different medicines, climates, and forms of diseases. The pupils kept notes of these lectures, and many of these compilations are still in existence.

At present the Teacher instructs three or four pupils, in many cases his relations, who are maintained at their own houses. In other cases the Teacher supports them. They continue five or six years reading the shastres, seeing the preparation of medicines, and their employment, for the cure of the sick. The teacher in many cases receives no emolument from his pupils, being content with the honor and merit of bestowing knowledge. This merit is considered to be of the very first order; procuring for him renown in this world, and the highest benefits in a future state. In most cases however, an allowance is made to such Teachers by their rich neighbours.

" A good teacher is like rain falling upon the germinating seed, and should possess the following qualifications :—A perfect knowledge of the shastres, joined to extensive practical knowledge and skill. He should be kind and humble to every one; he should have no defects of body, and should always be ready to expose the good, rather than the bad qualities of others ; he should be clean and neat in his person, and possess and exhibit to his pupils all kinds of medicines and instruments. He should always be increasing his knowledge of books, and should neither be angry by the improprieties of others, nor fatigued by their importunities. He should be kind and considerate to his pupils and be able to explain the most complicated statements, in the simplest, and most perspicuous language. Such a person as this, who instructs a pupil, when of good parentage, is like the seasonable cloud and rain upon the corn field, which quickly matures its valuable produce."

" Such a man is not therefore aged, though his hair is gray. The Gods considered as aged, the person who, though young in years, has read, and understands the vedas. As an elephant made of wood, or an antelope made of earth, such is an unlearned Brahman : who has nothing but the name." (Menu, p. 44. and 156 157.)

Should a Teacher give improper instructions to his pupil, or peruse with him bad books, he will bear the weight of the sin of his pupil, and the seeds which he sows will not produce good fruits.

These vaidya teachers are often more learned, and have less pride than the Brahmans.* "They are usually poets, grammarians, rhetoricians and moralists; and may be esteemed in general the most virtuous, and amiable of the Hindus. Instead of the vedas, they study the Ayur ved, and Rajaniti, or instruction of Princes, and instead of law, the Nitisastras, or general system of Ethics. Their Sahitya, or Cavya Sastra, contains innumerable poems written chiefly by physicians, which supplies the place of the Puranas, since they contain all the stories of the Ramayan, Bharata, and Bhagawata: they have access to many treatises of Alankára or rhetoric, with a variety of works in modulated prose; to the Nátaka, which answers to the Gandharvaveda, consisting of regular dramatic pieces, in Sanscrit and Prakit. Besides which they usually get by heart some entire dictionary and grammar."

CHAPTER III.

Character and duties of Pupils.

Brahmans should teach the sons of Brahmans, of Khetriyas, and of Vaidyas, who belong to the third order of Hindu castes. The last are the professed, though not the exclusive medical class among the Hindus. Other shastus state that a Khetriya should teach the son of a Khetriya, and Vaidyas a Vaidya, &c.

"In all cases the Medical student should be the son of a respectable and ancient family, who is either the son of a practitioner, or of one who respects the medical profession. He should be inquisitive and observant, not covetous, zealous, or lazy; he should be a philanthropist, possess a generous heart, and his disposition should be amiable, and happy. The indications of such qualifications are, an agreeable voice, a small tongue, eyes, and nose straight, with thin lips, short teeth, which do not expose the gums, and thick hair which retains its vigour."

"With such qualifications even the son of the Sudra may be taught the shastres, with the exception of certain prayers (mantras). The teachers faith in God will thus remain, and be conveyed to such a pupil; and the teacher will afford glory to the scholar, even should he be a

* The reverence with which a Brahman is held is not surprising when it is considered that they are sprung from the mouth of Bramha, that they are the guardians of the sacred books, that all the offices and benefits of religion must proceed from them, and, as Gods, they hold the destinies of man at their disposal.

Rajah, and after death the Teacher will go to the heaven of Indra (Indraloka).

The successful student should be active in his duties, and not fatigued by his studies, he should possess gravity, a good memory, acute senses, and considerable acquirements.

Without such qualifications and indications the youth should be rejected.

These students of medicine enter their names as the pupils of some celebrated Brahman or Vaidya, who teach the science of medicine. When the student has learned one branch of the medical art, or that followed by his Father, he is not allowed to change it for another branch, although he can change his profession at any time.

A fortunate day is to be selected for the pupil to commence reading the shastres. On that occasion he is to be clean in his person, and the place in which he is to study should be purified. A raised part of the room, a cubit square, is to be cleaned with cows' dung and strewed with Kusa grass, after which fire is to be placed upon it, with several kinds of sacred wood, upon which ghee is to be poured, while prayers (mantras) are repeated. The pupil while being initiated should stand near the fire with his face towards the east.

The master (Guru) and other Brahmans are then to pray over some dried rice, and the Guru should sprinkle water over the assembly. He is then to place a Brahman on his right hand, over which he prays as he throws a mixture of curdled milk, honey, and ghee over the sacred fire. The scholar does the same, and his lesson begins. The Guru declares that he must henceforth discard lust, anger, covetousness, ignorance, laziness, vanity, pride, envy, revenge, cruelty, lying, and evil actions. He must always be engaged in the search after truth, and in the performance of good actions; he must be clean in his person, wear a humble and peculiar kind of cooured clothes; and his beard and nails should not be cut during the period of his study.

He must always respect his teacher and parents; put the dust of their feet upon his head, and obey them in every thing. He is thus addressed by the guru :—

"When I say you may eat, drink, sleep, and rise from bed, you must immediately obey. If the scholar does not perform all this he sins, his understanding will diminish, and his glory will be quenched."

"Whatever I say you must believe, and carefully follow my instructions. You must be careful to act so as to please me, and if I do not acknowledge your good actions, I shall sin and my knowledge will be barren."

" In the treatment of the diseases of Brahmans, Gurus, and the poor and helpless or people who come from a distance, you must be as careful as you would be of your own relations, by which you will make more friends, acquire virtue, wealth, and a good name. You must not be displeased at my treating you as a son, a servant, or a beggar, you must harbour no bad thoughts, you must be moderate in the indulgence of your appetites, and you must be contented with a small recompence. By night and by day your anxious desire should always be to consider how you are to cure the sick under your care. You will avoid bad company, and neither give medicines to a culprit who has been condemned by a Rajah, to a woman whose husband and guardians are absent, nor receive any thing but food from a wife, without the consent of the husband. You must avoid entering a house, as a medical man, without an invitation, you must walk slowly, without gazing, and observe deliberately, but you must only observe the patient, and the symptoms of his disease ; and you must not express the period of a fatal disease. You must not vaunt your own knowledge, for although the learned may be pleased, the ignorant will be angry at the exhibition of learning in such a situation. After visiting the sick, should the disease be complicated, you must detail the symptoms, and consult other physicians as to their nature and treatment."

" As the shastres contain the precepts of numerous prophets and great physicians with their descriptions of diseases reduced to a proper order, you must study them with care ; by which the stupid and illiterate pupil will be instructed in his duties, and the intelligent and industrious in the manner in which that knowledge is to be improved and extended."

" The shastres are not to be read on unlucky (astami) days, or when the sun is obscured by clouds ; on the two first days of a new moon ; when it thunders ; at unseasonable times ; at the morning dawn, or evening twilight. The student must not study on holidays, or the day on which he meets a corpse, on which the Governor of the province is sick, when fighting occurs, or when war approaches."

The Brahmans were first called Brahmanha, and when they have received the string they are called Dwíja, or twice born ; in like manner, the Physicians are called Ambashta, and Vaidya (बैद्य) from Veda (बेद) when they have acquired the ayur-veda, or medical shastres. Besides the Ayur-veda, the physician requires to know different other sciences. But if a Vaidya does not know or does not follow the precepts of the shastres, he will be like a thief, and such a person exercising medicine, will commit as great a sin, as beating a Brahman.

The preceptor, during the time he teaches his pupil, should wear two pieces of cloth, his mind should be calm, and he should be regular in his attendance.

In teaching, the progress of the student must be at first slow, commencing with the nomenclature of the profession, and then acquiring single subjects, and lastly the whole system. He must first read slowly and distinctly, without much effort, and avoid a monotonous intonation, or acquiring a dislike to the subject. The instruction should be given without pain to the instructed ; and sweet gentle speech must be used by a Preceptor who cherishes virtue. When at his lesson, care must be taken not to allow any one to pass between the pupil and Teacher, as it will interrupt the supposed passage of good qualities from the latter to the former.

If the Student seek for long life, he should eat with his face to the east ; if for exalted fame, to the south ; if for prosperity, to the west ; if for truth and its reward, to the north. (Menu p. 28 ch 2 52)

When a student has studied medicine, and has understood, examined, and remembered the symptoms of disease with the actions of medicines and has acted for himself, he is to receive the authority of the Rajah to practice medicine.

CHAPTER IV.

Duties of the Physician, of his attendants, and of the Patient.

There are four circumstances required in the cure of a disease,—a physician ; a disease that is known ; a reasonable patient ; and medicines, instruments, and attendants. Each of these subjects will be considered in this order.

Duties of a *Physician.* The duty of a Physician relates to his person, character, acquirements, and observances.

Person. The Physician should possess a healthy body ; he should keep his nails and beard short ; his body pure, his clothes clean, and wear shoes, and a small turban. He should carry an umbrella, and stick in his hand.

Should the Practitioner not know his duty, the cure of the disease will be tedious and imperfect ; it will also be so when the pulse cannot be felt at the root of the neck, and when the senses are affected. In such cases the Practitioner should always inform the relations and friends of the sick person of the state in which he is in, before prescribing.

Character. The successful student, after leaving his preceptor, should be cleanly in his person, love and obey his Teacher, and should be active and studious to find out the proper meaning of the difficult passages he had learned by heart. Should these passages not be understood, or should the student know the shastres, and not practice the profession, he will be like an ass carrying a heavy load of fragrant wood without discovering, and enjoying the fragrance of his burthen.

The Physician should possess a good memory, and be always amiable, cheerful, and collected. His language should be mild, candid and encouraging, rather like that of a friend than an acquaintance, and he should be always ready to assist the sick. His heart should be pure and charitable, and he should carefully follow the instructions of his Guru, and of his predecessors. Such a physician should possess a character for strict veracity, of calm temper, and of the greatest sobriety, and chastity. He should be a man of sense and benevolence, and his constant study should be how he is to do good. As a person may be afraid of his father and mother, friends, and guru, but not of his Physician ; so the physician should be more kind and considerate to the sick than a father, a mother, a friend, or a guru. To these qualities should be added, that of affection for learned friends, the constant habit of visiting the sick, and seeing them treated by experienced persons. Without such a combination of qualities, knowledge will retard rather than advance his progress. He should know the causes and varieties of disease, and the means of preventing and curing them, and have the reputation of accomplishing cures quickly. He should study to remove curable diseases, but must avoid treating healthy persons. A good physician will continue to visit his patients diligently, examine them carefully, and be not fearful, but give medicines always when the patient can live : But if a physician attempts to treat an incurable disease, it will diminish his reputation, friends, and riches.

Acquirements. A good Physician should be acquainted with his profession, but so various are the qualifications that the combination is rarely to be found, even in heaven. He should be acquainted,—

1*st.*—With the introductory remarks of *Sutrusthána,* which considers the relation of customs and habits, and the knowledge of those duties which the shastres regulate, with reference to disease.

2*nd.*—*Sárira,* or structure of the body.

3*rd.*—*Nidán,* which includes the invasion (*Purbura*) ; and symptoms (*Rupa*) of diseases.

4*th.*—*Chikitsa* and *upasáya* concerning the regimen and the Medicines which cure diseases.

5th.—Upadraba, including all unusual symptoms which develope themselves in the course of disease ; as delirium, thirst, &c.

6th.—Kolpa, concerning poisons.

To such acquirements, the physician must have practised his profession as well as studied the shastres, which were compassionately revealed by the Gods. Without such a knowledge of books he will be confused, like a soldier afraid in the time of action, will be a great sinner, and should be capitally punished by the rajah. On the other hand, a want of practical knowledge will impede his advancement, and his senses will be bewildered, when called on to treat acute diseases. Such a physician will not be esteemed by the great, as he cannot pratice with success when only instructed in half his duty. Such a person is the murderer of his species, and the medicine prescribed by him may be compared to poison, or lightning—such ignorance prevents all the good effects of remedies. As the two wheels of a chariot, or the two wings of a bird, assist in their progress, so will the knowledge of the shastres, and of practice, lead the physician to proceed with safety and success in the treatment of the diseased ; but, should the physician want either of these essential qualifications, his progress will be impeded, as one wing or one wheel will impede the progress of the bird, or the chariot. It is the combination of both these qualifications which is required ; when medicine becomes like the water of immortality (*Amrita*). Such a physician, if he is to acquire celebrity, must still daily endeavour to improve his mind by an attentive perusal of scientific books. If such a physician does not gain money after he has been taught the shastres it is his own fault.

When such a *Vydya* is spoken to by a patient in a peevish or hasty manner, he will remain calm, mild, and courageous ; and cherish a cheerful hope of being able to save the sufferer's life. The practitioner should avoid frivolous or improper language, particularly with females ; he should not sit down upon the same bed, and the only presents he should receive from them is food. He should be frank, communicative, impartial, and liberal, yet ever rigid in exacting an adherence to whatever regimen or rules he may think it necessary to enjoin. Should death occur under the care of such an earthly saint, it can only be considered as his inevitable fate, and not the consequence of presumptuous ignorance.

The presence of a physician for the cure of a disease is most important ; indeed, as indispensable as a pilot is to a boat, as a coachman in guiding a chariot, or as a general to an army. If a physician is not consulted when a person is ill, he will soon die, as a lamp exposed to wind is continually liable to be extinguished.

Some severe diseases are cured immediately, by a good physician ; but simple diseases are increased much by the want of early assistance. At the commencement, like a young plant, it is readily rooted up, but as it expands and grows in strength the difficulties are much increased. Even for a slight disease the assistance of a practitioner will be of much use ; for as a large man at the bottom of a pit may get out by long continued exertion, his extrication will be much facilitated by the assistance of a friendly hand. As in war, a sword may defend many, so in the hand of an enemy it will destroy. In like manner the shastres and water may become the cause of destruction instead of benefit to mankind.

Some practitioners have many instruments and medicine which they do not know how to use, such are calculated to deceive ; and by their arrogant manners, and being without a knowledge of the shastres, are enemies to mankind, and are called *Chhadmachara.* Those who possess the favourable qualities of Physicians, without the necessary knowledge, are called *Pratirúpaka* ; and those who know the medical shastres, and are well acquainted with the causes, symptoms, and means of curing disease, and their prevention, will be fit to be the physician to a Rajah. Such persons are called *Sidhi Sádhaka.*

The first two are sometimes allowed to practice by the neglect of the Rajah, and they may be known by their vanity, and ill will towards the good physician. Such persons flatter the patients friends, are diligent, take reduced fees, are hesitating and doubtful in performing difficult operations, and pretend that their bad success is caused by the bad attendants, &c. ; such persons avoid the society of learned persons as they would a jungle.

Still some patients will be saved when under the care of such a physician, as a worm in destroying one of the sacred shastres will sometimes leave in its depredations the rude representations of some of the sacred letters. A bad physician may cure one patient, by which he endeavours to establish his fame, without considering the thousands he has killed ; such a person is like a boat in a storm without a pilot, or a blind man in the performance of any work, and is to be looked upon as the angel of death. If such a fellow has his fancy inflamed, he is like a deadly serpent, and should be avoided.

The Practitioner who knows the value of quicksilver, &c. ; is like a god ; one who knows the qualities of herbs and roots is like a man ; one who knows the use of the knife and of fire resembles a demon (Asur) ; and those who know the proper prayers to be offered up in the time of sickness is like a prophet.

The following characters will never be respected as Physicians :— When the person is born in, and inhabits a village which has a bad name, or visits the sick without being called. A bad Physician does not pay respect to the Brahmans, spiritual Teachers, or superiors ; he leaves the duties due to the memory of his father unfulfilled ; wears bad clothes, speaks on improper subjects, and in an improper manner, or neither speaks nor gives medicines. Such a person does not pay respect to astrologers, to the seasons and times, to the influence of the planets, to the opinion of friends, or acknowledges the power of holy men. Such a physician will never be respected ; and the great physician, *Dhanwantari* himself, possessed of such qualities, would not be liked or esteemed.

Should a proud physician reject the shastres, and the advice of his Guru, all sorts of evils will follow him ; and if he cannot repeat the usual prayers, is ignorant of the nature of disease, and takes money, he should be punished by the Rajah, as a thief. Should a physician speak disrespectfully of the shastres, or incorrectly of the *Ayur-veda*, or of astrology, the same punishment shall be inflicted, on him as that for killing a Brahman.

From these observations, it appears that the duties of a physician requires the exercise of sound judgement, unimpeachable integrity, profound learning, embracing an intimate acquaintance with many shastres, and a constant and extensive practice of his profession. To these qualities must be joined unremitting attention, a good heart and disposition, a knowledge of the appearance and varieties of disease, and the manner of preparing, and exhibiting the proper remedies.

A physician should not visit the enemy of a Rajah ; as he should always speak the truth, avoid speaking disrespectfully of ancestors, and of other good, exalted, and pious persons. He is not to walk with the wicked, foolish, or low-born persons, or with the patients enemy. He must avoid riding on wicked horses, elephants, or the like, living in empty houses, or in places where bodies are burnt ; in very retired places, containing wild beasts or reptiles, where people are quarrelling, especially with cutting instruments in their hands, or animals armed with horns. He is carefully to avoid walking behind biers containing dead bodies, moving in the shadow of the images of the Gods, of cows, Brahmans, or in the smoke of burning bodies, diseased persons, or great sinners. The physician as well as other persons should neither look at the rising nor setting sun. He should neither inform a person that a cow is eating what belongs to him, nor speak ill of a Rajah. He should not walk upon the tops of rocks, beat the water or earth with his hands or feet, prevent or resist any inclination of the body, to discharge any thing. He should avoid drinking or eating out of a broken vessel, or out of the hand ; and should not sleep with his face to the north. Ganesah had his head chopped off for so doing by Sunni, and the head of an elephant substituted, as it was found sleeping with its head in the same direction.

Observances. When called upon to attend a patient, the physician is to mark the following circumstances:—He is to observe the manner, speech, and dress of the messenger ; the state of the planets, and the time of the day; and the good or bad omens. He should note the occurrence of accidents, in walking, or in seeing impure, weak, imperfect, or divided objects : In such cases the person will die of the disease. This will be rendered more inevitable, should neither presents nor respect be shewn to the practitioner.

Before a physician visits a patient, he should first remark the position he is in when the messenger arrives to consult with him; and, by the persons countenance and conversation, endeavour to ascertain, whether or not the patient will survive. As he proceeds to visit the sick person, he must carefully note any good or bad omens that may occur regarding the messenger, the flight of birds, the relative position of animals, &c. Seeing cows, or Brahmans on the right hand side are favourable, as also corpses, jackals, vessels of water, &c., when seen on the left side. It is unfavourable when lizards are heard when leaving the house, when vultures, or bad characters are seen, or when the Physician is called by another person, or is hit by any thing behind, or when a person sneezes.

If the physician meets a person carrying out a vessel of water, earth, seeds, fruit, ghee, sees a bull, Brahman, or scorpion, when coming out of the sick person's house ; or the figure of a geni, a fire vessel, or a bow for arrows, the person will die. Seeing animals in unclean situations, on the right and left hand, bad sinners, very old and blind persons, or an enemy, are bad omens.

If the Physician arrives at the same time at the patients house with milk, the omen is favourable.

The physician should avoid visiting a sick person during the night. When he gets up in the morning, and has performed the necessary purifications, he is to visit the patient residing in a clean place.

The physician should avoid visiting a patient in a place where there is hair, bones, spikes, stones, chaff, ashes, broken stone vessels, charcoal, or in impure situations.

If the first object seen in the morning is a holy man, the person's money will increase ; and if a bad man it will diminish. Should the person be at enmity with a soothsayer, he will become poor ; with a physician, he will soon die ; and with a Brahman toil will be the only recompence he will get for his exertions, and he will soon lose his life.

Should the air at the time be cool, and pleasantly scented it is favourable ; but if with a strong wind blowing with a disagreeable smell, the prognosis of the disease should be more guarded. These and various other indications are explainded in the Medical works, and seem to be founded on the Hindu belief in fatalism ; a system, though sufficiently plausable with the ignorant, is fraught with many and great evils.

Useful indications are supposed to be derived from the dreams of the physician, as well as from those of the sick person ; and a long list of the good and bad subjects of dreams are given. In general, favourable dreams consist in seeing brahmans, cows, rajahs, clean water, splendid houses, &c. ; and the reverse in seeing the person cleaning himself, riding on an unclean animal, low caste persons, dead acquaintances, killing or fighting, unclean animals, falling down a precipice, loss of eye-sight, and other impure objects or defects, &c. The good and bad dreams in different diseases is likewise given, which seem to be good or bad according to the greater or less importance of the changes of the symptoms which they indicate.

The physician should first ask questions at the attendant regarding the disease ; what things he has eaten, and what he has done to produce, or to influence the disease. The physician should then mark the signs of longivity in his patient. These are long arms and fingers ; large eyes, forehead, trunk, teeth, mouth, and hands, feet, and shoulders. Persons will live to an old age who have long respirations, and a large space between the mamilæ, the fore-legs short and fleshy, the neck short, and speak and act sensibly. A person with a large body and good voice, deep navel, vessels and joints well formed, much hair on the body, the external ears long, the body strong, more particularly the head, quickly dries when wet with oil or water, from above downwards, and the senses are good: such a person will live long, and should be treated by the physician. The want of such signs will indicate a short life, not exceeding 50 years ; and when moderate in their manner of living, and rich, they will not exceed the age of 70 years. When such a person has not been diseased from his birth, has grown fat gradually, as well as in his knowledge of the shastres, he will live long. The person will live a moderate period when the lines on the palms of his hands, and long longitudinal lines on the back are well formed, but with large external ears, and the end of the nose prominent, the person may live 70 years. When the bones of the fingers and forearm are short, testicles pendulous, breast and back contracted, ears short, nose prominent, and gums are seen on laughing, and eyes are not steady, such a person will live 50 years. Then follows the proper proportions of both the large and small members, and the proportions of the size of each part of the body for indicating the length of the persons life.

It is necessary to recollect that a good Brahman, and a Rajah, will be cured of a disease with difficulty, as they will not always take the proper remedies, and the physician is afraid to urge his instructions strongly. The same is the case with women, children, and old people, who do not observe the proper directions. In like manner, those who do not explain their complaints, who are weak in intellect, are poor, and avaritious ; who will not spend their money, or have bad tempers or dispositions, are dissipated, and are without friends, will be cured of their diseases with difficulty, as they will not strictly follow the directions of the physicians. In such cases the disease may be rendered incurable.

2nd. The Nature of the Disease. The physician (chikitsáka) should next mark the nature of the disease, the seasons of the year, and enquire from what country the patient comes. He is to mark which of the humours (*dhátu*) are diseased, and how they can be cured.

There are three kinds of these duties :—

1*st.*—To cure the diseases of wind (vayu), bile (pitta), and phlegm (kaph) which occur without causing other diseases. These derangements are the usual cause of disease, and produce the change of disposition, and the peculiar feelings of the sick ; besides one disease may produce another, which sometimes diminishes the symptoms of the first.

2*nd.*—When a disease is present, how it is to be cured? and

3*rd.*—When a primary and secondary disease are present, and require to be cured?

The physician is to observe the general appearance of the sick person, his age, and the condition of his body, his temperament and strength, the state of the mind, and the food which he has been used to. He should examine the symptoms of the disease with his eyes ; consider the probable result of the disease by his judgement, and its similarity with other diseases ; as there is a good and a bad form of every disease. The symptoms enumerated in the shastres, should be observed, more especially the state of the pulse, of the tongue as to moisture and dryness, the condition of the bowels, urine, and sleep ; his general feeling, more especially the state of the nose, head, hands, feet and abdomen. The state of the patient's appetite and internal fire ; the part of the body attacked, and the state of the various vessels (*será*), and the abdomen (kastha) ; particularly where the stomach presses upon the food to digest it (pokasia) ; where the undigested portion is situated (ámasia) ; where digestion takes place (*pakasaya*) ; and where the dejections are retained (*molásaya*) next the bladder and pelvis. The seat of the blood (Jokerit, &c.) the heart (hit) and the lungs (phuspus) are to be considered ; and the period when the disease increases, and intermissions occur. The kind of caste, temper, and disposition ; the degree of fear ; the state of the dejections ; and, in females, the state of the cataminia, &c. If the patient cannot speak, those about him should be asked the usual questions about the disease.

The disease is next to be examined by the five active senses, and by speech. By the touch is distinguished the feverish heat or coldness of the surface, the dryness or moisture, the softness or hardness, the size of the vessels, and the irregularities of the skin. By the hearing, the passage of air in deep seated abscesses, wounds ; and in the intestines, by coughing, &c.

By the signs of longivity and strength of the body, and the changes in the colour of the skin, &c. ; as leprosy, and various forms of cutaneous diseases ; by the state of the tongue and of the urine ; the quantity of which is to be noted, and the quality, which is known by ants being fond of it, by the sight, and by the smell. In like manner the other secretions and discharges, as from ulcers, &c., are to be examined.

By speech, the Practitioner learns the time of invasion and progress of the disease, the sex and habit of body ; the nature and degree of pain ; and the state of the appetite, the strength, and the evacuations. Unless the disease is well explained, seen, and known the practitioner will not understand it, and will be made foolish by his ignorance ; whereas the knowledge, and judgment of the physician, like a lamp which illuminates a room, enables him to understand the nature of the diseases of the body.

The physician has special duties to perform to a Rajah as they differ from other men ; not in the formation of the body, but by their nature, which is to command and to pardon. These qualities are received from God ; and, as an exalted being, he is distinguished by the superiority of his voice and manner, by the pureness of his heart, and by the justness of his actions. The physician should be careful in the time of war, to point out the road he is to travel ; of his water. food, and shelter; and of the food of his horses and elephants. The physician is to live near the person of the Rajah, and be like his shadow, or his standard. Medicines and instruments should always be at hand; and he should be allowed to have free intercourse with the sick. But the care of the physician should not end here. It should extend to the water, and the food of the army, as well as of the beasts of burthen which the enemy may endeavour to destroy by poison*. The good physician will detect this, and may be the means of saving the army.

3rd. Medicines and Instruments. When called to a patient, the practitioner is first to remark if there is still life, and strength, in the sick person; his age, temperament, and country, and this knowledge will modify the kind and quantity of medicine to be given. As long as life remains in the root of the throat, and the senses remain perfect, the physician may give medicines, as the person, under such circumstances, may be cured. Even old, inveterate, and incurable diseases, may be alleviated by a judicious line of treatment. If, therefore, a practitioner, after the necessary examination, knows the disease, and that it may be cured even with difficulty, his duty is to endeavour to alleviate the sufferings of his patient. Should the alloted period of his life upon earth have expired, he will die notwithstanding the best directed means for his recovery. It is proper, however, that much caution be used in the employment of medicine in fatal diseases, as a physician may alleviate pain, but cannot give life; and by administering medicines in such cases, without previously stating the danger the patient is in to his relations, he will only bring discredit on himself, and on his profession. Taking such precautions, the practitioner may give medicine even when the patient is senseless, without any pulse, and only breathes.

The medicines proper for the individual case, and the manner in which it will be most proper to administer them, must be carefully observed; care must also be taken that the medicines be obtained from a good soil and neighbourhood. Those from Hímálaya Mountains are the best. The physician should, however, not only know the names but likewise the various qualities of these medicines. For this purpose he should penetrate forests, and climb mountains, to examine them in their natural situations; and should not despise the information obtained from hunters and shepherds, who may have had opportunities of witnessing their effects.

* The Burmese are said to sprinkle the decoction of some poisonous plants upon the trees, so as to destroy the elephants belonging to their enemies.

The medicines should be collected on a fortunate day, and at a lucky hour. They should be gathered by the physician himself, with suitable prayers. Should a person of another caste touch or prepare the medicines, and not the physician who prescribes, they will be rendered inert, even should a Brahmun have prepared them. When the proper medicine has been gathered and prepared in the prescribed manner, and administered at the proper time, the effect will be as if Vishnu had administered, and entered into the body of the sick person; but the medicine will be of no use to the sick unless administered by a physician, as it will otherwise be like the lump of prepared clay, without the aid of the potter to fashion it. A physician should, therefore, be his own apothecary, preparing and prescribing those medicines which are peculiarly appropriate to each particular case, and being unknown to others, constitutes one of his peculiar excellencies.

The qualities of medicines, depend on their colour, smell, and kind of juice. The active power of medicine should be great, but the quantity should be small. These quantities should be carefully observed, and the medicines given at the proper season, and stage of the disease.

The person's disease is then to be examined, the state of the humours and blood; the seven essential parts (dhâtu), and lastly the evacuations. He is next to decide on the nature of the disease, administer the proper medicines, and give directions regarding diet and regimen.

It is of much importance that the disease be treated at the proper time; and the patient be of the proper degree of strength to admit of the disease being cured. Active treatment should not be employed in a slight disease, nor a mild treatment in an acute disease. Should the treatment employed be doing no good, it should be changed; but when the symptoms are yielding, under a particular plan of treatment, it should be continued.

That kind of treatment will be successful which diminishes the disease, by equalizing all the humours; and that is bad treatment, which increases one, as it diminishes another humour. The treatment should be commenced from the first appearance, of the disease; as it is like fire, poison, or the enemy, and a small portion deranges health.

Should a physician exhibit medicines the first day he has seen the patient, without properly ascertaining the nature of the disease, he will be like the angel of death (Yama). Such medicines as cure vital air, bile, and phlegm when diseased, are not disagreeable to the person; do not produce any bad effects; and, given at the proper time, are the remedies to be employed. A Vaidhya should prepare the medicines ; although this is stated in other shastres to be the province of Brahmans. The susruta shastre says that any competent person may administer medicine, but the Vaidya declares whoever does not take medicine from this caste will go to hell. Even Brahmans are declared to have no authority in the practice of physic. Any other caste preparing or touching medicine, but the physician who orders its preparation, will render it inert.

4*th*. *Messenger and attendants.* The person who is sent for the physician should not be of low caste, a fool, one of questionable veracity, or a great sinner ; he should not appear before the physician distressed from fatigue, by a rapid journey, or appear to be fearful of the result of the sick persons ailment. The messenger who has his hair knotted, clothes old or wet, or is scantily or slovenly dressed, carries a cutting instrument, &c., as a sword or stick, holds ashes in his hands, will be as the angel of death. If he be a Dandí or Faqír, or is deformed, or defective in a member, or rides upon an ass, camel, or buffaloe ; or wears a band of red flowers round his neck, the prognosis is unfavourable. If the Messenger has his body anointed with oil, or if covered with the deposit of a river, or blood be flowing from his body ; or if he be of a bad temper or disposition, so as to speak hastily or indiscretely it will be unfavourable. If he rubs his shoulders, back, head, or hair with his hand while speaking, it will be like a decree of *Yama*, the angel of death. Should the Messenger arrive so as to meet the physician on the south, and the physician not wishing to visit the sick ; or if the messenger stands on one foot, sneezes, or stumbles at the patient or physician's house, these signs are unfavourable. Should he find the practitioner with his face turned towards the south ; with cutting instruments near him ; in an unclean situation ; naked, bathing, eating, sleeping, or making holes in any thing ; these signs are unfavourable. It is also a bad omen when the Messenger finds the physician preparing a body for the funeral pile, killing birds or the like, or boiling or preparing medicines with fire. Should the messenger arrive at the house of the physician at twelve at night, or at noon, or when certain stars are in the ascendant the prognosis is unfavourable.

The messenger should always present a present to the physician. He should be of the same caste as the sick person, and should be dressed in clean white clothes, have a good appearance, and be strong and intelligent ; of a mild disposition, and know the lucky seasons, and the shastres.

The medicines should be given by a healthy dependant, possessed of an amiable character, so as to prevent the machinations of the patients enemies.

The friend who relates the progress of the disease must be exact in his descriptions, and be careful that the patient takes the medicines regularly.

5th. Duty of the Patient. A person rejecting a Vaidya, or physician, will be punished in Hell ; whereas when a Vaidya is employed the patient will go to heaven, even should he not be able to see the sacred Ganges in his dying moments*.

The diseased person will carefully recollect the directions of the physician, must follow them with exactness, and must not be afraid of the effects of the medicines which have been ordered.

Should the disease commence at an unfavourable time, or if the physician visits the patient at night, or during an unlucky hour, or should he have been borne at an unfavourable moment, the person will die of the disease. A patient with a good disposition, with his body of the natural colour, and with the signs of longivity ; who is patient, has a strong mind, senses perfect, with no fatal symptoms, and has confidence in his physician, is easily treated, and will have the best chance of being cured. Should the patient be strong, the disease curable, and he has riches to defray the necessary expence, and follow the usual customs and directions of the physician ; and his mind is favourably influenced by the shastres, and has faith in his physician, he will recover. The prognosis will be unfavourable when the sick person is impatient, angry, and disobedient ; wanting in courage, is ungrateful, and desponds ; also, with those who have no confidence in the practitioner, fatal symptoms will quickly follow. Persons at enmity with the physician, and endeavour to deceive him, are cured with difficulty, and are to be avoided as much as possible. The patient will die who lives in the house of a person who despises the physician. The different appearances observed on the physician's approaching and leaving his patient will vary his prognosis.

The patient is to expect to be visited in the morning, after the customary prayers and ablutions, is to prepare the medicine as ordered, and is to sit in a clean, convenient part of the house for both the sick person, and the physician.

* Many respectable Hindus will only receive medicines from a Vaidya.

CHAPTER V.

Recompence of the Physician.

When a physician has cured a disease he is entitled to the usual gifts for the performance of a good action. These will vary with the rank and condition of the patient. Money will be the recompence bestowed by the rich; friendship, reputation, increase of virtue, prayers, and gratitude will be that of the poor. When a Guru, a Brahman, or a Dandí, a relative, a humble and good friend, or one without relations consults a physician, he must not accept of any pecuniary recompence: His reward in such cases will be an increase of knowledge, and the gratification of his desires in having an opportunity of performing a good action. His cures will ensure the admiration, and the esteem of all men; he will be honoured and respected as a master, and after death he will go to heaven. Should the patient prove ungrateful after being cured, his holyness and good fortune will pass to the physician. But the physician must avoid administering remedies, to hunters or great sinners. Such people do not deserve his assistance.

BOOK II.

—o—

ANATOMY AND PHYSIOLOGY.

UNDER THIS HEAD WILL BE CONSIDERED THE THEORY OF THE ELEMENTS; GENERATION, AND GROWTH OF THE BODY; NATURE OF THE CORPORIAL (ANATOMY), VITAL, AND SPIRITUAL PARTS; OF THE TEMPERAMENTS; AND OF DEATH.

CHAPTER I.

Elements of the Body.

At an early period the Hindu Philosophers reduced the material world to five elementary principles, and primary qualities; by the agency of which, they explained the appearance, composition, and condition of the world, and the structure and functions of the Body. The five elementary principles were earth, water, air, fire, and ether.

The peculiar qualities of each of the elements are as follow :—

The Earth has smell (gandha) ; the water, taste (rasa); the air, touch (sparsa); the fire, colour (rúpa); and the pure ether, sound (sabda). Besides these they have likewise the following qualities:—

Earth, which is the heaviest element, is possessed of the qualities of smell, sound, tangibility, visibility, and taste. It enters largely into the formation of the body, and of all solid and heavy substances.

Water possesses sound, tangibility, visibility, and taste; bestows the sense of coolness, fluidity, weight, and smoothness on bodies; and has much the quality of happiness (satwaguna), and of inertness (tamaguna), and is transparent producing light, and weight. It forms the different fluids of the body.

Air is possessed of sonorousness, tangibility, and lightness; and from having the quality of action (raja guna) in excess, it has the moving powers, and qualities of bodies.

Fire possesses sound, tangibility, and visibility, and gives taste. The medical property of fire is to afford heat, digestion, colour, light, and beauty to the body. It produces the passions, bodily strength, and valour of the individual; and from possessing much of the quality of goodness (satwa), and passion (raja guna), it gives it lightness, and movement.

In viewing the wonderful operations of nature, the Hindu Philosophers seem to have been soon arrested by the beautiful and varied adaptation of design to the end, by the order, harmony, and mutual dependance which pervades the whole of nature. This seems to have led them to the conclusion, that inert matter was insufficient of itself to produce such effects, and that there was a fifth element for performing the operations of the body, like the great soul which regulates those of the world. This induced them to add, at an early period, another or spiritual element to those of inert matter, which they called pure ether (ákása) ; which was supposed to be separated from the others, and possessed the property of sound, and form. It predominates in the organ of hearing, and fills up the porosities of living bodies, and their hollow cavities, as those of the bones, &c. ; and is full of the quality of goodness (Satwa guna). This Element is altogether undistinguishable by our senses, and is only made known to us through the evidence of our understanding.

These elements are all nourishing to the body, and are contained in different proportions in every sort of food ; so that after digestion, each element, by an inherent property, joins with that which already forms a part of the fabric of the body, in the following manner ; skin, vessels, bone, hair, and flesh, are made up principally of the element of earth ; alvine evacuations (mala), urine, semen, blood, and phlegm, of water ; hunger, thirst, and insensibility, are produced by fire ; movement, conscience, termination of a work, retaining happiness, by air ; and desire, revenge, stupidity, fear, shame, is produced by an excess of pure ether. There being both an active or warm, and a passive, or cold principle, which are increased and strengthened by the rays of the sun and moon.

The body or microcosm, is also divided into different parts, which correspond with those of the globe. It has its mountains, its cold and hot situations, with the various oceans. Each of the fluids are also influenced by one of the seven planets which regulate their condition.

The same reasoning, which was supposed applicable to the external world, was used for the explanation of the constitution, and fabric of the animal system. Hence, all living bodies, among which vegetable bodies are placed, are supposed to be composed of the five elements, with the element producing action or life superadded. Living bodies are produced from vapour, vegetation, incubation, and parturition ; as insects, plants, birds, fishes, reptiles, and animals.

Of the latter, man is the chief, and in proportion to the complicated structure of his body so is his liability to disease.

The essential or elementary parts, when mixed, form vital bodies, which are divided into two classes, one of which is stationary, the other moveable (jangama). This class is produced from the womb (jarâynja), as animals (pasu), and man (manusha). 2nd, from eggs (andaja), as birds, snakes (sadoso), &c.; 3rd, from the warmth of the earth, as worms, ants, mosquetoes, fleas, &c.; and 4th, (udjbidgo) such as break their habitation, and thus gain their liberty, as frogs, &c.

The second or stationary class consists of four varieties :—

1st. Vanaspati or trees in which the fruit is without flowers.

2nd. Vriksha trees with flowers and fruits.

3rd. Verada, creepers.

4th. Asudie, annuals.

The same elements and qualities, by their combination and actions constitute the human body; which is governed by an independent principle, or soul, which acts through the medium of the members; and is an emanation from the great soul of the world; into which after certain purifications, it is again absorbed. As long as the soul remains in connexion with the body, the diseases with which it is afflicted may be removed; and it is proper that during all this time, remedies should be employed for the purpose.

The following is the Hindu theory of the formation of the body :—

CHAPTER II.

Generation.

It is stated in medical works, that as the mould receives the seed which is to form the future plant, so the menses of the female receives the semen of the male, which germinates in it. Hence in treating of generation, the secretion of the menses is first considered.

When the menses appear monthly, the female is moist, plump, has desire; and is happy, with her hair flying about. Her eyes are languishing; her sides, arms, breasts, thighs, and hips are in a state of excitement. The menses continue for seventeen days, during which the woman may be impregnated, and not at any other season. During the flow of the menses the mouth of the uterus, which is like the mouth of a rue fish, is open like the water lily, exposed to the rays of the sun; and after this season, the mouth of the uterus again contracts, and closes like the petals of the lily, when the benign influence of the sun is absent.

The menses are of a red colour, like the blood of a hare, or of lac-dye. It should not stain cloth, when it falls upon it; and should be without smell. The menses are derived from the two vessels of the uterus, which discharge their contents by the influence of the vital air, into the uterus and vagina. The menses remain till the 50th year, when the woman is of a weak constitution; but it continues longer, when the individual is strong.

During the discharge of the menses, much attention is required to be observed regarding the conduct of the woman, as the state of the parents at the time of conception will affect the offspring in a very powerful manner. During the first three days of the discharge, the woman should remain pure, she must sit and sleep in a purified situation, upon the sacred grass (kush); she must eat out of a new earthen vessel, or from a leaf, she must not sleep during the day while the menses flow, or her offspring will be very sluggish: should she shut her eyes at the time of conception, the child will be blind; should she shed tears, the child's eyes will be sore; should she cut her nails during the flow of the menses, the child will be deformed; should she anoint or bathe herself during these three days, the infant will be afflicted with leprosy; should she laugh or speak loud, the infant will be unhappy and deaf; and should she fatigue herself, the offspring will be employed in low occupations.

The father should neither be very old, nor very young. If the father is not twenty-five, and the woman beyond sixteen, the offspring will die in the uterus, if it be born alive it will live but a short time, or if the infant lives the senses and other parts will be incomplete. Therefore a very young man, or a very old woman should be avoided. They should be in good health, the genital organs free from disease, and the female should neither be hungry, nor have eaten recently before connexion. The semen should be received into the menses as a seed dropped into a good mould, and like it germinate, producing conception. As milk taken into the stomach nourishes the child, so the semen requires to be animated with the menses to form the germ.

Should conception take place on the 1st or 2nd day of the menses, the offspring will die soon after birth. If conceived on the third day, the child will be weak, diseased, and deformed, and will die at an early age.

If the husband is not at home on the fourth day of the menses, the wife is first to regard the sun after bathing, as the best object; in order that her offspring may resemble that luminary in his qualities of bestowing strength and beauty, and should the first object she sees, after bathing on the 4th day, be a deformed individual, her offspring will also be so. The female is next to perform the necessary ceremonies to ensure offspring with the assistance of the Brahmuns ; she is to eat in the afternoon of the fourth day, bathe, rub her body with scented oil, put on clean clothes, and ornaments, and at night visit her husband. But should there be a great discharge of the menses on this day, she must not visit her husband ; as the semen will be washed away as by a swollen river, and will thus prevent conception. Such cases are to be treated as other cases of Menorrhagia.

When the female conceives on the 4th, 6th, 8th, 10th, and 12th days of the menses they are the fortunate days. It is when conception occurs, towards the last of these days, that the offspring will live long and have few diseases. If conception occurs after the 12th day, it is unfavourable to the offspring. When conception occurs on the unequal days of the menses, a female child will be born ; while on the equal a male will be produced.

Numerous forms of irregularities, and diseases of the menses prevent conception, the principal of which are derangements of the humours, in which cases the air, bile, and phlegm stop the flow of the menses, by closing the passages by which this evacuation flows.

When the menses are irregular, or are stopped, the woman should live on fish, a kind of pulse called *kulotha*, linseed (tel), masculi, butter, curdled milk, acids, and sura (a kind of wine).

Durga asked Siva the nature of the body, Siva answered ; know, O Durga ! that the body is formed by a mixture of the energy of the male and female, in this way : During a fortunate connexion the heat produced gives the semen the quality of the water, and the air conveys it to the urethra of the male, from which it passes into the vagina. When it enters the uterus it mixes with the heating qualities of the *sun*, which the menses possesses, and forms the embryo. It is when the mixture takes place, and has become solid, by their respective qualities of cold and heat to which the soul is added. Should the germ have more of the qualities of the semen, a male child will be formed, and of the menses a female child ; and should the qualities of both be equal, the child will be a hermaphrodite.

Signs of conception. The indications of conception, during the day it has taken place are ; the woman feeling fatigued, languid, and thirsty, a weakness of the two thighs, a retention of the semen and blood in the uterus, and a throbbing in the vagina.

The signs of Pregnancy, are the skin round the nipples becoming of a dark colour, and the hair upon the body becoming more distinct and prominent. The person feels weak, the eyelids heavy, and the eyelashes closed; much saliva is secreted; sickness and vomiting occur; and even pleasant smelling things are disliked, and produce sickness. In this condition the woman must not approach her husband; she must avoid fasting, vomiting, or strong purgatives; grief or fear; stretching or severe coughing; dragging heavy weights; riding on horseback; sleeping during the day; or sitting up at night. She must not be bled, nor strain in passing her dejections.

During Pregnancy, if the woman is not gratified with what she wishes to eat, and the air is deranged, the child will be crooked and cripple, or will be small in size, dumb, or cannot speak distinctly; will be blind, or have his eyes defective, or will be an unbeliever in the sacred shastres. In other such cases these defects are produced by acts of previous wickedness of his own, or of his parents in a former state of existence.

Whatever is wanted by the pregnant woman should therefore be supplied, when a perfect child will be born. If the woman desires to see a Rajah, the child will be great and rich; should the mother wish to adorn herself, the child will be well formed and vain; should the mother wish to see a holy man, the child will be holy, and just, and if she longs to see ferocious animals the offspring will be of that description. In like manner the desire for particular sorts of food indicates the disposition of the infant, and the form of his body. When the mother wishes to eat buffalo's flesh the child will have blood-shot eyes, much hair, and he will be warlike; and when hog's flesh, he will be sluggish, and sleepy.

If any injury be done to the mother, or she suffers in any way, the child in like manner suffers. The menses, after conception, goes in part to form the placenta, and as the blood flows every month, it coagulates to form the embryo; an upper layer being added every month to the embryo, and another portion to the breasts, of the mother by which the mammæ are increased in size.

The period of delivery extends from nine to twelve months, and after this time when the female is not delivered, the abdominal swelling must be considered as the effect of disease.

CHAPTER III.

Growth and functions of the Body.

There is no peculiar organ for the semen, but it is supposed to be contained in every part of the body, as butter is in the milk, or sugar in the sugar-cane. There is a duct on the right side of the mouth of the urinary bladder, where it is collected, and passes through the urethra in the time of coition.

The menses of the woman disappears when she conceives, and it circulates towards the mammæ where it is collected and produces milk.

The germ thus formed contains a small proportion of the five elements; each of which assists in promoting the developement of the other elements, and of the body in general. Jiva or the soul is last engendered, and like fire produced by a burning glass, the mixture of the menses and semen produce heat. When the air separates the particles of the semen it produces twins, triplets, &c. When one of the constituent parts of the embryo is unhealthy, the conception will be so; and, if both the menses and semen are impure, as when the parents are affected with leprosy, the offspring will also be afflicted with this disease.

The germ in the uterus is like a shrub, the vessels of which are connected with the uterus, by which the blood of the mother is circulated in it, and nourished. The germ is near the fire of the mother at the navel, is inflated by the air (váyu) and fire, which the embryo contains, by which it is expanded into its different parts, forming the vessels, circulating the juices, and from which its members are formed; like the potter giving figure to the piece of clay upon his wheel.

In the first month, the mixture of the semen and menses forms a small mass like a pea (kolala); seven days after conception it has the form of a bubble, or inflated bag. On the tenth it is red, and on the fifteenth it resembles a small round piece of flesh: This shortly enlarges in the same imperceptible way as the Moon enlarges in size (Jyotistatwa): At one month it has small fibres proceeding from it, and is animated with life (Prána). The point of the vertebral column, is to the body, what *Mount Sumeru* is to the world, and in that point the gods of the body reside (Bramha, Vishnu, &c.)

Should the germ become of a circular form (pinda), it denotes a male; an oblong form (Pashie) a female; and an iregular form (Arbuda) a hermaphrodite. In the third month five eminences appear, which when developed become the hands, feet, and head. The other smaller parts of the body are then but imperfectly formed.

In the fourth month the members are more distinctly developed; and the heart of the fetus being perfectly formed, life receives its active powers, and has a desire for the assistance of sense and activity. Life then acts as in its former state of existence.

In the fifth month, the powers of the mind are increased; and life performs its usual actions. The nose, mouth, eyes, throat, and abdomen may now be distinguished; and at six months all the members are formed, and the understanding is added.

At the seventh month, the body is completely formed, and the members can act separately, and possess life, mind, and understanding. The essence of the strength of the system (ozah) is imperfectly formed, even at the 8th month; and on this account, should the infant be born during this month, it will die. During the 8th month the joints are formed, the parts move on each other, the fetus requires food, and, by the heat of the mother strength is added. At nine months the mind and memory are active, it moves about, and it receives nourishment from the mother. According to some, by means of a vessel which passes from the mother's breasts to the mouth of the embryo; by others it is stated that the vessels of the umbeliacal cord have a communication with the vessels of the mother, and convey blood to the fetus, by which it is increased in size. In the 9th month, the woman is to remove to the house (sutiká grirah) prepared for her delivery.

At the tenth month* the fetus acquires knowledge, and prays to God, and sees the seven heavens, the earth, and the inferior regions. By the air of the pelvis (opana bayu) the fetus is then expelled; as an arrow is shot from a bow, and the child falls insensible to the ground. All his former knowledge is immediately forgotten, and on losing so many pleasing illusions, he cries (Jotis).

During the time the fetus is in the uterus it does not discharge its evacuations because they are in small quantities, and the air which discharges them is not present in the intestines (pokasia). The fetus does not cry in the uterus, as the mouth is closed by the fetal membranes, the wind-pipe is filled with phlegm, and there is no passage for air. The respiration, sleep, and turning of the fetus are performed by the mother, as she sleeps, &c.

By nature, the situation and form of the different parts of the body are developed. So that the hair is formed on one part, and is absent at another part of the body. If the quality of happiness (satwaguna) be in excess, the child knows the state it held in its former condition; and does good or bad actions accordingly, and acquires its former qualities.

The hard substances of the fetus, as hairs, bones, nails, teeth,

* Nine Calender months seem necessary for the perfection of the fetus; that is 39 weeks or 273 days from conception. The Hindu Shastres allow ten calender months or 300 days.

vessels, ligaments, &c., are produced from the semen, and resemble the same parts in the father; and the soft parts as flesh, blood, fat, marrow, heart, navel, liver, spleen, intestines, are formed principally from the blood of the mother, and resemble her.

The growth and strength of the body, the different colours and the duration of life, are produced from the (rasa) according to the qualities of the food of different kinds generally taken by the parents. The senses, knowledge of the arts, and life (jíva), happiness, misery, are produced from the parent's good or bad actions in a former state of existence.

The fetus in utero is bent on itself with his head upwards, and mouth towards the spine of the mother. His hands and feet are bent, and during parturition the air turns the body and brings the head downwards, and he knows his former history. The uterus is a dark and disagreeable place, which the Brahmans eledge is a kind of purgatory. If the mother eats proper food, the child receives its nourishment from the umbelical cord which is connected with the mother, and by means of the cord the blood is conveyed to the fetus which thereby grows.

The sex of the infant is known by the right mammæ containing milk first, the right eye being larger than the left, the woman wishing food of the masculine kind, and dreaming of the water lilies of different species, and her mouth, and the colour of her lips of an agreeable colour. The opposite indications are the proof of an infant being of the male sex. Twins are known by a depression along the centre of the abdomen; and when the two sides of the abdomen are depressed, and the lower end is a little prominent, with a depression in the middle, a hermaphrodite is known to be contained in the uterus.

The small vessels in the embryo produce first its growth, before the members are produced. The mixture of the semen and blood or embryo increase, and life enters it; the air separates the different members, the fire prepares the elements, the water moistens, the earth stiffens, and the sky (ákása) increases the fetus. When the embryo has hands, feet, mouth, nose, ears, buttocks, &c., then it is called the human body, and is composed of six principal parts; four extremities, the trunk, head, abdomen, back, umbilicus, forehead, chin, nose, neck, bladder, are the single parts of the body. The pairs are the ears, eyes, nostrils, eyebrows, temples, shoulders, cheeks, axillas, mammæ, testicles, sides, buttocks, knees, arms, thighs, &c. The body has nine orifices, like a house with nine doors. They are the urethra, anus, mouth, nostrils, eyes, and ears: The vagina forms the tenth in the female. There are ten fingers and ten toes. The other parts of the body are the skin, Kolah, (tissues) fluids (dhátu); dejections, (mala); and humours (dossoh); with the liver, spleen, lungs, pancreas, heart, stomach, urinary and gall bladders; the intestines, kidnies, vessels, ligaments, tendons, membranes, *median* connections of the body, bones, joints, muscles, vital parts, the veins, arteries, nerves, and capillary vessels, esophagus, wind-pipe, &c.

Saunaka says that the head is first formed, because; it is the principal part of all the organs of sense. *Kritabirya* says that the heart is first formed, because it is the seat of the mind and knowledge. Others that the umbiliacus is first formed, because from that centre the other members grow. Some say the trunk, and others that the hands and feet are first formed, as they are the root of the active members. *Dhanwantari* says that all these opinions are incorrect, and that all the members are formed at the same time but are, extremely small, as the first sprig of the bamboo contains the leaves, &c, of the future plant; and as a constituent part of the mangoe is only visible in its state of ripeness, and cannot be detected when the tree is green.

With the child is produced, the period of his life, his actions, whether virtuous or vicious; his acquirement of riches, or experience of the senses, and death, will be varied according to the actions he performed in his former state of existence. The acuteness of his senses, the extent of knowledge, the duration of his life, and happiness or misery, being produced from the soul; so the strength, colour, health, memory, will be derived from the nature of the food used by the parents.

As long as the elements remain in due proportion, the body remains in health, this state is called *Prakriti,* and when increased or diminished in its proper proportions it is called *Vikriti.*

On these qualities, and to these alone, the physician attends. From the elements, the eleven senses are produced to perform their peculiar offices, as the sound of the ear, &c., and is confined to it.

The parts of the fetus are formed in the following manner:—

The Liver and spleen are formed from the blood; Lungs from its froth; and the large intestines (cecum) from its impurities. The essential parts of blood and phlegm are concocted by the fire of the body, into which the air (váyu) enters, and forms the intestines, anus, and bladder. The tongue is formed from the essential parts of blood, phlegm, and flesh.

Air, with the assistance of a proper degree of heat, separates the soft parts, and forms canals, and passing between the flesh forms the different muscles. When these canals are filled up with marrow they form nerves. This opinion arises from their supposing that the brain and spinal marrow are the marrow of these bones. The air entering among the soft parts forms the different receptacles of the body, as the stomach and kidnies, which are derived from the essential parts of the blood. The *testicles*, and its appendages are formed from the pure part of flesh, blood, phlegm, and fat. The heart is formed by the essential parts of blood and phlegm, to which all the principal arteries are connected, by which life is preserved. It resembles a water lily, with its head turned downwards. When the person is awake it is in activity, and when asleep it is sluggish. It is the seat of the understanding ; and if the quality of darkness and ignorance predominates (tamaguna) the person sleeps, and when the (satwaguna) prevails the person remains awake.

Sleep is a kind of death, derived from Vishnu, and the ignorant sleep much, and those who have much sotwaguna sleep about midnight, and those who have much rajoguna sleep occasionally and without any reasonable cause. When the tamohguna and phlegm predominate in the heart, a kind of sleep (syncopy) occurs, from which the individual cannot be awaken : In this it resembles death.

Sleep during the day should always be avoided, except during excessive heat, as it is considered a sin, and is unfavourable to health by deranging the humours and producing disease ; such as coughing, asthma, catarrh, heaviness of the body, pain of the body, dyspepsy, fever. Want of sleep at night, produces the diseases of air and bile. But children and old people, and those who have indulged in an excess of venery, who have consumption, drink much, or are much fatigued by travelling, or other exercises, or those who are very hungry, or labour under indigestion, may sleep an hour (48 minutes) in the day time. If the person does not sleep during the night, he may take half the quantity of sleep during the day. Sleeping during the day deranges air, bile, and phlegm, and many diseases are produced by it ; as coughing, difficult breathing, &c. Night watching deranges air, and bile, and produces various diseases ; hence sleep should be taken at night. By sleeping at the proper time it will prevent disease, and will retain the heart, as well as strength, colour, and semen in their proper state. It will also prevent too great thinness or fatness, and such a person, with a good constitution, may live a hundred years.

When phlegm is diminished, and air and bile increased, by passions, and any humour of the body lessened by their causes, the sleep is disturbed.

If a person regulates sleep by his will, it will not be favourable. A certain period of sleep daily, is necessary to health. Too much air, bile, or grief, destroys sleep, diminishes the dhátu, and injures the health of the body. In such cases oil with turmeric and other like things applied to the head, and the body will promote sleep. Bathing has a like effect, as also champooing, eating good rice, flower, peas, cakes, sweet-meats, oleaginous food, milk, with the juice of flesh, especially animals that burrow in the ground, or the flesh of birds, rasins, and sugar eaten at night. The bed, &c., being soft and agreeable, will also promote sleep.

When sleep is protracted it is to be obviated by vomits (songsodhana) and a purge, by spare food, blood letting, and causes producing mental depression. When cough, or fat, or poison have produced it, exercise is to be taken at night. When there is thirst, colic, or hiccough, want of digestion, or diarrhœa, sleeping in the day is proper.

Dreaming. It is the soul which dreams. Whatever was seen or heard when awake, is represented by the mind, during sleep; and is the impression of good or bad actions, when there is much rajahguna in the heart.

Drowsiness, is indicated by the senses not remaining in their state of activity; the body is heavy, the person yawns, he is tired, is drowsy, and desires to sleep. It is produced by an excess of air, phlegm, and tomahguna.

Yawning. During a long inspiration the mouth is extended, followed by a short expiration, and a flow of tears from the eyes, is called yawning.

Langour is when the person is fatigued without a cause, and the respiration is weak, and imperfect.

Laziness when the person has the capacity, without the inclination to act; and wishes enjoyment without exertion.

Nausea is accompanied with an increased flow of saliva and tears, with pain in the breast, and an effort to reject the food, but it does not reach the mouth.

Fainting. When bile (pitta) and tamaguna are in excess, it produces this effect.

Swooning is produced by an excess of rajaguna, with bile and air.

Digestion. Six varieties of the digested part of food or chyle are distinguishable. When the food is astringent, sour, moist, &c., the chyle will become of the same nature. When digestion is accomplished, the respective elements unite with those which had entered into the formation of the body; the earth unites with the earth, the water with the water, &c., and they, acting on the inherent qualities of each of the five elements, mix and increase those in the body ; smell, the property of earth, with that of the body ; taste with water, touch with air, and noise with ether (ákása). The juice thus separated from its impurities is called chyle (rasa), which nourishes, strengthens, and gives colour to the body.

Some Pandits suppose that it requires a day and night to form and distribute the digested mass, to the last deposited part the semen and menses ; others suppose six days are required, and some one month before digestion is completed. The first class of Pandits suppose the fluids are formed and circulated as a wheel turning round, and supplying the various essential parts of the body (dhátu.) If an article of food or medicine increases much the semen, and fluids, they may require only a day and night to accomplish this, and such an increase cures some diseases of the body. As the beard does not grow, nor the flower yield its smell at an early stage of their growth ; so in the child, the semen, and the menses remain for a certain time undeveloped which is also the case in old age, like over ripe fruit.

The strength, or vital principle of the body (*Oja* or *tej*) is situated in the chest along its centre, and is produced by a mixture of the pure fluid ; in the same manner as a bee sucks the juice from different flowers, and produces honey. Oja exists as long as the person lives, and it is this which retains the body in its healthy state.

CHAPTER IV.

Structure of the Corporeal part of the Body (Anatomy.)

The Body consists of Humours, (*Dossoh*) and essential parts, (*dhátu*) with their appendages :—

Section I.

Humours.

The air (váyu*), Bile (pitta †), and Phlegm (kofa ‡), are the three pillars or supports of the system. If deranged they are

* Váyu from *Va*, to go, was first formed.
† Petu, from *Tapah*, hot ; from which the heat of the Body is derived.
‡ Kofa, *siliso*; from siliso, to embrace.

the cause of disease, and death; and, with the blood, they retain, and eventually destroy the body. Without these three Humours and the blood the individual could not exist. With the essential parts of the body, and the appendages, and impurities, they form the fabric of the body.

As the moon sheds moisture, and abstracts the Sun's rays, which dry up and bestow energy upon the earth, and the air moves from place to place, so does phlegm bestow moisture, bile withdraws it by its heat, and air wafts it about in the microcosm, or animal body *.

1*st*. Váyu, spirit, or air, flows through all parts of the body, and performs all its actions. It is of the active quality (rajaguna); is invisible, is of a cooling quality, is extremely light, and is always flowing more or less quickly; it conveys the essential parts over the body; performs respiration, and all the actions at the outlets of the body, the circulation of the fluids, and activity of the senses, and of the understanding. It dries up the fluids, is soft, but is affected by heat, and cold; and like the Sun's rays, it prepares and separates the fluids, and dejections. It produces happiness when healthy, and with heat increases the hot state of the system. It is principally found in the small intestines (puckassia), thighs, ears, eyes, senses, and all the canals, the testicles, and the anus. It produces the active properties of the body and its organs, and retains the body in its proper state. There are five kinds of *air* according to the situations they occupy.

a. Vital air (*Prána váyu*) which passes through the mouth and nose, and by it diglutition is performed. It is situated in the chest, and is the supporter of *prána*, or life. While this remains in health, so does the individual; it gives movement to the blood, and by it the food and drink are conveyed to the stomach, and strength to the body: when diseased it produces hiccough, and difficulty of breathing, &c.

b. *Apána váyu* is contained in the rectum, urethra, &c.; and is situated under the *puckasia*, It separates the dejections, urine, semen, menses, and expels the fetus. It is also situated in the buttocks. When deranged it produces diseases of the bladder, and the anus, diseases of the semen, and constipation.

c. *Samána váyu* is situated in the stomach, and small intestines

* This ingenious theory which has been so frequently renewed, and was for so many ages universally believed, seems to have been derived from the Hindus; from whom it was adopted by the Egyptian and Grecian Priesthood. It is defective, however, in excluding the blood which, notwithstanding, has been stated as one of the fundamental parts of the Body.

(amassia, and puckassia) ; performs the digestion of the food, separates the impurities, produces blood, and fat, and separates the urine, alvine evacuations, &c. When diseased it produces loss of appetite, goolmoh, diarrhœa, &c.

d. *Udana bayu* is situated in the hollow of the neck, above the sternum. In health it produces speech and singing ; and other functions of the voice, above the colar bones. When deranged it produces various diseases of the upper part of the neck.

e. *Beana bayu* is found acting in conveying the fluids over the body, and in performing its functions, and those of the juices. It produces the flow of the blood; and performs walking, jumping, opening of the eyes, raising or depressing things, &c. If diseased all the body becomes affected.

Vital air is thus supposed to flow over the body, to produce, and to retain the various vital functions of the body ; as joy, respiration, and its various actions : it also mixes with the humours, and regulates the movements of the body.

When the air is diminished weakness is produced, the person speaks little, he is melancholy, and it diminishes the understanding, &c. Vital air, is deranged by carrying heavy weights, by severe exercise, by excess in venery, much study, falls, or walking very fast : by always pressing the body, by injuries, fasting, jumping, or swimming ; by not sleeping at night, by riding upon horse-back, elephants, or in carriages ; by much walking, or using much sour, pungent, bitter, or dry substances, or light cooling vegetables, flesh or certain kinds of pulse, &c. Air may be deranged by the quantity and quality of the food which is eaten, by certain actions of the body, and by exposure to the cold, and moist air, early in the morning. If all the varieties of *Váyu* are diseased the person dies.

2nd. Bile (*pitta*) is a hot, bitter, oily fluid, having a peculiar smell, like that of raw flesh. It is of a blue colour and sour, when unconcocted ; and is hot and pungent like fire or pepper, and of a yellow colour when properly prepared. It produces animal heat, and it possesses the quality of *Satwaguna*. It is situated principally in the stomach (*Amassia*), and small intestines (*puckasia*) ; but it is also found in the liver, spleen, heart, eye, and skin ; where it is mixed with the blood, and other fluids. Its principal situation, however, is between the stomach and small intestines, from which it passes to the different parts of the body in which it is found. There are the following five kinds of Bile.

a. *Pachcha*, or that which assists digestion, and is situated between the stomach and small intestines. It digests the six kinds of food; and separates the chyle, urine, and feces. As the sun imparts its properties (*tej*) to the moon, so bile imparts its properties to the phlegm, situated in the stomach. The stomach is therefore like a cooking pot containing water and food, which is boiled by the heat of the bile underneath it. In this way digestion is performed, and the blood is rendered more fluid.

When digestion is performed its qualities are like fire, and dries up the thin part of the food, and is called *onola* or fire, and separates the pure part from its dregs. It gives strength to the body, and as a candle enlightens objects around, so bile conveys its properties over all the body.

b. In the liver and spleen the bile gives a red colour to the chyle, and is called *ranjaka.*

c. In the heart it produces sense, memory, pride, and is called *Sadaka.*

d. In the eyes it produces sight, and is called *álochoka.*

e. It gives the skin its shining, clear, and healthy colour; absorbs applications to the skin, and is called *brajoka.* Bile when not deranged produces the sense of sight, digestion, and the functions of organs by its heating and concocting properties. It produces appetite, and thirst, and retains the body soft, giving the proper colour to the body; and also joy, pride, memory, &c. Bile varies in different seasons; in July and August it is increased; in September and October it is liable to be diseased; and in March and April it is diminished.

When deranged, the internal fire or heat of the body is diminished, as also its colour, and digestion. In this case the nourishing chyle (rasa) is not properly separated in the organ called Amassia, and produces the indigestable dejections called *áma*, or more properly white slimey discharges. If the slime be mixed with air, bile, and phlegm it deranges the seven *dhátu.*

The increase of the five elements, and their five qualities, of which the body is composed, will be best understood by following the course and changes of the food when eaten. The food by means of *prán váyu* reaches the stomach (*amassia*), where it is softened and mixed with the phlegm in the stomach, and becomes red and sweet. By the air situated in the navel (*samána váyu*), the fire is increased, and it digests the food in the stomach, which becomes frothy and sour, it then passes to the place of bile (grinní), which is situated between the stomach and small intestines. When well concocted by the bile situated there, the food becomes pungent, being mixed with the chyle. It then passes to the *pukassia*, or place in which digestion is perfected, and is separated from its impurities.

The impure fluid part passes by means of vessels into the bladder; and the solid impurities by means of the *apán vayu*, passes into the *molásia*, or large intestines. The pure part of the digested food is of a milky colour, and is conveyed to the heart by means of the domonnic vessels, where it is mixed with the blood. Charaka calls these vessels the chyle carrying vessels (*rasyani*).

Should the fire be too strong it burns the food, and it becomes sour, and generates bile. When the fire dries the food, it produces a hard mass, which is bitter. After digestion the prepared food sometimes becomes sour, by its mixture with substances of this quality. When digestion is not properly performed, the internal fire and strength are diminished; the person becomes weakened, and diseases are produced, particularly the disease which is called *áma*.

When morbidly increased in the body, bile produces a yellowness of the skin, much heat, a desire for cooling articles of food, and a loss of sleep and strength. The person cannot see perfectly, and his eyes, feces, and urine become yellower than usual.

The hair of a person with such a temperament, becomes quickly grey, he perspires easily, his body is pale, his eyes are easily inflamed, and he is impatient, perverse, opiniative, vain, and consequential; is amorous, his conversation unguarded, is addicted to falsehood, is fond of abstruse studies, &c. Bile is deranged by anger, grief, fear, covetousness, malice, great fatigue, fasting, by eating roasted articles of food, by excessive venery, by sour, salt, and hot or heavy food, by mustard oil, or cakes; by certain kinds of pulse, as mustard seed; by vegetables, fish, flesh, curdled milk, butter-milk, spirits, and heat of all kinds.

3*rd*. The Phlegm (Kofa), is the impurity of the chyle, and it is conveyed by the *prana vayu* along the domonic vessels, and mixes with the rest of the phlegm in the body. It is cooling, moist, sweet, and when imperfectly prepared it is salt, and mixes substances together, &c. It is white, heavy, oleaginous, and glistening, and possesses the quality of *tomohguna* in excess. It is principally found in the stomach, in the breast, in the heart, at the root of the neck, in the head, in the eyes, in the throat, and tongue; and is found in the joints, in vessels, and all moist parts. There are five kinds described:—

a. In the stomach (*amasia*) it softens the food, and lubricates them together, and is called *Kledoka*.

b. *Abalambana*, is situated in the shoulder-joint, and neck, and it strengthens these parts, and also the breast.

c. In the tongue and throat, it produces the various tastes, and is called, *Rasana*.

d. In the head, it keeps the brain, the eyes, and other senses moist. It retains their respective qualities, and is called *Strehena.*

e. It keeps the joints moist and ready to perform their actions, and is called *slesona.*

If not deranged it retains the body in its proper state, produces its glistening appearance, and moist state. It strengthens the joints, produces the heaviness and strength of the body, and enters into the formation of semen. The temperament it produces is indicated by a greenish colour, and the person is fortunate, is of a fine colour, and is fond of sweet things. He is grateful, patient, and is without covetousness. He is strong with a white eye, his hair is black, and he dreams of water.

When morbidly diminished it produces impurities ; the body dries, the internal heat is increased, digestion is diminished, the joints move with difficulty, the person is incommoded with thirst, weakness, and watching. In this state it leaves its natural situations, and passes to other parts of the body. It is deranged by sleeping during the day, taking no exercise, using much sweet, salt, sour, or cooling substances ; as also oleaginous and heavy articles of food, as milk, and the like ; barley, various kinds of rice, the flesh of the buffalo, and those animals which live in water. It is also deranged by eating always the same food, or eating too often, or cooling things of all kinds. This humour is also deranged by the seasons ; in November and December it is increased, in March and April it is liable to be deranged, and in May and June it is diminished. When much increased it produce indigestion, loss of appetite, langour, lassitude, and vomiting.

It is supposed that the phlegm is contained in the parts above the navel, bile in the trunk above the pelvis, and air in and below the pelvis. In the morning phlegm predominates when the body feels cool ; in the middle of the day, bile predominates, when people feel hot ; and in the evening air is the strongest : at night the same order is observed. When these divisions meet, phlegm and air are the strongest. In like manner the age of man is divided into three periods ; to the 15th year phlegm is strongest ; to the 50th, or manhood, bile is the strongest ; and after that, or in old age, air predominates. In like manner where these periods meet, phlegm and air are strongest.

The same changes are observed in the seasons, and in the period of digestion of food, and physicians should be careful of them in the employment of remedies. On this account hot things should be given in the morning or to the young ; cooling things in the middle of the day, or to adults ; and tonic and pungent food in the evening, or in old age.

The seven *dhâtu* and the impurities remain at rest and incapable of action until acted on by air (vayu), and are wafted by it over all parts of the body, as clouds are wafted about by the wind, and through its influence they perform their respective actions. The air (vayu) presides over the ten senses, and is therefore the natural lord of all the actions of the body ; it acts quickly and strongly ; often deranges bile and phlegm, and produces many diseases. It is always present in the body, gives strength, and retains it in a state of health. It is diffused every where over the body, as well as in the world, of which it is the ruler, performing all the actions in it.

Sometimes the different humours are increased in quantity, either separately, or in combination of two or more together ; but bile and phlegm cannot pass from their own receptacles by themselves, without the assistance of air, which is the only active humour, as a high wind striking upon water, throws it about, so vital air acting upon the other humours increase them in quantity, and they are thrown about out of their proper receptacles. Thus, when air, bile, phlegm, and blood are increased, they pass from their own receptacles and mix with the other humours. Sometimes they are diffused over the whole body ; at other times to only a part which is irritated, and then form disease, like the cloud which accumulates over a part, throws down rain there.

If air is much deranged, it leaves its own receptacle, and passes to another situation, producing noise in an unusual situation. Bile in like manner produces heat, a burning sensation, and dryness ; when phlegm is increased, and is changed in its position at the time of its passage, it destroys appetite and digestion, and produces langour and vomiting. In cases where air, bile, phlegm, and blood are deranged, and accumulated in the abdomen ; they diminish appetite and strength, produce *gulmoh* and *bradrodrí*, or large abcesses in the abdomen ; also costiveness, cholera, dysentery, &c.

If deranged, air passes to the receptacle of bile, the medicines for this disease are to be employed for its cure ; and bile, if deranged, passes to phlegm. This is to be cured by removing diseased bile. If phlegm passes to the locality of air, this is to be cured in the usual way.

Brumha, the creator of the world, is full of the *rajaguna*, and resembles air ; while bile resembles *Vishnu*, and is like him full of satwaguna. In like manner phlegm resembles *Siva*, with his inactive qualities, and is the destroyer of the body.

When these humours accumulate in the bladder they produce diabetes, stone, disuria, and other diseases of the urine. When they accumulate in the penis they produce strictures, swellings, &c. In the anus they produce fistula-in-ano, piles, and the like. In the scrotum and testicles, they produce different forms of Hydrocele. If towards the head they produce the various diseases of the head, eyes, &c. When collected in the blood and flesh, the humours produce leprosy, different kinds of cutaneous diseases, and inflammation. If to the fat they produce different kinds of tumours and swellings, particularly of glandular parts. In the bone they produce inflammation, and other like diseases. In the feet elephantiasis, rheumatism, and the like. When diffused over the whole body, fever and other diseases of the body, as small pox, &c., are the consequence.

If such derangements of the humours remain for some time their effects may appear afterwards, and slowly produce the peculiar symptoms of disease.

SECTION II.

Essential Parts (Dhátu.)

The Essential Parts, or the supporters of the body, consist of the hard and soft parts, and fluids of the body.

These are the chyle (rasa), blood (rakta), flesh (mánsa), fat (meda), bone (osthi), marrow (majjá), and semen (sakra). These seven essential parts of the body form the fetus, nourish, and sustain life, and retain the system in a healthy state; they give the soft feel, the colour, and the strength of the body, and the action of the senses. When diseased or diminished, the body wastes, and the person dies. Thus will the period of life vary with the kind of food which is used. Good chyle produces good health, and with it bravery, strength, and a fine colour of the body, and retentive memory.

a. Chyle (rasa) that moves in the body is obtained, and is separated from the four kinds of food which is digested, and is said to be the essence (sára) of the food. It has a glutinous, cooling, and liquid appearance; is sweet, and is of a white colour. It is principally situated in the heart, liver, and spleen; and by means of the vessels called damanee, it is conveyed to the different parts of the body by the *samána váyu;* and nourishes the dhátu, and is changed by the bile (ranjaka) into blood (rakta) in the liver. This kind of bile is supposed to redden the fluids, when it is called blood. The chyle thus changed mixes with the blood, by means of the *samána váyu.* If the Bile be either too strong, or not strong enough; or the food is not properly digested, it becomes pungent, leaves a sour taste in the mouth, and like poison produces disease. The chyle then passes along to the heart, to nourish and increase the dhatu and parts of the body, as fields are irrigated by canals of water, which moisten, and afford them its qualities. When chyle is much increased it produces nausea, and an increased secretion of saliva. There are two varieties of chyle *áma* (chyme), slightly impure, and *pakwa* or chyle in its pure state which nourishes the body.

There is a difference of opinion as to the uses of the chyle, some supposing that it nourishes the parts directly, others suppose that by means of vital air (Prán-váyu), it is conveyed to the damanee vessels by which it is sent to the blood, and mixes with it in the spleen and liver, where it becomes red, is purified by the bile, and remains there for five days and a half. It then passes to the flesh, and remains there some time, and is purified by the bile (pitta), or a kind of internal fire, and is conveyed to the different parts of the body, which it retains at its proper temperature, and nourishes the flesh. In the same way it passes to and remains in the fat, bone, &c., which it nourishes, and purifies with one part; while another impure part (mala) is rejected. Perspiration is the impurity of the blood in the fat; as the tartar is the impurity of the teeth; and other secretions have impurities which are in like manner thrown off. The last dhátu to which the chyle passes is to the semen, which has no dregs: so that the chyle, like sugar, requires different processes to purify it, and at each stage it throws down impurities.

The chyle retains the person in good spirits, increases the blood, &c., and if not properly prepared, it becomes sour; and deranges the the dhátu. If diminished there is pain in the breast, the person shakes, has swimming in the head and moistness in the eyes, with thirst. In one month the chyle changes to blood, flesh, fat, bone, and marrow, from which semen, and the menses are produced.

b. Blood (rakta). The blood is derived from the digested parts of the chyle, and by being concocted by the bile becomes red, when it is called blood; which combines, and nourishes the other essential parts of the body (dhátu).

The blood is thin and limpid, like water, has a peculiar smell, is of a red colour, and light. These qualities are derived from the five elements; as the smell from the earth, the fluidity from the water, redness from the fire, mobility from the air, and lightness from the ether (ákása). When blood predominates it produces the redness of the eyes and body, and fullness of the vessels. In a healthy state it keeps the body of a good colour, increases strength, and the flesh or bulk of the body, nourishes the organs, and moves, lives, and retains their being. It preserves vitality (jíva) which it distributes over all the body; but in different quantities, being derived from the heart as its fountain.

The blood is known to be in a healthy state, when the nails, eyelids, palate, tongue, lips, palms of the hands, and soles of the feet are of a reddish colour, and of a shining appearance. It retains the fullness and hardness of the abdomen, gives the yellow tinge to the skin, reduces the heat of the body, and renders it heavy, and listless.

The blood is changed and produces the menses, which differ from the pure fluid, being formed by the internal fire of the body, and flowing continually three whole days during every month; from the 12th to the 50th year of age.

When the blood is diminished in quantity in the body, the skin becomes dry and rough, the vessels feel lax and feeble; it increases the internal heat of the body, and produces fevers, and other diseases; in which sour and cooling food and drink are desired.

Blood is never deranged by itself, as whatever acts unfavourably on it produces first its effect upon the air, phlegm, and bile, and then it acts on the blood. On this account the diseases of the blood are cured, by first curing the derangements of the humours.

c. Flesh (mánsa, muscles). Is produced by air (váyu) thickening the blood, which is digested by heat. This increases the firmness of the body. The air passes through the body, and being accompanied with the proper degree of heat, forms the large canals, and divides the flesh into different muscles; in which the vessels are lodged that contain blood. By means of these, it proceeds as the lily rises from the ground, and is nourished by water, &c., in its progress upwards. When the blood is digested in the flesh, with the internal fire, its essential parts nourish the flesh, and its dregs produce the wax of the ears, &c.

When diminished and dried up in the abdomen, cheeks, and lips, pelvis, thighs, breasts, armpits, nates, and neck; it produces pain, and the principal vessels are diminished in size. When it predominates it increases the size of the buttocks, cheeks, lips, thighs, arms, and calves of the legs, and gives a general heaviness to the body.

d. Fat (meda) is generated from the blood in the flesh, and is in large quantities round the eyes, throat, and breast, when properly digested by the action of its internal fire. It produces perspiration, keeps the body shining, and hard; is oily, and heavy;

and is the cause of the growth of the body, its obsity, and strength. It is diffused over the body, but its chief seat is in the abdomen.

When the fat is diminished the spleen may be easily felt, the joints seem dried, and moving them gives pain. In such cases animal food is always desired. When fat predominates, the body appears smooth and glistening, the abdomen and sides are increased in size; cough and asthma are produced, and the body has a disagreeable smell. It is supposed that the essential part of the blood and fat produce bone.

e. Bones (osthí), and cartilages (toruna) as new bone, are usually considered under the same head. These give form to the body, and to them all the soft parts are attached. When the bones are all united together, they form the skeleton (kankála). Bone, with blood are the parts from which the marrow of long bones, including the brain and spinal marrow, are formed. When digested the excretions (mala) of bone form the nails and hair. When the elements of bone are diminished in the system they become painful, the teeth and nails crack, become loose, and the body becomes dry. Where bone predominates, another portion grows over the old bone; and a more than usual number of teeth are formed.

Some authors say there are 300 (Susruta), others 306 (Charaka), bones in the body. This difference is owing to their counting the cartileges with the bones. The bones are connected together by capsular ligaments. The Bones are :—

1*st. Extremities.*

True Number.	*Up.*	*Lr.*	*Number—Sanscrit Authors.*	*Up.*	*Lr.*
Fingers and toes	14	14	Bones in the fingers and toes	30	30
Metacarpus and metatarsus	5	5	Long bones of each hand and foot	8	8
Heel bone	0	1	Wrist and ankle	16	12
Carpus and tarsus	8	6	Heel.........................	0	2
Fore arm and leg	2	2	Fore arm and leg	4	4
Patella	0	1	Knee	0	2
Arm and thigh	1	1	Arm and thigh............	2	2
	30	30			
	60	60		60	60
Number of bones of the extremities..............		120	Bones of the extremities *		120

* Sesamoid bones are not counted.

2nd. Head and Trunk.

True Number.

Brought over ...		120
Bones of the skull ... / Temporal bones	8	
External Cartilages of the ear	2	
Cheek bones	2	
Jaw bones	2	
Palet bone	1	
2 os nasi, and 1 cartilage	3	
Teeth of adult	32	
Throat { 3 Hyoid Cartilages, 1 Arytonoid Cartilage, 1 Os Hyoides }	4	
Neck, cartilages of the wind pipe	9	
Bones above the neck ...		63
Clavicles	2	
Vertebræ	24	
Sacrum	4	
Scapulæ	2	
Breast bones	4	
Cartilages between sternum and clavicle	2	
Enciformed Cartilage ...	2	
Ribs	24	
Sternal Cartilages	24	
Cartilages, tubercles, &c.	24	
Coccyges	2	
Sacrum	1	
Annominata	2	
Bones of the trunk		117
Number of Bones in the Body		300

Number—Sanscrit Authors.

Brought over ...		120
Bones of the skull	6	
Temples	2	
Ears, cartilages	2	
Cheeks	2	
Jaws, upper and lower ...	2	
Palet	1	
Nose	3	
Teeth in Adult	32*	
Throat	4	
Neck	9	
Bones above the neck		63
(Akoka) or clavicles......	2	
Back { 24 Vertebræ ..., 4 Bones of the sacrum, ..., 2 Scapulæ ...... }	30†	
Breast { 4 Breast bones, 2 Cartilages between the sternum and clavicle, 2 Pieces enciformed cartilages .... }	8	
Sides, 36 in each. { 24 Ribs ...., 24 Sternal cartilages ......, 24 Cartilages tubercles and the transverse processes of vertebræ...... }	72	
Pelvis.		
Coccyges	2	
Sacrum, ...	1	
Annominata	2	
Bones of the trunk		117
Number of Bones in the body		300

There are five varieties of bones :—

1. Flat Bones, *kapalá*; as of the knee, hip, shoulder, cheek, palet, temple, and head.

2. Teeth, *Ruchaka*.

* Charaka says there are 32 alveolar bones, and 30 teeth.

† Charaka says 25, with 24 ribs.

3. Cartilages (*toruna*) nose, ears, neck, and eyelids.

4. Round Bones (*bolia*) are those of the hands, feet, back, sides, abdomen, and sacrum.

5. Long bones (*nalaka*) as those of the arms, legs, metacarpal, and metatarsal bones, and the other like bones of the body.

Bones are insensible, immoveable, and as the centre of a tree is the hardest, so the bones are the most durable part of the body; and remain after all the other parts have decayed.

f. Brain and *Marrow* (*majjá.*) The Brain and marrow are situated within the bones and nourish them, and their impurities are the secretions from the eyes. The Majjá gives strength, and the shining appearance to the body. When the marrow is increased there is a heaviness of the eye, and of the whole body; and when diseased it diminishes semen, and produces pain in the long bones. The essential parts of marrow and brain mix with the blood, and produce semen.

g. Semen (*sukra*). Is the last essential part formed, and nothing is produced from it in the body. It retains the body in its proper state of health and strength, is the generative principle, and during its excretion it produces pleasure; when diminished, it causes pain in the penis, and testicles, and the person becomes impotent. When it predominates there is an increased flow, and it produces stone. The female has desire for the sex during the flow of the menses, which acts in them as the semen does in the male.

These seven essential parts of the body (dhátu) are contained in seven organs called kollá, or their receptacles.

The Blood retains all these parts in their proper state of health. Some Pandits believe that life is the blood, and others say that life is the sotwa, raja and tama gunas, with the five senses and the soul.

Ozah is the essential part to the seven *dhátu* above enumerated which gives them strength. It is cooling, oily, of a reddish, or slightly yellow colour; is diffusible and transparent, and is the principal supporter of life. It is spread over all the body. If destroyed, the body will soon die. It is deranged by severe wounds, by the diminution of any the seven essential parts; by the passions, anxiety, much labour, and hunger. If it is in a healthy state the body becomes firm, the proper functions of the organs are performed, a good colour is given to the body, the external and internal functions, and the organs of sense are retained in a healthly state. When deranged the person feels languid, with a loss of strength. The body feels heavy, swollen, and drousy, and its colour changes. If diminished, the person becomes thin, with fainting, delirium, and death.

Section III.

Excretions (Mala)

Are the impurities of the seven essential parts, the dregs of the chyle is phlegm; of the blood, bile ; of the flesh, the secretions of the ear, nose, &c. ; of the fat, perspiration ; of the bone, the nails, and hair ; of the brain and marrow, the secretions from the eyes, &c. The semen has no dregs or impurities, but others say that (Ozah), an oily transparent fluid, which is formed all over the body, is the essential part of life, and is its impurity. This is the strength of the body, and is principally situated in the thorax.

Alvine evacuations are the superfluous part of the nutritious food, which form the feces ; when diminished by dysentery, purgatives, or the like, pain is felt in the breast, and sides of the abdomen. When much increased it produces pain in the belly, with a gurgling noise. When in the proper quantity it keeps the body in a proper state ; and it supports the air, and internal fire in a healthy condition.

Urine is contained in the bladder, and keeps the parts moist. When diminished, pain is felt in the pelvis, and little urine is discharged. When much increased there is a frequent flow with pain in the pelvis, and swelling in the part.

Perspiration retains the skin in a soft and moist state. If diminished, the pores of the skin are closed, the skin becomes dry, tough, and deranged in its action. For the removal of this state, oil is to be rubbed over the body with warmth and moisture. When the perspiration is increased there is a bad smell of the body with itching.

Milk increases the size of the mammæ and is the food of the infant. When diminished, the mammæ become lessened, and little milk is secreted, and in these cases medicines which increase phlegm are to be used. When much increased the mammæ are enlarged, with a flow of the milk, and pain.

These impurities will be diminished by much purging or vomiting ; and also eating those substances in considerable quantities which diminish air, bile, &c., will have this effect. One mola when constipated, diminishes the others. In like manner disagreeable food or melancholy ; violent exercise, fasting, excess in venery, &c., have the same effect. There is however no certain quantities as they vary in different individuals, according to their size, &c. The increase or diminution of their fluids is therefore stated by comparison. When healthy, all the secretions and essential parts are supposed to be in a proper state ; and it is the duty of the physician to restore them to their just quantity ; if increased, they must be diminished ; and if diminished increased.

Others state that oily exudations, seminal fluids, blood, dandrif, urine, fæcis, earwax, nail-parings, phlegm, tears, concretions in the eyes and sweat, are the twelve impurities of the human frame." (Menu. p. 164. Ch. V. §. 135.)

Section IV.

Joints (*Sandhi.*)

The joints are of two kinds the moveable (*chala*) and immoveable (*sthira*).

Of the first kind are the joints of the extremities, jaw, and vertebræ. All the others belong to the second, or immoveable class. The moveable joints are :—

The 4 toes, 3 in each	12	
Large toe	2	
The foot, knee and hip, one each	3	
	—	
In each leg	17 both	34
Hand in like manner		34
		—
Joints of the extremities		68
The Loins	3	
Spinal Column	24	
Thorax	24	
Breast	8	
Joints of the trunk	—	59
Neck	8	
Throat	3	
Connection of vessels with the heart and organ of thirst (kloma)	18	
The roots of the teeth	32	
Pomum Adami	1	
Nose	1	
Eyelids	2	
Jaws	2	
Ears	2	
Temples	2	
Cheeks	2	
Above each eye-brows	2	
	—	
Carried forward	75	127

Brought up	75	127
Above each temples	2	
Head	5	
Crown of the head	1	
Joints above the neck	——	83
Total		210

There are eight forms of joints :—

a. *Kara,* hinge joint as those of the fingers, toes, wrist, ankles, knees, elbows.

b. *Udukhala,* as the ball and socket joint, shoulder, hip, teeth.

c. *Samudga.* Like the instrument for cutting beetlenut ; as the shoulder-blade, coxis, pubes, and innominata.

d. *Protara,* as the neck, back.

e. *Tunnosebanee* (sown as with thread), sutures of the skull, joinings of the illium, ischium, and pubes.

f. *Biosatunda,* the joints of the lower jaw, which resemble a crows beak (coronoid process).

g. *Mundala* (round) as of the orbits, throat (larynx) and thorax; in which the eyes, wind-pipe, bronchæ, and heart are situated.

h. *Sunkha burta* in the ears, as the os hyoides.

Section V.

Ligaments, &c. (*Snáyu*) *

Ligaments bind together and strengthen the frame work of the bones, like the strips of ratan which are employed to bind the pieces of a boat together, so as to prevent the entrance of water, and to support heavy weights.

These Ligaments are divided into those of the extremities, trunk, and head.

In each toe there are 6 ligaments	30		
Soles, sides, and joints of the feet	30		
Leg	30		
Knee	10		
Thigh	40		
Hip-joint	10		
	150	Opposite side 150 or	300
The proximid extremities	150	Do. 150 or	300
		Ligaments of the extremities	600

* This includes nerves which are not considered separately.

Brought forward		600
Ligaments of the Trunk.		
In the Loins	60	
Back	80	
Chest	30	
Sides, 30 in each side	60	
	—	230
Back of the Neck	36	
Head	34	
	—	70
Number of Ligaments of the body		900

There are four varieties of Ligaments.

a. *Protanobutee*, long ligaments, as of the legs, feet, and joints.

b. *Britto*, round ligaments and tendons, as of the penis, &c.

c. *Prithu*, thick ligaments and tendons; as along the sides, breast, back, and head.

d. *Susira*, those with holes in them, as in amasia, pokasia, and bladder (bustee).

The physician, by knowing exactly the situation of the external and internal ligaments, will be able to remove extraneous bodies which have penetrated far into their substance.

Wounds of these Ligaments (and nerves) are most painful and dangerous.

Section VI.

Muscles (*Pashee*)

Muscles cover, strengthen, and retain in their places, vessels tendons, bones, and joints.

The size of the muscles differ according to their situation and uses. They are :—

Bahala, or broad and large.
Peleba, small.
Unu, narrow
Sthulah, thick.
Birta, round.
Krussa, short.
Sthera, hard.
Mirdu, soft.
Sluckno, smooth and shining : and,
Korkasha, rough.

They are as follows :—

In the two hands and feet	400	
Trunk	66	
Above the nape of the neck	34	
	—	
1st. In the extremities		500
Each finger and toe 3 or	15	
In front of the foot (tarsus)	10	
Above the foot (metatarsus)	10	
Under the ankles	10	
In the leg	20	
Knee	5	
Thigh	20	
Hip	10	
	—	100 two feet 200
Two hands the same		200
		—
2nd. In the Trunk		400
Anus	3	
Penis	1	
Frenun of do.	1	
Testicles	2	
Hips, 5 on each side	10	
Above the bladder	2	
Abdomen	5	
Umbiliacus	1	
Vertebral column	10	
Side	6	
Breast	10	
Upper breast	7	
Place of life, and amasia	2	
Liver, spleen, and rectum, 2 each	6	
	—	
3rd. Muscles above the nape of the neck		66
Nape of neck	4	
Jaws	8	
Throat and upper part of the chest	2	
Pallet	2	
Tongue	1	
Lips	2	
Nose	2	
	—	—
Carried over	21	466

Brought up	21	466
Eyes	2	
Cheeks	4	
Ears	2	
Forehead	4	
Head	1	
	—	
Above the neck and head		34
		—
Total number of muscles		500
Females have 20 more muscles, viz:—		
Five in each mammæ	10	
Vagina, 2 external and 2 internal	4	
Uterus	3	
For conveying the semen and blood internally	3	
	—	20

In these positions the muscles vary according to their actions. The muscles of the penis and testicles of the male are retained internally in the body of the female. Besides which there are spiral muscles like those of a shell; the first circle being the vagina, the second the neck of the uterus, and the third its cavity. In the uterus is contained the fetus with the mouth of that organ turned downwards and shaped like that of a *ruefish*.

Section VII.

Vessels.

The vessels are distinguished from each other by the names *será, damanee* and *srota*. The appearance of these vessels is nearly the same; but they differ from each other, by their actions.

The navel is the origin of all the vessels, and the principal seat of the life (pran), as it is situated there in larger quantities than elsewhere. The navel may be said to resemble the root of a waterlily, from which the different vessels proceed to all parts of the body. The navel is thus the root of the vessels of all living animals *. It is surrounded by vessels like the central part of a wheel which receives spokes from the circumference. Among these, forty principal vessels are enumerated.

Será are the vessels which convey blood, air, bile, and phlegm.

* This idea is derived from the appearance of the vessels in their fetal state.

The branches of these vessels are like those of the leaves of trees, which ascend, descend, and cross. They nourish the body as a garden is irrigated by a small brook. These vessels, as a river, distribute nourishment in their course, and keep the body flexible, and ready for action. Of the forty principal vessels, ten contain air, ten bile, ten phlegm, and ten blood. Each trunk is attached to its own receptacle *dosa.* They are of all sizes, and life is contained in different degrees in different vessels. The midling size contain principally air.

The ten trunks of vessels which convey air are divided into			175	branches.
Do.	Bile	Do.	175	,,
Do.	Phlegm	Do.	175	,,
Do.	Blood attached to the spleen and liver		175	,,
		Total	700	

Air vessels have 25 branches in each lower extremity		50	
Do.	do. 25 in each upper do.	50	
			100

The air vessels of the trunk are as follows :—		
In the anus, penis, and buttocks	8	
Two sides	4	
Back	6	
Belly	6	
Breast	10	
		34
Neck	14	
Two ears	4	
Tongue	9	
Nose	6	
Eyes	8	
Air vessels in the neck and head		41
Number of air vessels		175

The vessels that convey bile, phlegm, and blood are the same in number as those which convey air. But, in the eye, bile has ten, air has two instead of four; and in the ears two. The phlegm and blood have the same number. All vessels, therefore, are supposed to contain air, bile, phlegm, and blood, but in different proportions.

When they contain more air, bile, phlegm, or blood, they are called air vessels, phlegm vessels, or blood vessels.

The colour of air vessels is red, and air appears in them ; those of bile are blue and hot, and those of phlegm are cool, of a whitish colour, thick, and their contents seem to remain at rest.

If *air* circulates properly in its own vessels, the person will act properly, and the functions of the body will be performed in such a manner that the individual will enjoy health ; his understanding will be good, and he will possess all the other good qualities of air. If deranged, various kinds of the disease of air, will be produced.

If *Bile* is in a proper condition, the person will have a healthy appearance, his appetite good, the internal fire will be strong and healthy, and he will possess other good qualities. But if deranged, the diseases of bile will be produced.

If *Phlegm* acts properly the skin will be smooth, the joints healthy, and the strength will be good, and he will have the other good qualities of phlegm. If deranged, it produces the peculiar class of diseases of phlegm.

Blood. This fluid produces and nourishes all the other essential parts of the body. If the blood is in a healthy state, the persons colour remains good, the surface is sensible, and it produces the other good qualities of blood, and when deranged it developes the various diseases of blood.

When the air vessels are alone deranged, disease is not produced, but when deranged, with an increased quantity of bile, and phlegm, disease is the consequence. By the state of the eight principal vessels the physician knows if the patient will die or live. There are two vessels in the hands, two in the feet, two in the throat, two in the temples, and two in the nose, which are thus to be examined. In the foot the vessel is behind the maleolus internus, and is in length two fingers breadth ; in the hand it is three breadths of the fingers, in the neck two breadths of the finger, and in the nose two, at which the pulse is felt. The two vessels of the hand are however the principal ; and if their contents flow naturally the person will live and do well. In these situations are the vessels containing the indications of life, and a sensible physician will examine them all, and if air flows naturally it will be favourable. If in any of these the semen is deranged in the vessel, and air flows naturally, the person will live, this air produces the pulse*. When the pulse is to be judged of, three fingers are to be put upon the vessel at the wrist ; the

* Physicians feel the pulse at the wrist, ankles, temples ; and sometimes at the nose, or neck.

first, next the hand, represents or indicates air or Brumha, the second bile, or Vishnu; and the third Phlegm, (Mahesur or Siva).

Should air be deranged in the vessels, sometimes it will be cured by pressing, champooing, or opening the vessel; or by perspiration or friction. These remedies must always be employed.

When air, bile, and phlegm are deranged, and increased in quantity, they do not remain in the same vessels, but pass into different channels, as into those of one of the other fluid.

The vessels carrying principally blood, are very red; but are neither very hot nor cold. Some of these vessels may be opened, others cannot be opened with impunity. Should they be wounded, the person will die, or the part will be rendered imperfect in its actions.

There are four vessels which should not be opened in each extremity:—

1 Ijálá dára		1
2 Urbee	deep seated	3
1 Lohetaka		
		4

There are in the trunk 136 vessels, of which 32 should not be opened; 4 are in the buttocks; 3 in each side of the spinal column; in the belly 4; and in the breast 14. Above the clavicles 50 are not to be opened. In the neck 16; in the jaw two on each side; 4 below the tongue, 4 near the nose, 1 in the soft palate, one on each side of the eyes, and one in each ear, one in each side of the forehead, two in the temples, two above it, one between the eyebrows; and six in the upper part of the head.

It is stated in some books that there are innumerable vessels consisting of those of a large and very small size, which are like decayed leaves in which the interstices of the leaves have been removed. They are said to form 3½ cotees* of vessels, or 300 lacks of all sizes and figures. These all arise from the navel.

Damanee vessels †.

These include vessels and nerves; by which the different functions of the body are performed.

* One cotee is equal to one hundred lacks.

† A tubular vessel of the body, as a vein, nerve, &c. Other shastres say that they proceed from the turtle situated in the navel with four legs; ten vessels from the proximid extremity, ten from the lower, two from the mouth, and two from the anus (Tantra).

There are 24 of these vessels, which for the most part proceed from the navel. There are 10 that proceed upwards, ten downwards, and two laterally. The upper ten perform the functions of hearing, touching, seeing, tasting, and smelling. They also perform breathing, gaping, sneezing, coughing, laughing, speaking, and crying; when these vessels approach the heart, the ten are divided into three each, forming thirty branches. Two of these are divided into twelve, of which two convey air, two bile, two phlegm, two blood, and two chyle. Eight others perform hearing, seeing, tasting, smelling, two being allowed for each function. By two speech is performed, two make a noise, two produce sleep, two waking, two convey tears, two the milk of the female, and two in the male convey semen. These constitute the upper vessels.

The actions of the ten lower vessels, situated under the navel, are to carry the air of the abdomen, for acting on the urine, dejections, semen, menses, and the like. They separate all these parts from each other; and by them the chyle is separated, and the body nourished, and retained in health.

These ten vessels become thirty in the stomach (amasia) and intestines (pukasia); two of which convey air, two bile, two phlegm, two blood, two chyle, two the solid, and two the fluid food, two for the urinary organs, and two for producing the semen, and two for conveying it externally, two for the menses, and by two the dejections are discharged.

From these, numerous other branches proceed; the whole body being enveloped by the branches proceeding from the four lateral trunks. These are innumerable and terminate in open orifices on the surface, and convey perspiration, retain the body in a healthy state, and by their communications convey external applications into the system. By these vessels feeling is produced, and by them the oil or water is drawn into the system, and they cool, refresh, and clean it.

Srotá (or canals).

These vessels convey prana or vital air; the food (onna); water (uda); chyle (rusa); blood (rokta); fat of the flesh (mansha); urine (mutra); feces (purica); semen (sukra); and menses (artobo). From each of these numerous other vessels arise.

Should the two vessels conveying life (prana) be wounded at the root; which is in the heart, the person screams, bends forward, becomes delirious, shakes, reels, swoons, and often dies. Should the two vessels conveying food, the root of which arises from the stomach be wounded, the symptoms will be flatulency, pain in the abdomen, loss of appetite, vomiting, thirst, blindness, and death.

There are two vessels, which convey *Chyle*, the roots of which are in the breast. If wounded the body dries up, and the same effects are produced as when the vessels conveying life are wounded: the person generally dies.

There are two vessels for conveying *blood*, the roots of which are in the liver and spleen, and if they, or the roots of the other blood vessels are wounded, the person becomes of a pallid or gray colour, with fever ; much blood is lost, and the eyes become red.

There are two vessels for conveying *flesh*, the roots of which are the veins (sira), and skin (twak), and the root of the vessels which convey blood which if wounded produce swelling, drying of the flesh, and enlargement of the vessels (sira) conveying blood (aneurism), and the person dies.

For *fat* there are two vessels, the roots of which are in the sides and loins, and when wounded produce perspiration, coolness of the body, the palate dries, the body swells, and there is thirst.

There are two vessels for conveying *urine*, the roots of which are in the bladder, and penis ; and if wounded the bladder is distended by the collection of urine, and the penis swells.

There are two organs for containing *dejections*, one of which arises from Pakwásaya, and the other forms the anus. If wounded costiveness (ánáha), and a bad smell are produced, and the intestines swell, or become knotted.

The *semen* has two canals the roots of which are in the breast ; and two from the testicles. If wounded they produce impotency, and the semen is discharged very slowly, and is mixed with blood.

The *menses* have two canals, the roots of which are the uterus, and the damanee vessels, which convey the menses. When wounded, they produce barrenness, and the menses cease.

Section VIII.

Cellular tissue, and fascia of the Body (kalá).

The cellular tissue connects, and surrounds, the different parts of the body, and separates the seven essential parts from each other. The tissues which thus retain the different parts of the body together are of seven kinds :—

Ist. Mángsadhará * is situated between the muscles, and in which the vessels (rugs) pass, and divide into branches, to nourish the neighbouring parts, as the lily rises from the ground, and receives its nourishment from the water and earth.

* From mángsa, flesh, and dhara surrounds.

2nd. Raktadhara * in which the blood is contained, in the spleen and the liver. They retain the blood, as the juice of trees is retained, and is discharged when cut into.

3rd. Medodhara † is the organ in which all the fat is retained, the chief place of which is in the abdomen (the omentum). When the fat is contained in the bones it is called majá.

4th. Sleshmadhara ‡ which forms the bags containing the phlegm ; With which the joints are lubricated, and rendered supple ; as oil is applied for the movement of wheels.

5th. Purishadhara, in which the dejections are retained in the abdomen, it is attached to the pakavása, and is situated between the liver and the intestines.

6th. Pittadhara, or organ which receives from the stomach the four kinds of food, taken by sucking, dividing with the teeth, drinking, and licking. These kinds of food are digested by the heat of the bile (pittateja).

7th. Sukradhara retains the semen, which is dispersed over all the body with other fluids, in the same manner as milk contains butter, or the juice of sugar cane, sugar-candy. The principal seat of the semen, is two fingers breadth on each sides the neck of the bladder ; and the semen passes along the urinary passages, and is discharged in a state of pleasure.

Section IX.

Organs or Receptacles (ásaya.)

There are seven of these receptacles, with an additional three in the female. They retain the Humours of the body in their respective situations ; such as air, bile, and phlegm, blood, chyle, chyme, urine, and feces.

The receptacle of the blood is the heart ; under which the organ of phlegm is situated. Still lower down (distid) is situated the stomach (ámásaya) between the breast and navel. Under which is the (pittásaya), receptacle of bile ; below which is the receptacle of air (pavanásaya), or place for the excretions § ; and below that is the receptacle of urine (vasti or bladder). The female has three more receptacles ; the uterus, and two receptacles for milk, or the mammæ.

* Rakta blood, and dhara retains.
† Meda fat, and dhara retains. Maja brain, saroia marrow.
‡ Sleshma phlegm, and dhara retain.
§ Charaka divides these into large and small intestines, and gives each a name.

Section X.

Orifices of the Body. (*Bahisrota.*)

There are nine orifices in the body of the male ; the mouth, two nostrils, two ears, two eyes, the anus, and the urethra.

Females have the orifices of the two mammæ, and the vagina, more than those of the male.

Section XI.

Skin. (*Twak*).

The skin is said to be in a state of health when it is soft, and has much hair. The skin consists of seven layers, or membranes ; as milk when boiled, forms a coating like that of the skin. The skin gives the seven different kinds of colour to the body.

1*st.* *Avabháshini* (cuticle) this is the external layer, and is transparent. Its thickness is about the eighteenth part of a grain of rice.

2*nd.* *Lohitá* is the sixteenth part of a grain of rice in thickness.

3*rd.* *Swetá* is a membrane of a white colour, and is the thickness of the twelth part of a grain of rice.

4*th.* *Támrá* is of a copper colour, the thickness of an eighth part of a grain of rice.

5*th.* *Vediní* is the sensible part, and is the thickness of the fifth part of a grain of rice.

6*th.* *Rohini* is the thickness of a grain of rice.

These membranes are not found in the head or fingers, but are distinguishable when there is much flesh in the part examined, as the belly, extremities, &c.

7*th.* *Mángsadhara.* These parts of the body are innumerable, and retain the muscles in their places.

Section XII.

Supplimentary Parts.

Principal tendons (kandará) are sixteen in Number :—

To each foot two	4
Do hands	4
Neck, and front of the body	4
Back	4
Carried up	16

From the tendons of the extremities the nails proceed. Those of the neck bind it to the trunk, and it is a tendon which extends to form the penis.

The back and buttocks are bound together by mere tendons; which pass down and form the testicles.

There are also 16 Jála (like a net) and are formed of vessels, &c., which strengthen, and bind the joints; and six *kurcha* which form bundles of parts.

Sebani (sowing or sutors), there are five sutors in the head, one in the frenum of the tongue, and one in the frenum of the Penis.

Section XIII.

Dissection of the Human Body.

All the Rishís are said to have recommended the dissection of the human body, as proper and necessary. Menu, the great legislator, and the one most respected by the Hindu sages, says (85) "one who has touched a corpse, is made pure by bathing"; and again (77) "should a Brahman touch a fresh human bone he is purified by bathing; and if it be dry by stroking a cow, or by looking at the sún, having sprinkled his mouth duly with water."

Charaka, one of the munís, and Physicians say, that a practitioner should know all the parts of the body, both external and internal, and their relative positions with regard to each other. Without such a knowledge he cannot be a proper practitioner.

Susruta, a Rishí of the highest rank, says that a jogí (a holy man) should dissect, in order that he may know the different parts of the human body; and a surgeon and physician should not only know the external appearances, but internal structure of the body; in order to possess an intimate knowledge of the diseases to which it is liable, and to perform surgical operations so as to avoid the vital parts. It is by combining a knowledge of books with practical dissection, that the practitioner will alone attain an intimate knowledge of the subject of his profession.

The body which is to be examined by dissection should be that of a person who had neither been destroyed by poison, nor had died of a long disease, as the structure of the body will be altered by the deleterious substance taken, or destroyed by the ravages of disease. In like manner the person should not have been very old, and all the members should be in a perfect state.

When a proper body for the purpose has been selected, the dejections are to be removed, the body washed, and placed in a frame work of wood, properly secured, by means of grass, hemp, or the like. The body is then to be placed in still water, in a situation in which it will not be destroyed by birds, fishes, or animals. It is to remain for seven days in the water, when it will have become putrid. It is then to be removed to a convenient situation, and with a brush, made of reeds, hair, or bamboo-bark, the body is to be rubbed so as, by degrees, to exhibit the skin, flesh, &c., which are each in their turn to be observed before being removed. In this manner the different corporial parts of the body already enumerated will be exhibited; but the life of the body is too etherial to be distinguished by this process, and its properties must therefore be learned with the assistance of the explanations of holy medical practitioners, and prayers offered up to God, by which, conjoined with the exercise of the reasoning and understanding faculties, conviction will be certain.

CHAPTER V.

Vital Parts (*Marma*).

The description of these parts, and the consequences of their being wounded, afford a convincing proof of the great practical experience of the Hindu writers. The advantages of having a good and attentive medical attendant, compared with that of an ignorant one, is emphatically declared to be as great as the difference of the individual, being restored from weakness and deformity, or even from death after much suffering to perfect health.

In Susruta the dangerous parts are all named and described; and the necessity of avoiding them in operations pointed out. The consequence of wounds near the great toe in causing tetanus; in the palm of the hand, in producing such a degree of hemorrhage as will require amputation of the arm; of the effects of wounds of the testicle and groin, and of the fractured bones of the head and breast, which are tobe raised or removed, &c., are all stated in this practica lwork.

There are five kinds of *Vital* parts :—

Flesh has (mángsa marma)	1
Vessels (sira marma) have	1
Nerves and Ligaments (snáyu marma).	1
Bones (ostí marma)	1
Joints (sandhí marma)	1
Carried up	5

Brought forward		5
The following are the varieties of vital parts :—		
Flesh has	11	
Vessels	41	
Tendons, nerves, and ligaments	27	
Bone	8	
Joints	20	
Varieties of vital parts of the body.		107
These parts are also divided as follows :—		
In each leg there are 11, in both	22	
In each arm 11, do.	22	
In the abdomen (udara) there are 3, and in the thorax 9	12	
In the back there are	14	
Above the trunk	37	
		107.

Vital parts of the distid extremities.

1. *Kipra.* The space between the great toes, and the one next it, if wounded or bruised, the person will die with tetanus. Hence a bite of a serpent is very dangerous in this part.

2. *Talahridaya.* Under and behind the 4th and 5th toe. If wounded death will be produced with great suffering.

3. *Kurcha,* above the *Kipra,* and on each side of it. If wounded there will be an unsteadiness of the foot.

4. *Kurchaṣira,* under the ankles, it will produce pain and swelling.

5. *Gulpha,* the ankle joint, which produces pain, and the joint becomes stiff, and the person lame.

6. *Indrabasti,* along the anterior and posterior part of the leg. If blood flows largely, the person will die.

7. *Janu,* or vital part in the knee. When hurt, it will produce lameness.

8. *A'ni Marma.* Three fingers in size above the knee. When wounded it will be followed by much swelling and stiffness of the joint.

9. *Urbi,* middle of the thigh. If wounded much hemorrhage will follow, with death.

10. *Lohitaka,* a little above the last, and below the groin. When wounded, from the great hemorrhage, paralysis of that side will occur.

11. *Vitapa.* If the part between the testicles and groin be wounded, the person will become powerless with a loss of semen.

Both upper extremities have the same vital parts as the lower, differing only slightly from each other.

Vital parts of the Trunk.

1. *Guda.* If that in the anus be hurt, it will soon kill the person.

2. *Basti,* or urinary bladder, if wounded the person will soon die, excepting after the extraction of the stone. If one side be wounded, a fistula will form, but the person will not die. Should the vital parts in both sides be wounded, the person will die.

3. *Nábhí,* between amasia and Pukasia, when wounded where the vessels originate, the person will die.

4. *Hridaya* or heart, which is between the two breasts within the thorax. If wounded the person will soon die.

5 *Stanamula* is in two parts, situated below the breast; and is two fingers breadth in size. If wounded death will be produced by the severe cough, and asthma thus produced.

6. *Stanarohita,* above the breast two fingers breadth, if wounded severe cough and asthma will take place, by the visera being filled up with blood.

7. *Apalápa,* in the axilla. When wounded under the axilla, a great discharge of blood and pus will precede death.

Vital parts of the Back.

Should the loins on each side of the back (*Koteekotorna*) be wounded above the sacrum, from the blood lost, the person will become of a yellow or bad colour, and die.

1. *Apastamba.* The two vessels which convey bayu in the chest. If wounded cough and asthma will produce death.

2. *Kakundara.* The side of the spine near the buttocks when wounded is followed by a loss of feeling, and the person cannot move the inferior parts of the body, which become paralized.

3. *Nitamba.* When the sensible parts of the two buttocks have been wounded, the lower limb shrinks up, and becomes weakened, and the person dies.

4. *Párswasandú* is situated on each side of the trunk and lower part of the abdomen (iliac region); when wounded the person will die, from the flow of blood from the organs.

5. *Vrihati,* on each side of the spine, near the breast; the man if wounded there, will die from the great hemorrhage.

6. *Angsafalaka*, at the upper part of the spinal column, when wounded, the arm becomes insensible, immoveable, and dries up.

7. *Angsa*. If the shoulder joint be wounded it disables the arm.

Vital parts above the trunk.

There are 37 vital parts above the trunk ; of which two are on each side of the trachea. There are four vessels called necla (blue) and two (manya) ; which if wounded or bruised the person cannot speak, or the voice becomes changed, and he loses his taste.

2. *Sira Matrika*, on each side of the neck, there are two vessels ; if wounded the person will soon die.

3. *Krikatika*, or the joint between the head and neck, if wounded, the head is always in motion.

4. *Bidura*, under the lobe of the ear, if wounded the person becomes deaf.

5. *Fana*, should the inside of the two nostrils be wounded, he cannot smell.

6. *Apanga*, below the extremities or above the eyebrows, if diseased or wounded the person will become blind.

7. *Abarta*, above the eyebrows, if wounded, they produce blindness, and diseases of the eye.

8. *Sangkha*, the temples, if wounded the person will soon die.

9. *Utkhapa*, above the temples, if wounded, the individual will live as long as the instrument is in the wound, but if removed he will die. Should it be allowed to remain, and medicine be given to discharge the instrument it may drop out of the wound, and the person may live.

10. *Sthapani*. Between the eyebrows, the same effects will be produced as in the last case.

11. *Simanta*, the five joints of the head, if wounded, will produce fear, insensibility, madness, and death.

12. *Sringataka*, should the vessels at the union of the eyes, nose, ears, and tongue be wounded, the person will soon die.

13. *Adhipati*, inside of the upper part of the head, at the passage of the vessel along the bone (lateral sinus) wounds will soon destroy the person.

In operations, sensible parts are to be avoided and a surgeon and Physician should know all these parts.

When a member is cut off, the parts contract, and less blood will often flow ; but if wounded in a vital part it will generally cause death, by the number of vessels that are divided, while the deranged air produces much pain. The person dies in such cases, as a tree will die if the roots be divided. Hence if the vital parts be wounded, as in the palm of the hand, the arm is to be amputated to save the individual's life. Should a person live after such injuries, the parts will be left in a state of weakness, and his recovery will depend entirely upon the skill of his medical attendant.

If a bone of the head or breast be broken, it is to be raised or removed by the assistance of instruments. Wounds of the legs or arms will not be fatal, if the vital parts have escaped. In these vital parts the qualities of the moon, air, strength (tej), and raja, satwa, and tama gun, and also life (Jívátmá) are retained in considerable quantities. Hence, the fatal effects which usually occur from injuries of these parts. The senses become imperfect or destroyed, the understanding becomes changed, and various kinds of pain are produced in such wounds, followed by death. When the fatal termination of wounds of vital parts is prevented at the time of the injury, death will be produced, some days after, with much suffering and weakness. In those situations, where injuries do not produce fatal consequences, but an imperfect action of the part, they are cured by the skill and care of the surgeon. By wounds in such situations death is produced on the instrument being withdrawn, by the escape of air (váyu), &c. If wounded near a vital part, and there is a bad surgeon, the person will become a cripple.

There are five varieties, or degrees, of vital parts. In one variety the person when wounded dies quickly, of which there are 19 ; another in a few days, of which there are 33 ; one when an external substance enters, it produces a fatal effect, as soon as it is withdrawn, there are 3 such parts ; another kind produces lameness, 44 are of this kind ; another produces only pain, of which there are 8.

When any of these parts are injured, it destroys the individual, from the portion of life it contains. Those that produce death suddenly, have the quality of fire and, like it, quickly destroy. The kind that destroy life only on the instrument being withdrawn, which had inflicted the wound, is in consequence of the part having the qualities of air (váyu) : In this case, the external instrument closes up the air, &c. ; and as soon as it is removed they escape, and the person dies. That which produces pain and lameness has the qualities of the moon ; as it is cool, and steady, and retains life. That which produces pain has the quality of fire and air ; by increasing which, the pain is produced. Some Pundits suppose that pain is produced by the injury of the five elements.

When the five varieties of sensible parts, the vessels, &c., are wounded ; the effect is increased by the number, and the person dies. If only four are wounded, he will live a few days. When three are wounded, and the instruments removed, the person will die soon after its extraction. If two are injured, an imperfect action of the part will be the consequence; and if only one be injured, there will only be pain.

These four varieties of vessels are generally contained in sensible parts; and retain the body in a healthy state: but if the sensible parts are wounded, the air is increased; it passes through the four species of vessels, produces much pain, and causes fainting, and death. Should an external substance be required to be withdrawn from a wound, the surgeon must first carefully observe the sensible parts, and then remove the instrument. If the vital parts are wounded towards their centre it will produce death in a few days; and it will produce an imperfect action of the part, when wounded on one side. Those vital parts which produce death on the instrument being discharged, when wounded near the edge, will give much pain. The other parts give much pain when wounded directly; but will produce little pain if wounded on one side.

The same symptoms and consequences will take place should the parts be lacerated, crushed, or burnt, as when wounded with a cutting instrument.

CHAPTER VI.

Spiritual part of the body.

Life (*Prána*) consists in the combination of the soul (*bhútátmá* purusha, jívátmá); the mind (manah); the five senses (Indriya); and the three qualities of goodness, passion, and inertness, (Satwa, Raja, and Tama)

The soul (purusha) is a shadow or emanation from God (Paramátmá, Ishwar), the eternal, who is without beginning or end, is invisible, immortal, and is only known by reflection. When it bedews the five elements it produces the living body, and becomes by its actions evident. It is liable to decrease, and is influenced by medicine. There is no difference between the human soul and the soul of the world; this being only the exterior and condescending manifestation of God, while the human soul is its reflection into itself, and its elevation above itself is the Divine soul. The presence of the soul is necessary to animate the body; is full of knowledge and happiness, and is possessed of judgment. It produces waking and sleeping; and combined with mind is like a coachman who directs the senses, and regulates the body, suffering from its wickedness, or enjoying its beatitude. The soul is always in a state of purity, when separated from the body; but neither acts usefully, nor otherwise, useless when united with mind, and the female energy (prakriti).

When the soul enters the embryo it forms the knowledge (vidyá), and ignorance (avidyá), wickedness, &c., of that individual. In some medical works the soul is represented to exist in beasts, animals, and demigods according to its conduct in former states of existence. When the soul (Jívátmá) has bedewed the body with its twenty four qualities, it performs all the corporeal functions, and sensible actions; as vision, hearing, touch, &c.; and by it we speak and act. If it acts on good works, the person will be good, and his soul will go to heaven after death.

When the soul is united with the mind (manah); it produces desire, activity, enmity, happiness, grief, misery, intelligence, exertion, judgment, memory, dexterity, and useful knowledge. It produces expiration and inspiration, closing and opening the eyelids, understanding, reflection, consideration, memory, the exercise of the arts, and performs the action of the senses.

The mind (manah) is a quality or power of the soul by which the person thinks and reasons. It is incomprehensible, and is known by its actions through those of the senses. As it is single only, one sense can act at the same time, as it requires the presence of the mind for the comprehension of any thing, and the understanding with ideas of its own operations.

The mind is chiefly situated in the head, between the eyebrows; others suppose that it is in the heart, and resembles the light of a lamp, by which the person knows, sees, hears, tastes, and moves. It proceeds from itself, as the silk worm weaves its thread from itself, and forms its own house, which it regulates, and in which the different qualities (guns) are produced. When disposed to separate from the body it is drawn back by these qualities, as a loadstone retains a piece of iron, by their mutual influences; in which situation it remains immoveable. (Tantra).

Some Pundits say that the soul (Jívátmá ?) and the mind (manah), are the same essence; as there can be no soul without mind, nor mind without the soul.

The five elements form the five organs of sense, (Indriya) as the nose, ears, &c. ; the five objects of sense (Indriyártha), as sound smell, &c. ; and the five perceptive judgments. Above these is placed the mind, which is incomprehensible by them, and is alone rendered evident through the action of the senses. These are deranged by too great or too little exercise, while moderate exercise retains them in good health.

From these remarks it appears that the soul, the emanation from the deity, united with the mind and senses, perform all the vital actions of the body. The body, mind, and soul are considered, therefore, as the three pillars which support the living system.

CHAPTER. VII.

Nature of Temperaments.

The opinion of the Hindus as to the formation, and condition of the world, afforded a natural means of explaining the temperaments, or peculiar qualities, of the body. The predominance of one or more of the humours ; and the qualities of goodness, passion, and inertness, explained the peculiarities of habit, and character ; and, as more shades were observed, in these the simple excess of one or more of these agents, were explained by their peculiar mixtures which produced the dispositions of the Gods, sages, demons, and the lower animals. The latter being only supposed to be inferior states of the animal body, which in a higher condition form man. These explain the theory of the temperaments found in Hindu Medical works.

At the time of the mixture of semen and female blood whatever humour, whether air, bile, and phelgm, is in excess produces that particular temperament. Hence there are seven temperaments, one being produced by an excess of air, another of bile, and a third of phlegm ; a fourth, fifth, and sixth, from an excess of two of these humours ; and a seventh temperament is produced by an excess of three humours, air, bile and phlegm.

1. When air is in excess the person is not inclined to sleep, or to become warm. His disposition is bad, and he becomes a thief ; is proud, and has no honor ; is always singing and dancing ; his hands and feet split, his hair and nails are dry, and he is always angry and boisterous. He speaks untruths, he is always grinding his teeth and biting his nails, he is always impatient, is not a firm friend, is changeable, and forgets good actions. His body is slender and dry,

he always walks fast, is always in motion, and his eyes are always rolling. He dreams that he is flying about the air, friends are few and his riches of little value. Such persons as have an excess of air have the disposition of the goat, jackall, hare, camel, dog, vulture, crow, and ass.

2nd. A person with an excess of bile perspires much, and he has a bad smell. His skin is of a yellowish colour, his flesh is soft; his nails, eyes, pallet, tongue, lips, and the palms of his hands, and soles of his feet are of a copper colour; his fortune is bad, and his hair becomes soon gray, the upper part of his head bald, and his skin wrinkled as if by age. He eats much, and dislikes warm articles of food, is soon angry, and is as soon pacified, is of moderate strength, and does not live long. His memory is good, he is a good man of business, and speaks accurately, and to the purpose. His appearance is fine, and in company he excells in speaking. He dreams of gold, and yellow flowers, fire, lightning and falling meteors, dislikes saluting a person, and is angry at others not doing so, is never content, &c. His disposition resembles serpents, owls, cats, monkies, tigers, and bears.

3rd. Phlegm in excess produces a light greenish or blue colour of the body. The person's fortune is propitious, he is pleasant to look on and handsome, likes sweet things, is grateful, constant, just, and forgiving, and is not covetous, is strong and understands with difficulty, and is an implacable enemy. His eyes are white, his hair is fine, black, and waving. He is wealthy, and his voice is strong and loud. He dreams of lilies, geese, and large fine tanks. The angles of his eyes are red, his colour pleasing, and his members are well formed. His regard mild, his disposition is very good (satwaguna), and he is charitable. He is active, honors respectable persons, and is kind to them; and knows the sciences. He retains his friend, and health remains constant; he is careful, but gives much. He is of the nature of Bramhá, Indra, Shiva, and Varuna; of lions, horses, elephants, cows, and bulls, and of the bird upon which Vishnu rides (Gaṛura) (something between a man, and a bird like a goose).

When two or three humours are in excess, they are known by the combination of the two or three classes of symptoms.

Some suppose that the disposition is derived from the elements of the body. In this case air, fire, and water resemble the temperaments of air, bile, and phlegm; and the temperament of earth produces a large and strong body, and the person can suffer much. When there is an excess of pure ether the man is holy, lives long, and the external openings of the body are large. The disposition of individuals are either satwa, raja, or tama ; that is good, passionate, or inert.

When the qualities of the Gods predominate in the embryo, the following will be the indications. When the qualities of the God Bramhá predominates in the body, the person will remain clean, religious, and learned in the *Vedas ;* is charitable, hospitable, performs ceremonies, and prays to his Guru.

If the quality of *Indra* be in excess in the body at conception ; the individual will be great, magestic, and powerful, and employs many dependants.

If the qualities of neptune (*Varuna*) be in excess he is always desirous of cool things, is patient under suffering, is of a yellowish colour, and his hair is like that of a lion. He speaks pleasantly or kindly.

The qualities of the God of riches (*Kuvera*) predominating, the person will be a peace maker, have much wealth, have many children, will be careful, rich, and fond of collecting wealth.

With the disposition of the God of music (*Ganddharva*) predominates, the person will have a desire for good smelling things, and flowers, and will be always wishing to dance, sing, and play.

The disposition of the angel of death (*Yama*), or judge after death, are as follows : The person acts agreeable to orders, and acts properly, has no fear, has memory, is always clear, is not angry, is not ignorant, has no hatred.

The person with a disposition of the sages (*Rishis*) is always pronouncing the names of the Gods ; follows the orders of the shastres, and always remains pure and prays frequently. He has much knowledge, especially of the arts. When the Satwa gun predominates in the embryo, the individual will possess these qualities.

The bad in disposition are those in whom the qualities of the demons (*Asuras*) predominate. These persons will be very rich, and inspire terror ; they are great warriors, fierce, and always inclined to oppress people. The eat once a day, and require good things and never perform the usual ceremonies, on such occasions.

With the qualities of *Serpents,* such persons are always hot, are jugglers, fearful, fierce, forget persons, and do not act fairly.

Birds. A person with this disposition is not inclined to change his work ; indulges in lust, is always eating, angry, and restless.

Rákhyasa or Giants. Such a person is constant to one work, he produces fear, and calumniates, acts unfairly to others, and has much pride.

Pihsách or devil. The person always wants to eat the fragments of others meals, is of a hot disposition ; rejoices in wickedness, is courageous, and has no shame.

Preta (demon). His disposition is difficult to discover. The person is always lazy, and always wishing to act improperly, is covetous, and is not generous. The above six disposition have much passion.

Persons with much of the qualities of *Beasts* (*Pashu gana*), have a bad memory and act badly ; they are always dreaming that they are with women ; do not work themselves, and entice others from work.

One with the disposition of *Fish* is always changing, has no sense, is always fearful, always wants water, and will injure others.

Men having the disposition of *Trees*, always wish to remain in one place, are always eating, will not work.

A physician is to notice such dispositions, and in his practice to act so as to remove an excess, or increase a deficiency.

CHAPTER VIII.

Ages.

There are three ages, childhood (Bályа), manhood (madhya), and decrepitude (várddhakya).Ist. childhood extends to the 15th year, and is distinguished by three stages :—

a. Period of suckling to 1 year.

b. The period in which milk and rice are the food ; which extends to the second year.

c. When the food is rice ; which extends from the 3rd to the 15th year, during which time Phlegm is in excess.

2nd. Manhood (madhya) extends from the 16th to the 70th year ; and is divided into four periods.

a. *Vriddhi* or growth, which extends from the 16th to the 20th year.

b. *Jauvana.* From the 20th to the 30th year.

c. *Sampúrnatá,* from the 30th to the 40th year ; when all the humours, senses, strength, (bala) are in their full developement.

d. *Háni,* from the 40th to the 70th year ; when all the powers of the organs are gradually diminishing. Bile is at this period in excess.

3rd. Decrepitude (*Várddhakya*) extends from the 70th year till the person's death ; during which the humours, senses, strength, and animation diminish daily. The muscles become soft, and flaccid, the hair turns gray, and falls off, the body becomes bent, and the person is afflicted with coughing, asthma, and other such diseases. He cannot perform any work ; and other signs of decrepitude appear ; like an old house in the rainy season with many props. In this period of life, air is in excess, and nervous diseases prevail.

It is supposed the male at 25, and the female at 16 years of age, arrive at their perfection in figure and strength.

In youth and in old age, the application of fire, caustics (actual and potential cauteries), blisters, &c., and the use of strong purgatives are to be avoided ; or when required they are to be administered in a weaker form than usual, and administered by degrees. There are likewise fat, thin, and middle sized individuals. In the first the humours are to be diminished ; in the second increased ; and in the third the humours are to be preserved in the same state. Some of these thin persons are strong, and fat individuals weak. Among all the principles of our treatment the strength of the person should first be observed ; as without it, the administration of many medicines, and the performance of operations is improper.

CHAPTER IX.

On death (Mrityu)

Death is the separation of the soul from the body ; of which there are one hundred and one ways in which a person may die ; one of which at the time appointed, is natural death, which takes place about the hundredth year of age ; the others are accidental, which occur from numerous causes, as bad living, intemperance, poisons, fire, lightning, drowning, sin, &c. ; these are to be guarded against by care, medicines, and prayers. Man is like a coachman driving his own carriage ; if this be well made, and if he continue to drive cautiously, it will go a long time ; but, if he drives it upon bad roads, the wheels will get injured, and the carriage will be soon worn out.

Should he indulge too much in the gratification of the senses, he will die like a deer, which is supposed to be deluded to its destruction by the sweet sounds of the lute which the hunters use ; should he indulge in lust, like the Elephant ; in sight, like the butterfly in approaching the lamp ; in smell, like the bee which is inclosed and crushed in the flower, which has attracted it by its smell ; in taste, like the fish by the fisherman's hook : So beware of indulging too much in any of the pleasures of sense, else it will lead, in like manner, to your destruction !

Death is always near ; and when it occurs, nothing but the sins and virtuous actions which have been performed, accompany the soul*. " When a person leaves his corpse, like a log or a lump of clay, on the ground, his kindred retire with averted faces ; but his virtue accompanies his soul. Continually, therefore, let him collect virtue, for the sake of securing an inseparable companion with which he may traverse a gloom, how hard to be traversed ! For, in his passage to the next world, neither his father nor his mother, nor his wife, nor his son, nor his kinsmen, will remain in his company: his virtue alone will adhere to him. Single is each man born ; single he dies ; single he receives the reward of his good, and single the punishment of his evil deeds †."

The wise and foolish, the great in rank, the low in condition, all die in the same way. As a rich man has more foresight than the poor and ignorant, so the former is more anxious about his death, which must happen to all ; but it is the holy man who has least dread of its occurrence, as being more prepared than others for the necessary change.

After death, the body is like a house without a tenant ; and the five elements slowly separate and join their like ; the atoms of earth join the earth, the watery mix with water, &c. Death is therefore called in Sanscrit *Panchatwa*, or separation and passage to the five elements. To promote this separation of the elements after death, which would be defiled if buried, and to purify them in their passage from the body, so as to enable the earth, air, fire, water, and ether, of which the body is composed, to join the mass of the same elements which compose the world, the bodies of Hindus are burnt. " What then dies? not the body, for it only changes its form ; and certainly not the soul ! Why then regret the death of relations and friends, if they have passed through life with propriety ! such grief is indeed natural, for it is universal, but it is the offspring of our igorance and our selfishness.

As the body is continually changing in its progress through life, so death is merely one of these changes. The body is frail, but the soul is incorruptible. Some say that an infant is born, that a person

* " A mansion infested by age and by sorrow, the seat of maladies, harrassed with pains, haunted with the qualities of darkness, and incapable of standing long ; such a mansion of the vital soul let its occupier always cheerfully quit" Menu, Ch. vi § 77 p. 183.

† Menu Chap. IV § 239, 240, 241, 243. The same idea is thus expressed in another sanscrit work. " The wise man meditates on the acquisition of knowledge and riches, as if not subject to sickness or death ; and cultivates virtue as if death had already seized him by the hair." (Hitopadesha).

is dead ; that this one is the murderer, and that body the murdered : but these are foolish exclamations ! The body is alone destroyed, not the soul ; as it only changes its position, like a person who casts off his worn-out garments. Cutting instruments may wound him, water may purify him, and air may dry him up, but the soul remains always the same. Those who are born must die, and whoever dies must be born again ; and as the elements were invisible and separated, before the formation of the body, in like manner they are again separated and dispersed upon its dissolution.

At the moment of death the material elements of the body separate, and the vital soul, which has an invisible body (*linga sharíra*), resembles the form of the body it had inhabited, and retains the organs of sense and of action. On separating from one, it joins itself to another, and according to the actions the person had performed in his former state of existence, so will be his future condition. As a seed of an inferior or superior order, so will the plant be ; thus may the soul animate a man who will grow old in a deformed and diseased body ; with a mind wicked and miserable. This union of the liberated soul, and its juncture with the seed of another body, takes place immediately ; as a leech on leaving one piece of grass, must immediately attach itself to another. Thus that immutable Power, by acting and reposing alternately, revivifies and destroys, in eternal succession, this whole assemblage of immoveable and locomotive creatures.

Beatitude is to be obtained by the coercion of the members, by abstaining from hurting and afflicting, or giving pain to sentient creatures ; when the individual becomes fit for immortality." Menu, § 60. When the vital soul has been purified by the good deeds which have occurred in the body, it is absorbed into that supreme essence, the divine soul of all beings, which withdraws his energy, and placidly slumbers. Menu adds—" Let him not wish for death let him not wish for life ; let him expect his appointed time, as a hired servant expects his wages." (Chap. VI. § 45, page 178).

BOOK III.

—o—

THERAPEUTICS.

The Hindu sages suppose that diseases are either produced by sins committed in a former state of existence; by derangements of the humours; or by the combination of these two causes. The former class can only be removed by certain sacrifices, prayers, penances, and gifts; the second class only, are those which may be removed by the employment of remedies. By this means, the physician knows that when a disease does not yield to the employment of proper remedies, it must belong to the first class of diseases, and will be only cured by the means prescribed in such cases. The third class of diseases are produced by a combination of sins and derangement of humours; these require for their cure the employment of prayers, and of a proper course of medicine.

The means employed by the physician for curing diseases, will be considered under the following heads.

1stly—*Hygeology* or regimen.

2ndly—*Materia Medica* and *Pharmacy*, or preparation of Medical agents; and,

3dly—*Surgery*, or all manual applications for the cure of injuries and diseases.

CHAPTER I.

Hygeology.

The Hindu Legislators appear to have been convinced, at a very early period, of the importance of a knowledge of the means of preserving health, as we find various laws were enacted for this purpose; and in order to enforce these precepts among a rude people, incapable of appreciating their importance, and disinclined to obey them, religion was employed to afford its powerful assistance. This explains the numerous precepts of Hygeine which we find in the sacred works of the most ancient people ; and which necessarily vary in their nature with the climate, and the character and habits of the people. In the sacred works of the Hindus, these laws are so numerous that it is impossible that any single individual should follow them. On this account they are probably more generally neglected than they would have been had the catalogue been less numerous. A fact much to be regretted, since the climate requires so much more attention to Hygeine than a more temperate one. The most important Hygeian precepts will be considered under the heads of relative and personal precepts.

Section I.

Relative duties.

Climate of India.—The extensive country known among the ancients by the title of *India* within the Ganges, has been famous, from the earliest ages, for the wisdom of its sages, the richness of its productions, and the fertility of its soil. It is now named Hindustan*, and is bounded by the River Indus on the west, and north by the Himalaya mountains ; on the south by the Indian ocean, and on the east by the hills and forests of Assam. From the magnificent range of Mountains in the north, Hindustan consists mostly of extensive plains, which possess a rich and black loam, consisting of clay with a considerable proportion of silicious sand, fertilized by various salts, and by decayed animal and vegetable matter where it is watered by the Ganges. In other parts of the Panjáb, in Bengal, and the adjacent provinces, there is a considerable extent of clayey soil. In Sind and Gujerat the soil is sandy, and in Malwa a rich deep black mould prevails. The soil is generally unproductive in Gundwana, and Orissa ; and near the coasts, of the Malabar and Coromandel sides, the soil is sandy and generally very poor, while the Table land of the Peninsula of India is generally fertile. The eastern part of Hindustan is intersected by numerous branches of large rivers, which

* The word *Hind*, from whence *Hindu* and *Hindustan* are derived, is of Persian origin, from Hindu, black, or dark and st'han, a place, or country of blacks. Others suppose it may have been derived from *Hind*, the supposed son of *Ham*, the son of Noah.

irrigate the rich plains of Bahar, and at not a very distant period seems to have formed, from its rich deposits, the large, flat and fruitful province of Bengal, to which the following remarks principally apply :—

In the Hindu medical works three climates are mentioned, the moist, the hot, and the mixed, or temperate.

The moist country (Anúpa) is distinguished by having much water upon its surface, by being intersected by rivers and being irregular in its surface, with high mountains, and tall trees. In such a climate the air is cool, and the wind temperate. There lillies and other water flowers abound; geese, ducks, cranes, and other such birds are common; and fish and serpents are numerous. In such a situation the inhabitants are unhealthy, and are short-lived. There diseases of air and phlegm abound, and the inhabitants are fat, indolent, and weak. In such situations the juices of the body require to be dried by the use of hot, dry, and light food, in small quantities; so as to strengthen the internal fire.

The second or Hilly country (Jángala), is characterized by the heat of the air, and by the prevalence of hot winds, by large and arid plains covered with dwarf trees and prickly shrubs, growing at a distance from each other. In such a country there is little water upon the surface, and it can only be obtained by digging wells. In such a climate the bamboo, the ákanda (Calotropis gigantea), the kúl (Zizyphus *Jujuba*), Yagyadumur (Ficus glomerata), the Gáb and Kenduka (Diospyros glutinosa and Diospyros melanoxylon), and the like trees are found. The inhabitants of such climates are remarkable for having little muscle, for having large bones, and being good workmen. The diseases of air and bile are most frequent; but the climate is healthy, and the inhabitants are long-lived.

When the two above climates are found in the same country it is called mixed, or temperate (Sádhárana). The heat and cold are more equable, the derangements of the air, bile, and phlegm are equalized, and the climate is favourable to life. The inhabitants of such a fortunate region are stronger, more vigorous and healthy, than in either of the other two climates. It is, however, worthy of remark that a person who is attentive to his regimen may live with impunity in any of the above climates.

When a person is born in a particular climate, and has air, bile, and phlegm deranged, on going to a worse one, the derangement of the humours increases and will destroy the person; or if he journies to another and better climate the tendency to disease will be removed.

Whatever is the custom of a climate as to food, clothing, &c.,

is to be followed, when the change will not prcduce any bad effect. If the disease is recent, and the individual strong, it will be cured easily; but this will be retarded or promoted, by the predisposition of the climate and season to affect such diseases. A complicated disease will always be cured with great difficulty. When one remedy does not produce the expected good effect, another should be substituted for it. But if a remedy does some good, it should be continued, in preference to a hundred others which have not been tried. If no other treatment can be devised in such severe diseases, the one adopted should be continued. The remedies must be varied according to the climate, season, age, and constitution of the affected person. If this is not observed, bad effects will follow, and other disorders will be produced.

Time (kála) like a God is produced perfect in root, stem, and branches. It has neither beginning nor end ; or is like a wheel which is always turning. It produces life and death, and the good and bad qualities of every thing, excepting that indistinguishable something, called the ultimate elements of the world (Paramánu), from whence another world will be ultimately formed.

2nd. Of Time and of the seasons. Time is divided as follows :—15 winks of the eye are equal to a káshṭhá; 30 káshṭhá 1 Kalá ; 20 kalás 1 Muhúrta; and 30 Muhúrtas to a day and a night; 15 days 1 Pakhsa or fortnight; one of which is the dark (Krishna) and the other light (Shukla) ; 2 Paksha 1 month (mása); 2 months are equal to one Ritu or season; 3 Ritu 1 Ayana; 2 Ayana 1 year ; and five years make one Yug. The sun forms the distinguishing qualities of the seasons. It dries the Earth, which is softened by the moon ; and with the assistance of wind it promotes the growth, and life of organized matter.

Seasons (*ritu*) are divided into *uttaráyana,* when the sun is supposed to be north of the equator; and *Dakhsináyana,* the six months when it is supposed to be south of the equator.

The seasons are six in number, each consisting of two siderial months each. The succession of them is always the same; but the vicissitudes of climate in them will depend on the position of the Equinoctial colure. Sometimes the year is reckoned by *Ayana,* from September (Shrávan), and January (mágha).

a. Cold Months, Shishira, (Mágha and Phálguna or January and February), during which warm clothing is to be used. Air is in excess during this season ; when the broths of animals, fish, amphibious animals, and substances mixed with ghee, are to be taken. The wine called *Sídhu* is to be used, and honey mixed with water; milk and different sweetmeats ; fat, and new rice; and warm water is always to be used. The body should be well rubbed with oil, which should also be applied to the head. The person should sleep in a room near the centre of the house, so as to be warm, and removed from the wind. Warm clothing should always be used during this season. The food should be in small quantities, and hot and dry substances should be avoided.

b. Spring Months, Vasanta (March and April). All organized bodies are generated during this, or the spring season. The air is then clear, flowers are numerous, and the country looks beautiful, with the new leaves on the trees; and man is cheered by the song of birds and the hum of bees. The south wind now begins to blow. In this season the phlegm predominates, and its diseases appear. The internal fire is diminished. Emetics and purgatives should be employed, and heavy, oily, and sweet substances are to be avoided, and sleeping in the day time should also be guarded against. Bodily exercise should be used. Tepid water should be used for every purpose, and the body should be rubbed with sandal and other fragrant woods. Use barley and wheat, the flesh of deer, hares, and wild fowls. Drink sídhu and *Mada* (wine) and reside in a garden with women.

c. Hot Months, Ghríshma, (May and June), The hot season, in which the rays of the sun are powerful, with warm wind from the south, which makes this season oppressive and unpleasant, increases air, produces debility, and affects even the understanding. The earth becomes hot and dry, the rivers diminish, the water is warm and light, and the earth appears to smoak. Birds and deer proceed in search of water; and the juice of plants is raised, and their qualities are diminished; creepers, grass, and the leaves of trees are diminished and fall off, dried and decayed.

During this season the diseases of air prevail. In it use cool liquids and food prepared with ghee. Drink different sherbets, and use broth of wild animals and birds; eat rice with milk and ghee; by which means a person will not lose his strength. Little wine is to be used, and always mixed with much water. Salt, acid, and hot things are to be avoided. Do not take much exercise. Reside in a cool garden with a large tank and flowers; avoid excesses in venery. Sleep during the day in a cool room, and at night repose in the upper rooms, and use the hand *pankha* (fan) sprinkled with sandal wood and water.

d. The *Rainy season, Varshá* (July and August). During this season the sky is loaded with clouds; the wind easterly, with much lightning and thunder; new grass and leaves appear; the rainbow is beautiful; numerous graceful creepers of the class of convolvulus appear, of various colours, white, blue, and pink. The banks of the rivers, and the trees upon them are broken away by the force of the torrents; the tanks and lakes are adorned by varied coloured lilies; much clear water continues upon the surface of the earth, and vegetation proceeds rapidly. There are many clouds which obscure the sun and planets, and much rain falls. Towards the end of the season there is little thunder. The clouds diminish the light and heat, and with the water of the moon (dew), reduce the juices of living animals, and their strength. Water is impure, during this season; the body is soft, the cold damp air affects the strength of the internal fire, and the food is burnt in the body, by the increased quantity of bile.

In *Varshá* the appetite is diminished by the derangement of the humours, caused by the heat and moisture; and new water has an acid quality. The food should be sparingly given, and should neither be too hot nor very cold; sleeping in the day time and exposure to the climate are to be avoided, as also the use of river water. Too much exercise, exposure to the sun, and venery are to be avoided. Water mixed with honey is to be used, and in a cloudy day take food mixed with salt, acids, and ghee; barley, wheat, and old rice are to be used, with the broths of wild animals and fowls. The wine of grapes, and fresh water which has been boiled, are to be drunk. Anoint the body with fragrant oil, and bathe daily; use light and white clothes, and live in a high and dry house.

5 The *Moist Season, Sharat,* (September and October). During this season the sky is overcast with white clouds, and the tanks are full of water lilies. The earth is covered with *salt*, and many trees are rooted up and die. The surface of the earth appears irregular.

During this season the sky is clean, with white broken clouds; the air is sultry, the moisture on the ground dries, the sun's rays increase in strength; and by the changes in temperature bile and cough produce diseases. In this season the water is pure, and may be used freely for bathing, and for drinking. Vegetation is vigorous, the country beautiful; and food produced during this season is not good, but is improved by keeping, if it admits of this. The lakes are covered with lilies, reeds, and white flowers. Ducks, &c., abound.

Diseases of the Bile prevail in this season. The food and drink to be used should be light, cool and sweet; with tonic and bitter articles. Such food as wild fowls, hares, and animals of the same kind; mutton is also good, with rice, barley, wheat, and the like. Use purgative medicines and blood-letting; while exposure to the sun and heat and night air are to be avoided, more particularly the east wind ; sleeping during the day, too, is to be avoided ; as also fat, oil, fish, the flesh of amphibious animals, and acids. The clothes should be light, and clean.

6 *Cold season, Haimanta* (November and December). The water during this season becomes clear, cool, and heavy. The rays of the sun diminish in influence ; and phlegm is increased, as is exemplified in its discharge from the nose, from colds.

The Bilious diseases, which were common during the last season, diminish during the present, in which healthy, cool, northerly airs prevail. A mistiness hangs over tanks and rivers, like clothes which cover the body. The cows, sheep, buffaloes, and elephants look clean, and several trees such as priyangu, punnága, &c., are in flower.

The seven last days of one season, and the seven first of the new one, are called ritusandhi (the junction of seasons). During this time the regimen of the former is gradually to be left off, and that of the succeeding one substituted.

Diseases from Bile are cured by the cold season ; those from phlegm diminish in the hot season, and from air during the moist months. The morning is like the spring season, noon like the hot, and evening like the rainy season. The same changes occur in the night ; the first watch being like the rainy season ; the second like the moist ; and the morning watch, like the cold season. In these times, air, bile, and phlegm increase like the seasons ; and in the process of digestion they increase in the same manner ; during the first stage phlegm predominates, then bile, and lastly air.

The irregularities of the seasons produce an unfavourable effect on health, and both food, water, and medicines lose their good effects, and various diseases are produced. It is during these irregularities that plagues appear, devils rage, and sin prevails. Poisonous air often produces the same effects. The odours of flowers mixed with poisonous air produces derangements of phlegm, difficult breathing, vomiting, discharges from the mouth and nose, headache, and fever. There is an influence of planets and stars, from the bad situation of dwelling houses, the place in which persons sleep and sit, and the diseases of the horse upon which he rides, is liable to effect the rider. These are to be prevented by changing the person's residence, by prayers, by the removal of sin, by different sacrifices and ceremonies, by the intercession of Brahmins, and by visiting holy places.

In these remarks we have the evidence of considerable correctness of observation ; as the increased communicating power of moist air, the unhealthy nature of certain situations, for preventing or curing diseases ; in which a change of situation is very properly recommended. But these remarks are mixed up with false statements, from the desire of the writer to explain all difficulties by superstitious fancies; thus whenever a child is attacked with sickness, it is supposed to be produced by the attack of certain devils; such as graha, asura, rákhyas, bhúta, &c.; to relieve which different prayers (mantras) and ceremonies are performed, with generally the addition of certain remedies.

When a disease continues long, the situations of planets and stars are calculated; by which the long continuance of the disease is explained, and for the relief of which certain ceremonies and gifts are performed.

The heat of the fire cures diseases of air and phlegm. It also removes passing pains. It promotes the dejections, and removes shivering and discharges from the nose, mouth, and eyes, It increases the diseases of blood and bile, and during sleep retains the humours in a good state; it improves the colour of the body, strengthens it, removes dozing, and promotes happiness and internal warmth.

The heat of the sun when very strong, is drying; and promotes perspiration, faintness, giddiness, thirst, and the heat of the body.It increases the bad smell of the body, deepens the dark colour of the skin; and increases the diseases of the bile, and blood.

Shadows remove the bad effects of heat, as they have a sedative, cooling, and pleasant quality.

The smoke of fire increases bile and air.

Dew and mist increase phlegm and air.

Moonlight cures diseases of blood and bile.

Rain increases strength, is cooling, increases semen, sleep, languor, phlegm, and air.

Easterly wind increases phlegm, is cold, has a saltish quality, and is heavy. It diminishes appetite, increases laziness, the heat of the body, and strength. It produces diseases of the blood and bile, is bad for those with sores, or who are affected with poison, and diseases of phlegm. It removes the derangements of air. It is good for persons fatigued, and it diminishes the form of consumption produced by phlegm. It also give strength, and softens the body. A Southerly wind is pleasant, does not produce heat, and has a light and sedative quality. It is good for the eyes and strength, it cures diseases of blood and bile, and the air is not deranged by it. Westerly wind increases internal heat, dries the body, and diminishes the bulk of the body and strength; it produces a roughness of the skin, diminishes the strength, and health. It dries up phlegm and fat. Northerly wind is soft, cooling, light, agreeable, and slightly sedative. It promotes the dejections, and increases diseases of air, bile, and phlegm. In healthy individuals it increases the phlegm, and the strength. It is good for severe cough with bloody sputa, for diseases from poisons, and does not derange the humours.

The air from Pankhas, removes faintness, thirst, perspiration, fatigue, and heat. The Tál Pankha (common hand pankha) and chowry and cloth pankahs, cure deranged air, bile, and phlegm ; are cooling, and increase happiness.

There are three prevailing seasons in Bengal, the cold, hot, and rainy seasons. From the end of February, and during March and a part of April, may be considered as spring months, and are the most agreeable of any of the year. Towards the end of March, and during the months of April, May, and a part of June the weather is very hot ; and in the northern and more inland provinces a violent hot wind blows from the west, loaded with almost imperceptible particles of sand. In this season the weather is so oppressive as to confine the inhabitants to their houses, during the great heat of the day. Vegetation is destroyed, and these provinces are reduced to a burning tract of sand ; while the air of the neighbouring mountains remains cool and pleasant, during these hot months.

In the upper provinces the rains begin in April and May ; but in the plains they do not commence till the beginning of June, and continue to full till the end of July. The rain disperses the accumulated heat, which would otherwise be insupportable. During the months of August and September the rain falls less frequently and copiously, and the long day and high altitude of the sun, with an atmostphere loaded with moisture, render the weather excessively oppressive and sultry ; particularly when the air is calm, which is of frequent occurrence, as the Monsoon changes at this time. The cold season commences in the month of October, when dews are heavy ; the cold increases, and during the months of November, December, and January, it is often intense in Bengal and Behar. In these provinces the cold has generally a damp disagreeable feel, whereas, in the northern and western provinces, snow and ice are common on the Mountains, and the air is dry and bracing.

From such an extensive country, and variety of soil and climate, the vegetable and animal productions are of the most varied description in the different latitudes, heights, and exposures ; and man himself affords great varieties in his physical and mental powers in the different situations and climates in which he resides. In the Northern Provinces of Hindustan, the men are tall, strong, and active, and are distinguished by their courage and mental qualities ; as we advance to the more sultry and moist climate of Bengal, the inhabitants become of lower stature, possess greater agility, and are capable of enduring great fatigue, have little courage or mental aptitude, but great cunning and retentiveness. They are generally of a fair olive colour, handsome in their youth, and in after life in proportion to their rank, and healthy and guarded occupation ; but become of a dark olive colour and plain exterior, in proportion as they inhabit low and damp houses, live on unhealthy food, and are much exposed to labour, and to the inclemency of the weather. In general the head and face of the Hindu are small and oval, the nose and lips prominent and well formed, the eyes black, and the eyebrows regular, and full *. The females are distinguished for the gracefulness of their forms, the softness of their skins, their long and black hair, dark eyes, and delicate persons. These peculiarities are marked in youth, but rapidly fade. The fairness of the skin also differs—depending on that of the parents, and on the occupation and exposure of the individual to the sun, &c.

Section II.

Personal Duties.

The practitioner should give instructions to persons not only as to the manner of curing, but also of preventing the occurrence of disease †.

The following remarks will be considered under the heads of duties—*a* rising from bed in the morning ; *b* cleaning the mouth ; *c* anointing the body ; *d* exercise, shampooing, and rubbing the body ; *e* bathing, *f* clothing, *g* food, and *h* sleeping ‡.

* The intelligence of the Bengálís is much more marked in the higher classes than among the lower. In the former, the brisk and intelligent boy, that receives instruction readily, is fickle and restless ; and from the short period he attends school, from the enervating nature of the climate, and the vitiating influence of Híndú Society, is too often transformed into the stupid and sensual man.

† Bodies are cleansed by water, the mind is purified by birth, the vital spirit by theology and devotion, and the understanding, by knowledge (Manu. p. 161. ch. v. §109.

‡ So careful were the Hindu authors of the regimen of the sick, that they even noted the hour at which the disease commenced, the length of time to be devoted to sleep in different diseases ; how often the patient is to clean his teeth, and wash his mouth ; and the kind of house in which he should reside. Such particulars captivate the ignorant patient and his friends, who fancy the practitioner possesses a great extent of knowledge from the care with which these trifles are attended to, while they often neglect important indications.

a. It is proper to rise from bed sometime before sun-rise, to perform the duties of nature, with the face towards the north.

b. After these duties the teeth are to be cleaned with a piece of a fresh branch of the nim or catechu tree, and the mouth and eyes and face are to be cleaned with water. Should these not be got, branches of any other kind of wood, not hollow, may be used. Persons are not to clean the teeth when it produces vomiting, when the food is not properly digested (ajírna), in diarrhæa (atisár), in shúl, in diseases of the teeth, during the first eight days of fever, in asthma (shwása), when the mouth is dry, in cough, in epilepsy in fainting, in headache, and in diseases of the eyes. The teeth should not be cleaned before the tenth year of the child's age.

When a powder is used for cleaning the teeth it is to be formed of honey, long pepper, black pepper, and dry ginger, &c. This is used daily, and a soft brush of the above wood may be used. Cleaning the teeth promotes appetite and happiness.

For cleaning the tongue, a piece of gold, silver, or wood ten finger's breadth in length, with a thin edge, may be used as a scraper.

The mouth is to be washed with water, ghee, oil, or the like ; which strengthens the teeth, and promotes appetite.

c. The Hindus, and all Asiatics, anoint their bodies daily with oil, more especially their heads, ears, and feet ; which they suppose is conducive to health, by increasing good fortune, improving the colour and softness of the skin, increasing happiness, sleep, life, strength, and curing perspiration, bad smells, and lassitude. It also diminishes the diseases of air and phlegm, increases the seven dhátu, and improves the marrow, and the colour of the skin, and the organs of sense. It also cures diseases of the feet, prevents painful cramps of the fingers ; and as long as the head is kept moistened with oil, it prevents headache, improves the hair, and prevents its becoming gray. In all cases in which bathing is to be avoided, the anointing of the body will be advantageous to the person's health.

Mustard, or any other fragrant oil, is used for anointing the body. Anointing the face with sweet smelling oils, as females often do, retains the eyes healthy, and the face soft and pure, the mouth and lips like the lily, the eyelashes beautiful, and the skin clear like light. Using such, increases riches, children, and other desirable objects. Anointing the ears prevents deafness, &c., and the diseases of the nape of the neck, and of the condyles of the jaw. Anointing the feet improves the eyesight, and prevents the feet from cracking. The Body should not be anointed at the beginning of fever, when the food is not digested, or after purging, vomiting, and enemas. The Hebrews, in like manner, especially their females, made much use of oil ; and it was considered by them as a mark of esteem, and honor to offer oil to those that went to see them, so that they might anoint their heads *. The modern method of anointing the head at the coronation of kings is derived from this custom.

The hot climate and slight clothing, and exposure to a burning sun, increases the action of the cutaneous vessels, and renders the skin hard and dry ; and if perfect cleanliness is not observed, it becomes incrusted with its own discharges, and with foreign matter which irritates the part, and prevents the proper action of this important organ. To prevent such a consequence, oil is ordered to be rubbed over the surface before it has been washed, by which it is rendered soft, and pliant ; it also promotes an equable perspiration, and an excessive degree is avoided which would weaken the body. Whenever the Hindu feels indisposed, the body is anointed with oil, on the same principle that Solomon, in his Proverbs, speaks of administering ointment, " which rejoices the heart, which may be a healing medicine to the navel, &c". In this case the oil was mixed with other vegetable oils to render its effects more permanent. The metallic oxyds were sometimes added so as to form ointments, liniments, and plasters. The latter medicines giving them a due consistence by their drying effects on the oils.

Several oils are prepared with those medicinal plants which are used internally, and are applied externally in different cases of disease ; especially in old fevers, spasmodic, paralytic, rheumatic diseases, in affections of the mind, as madness, &c. ; and these oils are supposed by the Hindus to be thus used more advantageously than when given internally. Medicines keeping the feet and the outlets of the body clean, promote health, and are good for the eyes and skin. After the person has adjusted his dress, prayers are to be offered up to the gods.

d. Exercise increases strength, prevents and cures diseases, by equalizing the humours; it prevents fatness and laziness, and strengthens the firmness of the body. It removes grief, increases the internal fire, and the body becomes lighter, more vigorous, and ready to work. If daily used, it prevents the bad effects of indigestible and unusual articles of food, and fat food so desired. Walking is always to be used, particularly by those persons who live on rich food ; such exercise is to be used evening and morning, especially in the cold and spring months, while fatigue is avoided.

Persons with diseases of the blood and bile, with fever, difficulty of breathing, dizziness, asthma, fatigue, and all kinds of cough, and

* See Luke vii. v. 46.

dryness of the body, should avoid exercise. When the mouth is always dry, with difficulty of breathing; in diseases of the air and bile, in boyhood and old age, after eating, and before the food is thoroughly digested, or when there are sores upon the body, exercise is to be avoided. When reduced in flesh by lust, such exercise tires and increases fever, phlegm and thirst; and increases diseases of the blood and bile. Should much exercise be taken, it produces cough, fever, and vomiting; after exercise quietude is proper, as it increases strength, cures a superabundance of fat, and removes the feeling of fatigue.

e. Shampooing cures diseased phlegm, air, and fat; the members are retained healthy, as well as the skin, and it increases internal heat. *Rubbing* the body is pleasant, cures *amasia*, improves the skin, and the body feels light; it also cures itching, small pimples, diseased air, and impurities in the abdomen. If the body be rubbed with a brush, the fire of the skin will be increased, and perspiration then cures itching, and small tubercles. The nails, beard, mustachoes, and hair are to be cut every fifth day. The hair is to be combed and cleaned, which improves health.

f. Bathing. There are several kind of baths (*sweda*). The following are the most common:—1st. Cold bathing removes the inordinate heat of the body, fatigue, perspiration, itchiness, thirst, and promotes happiness and pleasure. It removes the impurities of the body, clears the senses, removes drowsiness and sin, increases semen, retains the blood pure, and increases the internal heat. If warm water is poured on the head, it is not good for the eyes; but the use of cold water strengthens vision. Bathing in very cold water in the winter deranges phlegm and air, and during the hot season warm bathing increases bile and blood. Bathing is not proper in diarrhœa (*atisár*), in the beginning of fever, in diseases of the ear, or in those of the air, in swellings of the abdomen, in indigestion, and after eating. Bathing the feet is to be used for removing impurities, local diseases, and fatigue. It retains the eyes clean, increases semen, and prevents the approach of devils. Independent persons, such as rich merchants, bankers, talukdars and others, generally bathe at 10 or 11 o'clock, and after performing these ceremonies they breakfast. Shop-keepers, day-labourers, &c. eat, at 10 o'clock, a handful of rice which has been moistened for half an hour in water, or a handful of gram moistened, and do not generally bathe till after 12, 2, or even 3 o'clock. There are some who bathe twice or thrice a day, but they are few in number. This description applies to the male inhabitants of towns. The higher class of females seldom bathe in rivers, but do so in tanks, in their respective gardens; or in warm water, between 10 and 11 o'clock. Widows of the lower class are not strict, and do not observe the rules of the Shástras regarding bathing.*

The cold bath is used in some inflammatory fevers, and in madness (*unmáda*); and locally in some external inflammatory swellings (*vrana*).

2nd. *Avagáha sweda,* or warm water bath. It is prepared with several medicinal plants, and is used either locally or generally; for relieving pain, in different kinds of fevers, spasmodic affections, &c.

3rd. Vapour Baths (*Ushmá sweda*) are much employed by the Bengálís, more particularly for removing pain. They are made by heating a quantity of water in an earthen pot, over which a lid had been placed. The patient is first well rubbed with oil, and then sits on a chair over the pot of hot water, with a covering of clothes thrown over both. When any particular part of the body is pained, this only is exposed to the steam bath, and in other cases medicinal plants are added to increase the good effects of the remedy, as milk, *ním* leaves, and other such drugs.

4th. *Upanáha sweda* or hot cataplasms of medicinal plants. These are made into a paste, heated, and applied locally to relieve pain. In other cases these medicines are applied locally, with hot vapour. A tube is used to convey the vapour to the diseased part.

5th. *Tápa sweda* is the frequent application of a hot hand, a heated cloth, or a bag filled with hot sand or salt.† It is used for relieving local pain, and for promoting the warmth of the body, when it becomes cold, in any disease.

After bathing apply *Surmá*, or antimony, to the edges of the eyelids; which improves the sight, clears the itchiness, or any unhealthy humors of the eyes, and prevents the bad effects of the

* The Hindu men and women may be seen proceeding towards the sacred Ganges in the cool of the day, the one with his small copper lota, the other with her antique earthen pot perched upon her head, amidst the rustling of the beautiful palm trees, which almost hide the graceful cupolas of the neighbouring temples. After washing their heads with some of the mud and water of the Ganges, they proceed to clean their teeth with the branch of a tree which they have brought with them. They then wash their bodies, using mud for soap, fill their vessels with water, and return home.

† In some cases the earth is heated, and a plantain leaf is extended over it, upon which the person lies.

glare of the sun, and the diseases of the eyes in general. Persons should not use Súrmá who have sat up during the night, who are much fatigued, who have vomited, who have eaten recently or are feverish. Medicines are sometimes added for increasing some particular effect.

g. Clothing. After bathing, the body is to be well rubbed with a piece of clean cloth, which produces a good colour of the skin. Silk, and warm *red* clothes diminish the diseases of air and phlegm, and should be used in the winter season. The clothes should be light, cool, and thin during the hot weather. In rainy and cold weather, warm *white* clothes of a medium thickness are to be used. Care must be taken always to wear clean clothes, which is good for the skin, looks well, and promote happiness and longevity.

A piece of cotton cloth tied round their middle is all the clothing the poorer classes of natives have ; it is only when they appear in public that they add the turban, or piece of cloth to cover their heads and shoulders. The turban defends the head from heat and cold, and prevents the determination of the humours to the head. If the person uses it continually he will live long, and his head will remain clear, and cool. A single piece of coarse cotton cloth, several yards in length, is the usual dress of females. Such clothes, particularly with the addition of ornaments, prevent the approach of the Rakshyasas or devils, increase strength (ojas), improve good fortune, and retain the heart happy and contented. Sandals are to be put upon the feet to strengthen, and to protect them.

A paste of sandal wood, and other fragrant drugs, is then to be rubbed over the fore head, chest, and upper extremities. A prayer is offered up to God, and gifts presented to the Bráhmins.

The *Umbrella* protects the person from rain, wind, and dust ; it diminishes perspiration, protects him from the influence of dew, retains the colour of the skin and eyes, and promotes health. A stick protects the person against beasts, and it prevents fatigue.

h. The Native *Houses* are well adapted for the climate, being raised from the ground by prepared earth ; with which the walls are likewise formed, and a thick thatch covers it, and extends beyond the walls so as to form a protection from the heavy rains. They are usually well ventilated in consequence of a space being left between the walls, and the thatch. These houses are divided into apartments to suit the convenience of the family, and the mud walls and thatched roof keeps them in an equable temperature. In consequence of the unsettled state of many parts of the country, the houses of a family or tribe are usually built in the form of a square, or a series of squares, for their mutual protection. The open central space is usually kept clean, and is covered above, in days of festivity, when the prescribed ceremonies are performed to their tutelar Gods, placed in a separate house on the north side of the square. In some parts of the country their houses are made of sun-burnt or fire-burnt bricks, and the houses are often two, or more stories high. In many parts of the country the houses or villages are fortified to protect them from wild beasts, and from their enemies.

i. Diet. The Hindu medical writers usually commence the cure of a disease by arranging the diet that is to be followed by the sick person. So much do the Hindu Physicians rely upon diet that they declare that most diseases may be cured by following carefully, dietetic rules *; and if a patient does not attend to his diet, a hundred good medicines will not remove the disease. The generality of diseases being supposed to be produced by derangement of the humours, if one or more are morbidly increased in quantity, their indications of cure are commenced by promoting the just balance of the elements and humours, by a judicious choice of aliments, and by such means as assist the vital principle on the completion of the assimilation. On this account they have not only been careful in describing the regimen, but also the food and drink for the different seasons, and even the vessels in which they should be kept.

Food gives strength, and colour to the body, and the essential part of life (*ojas*). It also supports the heat of the body, increases and diminishes the humours, retains these in their equilibrium ; keeps the person happy, the senses active, and the memory retentive, while it supports life, and promotes longevity.

The different articles of food which are employed to nourish the body will be considered under the head of general remarks on food derived from the vegetable, and animal kingdoms ; with a few remarks on condiments ; under which will be considered articles derived from the mineral kingdom, including water and medicinal liquids. The form in which food is taken into the body will vary its effects upon the system ; but some articles of food are always wholesome, even from birth to old age ; as water, milk, rice, ghee, &c. A second kind is always dangerous to health as fire, escharotics, and poisons ; the one burning the part, the second destroying it, and the third killing the individual.

* Or as Baglivi expresses the same opinion, as the heading of one of his chapters " de ciborum delectu, sive de methodo curandi morbos quamplures per opportunum ciborum genus, sine ope remediorum. Op. omnia, T. 11 p. 530.

Some substances are injurious to the system when mixed and prepared in a particular manner, when they become like poison: Thus pumpkins, mushrooms, bamboo-shoots, plumbs, dried vegetables, unleavened bread, goats or sheeps flesh, pigs flesh, salt, spirits, when eaten, or drank with milk, resemble poison. Sometimes articles of food act on the humours favourably or unfavourably, according to the state of the body. One article will be good for deranged air, and another bad for deranged bile, &c. Again the state of the article will modify its effects. Red rice, which grows in the cold season, wheat, barley, and other grain of the same kind are good, and preserve health; whereas rice which has sprouted, *másh kaláy* (Phaseolus radiatus), fat, honey, milk, jagree, when eaten with the flesh of domestic or amphibious animals, or with fish, are so bad as to resemble poison. Milk with honey, and vegetables in general should not be used together. Pepper and a kind of vegetable called kákámáchí are notto be used; as also honey, and hot water. When animal food is to be used, the bile is to be carefully evacuated, or it will derange the person's health.

Butter-milk, with honey, ghee, a variety of fishes, and the flesh of deer, are not to be eaten together; fish and milk, or its preparations, or fish and sugar, and its preparations; hogs-flesh prepared with honey, are to be avoided; plantains with butter milk, curdled milk, or milk with sour fruits, before or after eating, are improper. Pigeons fried with mustard oil; honey mixed with rain water, and kept in brass pots for ten days, should be avoided. These remarks are particularly applicable to boys and strong persons, and those who take violent exercise.

2nd. Food may act unfavourably by the quantity which is taken. Thus honey and ghee, oil and marrow, or honey and water, oil and ghee, or fat, are bad when eaten in large and equal proportions.

3rd. The following mixtures of articles possessing certain tastes are improper, as sweet and sour articles, sweet and salt, sweet and pungent, sweet and bitter substances, or bitter and salt articles. Such mixtures should therefore he carefully avoided; as they form bad chyle, and thus the appetite &c. is deranged. Such mixtures, however, will not injure the health of the young and strong, those who live in a pure air and take much exercise; and those accustomed to their use, by whom they may be eaten in small quantities with impunity. But in ordinary circumstances, when their bad effects are felt, recourse must he had to the use of emetics and purgatives, and such medicines as have a tendency to equalize the humours. The articles of food which are wholesome from mixture, and preparation; are those which derange air, and diminish bile. The opposite articles of food which moderate air, and derange bile, are unwholesome. By improper mixtures wholesome articles of food may become as poisons. But the kind of food to be used must be varied according to the age, habits, and seasons as well as to the individual's idiosyncrasy.

There are four forms in which food may be taken—one kind is taken without being chewed as drinks (píta); another is lapped (lírhá); another sucked (chúshya); and another kind of food is chewed (káṭita).

According to Charaka there are six varieties of food.

1. Soft food (bhojya) as rice, &c.
2. Soft sweetmeats (bhakhya).
3. Hard food (charbya), that requires chewing to prepare it for digestion.
4. Drinks (Peya).
5. Liquids that are lapped (lehya).
6. Food that is sucked (Chúshya), such as mangoes, sugar-cane, &c.

Food and medicines are also divided into six different classes, according to their effects on the senses. These are into sweet, acid, salt, bitter, pungent, and astringent. These tastes are however, modified by disease.

a. Sweet articles of food increase the semen, the milk, and the fat; while they improve the eyesight, asthma, worms, and affections of the throat. They also increase phlegm, the strength of the tissues, and humours; retain the body in health, and promote longevity. These substances are good for the soul, and cooling for the body. They cure derangements in air and bile, promote appetite, and are useful in correcting the effects of poison.

b. Acid articles of food promote appetite, are cooling before, and heating after eating. They are agreeable to the taste, promote digestion, and increase bile and phlegm. They increase the blood, and restore irregularities and derangements in the air, bile, and phlegm. When they have been often taken they produce weakness, and emaciation of the body, and sometimes they produce blindness (nyctalopia). Acids act quickly, and produce itching, irruptions over the body, a palor of the skin, and a swelling of the body, with thirst, fever, and boils.

c. Salt articles of food relax the bowels, promote digestion, and increase appetite. They also promote perspiration, remove derangements of the air, bile, phlegm, and blood; produce a glossiness of the surface of the body, diminish or cure aphrodisia, are cooling, and heal sores. They are, however, bad for the eyes; and if long continued, they derange the humours; the skin becomes covered with irregularities upon its surface, followed by leprosy, weakness, and by symptoms produced by poisons having been taken (visarpa).

d. Bitter food is not pleasant to the taste, but is dry, and light to the stomach; increases bile and air, and produces dryness, heat, and diseased milk. If taken before eating it improves the appetite, removes worms, thirst, poison, leprosy, epilepsy, nausea, heat of the body, and fever. It corrects too much bile, and phlegm. It also improves the flesh, fat, marrow, urine, and dejections; increases memory, is cooling, and is good for the palate and throat. But if always eaten it has a bad effect, deranging the humours, and producing diseases of air.

e. Pungent articles of food are of a drying nature, increasing the appetite and milk, and diminishing thirst and fever. They cure diseases of phlegm, diseases of the throat and head, itchiness, and internal pain. But if eaten for some time in considerable quantities they produce thirst, weakness, shaking, pain over the body, and derange the spleen.

f. Astringent articles of food are cooling, and cure diseases of the bile and phlegm. They increase air, particularly flatulence, they clear the blood and flesh, and are heavy to the stomach. They produce costiveness, and stop diarrhæa, and thicken the dejections; they remove diseases of the skin, and heal wounds and sores. But if taken for some time they produce costiveness, a swelling of the abdomen, thirst, and weakness, and retard the circulation of fluids in the body.

For ensuring good digestion the patient's passions must be regulated. He must sleep at night in a protected room; must use warm water to bathe with, and take bodily exercise. Such observances are considered to be most necessary to health.

I. *Articles of food derived from the Vegetable Kingdom.*

There are seven parts of vegetables employed for food. These are the leaves, flowers, fruits, wood, branches, roots, and mushrooms. They are more easily digested in the above order, which is followed in the Hindu medical works. I prefer the order in which the different articles came into use as the food of man.

Fruits. The form and size of fruits would soon fix the attention of mankind, and with the culmiferous and leguminous vegetables would form the primordial food of man. In Hindustan there are a great variety of indigenous specimens of these articles of food. The following are the principal :—

English.	*Scientific.*	*Sanscrit.*
Pomegranate,	Punica Granatum,	Dárima.
Myrobalan,	Phyllanthus emblica,	A'malaká.
Custard apple,	Annona squamosa,	Sleshmátaka, or átá.
Plumbs,	Prunus,	Badari.
Apples,	Pyrus,	Simbítiká.
Quince,	Pyrus Cydonia,	Táhár.
Wood apple,	Feronia Elephantum,	Kapittha.
Lemon,	Citrus acida,	Mátulunga.
Mango,	M Mangifera,	A'mra.
Hog plumb,	Terminalia Chebula,	Harítakí.
A Species of Bread fruit tree,	Artocarpus Lacucha,	(Rox,) Lakucha.
Karinda	Carissa Carandas,	Karamarda.
Guava,	Psidium pyriferum,	Párábata.
Tamarinds,	Tamarindus Indica,	Amliká.
Rose apple,	Eugenia, Jamborosa	Jambúl.
Jack fruit,	Artocarpus Integrifolia,	Kanthaphal or Kántál.
Pine apple,	Bromelia Ananas,	Shátanetra.
	Palms.	
Cocoanut,	(Cocos Nucifera ;)	Nárikela.
Date tree,	Phœnix dactylifera,	Karjúra.
Fan Palm,	Borassus flabeleiformis.	Tála.

Pamplemus, Plantain, &c., &c.

The following varieties of oranges, lemons, citrons, &c., are indigenous to Hindustan, and were well known to the Greeks and Romans. They increase bile, improve the appetite, and cure dyspepsia.

There are several varieties of oranges (Kamalá), but they are not distinguished by different names.

There are different sorts of Lemons, (Nimbu,) such as Limpáka, Kágaji, Nárángi, Batábi, Kamalá, &c.

Drupes.—These fruits are of the genus Amygdalus, &c.

Prunes.—Apricot, Prunus Armenaica ; Cherry, P. Cerasus &c.

Cucurbitaceous fruits or Gourds.

Water Melon,	Cucumis Melo.	Kharbuj.
Sweet Melon,	C. Momordica,	Phutí.
Common Cucumber,	C. Sativus,	Sashá B. or Khírá. H.
Bottle Gourd,	C. Lagenaria,	Kadu.
Pumpkin,	C. Pepo,	Kumrá. B.

Squash Gourd,	C. Melopepo,	Sapharí Kumrá.
Fig tree,	C. Citrullus,	Tárbúj.

These fruits have from the earliest times constituted an important part in the diet of the Hindus.

Vegetables. In general vegetables are not easily digested, as they increase air, bile, and phlegm, produce worms, and constipate the bowels. They are rendered more wholesome when boiled and seasoned. If employed alone for food they derange the system, affecting particularly the colour of the skin and eyes, and diminishing semen, blood, and memory.

The leaves of the *chílu, bastaki, sunishannaka, tanduliyá,* and *mandúkaparní,* are considered the most wholesome kind of vegetables. They are usually prepared by being boiled in water, fried in ghee, and then seasoned with salt. In some cases they are dressed with butter, and tonic compounds called Ticta barga; such as Prapunnára (a kind of Cassia), Somarájí (Serratula Anthelmentica), Patola (Tricosanthes diœcia), Várttákí, (Solanum melongela or the egg plant, &c.

The *Esculent roots* are very numerous. The following are the chief varieties. The Arum Colocasia; A. Marcrorhizon, and A. Peltatum; the roots of the different varieties of lotus (Nymphœa Lotus), &c. (Shálúk) Nelumbo (Padma); Yams (Dioscorea); Spanish potatoes (Convolvulus Batatas), beet root; onion; garlick; lecks; white and red Carrots; raddishes, &c.

The generality of European pot and salad herbs are found indigenous in Hindustan. The following are a few of these :—

Cauliflower (Brassica), broccoli, parsley (apium petroselium), spinage (spinacea oleracea), common lettuce (Lactuca sativa), Garden cress (Lepidum sativum), endive (cichorium endivia), mustard (Sinapis nigra et alba), with many others. The properties of each of these are given in the Hindu medical works, with their effects on the different humours, and on diseases.

The *Graminivorous* seeds form a numerous class which afford the chief article of diet to a large proportion of the inhabitants of Asia. The principal varieties of corn and pulse were derived from Asia, and they are peculiarly fruitful in Hindustan, and from their hard consistence they may be kept in a good state for long periods. Rice (oryza sativa) in the form of paddy, when covered with its husk, in a dry situation will keep for years perfectly fresh and good, and may be transported from one part of the country to another with great facility. A large population almost entirely live on this grain, of which there are numerous varieties. The *shálí* rice, when of a red colour, cures diseased air, bile, and phlegm ; clears the eyes, increases the strength, semen, and urine, and removes thirst. *A'tapa*, or Sun-dried rice, increases the diseases of air, bile, and phlegm ; is heating, increases the perspiration, alvine evacuations and urine. It is considered indigestible, and weakens the body. When the plant has been transplanted, the rice is rendered lighter, and more easily digested.

New rice is heavy, increases phlegm, gives an oleaginous appearance to the body, and promotes the secretion of semen.

Old rice is pleasant to the taste, is drying, improves the appetite and internal heat. It is light, and increases air. The rice of sixty days growth, which is produced in the rains, or in the months of August and September, is considered as forming the most wholesome food ; and is called *Shashtiká*. A small red rice, called *Raktasháli*, is considered wholesome ; and the kind called *Kanguka*, is considered good. There are twenty other varieties, which are distinguished by the size, and colour of the grain.

Parched rice is much used, and is considered nourishing, increasing appetite, and curing the diseases of phlegm. When the parched rice has been preserved unhusked (khaï) it is considered more wholesome, increasing appetite, removing thirst, vomiting, dysentery, and great fatness. It also removes the diseases of bile and phlegm.

Rice-water, and rice and milk, are also considered very wholesome. The particular qualities of each preparation are given at length in the Hindu Medical writings.

Wheat (*godhúma*) has been used, and has been an article of food from time immemorial in Hindostan. Several varieties are cultivated with success. It is considered nourishing ; increases the appetite, flesh, and strength, and the seven humours, improves the general health, and increases the semen. It cures the diseases of air and bile, and increases phlegm.

Barley (Yava) is considered nourishing.

Sesamum seed (Til) is now principally used as a condiment.

Leguminous Seeds, or Pulse. The list of these seeds is very long ; the following are some of them :—

Pea, mattar (Pisum Sativum,) ; Bean (vicia) ; the different varieties of Dolichos, the black seeded (D. Lablab,) the D. Labea, the D. biflorus, or horn-grain, and the D. Catjang. The Phaseolus communis (common bean), and the P. maximus ; P. nanus ; P. minima ; P. mungo, &c. The chick pea (cicer arietinum) ; the Cytisus (cajan) ; the Frigonella (Tænum Græcum) are enumerated with many other excellent varieties of pulse. They should be eaten after being well boiled, or in the form of porridge, or soup.

Animal Food.—It is probable that for many ages the use of

the flesh of animals was unknown, from the want of weapons and the strength and activity of the animals ; but when this kind of food was brought into use, it seems to have been considered as a great luxury. In these ancient times, the chief of the household usually acted the parts of the butcher and cook. The flesh of animals was then considered as agreeable to the taste, increasing the bulk of the body, and the strength, and curing the diseases of air. It is also said to be heavy to the stomach, and when digested is sweet. The writers of the more ancient shastres lived in a cool air, and were accustomed to an active life, which required the use of more animal food than is proper in Bengal. This was probably one reason of the superiority of the ancient Brahmins over their more degenerate descendents ; who are small in stature, and incapable of those mental and corporeal exertions which raise a people in the rank of nations. The indigestible nature of the flesh of some of the animals of the country, with their unclean habits, rendered them objects of disgust. Pork, even in Europe, is sometimes unwholesome, producing diarrhæa, griping and vomiting, and sometimes resembling the effects of the most violent poisons. The flesh of this and other animals is not so digestible as in more temperate climates, where their food is of a superior quality. The want of exercise and food during the greater part of the year, renders the flesh of such animals peculiarly unwholesome ; and seems to have induced the Hindu Legislators to inculcate the transmigration of souls. Such an opinion must at once have prevented the general use of animal food. It was most probably introduced into Greece by Pythagoras.

It is stated that, during the three first Yugas, cow's and buffaloe's flesh were used for food. Its prohibition is thus accounted for :—A prophet had a favourite cow killed by his scholars during his absence. On his return he was much displeased, and directed that, in future, should a Hindu use the flesh of the cow during the kali yuga he should loose caste. Another legend states that a prophet, in performing a religious ceremony which required the offering of cow's flesh, with gur, honey, and oil, used such powerful prayers that the cow rose up out of the sacrificial fire. It was, however, found that a part of the animal was wanting ; on enquiry the Brahmin's wife confessed that she had taken a part of the sacrifice to eat it. On producing it, two vegetables were found growing from it (the Lashun, garlic ; and Pyáj, onion). The flesh thus recovered was put up on the cow, and it adhered and completed the animal, which was, in consequence, directed not again to be eaten. Cow's flesh is said to cure the diseases of bile, sores in the nostrils accompanied with want of taste, and prevents relapses in fever. The flesh of calves cures the diseases of air, and increases phlegm. Besides the flesh of cows and buffalows, deers, hares, hogs, goats, and sheep were used by the ancient Hindus as food. The flesh of animals are digestible in the following order, the first being the least so ; the pig, tiger, cow and deer.

Flesh boiled with oil is heavy, increases bile, and is heating. Dried flesh removes fatigue, is of use in diminishing bile, in curing the diseases of phlegm, and sores in the body.

The flesh of domestic animals was not given to the sick as it was considered heating. On this account the flesh of wild animals was substituted, as they were supposed to be more wholesome, such as deer, of wild fowls, &c ; the fat in these cases being carefully removed. Animal fat and marrow were supposed to cure diseases of air, and increase the diseases of blood, bile, and cough. *Broths* were made of the flesh of these animals, and given to invalids ; they cured old fevers and increased strength, improved the voice and eyesight, increased the strength and semen, and cured boils. They strengthen the joints, and promote their cure when wounded. If given with rice, broths cure old fevers, strengthen the individual, while they lighten the heart, and cure the diseases of bile. The Hindus are directed, at the same time, to abstain from hard and indigestible food, such as curds, milk, oil, jagree, with various kinds of pulse and leguminous plants.

Animal Secretions.—*Milk* is heavy, cooling, and sweet, gives a shining appearance to the skin, strengthens, fattens, and increases semen ; it cures the diseases of air, bile, and phlegm. *Goat's Milk* is sweet and cooling ; it is binding, promotes the internal heat ; cures *ractapitta* (Hœmorrage) and diseases of air, bile, phlegm, and blood ; as Goats eat many medicinal plants, drink little water, and are very active. *Sheep's Milk* is sweet and heavy, and increases phlegm and bile. *Buffalo's milk* is drying and heating, but cures swelling of the abdomen, and diseases of air and phlegm. *Mare's milk* is saltish, sweet, and light. *Woman's milk* strengthens the soul, increases flesh, and the consistence of the circulating fluids : it should only be drunk fresh. *Cow's Milk* is pleasant, and very wholesome. It is cooling, sweet, promotes semen, cures diseases of air, blood, and bile, and promotes memory, strength, and longevity. Early in the morning this milk is heavy, and constipating. It is not good when the cow is near calving, or when there is no calf ; the best milk being when the calf and mother are of the same colour, particularly when of a white or of a black colour, with erect horns ; and when the cow has eaten the leaves of the sugar-cane. Milk that has been kept a day is heavy, and constipates; and fresh milk increases the secretion of phlegm from the nose. When boiled and drunk warm, it cures diseases of phlegm and air; when allowed to cool, it cures the diseases of bile. The milks of goats and asses are not so wholesome as that of the cow. They should not be drunk fresh; and salt may be added or the milk may be boiled.

2. *Curdled Milk* is formed by adding a little sour milk, or daï, to milk which has been boiled and cooled. It should be allowed to stand for a night before being used. It is cooling, increases the internal heat, and is useful in the cure of agues, diarrhæa, dyspepsia, and strangury; it increases the phlegm, and the secretion of semen.

3. *Butter-Milk* (Ghol) is made by stirring about curdled milk, until butter is obtained; or this is produced in the ordinary way. It is good for persons who have take poison, who are labouring under diarrhæa, dyspepsia, vomiting, strangury, jaundice, piles, spleen, or ague. It diminishes fat, phlegm and air. *Fresh Butter* is sweet and nourishing; it is cool, agreeable, diminishes bile and air, and promotes the secretion of semen. It cures consumption, chronic cough, asthma, ulcers, piles, and tetanus. It increases strength, and is good for children. *Ghee* is made by boiling butter for a few minutes to dissipate the watery part, when it may be kept for a long time. It is sweet, and softens parts. It is useful in madness, epilepsy, and ague. It diminishes air and bile, and improves the appetite, memory, and the beauty of the body. It also promotes longevity, and preserves the eyesight. Ghee which has been kept ten years and upwards is called old ghee, which is said to cure sudden blindness (timira), morbid discharges from the nose, eyes and mouth; difficulty in breathing, fainting, leprosy, and epilepsy; diseases of the vagina, pains in the ears, eyes, and head; old fevers, carbuncle, and diseases of air, bile, and phlegm.

Flesh of Birds. Their general properties are, that they cure the diseases of air, bile, and phlegm; improve the colour of the skin; are slightly heavy, and sweet; increase the semen, memory, and appetite; and give consistency to the alvine evacuations. The principal of these are partridge; jungle-cock; common cock; peacock; pigeons; water-wagtail; taylor-bird; duck; paddy-bird &c.

The flesh of animals and birds is not good the second day, when they are tainted. Such as have been drowned, or killed with an arrow, as this may have been poisoned, are digested with difficulty, and produce diseases, particularly of air, bile, and phlegm.

The upper (atlanted) part of the male, and the lower (sacral) part of the female are the heaviest. The flesh of female quadrupeds, and male birds, is the lightest. The flesh of large animals which work much, and eat little, is heavy, in the following order : head, shoulders, spleen, skin, liver, fore-feet, and hind-feet, tail, testicles, abdomen, and urinary organs. The humours are heavy in the following order :—blood, flesh, fat, bones, marrow, and semen.

Such Birds as live on flowers are thin, and increase the bulk of the body ; such as live on fish, increase bile ; and such as eat rice, remove the diseases of air.

Flesh should be eaten the same day it has been killed ; rice shonld be prepared ıapidly, and a man should live with a *young* wife, use milk, ghee, and boiled water which has been allowed to cool, as they promote health and strength. The opposite articles have a contrary effect on the health ; as putrid flesh, exposure to the morning sun, new curdled milk, sleeping in the morning, &c.

Fish produces a shining appearance of the body, is slightly heating, and sweet ; and increases the air, urine, and alvine secretions. When white, fish increases the strength, phlegm, and bile ; it is of advantage to health when the person labours under diseases of air, when used by wrestlers, by those accustomed to violent exercise, and those who are tired. Black and small fish are light, and constipate. They increase the appetite and strength, cure air, and are of use during convalescence. White fish increases air, bile, and phlegm, gives a shining appearance to the skin, is digested with difficulty, and produces a laxative effect upon the bowels. Fish roes are pleasant and increase air, phlegm, and semen, diminish the appetite, and produce a bitter state of the stomach.

Fish when boiled is heavy, and cures the diseases of air ; it increases the strength, removes fatigue, enlarges the muscles, and improves vision. Dried fish constipates, and weakens the body, and is digested with difficulty ; when roasted, fish is heavy, increases the semen, flesh, and strength. In such cases fish should be prepared with oil. These properties of fish are increased and modified, by mixing them with other articles of food, as with the leaves of certain trees, pumpkins &c. Ruï is the best of all fish, and others in the following order ; bekti, chital, shol, garaï jheṇyá ilísh, baül, gágará, gaṛká, balsguní, chenga, kaï, páṭí, teṭí, chuná, chándá calsá, ḍáinkoná, chingri. Turtles were used, and were stated to cure diseases of air, to increase strength, semen, and memory, and to improve the eyesight.

The following are supposed to be the proportionate nutritive qualities of certain articles of food :—

Rice is eight times lighter than cakes.
Milk „ „ flesh. „
Flesh „ „ oil. „

Sugar, Saccharum Officinarum, has been known in the east from the earliest antiquity; it is the sweet cane of Scripture "brought from a far country," and offered up by the Jews among other sacrifices to Jehovah (Isa. xlv. are 24. ; Jer. vi. 20.) The fresh juice is cooling, increases semen and urine, is pleasant, increases, strength, and cures the derangement of air ; it improves the dejections, and diseases of blood and bile, is sweet, gives a shining appearance to the skin, increases happiness and flesh, and is heating.

After the juice has been exposed to the air for some time, it is heavy to the stomach, is heating, cures derangements of the air and phlegm, and increases the shining appearance of the skin. *Gur* or the inspissated juice, is sweet and pleasant to the taste, and gives strength, and a shining appearance to the skin. These qualities are improved by keeping, when it removes derangements of the air and bile, and purifies the blood. It is heavy to the stomach, increases semen, purifies the urine, increases the strength and flesh, and produces intestinal worms. Sugar is of use in diseases of the blood and bile, in fainting, vomiting, and thirst.

Oils—There are numerous plants which furnish a large supply of oil from their seed, which is extensively employed by the Hindus for the purpose of unction, for their subsistence, and as an offering to their Gods. Besides the oils extracted from the different palms, and the madhurá, (Anise) it is obtained from the almond (Pistacha vera, or Pistachio nut) ; sesamum indicum ; sinapis alba et nigra, or mustard oil ; S. Orientale, the til oil ; Ricinus or Palma Christi, the Rám Tila of the Hindus, and the Huts-ellí of the Mussulmans, &c. i. e. castor-oil ; the tillee, or linseed oil ; curumbo oil ; and Coringa oil. Other oils are also used in medicine, but they possess the same qualities as the seeds from which they are extracted. On this account they are used for the same diseases. Vegetable oils are bitter and sweet, and are good for the skin, and alleviate all diseases. Oil is heating, when taken internally ; it increases the diseases produced by bile, and constipates the bowels, and lessens urine.

Liquids.—These may be considered under the heads of water, and medicinal drinks.

Water—The Hindus were very careful about their drinking water, and ascribed the appearance of many diseases to bad water. Pure water has no taste and is considered as cooling, relaxing the body, and improving the senses, and the general health. They considered the water of wells, or natural springs in the sandy beds of rivers, as the most wholesome, as they promote digestion and strength ; the river and fountain water at the bottom of high hills, was considered less wholesome ; and the most unhealthy was considered to be the water from brooks, and the stagnant water of tanks, and reservoirs : this water was supposed to produce indigestion, obstructions, and lethargy, with a predisposition to fever.

Rain Water, when preserved in a clean vessel, was supposed to cure the diseases of air, bile, and phlegm, and improve the health. It keeps the mouth clean, and improves the state of the tongue, teeth, and memory. It was considered to be heavier during the rains than in the cold, and hot weather. Hail-water was considered peculiarly wholesome.

Water was supposed to be improved by boiling, and its effects were varied according to the quantity dissipated by evaporation. Water which has been boiled and drunk cold cures air, bile, and phlegm, also cough, fever, and constipation. It removes great fatness, and increases the internal fire.

Water mixed with the other elements produces six tastes, or sweet, sour, salt, pungent, bitter, and astringent. When the food contains a large proportion of water and earth, they produce a sweet state of the stomach. The sweet, sour, and salt articles, diminish air ; the sweet, bitter, and astringent, diminish bile ; and the pungent, bitter, and astringent, diminish phlegm.

Medicinal Drinks.—The usual *drink* for the sick, is water in which a little of the infusion of cinnamon and cassia has been mixed. By others the drink is varied with the nature of the disease. When *air* is deranged, water in which the infusion of such medicines as cure this class of diseases, as long or black pepper, sugar, &c. is to be added. When *bile* is deranged, pure water is either given, or its cooling qualities are increased by the addition of the infusion of ushira, or kaskas ; gandhatrina, a fragrant grass ; Sugar-cane, Ikhyu ; kusha, a kind of sacred grass &c. When *phlegm* is deranged, the infusion of cinnamon, black or long pepper, cloves &c. is to be added.

. In fever, produced by derangement of air, bile, and phlegm, the fresh juice of the kau, a kind of grass, is recommended instead of water.

In hemoptysis (Rakta Pitta), the fresh juice of the Káshanda (pumpkin) and pomegranate are the best additions to the drinks. In cases of swelling, or *Dropsy*, an infusion of dry raddish (múlaka), ginger, soot, &c., are to be used. In *Leprosy* the infusion of catechu (khadirá) is to be used, with the infusion of black pepper, and sugar candy.

Condiments. In weak digestion, water mixed with camphor, or infused in native mint (Padiná) is to be used. Beetlenut, camphor, cloves, long pepper, pepper, dry ginger, and other spices are mixed with slacked lime, surrounded with the leaves of pán, and chewed as a condiment. It cleans the throat and voice, promotes digestion, keeps the breath sweet, improves the senses, and gives an agreeable appearance to the person. It increases semen, and should be used after vomiting, bathing, and sleeping. The Hindus also use as condiments, nutmeg, cloves, cardamum seeds, cinnamon, turmerick, mustard, sandal-wood, debdáru wood, ginger, black, and long pepper, capsicum, coriander seed, aniseed, assafœtida &c.

Wines. Within the first year after the debarkation of Noah from the Ark, he made wine from the grapes of Mount Ararat (Gen. ix). The vine also thrives well in the northern parts of Hindustan, but not in Bengal. It is only in the northern parts of Hindustan that the grape is sometimes converted into wine, from the fermentation being too quick, and from the heat and moisture of the lower provinces. The grape is considered cooling and aperient, by the native practitioners. All wines are moderately strong, and are divided into sweet, and sour. They all increase bile, and diminish phlegm, and air. They are also tonic, stimulating, increasing the acuteness of the senses and appetite, and promoting digestion and health, when properly used. There were different kinds of wines used by the ancient Hindus, which received different names according to the fruits, flowers, and other substances from which they were derived. The wine which was made from the grape was called *Siddha ;* from raisins (kismis)*márdhwíka ;* from the flowers of the Bassia latifolia, mádhwaka ; from jagery or gur, *goura* or *surá.*

In the *Veda* shástras the use of wines and spirits are forbidden ; but in the Tantra they are allowed, and the worshippers of Shiva indulge in their use.

When digestion has been completed, the state of the stomach will depend on the qualities of the food or medicine which has been taken. When bitter and astringent articles of food or medicine have been eaten, they produce a bitter state of the stomach ; sour food produces a sweetness after digestion ; and sweet and salt food produce sweet eructations from the stomach.

During the rains, light and stomachic food with bitters should be preferred, while liquids and oils are not to be used too freely ; the drinking water should be boiled, and drunk with a little honey. In cloudy days exercise is not to be taken in the open air ; the bedroom should be warmed with fires, and all persons should sleep upon a chárpáy, during the night. In Autumn (sharat) bitter and sweet articles of food are to be preferred, and light and clean water is to be used freely for drink. Exercise is to be taken in the evening ; and deranged bile is to be cured by bleeding or purging. Sherbets and spirituous liquids, especially such as relieve the increased secretion of bile, are be used.

In winter (Shishira) saline, bitter, pungent, and warm articles, prepared with ghee and oil, are to be taken for food. Meat is to be used, and the drink warmed, and accompanied with spirituous liquors. The warm bath and frictions with oil are to be used, and exercise taken in the morning.

In spring (Vasanta) sour, sweet, oily, and saline articles are to be used. The drinking water is to be boiled, and spirituous liquors are to be mixed with it, to diminish the increased phlegm. The warm bath, and foot exercise are also to be used.

During the hot season (Gríshma), sour, pungent, and strong warm substances are to be avoided, and rice, barley, and curries of light vegetables are to be used. Food possessing warm qualities is to be avoided, and the breakfast should consist of cooling fruits and sherbets. The Cold bath is to be used, and thin light dresses are to be worn. The surface of the body is to be smeared with cooling aromatic applications, cool water should be used for drink, and sleep is to be allowed during the day.

The highest classes of Brahmins, as officiating priests, attend rigidly to the performance of religious ceremonies, and generally bathe in the morning at sunrise. After performing the ceremonies of their guardian Deity, they take for breakfast small sweet cakes, or a handful of moistened rice, at 10 or 11 o'clock ; as they must always purify their body by washing, before eating. They dine on boiled rice, peas, and vegetables, and some of them have fish curry at 1 or 2 P.M. *

From eight to eleven o'clock, supper is prepared, and consists of the same food as at dinner. The middling and higher classes mix a small quantity of milk and ghee with what they eat at dinner and supper.

In some houses instead of boiled rice at night, unlevened flour-cakes are eaten, with a little ghee spread over it. They are often eaten with vegetable curries or boiled peas, or with the flesh of kids,

* The months of October, April, and January are considered holy, when not only the priests, but many others, who are desirous of an easy entrance into heaven, repair to the river side to bathe, immediately before sun rise, and to perform the morning ceremonies.

pigeons, and other birds. These are often eaten with butter by the rich. Shop-keepers eat late, and sleep for an hour or two after mid-day. Their drinks consist of plain water and sugar-candy, or sugar and water, to which lime-juice is sometimes added.

The principal precepts with regard to personal duties are—use boiled water for drink, sleep all night in a cool, dry and elevated situation, and take exercise ; wash the eyes with cold water, which will keep them cool, clean, and diminish heat ; and anoint and keep the body clean by frequent bathing. Rest after labour will increase strength, prevent fatigue, and promote the freshness of the body.

The diet of the sick is to be regulated by the nature of the sickness, the constitution and strength of the individual, and the situation, period, state of the appetite, &c.

k. *Sleep.* "Early to bed and early to rise," is one of the old and most approved maxims of the Hindus ; which indeed is peculiarly applicable in a hot enervating climate like Bengal, where the night air is so pernicious, and the mornings so cool and healthy. The Hindus sleep on a pretty large mat, with a small sized pillow for the head, generally upon the plain ground, or upon a charpay. The mat is to be soft and clean, and not circular; the head is to be turned towards the east, or rising of the sun ; or south, towards *Yama*, where the person goes after death, and where is the residence of the gods. Care is taken not to turn the feet towards their father or mother, or superiors. To have refreshing sleep, the mind of the person should be tranquil and contented. This will also be promoted by music, and rocking ; by anointing the body with oil ; by the use of the bath ; by eating new rice, milk, ghee, and the like ; by sherbuts and spirits, and such articles as improve the health ; by sleeping upon a large mat, in a comfortable house, and at the accustomed time. Sleep keeps the humours in a healthy state, improves the colour of the skin, the health, appetite, and strength.

Watching increases air, dries the body, and diminishes cough and fat, and retards the action of poison. Sleeping during the day increases cough and fat, and should be avoided in those in whom phlegm is increased, and during the spring, in the rains and winter months, &c. It may be indulged in during the hot season, when the habit has been acquired and when the air is deranged.

The Hindus generally rise at 6 o'clock in the morning ; but before getting up in the morning and going to sleep, they repeat certain prayers. The person next proceeds to perform the duties of nature, and then washes his face, mouth, &c. They brush their teeth with a small fresh branch of a bitter tree or plant ; afterwards they change their night-clothes, and go to their business. The smoking of tobacco is used morning and night, at bed time, and after dinner and tiffin. It should be smoked slowly by means of a long tube.

CHAPTER II.

Materia Medica.

The following remarks on Materia Medica will be arranged under the heads: 1st, general remarks on simple Medicines; and 2nd, regarding the most common preparations and uses of Medicine.

SECTION I.

General remarks on Simple Medicines.

The Hindu medical writers have recorded many observations on the properties and choice of medicines, the situations in which they are to be found, the time at which they possess their peculiar properties in the highest degree, and the manner of preparing and preserving them. These medicines are very numerous; but from the few and indistinct remarks which are recorded of some of them, they cannot always be identified.

The following remarks will be arranged under the heads of the vegetable, animal, and mineral kingdoms. A list of the principal medicines will be given in the next Chapter, arranged according to their effects.

A. *Simple Medicines from the Vegetable Kingdom.* The belief of there being a remedy for each disease, led the Brahmins to make a very careful examination of the vegetable kingdom; and a large number of Medicines were discovered, some of which were very powerful. The success which followed the employment of these remedies in the cure of diseases was invariably supposed to rest on individual sanctity, and the divine pleasure which imparts it. Hence the great difficulty of obtaining information; as it is believed that if such secrets are revealed to others, the medicine loses its effects, not only in the hands of the person to whom its qualities have been revealed, but also of the person who had known them before. It is from such selfish motives that the properties of many valuable medicines have been lost. There are nine such secrets which should not be revealed to any one :—these are the age of a person ; his wealth ; family occurrences ; his bad actions ; or those which reflect shame, or dishonour upon him ; his intercourse with his wife ; his prayers to his tutelar gods ; his charities ; and the virtues of nostrums the ingredients of which are known to him.

The simple vegetable medicines are procured from the bark, roots, leaves, flowers, fruit, seeds, juices, gums, and wood of plants. These medicines are arranged in the following order :—

1. *Bánspáti*, or those trees which contain fruits without flowers.
2. *Vrikshya*, those which contain both flowers and fruit.
3. *Virut*, creepers with flowers in clusters.
4. *Oshadhi*, those plants which die after the ripening of their fruit, as rice, &c.

The effect of medicines from the vegetable kingdom will vary with the period at which the medicine is gathered, according as the air is agitated with wind or not, as it is in the sun or shade, as taken during the day or night, during the cold or hot weather, during dry or rainy weather, and also according to the interval between the time when the medicine is gathered and that when it is used.

Medicines from this kingdom should not be procured either from the jungly, or from a country covered with water ; neither from a dry and sandy ground, nor from one that is unequal or has many holes, stones, or broken vessels upon it. Situations in any way destroyed by insects, or in which white ants have their nests, as these are supposed to remove the strength of the earth, or where water drops from a choppered roof, where bodies have been burnt or buried, where persons have died, or sacred situations are not proper places for raising medicinal plants. Soils in which there is much salt are also unfavourable for the growth of medicines ; and plants that grow at unseasonable times, or when very old, and those which water forms, or insects have injured are to be thrown away.

The soil most favourable for the growth of medicines is of a soft black, yellow, or red colour ; is equal, or heavy ; is situated near water, and where trees grow luxuriantly, and the grain is moist and glistening: in such situations the soil has its proper quality of taste. Those of water are found where the place is sweet, and the plants glistening. The qualities of fire are greatest, when the soil has several colours, and where the earth is light, the trees small and growing at a distance from each other, and where the young leaves of grass, as they burst through the earth, are of a light yellow colour. The qualities of air predominate in dry places, of a grayish colour, like the ashes of wood. In such situations the earth is light, the trees are few, small, dry, and have holes in them, with little juice. The qualities of ether (ákásh) are in excess in such situations as are of a greenish colour, are soft in the centre and equal, with many holes. The water in such situations is without taste, and the mountains and trees are large.

The rays of the sun and moon produce the colour, &c., of plants. Thus the yellow colour of trees is produced by the sun, and such medicine should be gathered during the hot period of the day. Emetics are to be gathered at such times, from soils possessing the qualities of ether and air. The moon produces the white and cold plants, which should be gathered during the cold season, when the qualities of these plants will be most energetic. They will then be sweet, moist like oil, and cold like water. Purgatives are thus to be gathered in a soil possessing the qualities of taste and smell.

The physician should observe the lucky days and hours, and the most favourable period of the moon's age, in order to ensure the cure of the disease. The Stars which are predominant on particular days are to be observed, particularly those which occur on odd days. Medicines which are to be exhibited internally, are to be taken for the first time on Mondays, Thursdays and Fridays. They are also to observe the most favourable period of the moon's age, and that fortunate stars are in the ascendant *.

Before a medicinal plant is gathered in the morning, a prayer should be said by the person with his face to the north. The following is such a prayer, which is supposed to remove any devils which may be hiding near.

'O God! if any devil be lurking here—begone! whether it be Vetal, Pisháchá, Rakshas, or Shri sarpa (the devil of serpents).' As the shrub is being gathered, the person is to say: 'O, shrub! as Brumhá, Indra, and Vishnu plucked you, for the same reason I now remove you.'

B. *Simple Medicines derived from the Animal Kingdom.*

These are skin, hair, nails, blood, flesh, bones, fat, marrow, bile, milk and dejections. These medicines should be obtained from healthy animals, which are neither very old nor very young. The urine and other dejections should be obtained from the female.

a. Skin, nails, and hair, are used for fumigations in intermittent fevers, &c.

* There are twenty-seven Stars, one of which presides over each day of the week.

b. Blood. When there has been a great loss of blood, it is sometimes exhibited internally.

c. Flesh is mixed with oily and other medicines, and vegetables; and is given in weakness, phthisis, and in nervous diseases.

d. Bones. The ashes of bones, mixed with other medicines, are exhibited in nervous diseases and those of children. They are also used to fumigate.

e. Fat is used principally externally, as in the form of ointment, &c.

f. Marrow is used externally in the form of ointment, and internally in cases of weakness.

g. Bile is considered a stimulant, and is used in fever; also as an external application, as to the eye.

h. Milk is one of the principal articles of food. It is used in combination with decoctions, and given internally in diseases of children, and for nervous diseases. It is often used with oil as an external application.

i. Urine is pungent and slightly bitterish and saltish to the taste. It is slightly laxative and cures diseases of phlegm, air, worms; and diseases produced from poison: it is also of use in leprosy, and in dropsical swellings, jaundice, and dyspepsia. Cow's urine is generally preferred.

k. Dung. The moisture contained in cow's dung is used in inflammation, and in discolouring of the skin. It is also given internally, and prepared with other medicines.

C. *Simple Medicines derived from the Mineral Kingdom.*

These consist of metals, (*Dhátu*) and inferior minerals (*Upadhâtu*).

Of *Salts* (*Lavana*), *Saindhava* is the best form of Rock-salt.

There are four kinds of *kshára*, 1 Java, (salt-petre) 2 Sarjiká (natron) 3 Páksham (Bitloben) 4 Tankana (Borax).

I. To Yavakshár, add Sajímáti (natron or alkali) and Sohága (borax), &c.

Sámudram, or common sea-salt, is less powerful than the black salt (bitlaban). It is stomachic, and cures air and indigestion.

Sarvakshár or Sachal, (an impure soda) is used in spleen (gulmo), cholic (shúl), and dyspepsia. There are other salts, such as Vámaka, Udhada, &c.; but their qualities are the same as above.

Salt increases appetite; produces diseases of the blood and bile. It cures gulma, piles, dysentery and stone.

Metals (*dhátu*).—Iron and tin were the only metals used internally by the Hindu Physicians; but in the more modern works the other metals are described, and were probably introduced into Hindustan two or three hundred years ago, probably for mercenary purposes ; as the Physician, before the recovery of his patient, only eceived his recompence for the medicine he prescribed.

The metals now used in medicine are as follows :—Quicksilver, gold, silver, copper, iron, lead and zinc.

1. Mercury (Sútam, Rasa or Párada.)

Quicksilver is found in Thibet ; in the form of cinnabar, and in its native state in Nepál.

Shiv declared to Durgá that, if properly prepared, quicksilver will cure all diseases, even should they be of a fatal nature. Quicksilver is used either in its metallic state, or reduced so as to lose its peculiar properties. In both forms it is useful for the cure of diseases.

Quicksilver is often in an impure state, as when it is mixed with blacklead, stone, poison, tin, or other impurities of the same kind ; another bad quality is when it resembles fire, and when it disperses in different directions. Good quicksilver is of a slight blueish colour, like water internally and externally, and bright like the sun at mid-day. It is also good when it has a brownish, or whitish colour ; but if it has a mottled appearance it is not good.

To purify quicksilver from lead ; mix it with rice-water and expose the mixture to fire, which will remove its bad ingredients. To purify quicksilver from *tin ;* mix it with the powder of Vishál (Cucumis colocynthis) and *Ankoṭha* (Alangium hexapetalum), and then expose the mixture to fire. To remove the other impurities, add the juice of Cassia fistula. To purify quicksilver when it separates into globules ; mix it with the juice of datura and lime, and then expose it to heat. To destroy the poisonous qualities of quicksilver mix the three kinds of Myrobalan, and then expose it to heat. It is thus fit for use.

Quicksilver is the semen of Shiv ; and being difficult to prepare, the practitioner is first to pray to Vishnu, &c., on a lucky day ; and agreeable presents are to be made to virgins, and families of Brahmins before the process is commenced. The following prayer is then to be offered up to Shiv.

'O Ugra (wrathful one!) I salute you ! and O Ugra, I pay my reverence ! Goraksha, Ishwara, Sarva, Shiva and Bhadra ; I salute your different forms ; and ask your gracious assistance in rendering this medicine successful.' The quantity of mercury to be prepared should not be less than one pala ; and some say when only a small quantity can be obtained, prepare two tolás.

To purify mercury so as to render it fit for being used as medi-

See Pages 118 & 119

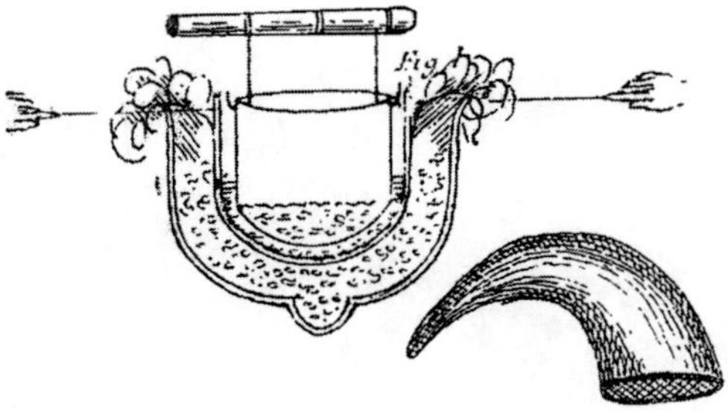

Fig 1

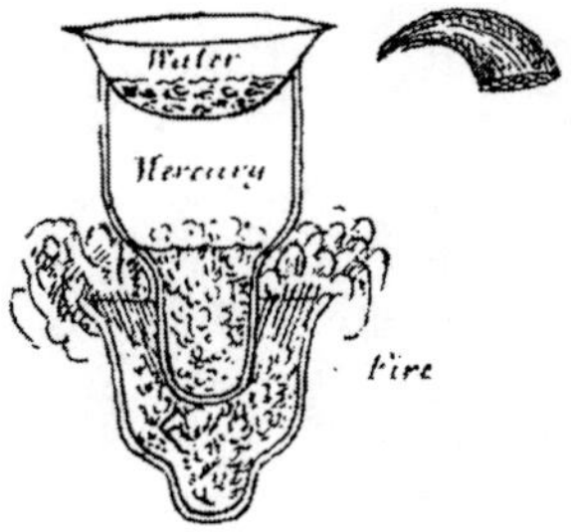

Fig 5

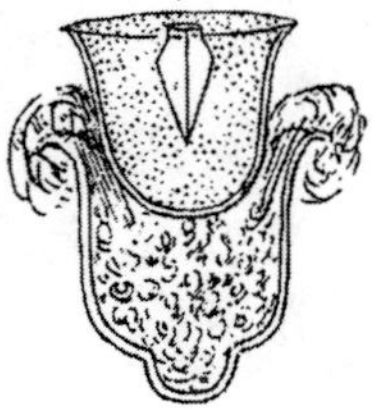

Fig 2

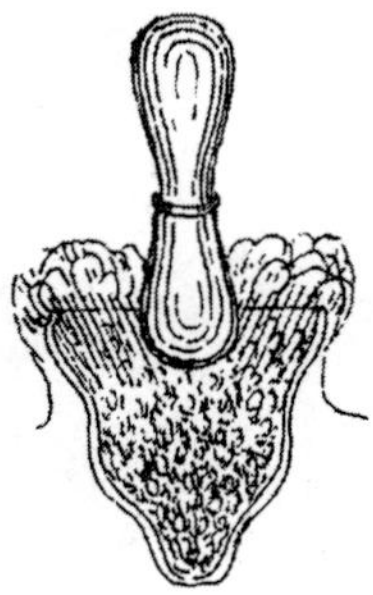

Fig 6

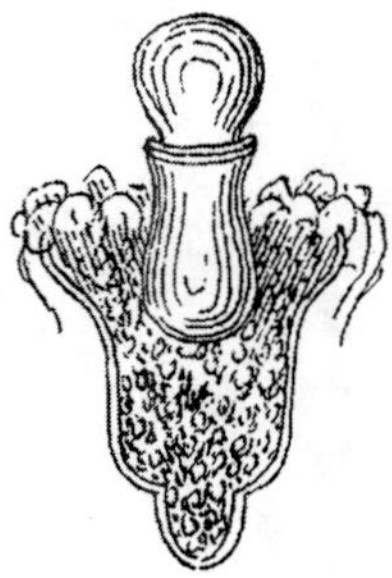

Fig 3

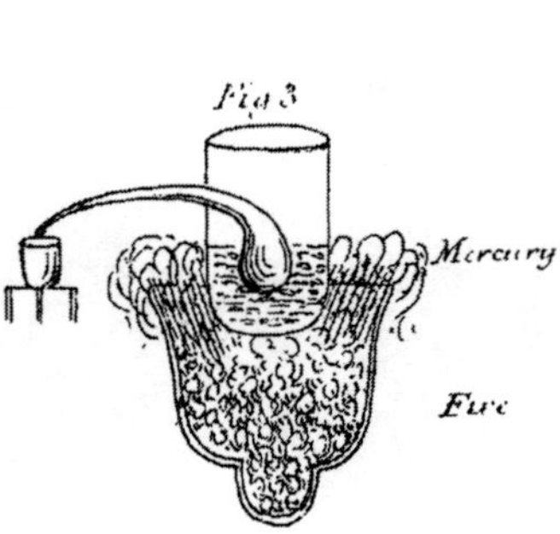

Fig 6

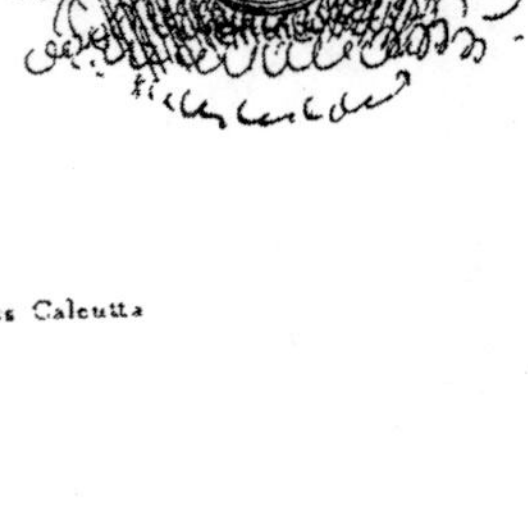

T. Black Asiat. Lith: Press Calcutta

cine, take of turmerick, brick-dust, suet, the juice of lemons (or congee, if limes are not procurable), and the wool of sheep, of each one chhaṭák, and mix it with one ser of quicksilver. The mixture is to be well rubbed in a mortar, for one day, and wash the product carefully with water.

Another means of purifying mercury is to place it in a bag which is then to be immersed in congee, and exposed to heat. This is called a ḍolájantra. By this means the quicksilver is completely purified. See fig 1.

Another way of purifying mercury is by sublimation. The apparatus is called *Urddhwapútanajantra* ; and is used in this manner. Take vermilion and the juice of lemons ; dry it in the sun and then sublime. It is then to be rubbed with more of the lime, or the juice of the Páribhadra (the coral tree or Erythrina fulgens) and nimba (Melia azadirachta). They are to be mixed for three hours and again sublimed. See fig 2.

Quicksilver is also purified by evaporation, by means of Vakajantra or retort of this form. See fig 3.

Before quicksilver is mixed with sulphur the following prayer is to be offered up. 'O Shiv, may you so order that this preparation may be so made as to enable it to cure all diseases.' When such prayer is offered up with faith, by a holy Brahmin, it will be granted. Then mix six parts of sulphur with one of quicksilver, put it in a crucible of this form (fig 4 *) with its opening properly luted, place this in a sand bath, which is formed in this manner—(see fig. 5) and apply heat slowly. When the mixture is completed, take the crucible off the fire and break it ; the contents may then be used for medicine.

There are four forms in which quicksilver is used in medicine ; the black, white, yellow and red forms.

The *black* kind is formed by dissolving equal parts of sulphur and quicksilver over the fire, when the residue will assume this colour which is the most common form in which mercury is used in practice.

To form *white* mercury (hydrargyrum precipitatum album). Take of Borax, honey, lac, and the wool of sheep ; mix, and add the juice of the Bhringaraja (Verbesena scandens) ; then add sulphur, and mix for one day ; after which expose it to the heat of a sand bath until it is reduced to ashes. It will be white like pure camphor, and will resemble the corrosive sublimate. Another kind of white mercury is made by mixing turmerick, brick-dust, suet, ámalakí, (phyllanthus

* The crucible is made by mixing two parts of the ashes of paddy, one of the earth of white ants, one part of iron cinders, one part of white stone (safied miṭi) and one part of hair ; mix with goat's milk, and beat half a day. The crucible is then to be formed, and dried in the sun or fire, for use.

emblica or emblic myrobalan) boirá, (beleric myrobalan) and harítakí, chebulic myrobalan) chítá (treacle), congee, and the juice of the ghritakumárí, or Indian aloes, mix for one day, and then add half the weight of prepared sulphur.

Another form is made with rock salt, blue vitriol, sulphur, chalk, alum and quicksilver in equal quantities ; mix the whole with the juice of the lemon. This is to be put in an earthen vessel over which another is to be placed and the juncture luted (Seefig 5). The mixture is then to be exposed for a day to the action of fire, when the mercury will be white and prepared for use.

The use of the white form of mercury is very important. It cures rheumatism, and the eighty diseases of air, as well as the diseases of bile and phlegm. Should it affect the gums, a gargle of curdled milk should be employed. This preparation of mercury will also be found useful in shúl, (colic,) fistula in ano, in diseases of the eye, in diseases of the arms, and in general debility ; as it increases strength, appetite, and the general colour of the body.

The *yellow* preparations of mercury are made in the following manner. Mix equal parts of sulphur, quicksilver, and the sundu plant and myrobalan. Dry the mixture and put it in a sand bath, and apply heat for twenty-four hours. When properly prepared it has a yellow colour. This preparation increases the appetite, and cures dropsy and dyspepsia.

Red Factitious cinnabar or red sulphuret of mercury, when in powder vermilion (Hingula) is prepared as follows : mix one pala of sulphur, and one pound of black lead with the juice of the ghritakumárí ; place it in a clean vessel, put a lute or coating of mud and cloth, or a mixture of lime and chalk over it. It is to be exposed in a sand bath for three days, when it will be found of a red colour.

It cures all diseases, even of the fatal kind. It removes weakness, improves the appetite and memory, diminishes fat, and cures leprosy. It requires to be given a proper menstruum and mixed with other medicines. The dose is then one ganja.

Another form of mercury is prepared by mixing the black preparation in an iron spoon. Add a little ghee, and then expose it to heat. When melted throw it into a leaf of the plantain. It is then called Rasaparpatí or *cake* mercury and is very useful in dropsy, chronic dysentery, and as an alterative.

2nd. *Gold.* This, as well as the other metals, is first to be reduced by beating to small thin plates. These are to be exposed to a red heat, and in this state cooled separately in oil, curdled milk, cow's urine, congee, and a decoction of kulattha (a kind of pea). This process is to be repeated seven times in each liquid. The metal is then considered as prepared for use. Some only quench the hot metal in the above liquids three times. It is also recommended that metals should be cooled twelve times in a mixture of the juice of the leaves of the tuk and ákanda trees, with brimstone. In other cases three parts of the metal are mixed with one of quicksilver and exposed to heat. Other mixtures are recommended by different authors for oxidizing the metal.

The preparations of gold are considered as most valuable medicines, curing nearly all diseases, even those in which other medicines have been used without any good result. The general effect of these preparations is to increase memory, and restore the vigour of manhood.

The usual manner of preparing gold for use is to mix 16 times the quantity of the gold plates to one of lead, and add lemon juice and *ghritacumárí*, or Indian aloes. They are to be rubbed together, exposed to heat, and made into boluses of the usual size. Or take of the mass of gold plates, mix with quicksilver and sulphur, add a little water, or the juice of *ghritacumárí*, make it into a large mass ; put it in an earthern pot with a mouth well secured, surround the vessel with a mixture of clay and cow-dung, and expose it to the sun to dry. It is thus to be exposed to the fire twelve different times, until it is reduced to powder. Some practitioners mix lead, sulphur, and quicksilver together with the gold, and the mixture is then prepared as above. The oxide of gold thus prepared is often mixed with other metals ; and is considered a valuable medicine in chronic diseases, in intermittent fevers, in gonorrhœa, and in diseases of the spleen. It is considered an excellent tonic, improving vision, reducing the bulk of the body, and is good for consumption, and pregnant women and children. It is useful in diseases of air, bile, and phlegm.

Silver. This metal is prepared by mixing two parts of it reduced to small thin plates, with one of brimstone. These are to be well mixed, lemon juice is to be added, and the whole surrounded by a mixture of cow-dung and clay, and exposed to a high heat in a furnace, in the same manner as that in which gold was stated to be prepared. This preparation is sour, cooling, and astringent ; and it cures deranged air, promotes appetite, strength, digestion, and the colour of the skin. It also lengthens life, and is of much use in all chronic diseases, as it purifies the body and the dejections.

Copper. This metal is found in the north of India. It is purified by boiling for three days with a strong heat, the small thin plates in cow's urine. The metal is then to be mixed with two parts of brimstone and one part of rock-salt, to which the juice of the lemon has been added. The mixture is then to be surrounded with a coating of cow's dung and clay, and exposed to the fire of a furnace, when it is ready for use. To prevent its producing vomiting and purging, put the mixture into a bulbous root called *Súrana*, which has been hollowed out ; it is then to be covered with a mixture of dung and clay, and exposed to heat.

The sulphuret of copper (Tútaka) is prepared by mixing two parts of the thin plates with one of sulphur. It is then to be exposed to heat for two hours. The medicine will neither produce giddiness, vomiting nor purging.

These preparations of copper are found useful in fevers, particularly the intermittent kinds, diarrhœa, spleen and diseases of the liver and blood. It is also, useful in leprosy, colic, piles and indigestion*.

Lead (sísaka). This metal is found in many parts of Hindustan and is prepared for use by mixing it with the juice of the *ákanda*, tree. It should remain immersed for three days ; then wash the metal in water, and mix it with the juice of the leaves of the vásaka tree (Justicia ganderussa) and sulphur. Put it into an earthern vessel, and expose it to a high heat. It is then ready for use, and is recommended in gonorrhœa, chronic diarrhœa, in leprosy and in ulcers.

Tin (Trapu and Ránga). One part is to be mixed with the same quantity of sulphur, mix it with the milk of the arka tree (calotropis gigantea), and the dry bark of the Banian tree. Rub them together in a hot mortar for many days.

It is then prepared for use, and is bitter and sour to the taste. It diminishes fat, the diseases of phlegm, is an Anthelmintic, and cures gonorrhœa and jaundice. It is to be avoided in diseases of air.

Zinc, and other metals are prepared in the same way as copper, and their effects upon the system are the same.

Sulphuret of Antimony (Rasánjana Sanvira) is generally obtained from Nepaul or Siam. It is prepared for use by placing it in lime water, and exposing it for several hours to the sun. It is exhibited in diseases of the eye, in the form of a collyrium, mixed with the juice of the ripe pomegranate. It is applied to the edges of the eyelid to increase the brilliancy of the organ ; and it is also used as an emetic in the first stage of the fever, and in combination with other medicines.

Iron (Lauha). is found in many parts of Hindustan in the

* This preparation is also used for strengthening the teeth, and for cleaning and improving their colour,

form of oxide, in ochres, bog ores, and other friable earthy substances. The two following ores are almost commonly used by the Hindus as medicines :—

Sulphate of Iron (káshísha). This is prepared for use by macerating it in a decoction of the leaves of hemp. It is bitter to the taste ; and is useful in epilepsy, in white leprosy, in diseases of the eyes, in diabetes, in amenorrhœa, and in phthisis. It is considered tonic, amenagogue, anthelmintic. An *Iron Oxide* called *Sarnamanku?* is prepared by mixing two parts with one part of rock-salt, and with lemon juice in an iron vessel. Apply heat, and rub it with an iron pestle, until it becomes of a fine red colour. It is then slightly bitter and sweet ; and is of use in gonorrhœa, in diseases of the urine, in worms, and in various diseases of the bile and phlegm. It is usually exhibited in combination with other medicines for improving the strength.

There are also other varieties of iron. The Kánta (steel ?) is the best, and is prepared as follows :—The iron is to be made into three small plates—exposed to heat, and quenched in the juice of the plantain tree. Repeat this seven times : make a furnace by digging a hole one cubit in depth, and the same in circumference —fill it with live charcoal, mix the iron with half its weight of (Swind Maaker) the common Pyritic iron ore, mix them in the juice of the three Mirabuli—add one fourth of red arsenic (Manahshilá), rub them together with sour congee—expose them to heat in the usual manner with a blast furnace, which is to be well covered ; remove the iron when in a red hot state, and quench it in a mixture of the three Mirabuli—beat on an anvil to separate the oxidized part. Again expose the iron as before, so as to reduce all the iron to this oxide, which is used by rubbing it with cow's urine ; make it into small boluses, put them in an earthen vessel, and expose the mixture to the heat of a fire of cow's dung. Repeat this a number of times—from 10 to 1000.—It should never be used unless prepared at least with an exposure to heat more than ten times, and it will be so much better if repeated a great many more times. In this state it does not sink in water, and there is no alterative so good as this. It is an excellent tonic, improves digestion and removes all diseases.

When iron has been exposed for many years in the earth it is changed to a red colour, easily powdered. It is called mondulo, and is used for the same diseases as the above preparations of iron.

Arsenic.—The *yellow* sulphuret of *Arsenic* or *yellow Orpiment* (Haritála) is brought to India from China and the Burman dominions ; is purified by boiling it in the water of a kind of gonaro Kushundo ; in lime water ; in oil ; and in sour congee, for two or three hours in each. This medicine is also purified by mixing it with four parts of nitre, and then subliming it. This is done by placing it in an earthen pot with another over it, and applying heat for a day and a night.

This is a very celebrated medicine in the black leprosy, and in fever. It also improves the colour of the body.

Red Arsenic, or *red Orpiment* (Manahshila) is brought from Japan and is prepared by macerating it in the juice of the Boke tree, or in the juice of the fresh ginger. It is tonic, and is used for removing diseases of phlegm, for Asthma, &c.

White oxide of *Arsenic* (Daarmuch) is prepared by being macerated in the juice of the lemon, and then boiled in the juice of the plantain tree. It is used in doses of the fourteenth part of a grain, in conjunction with aromatics, to check obstinate intermittent fevers, in glandular and leprous affections, in the same way as the yellow Arsenic.

Minerals (*Upadhátu*).

The minerals which are employed in medicine are mica, diamond, precious stones, brimstone, ammonia, a particular shell, and the fragrant earth obtained from Surat.

1. Mica (abhra) is first to be exposed to a high heat, and then thrown into the juice of the *Justicia Gandarussa*, rub them together, and expose the mixture to a high heat. This is to be repeated ten times; when it is considered ready for use. It is reduced to powder, and is then said to cure all diseases. As it increases the the secretion of semen it is used for curing impotency, lengthens life, and strengthens judgment.

2. *Diamond* (híraka, vajra) there are four varieties; white, yellow, red, and black. The first is said to resemble the brahmun class, the second the kshattriya; and the other two the vaishya and the shúdra. The large, soft, round, square, and bright, without inequalities or cracks, is considered masculine; the small, hard, five angular, and cracked diamond is considered feminine, and the oblong and triangular kind is considered as neuter. The first is the best kind, it alone should be used in medicine.

It is prepared by being covered with clay and cowdung, and exposed to heat for a day and a half. Soak it then in the urine of a horse, expose it to heat seven times, when it is considered prepared for use.

Use. It lengthens life, and improves the strength and colour of the body; and cures many diseases.

Precious Stones (mánikya)—these are pearls, and corals. They are prepared by mixing them with lemon juice for a day. Then boil them in a mixture of the juice of the three mirabuli. This is done by exposing them in a bag, covered with a coating of clay and cow-dung—(See fig. 6) and reduce the medicine for use. It is considered a good tonic, and cures many diseases.

4. *Sulphur* (gandhaka) is prepared by mixing it with lime, water, oil and congee, and exposing it to heat, upon an iron vessel, for three hours. It is then ready for use as a medicine, and is administered in combination with other metals.

5. *Ammonia* (nishaadul) is prepared by mixing it with lime water in a bag (golaaguntro) for several hours. It is used in preparing mercury, and some other medicines. It is not used by itself.

6. A shell called (shankanábhi) is sometimes used as a medicine, in combination with others. It is prepared by being macerated in lime-juice.

7. The fragrant earth obtained from Surat called Saurásbtramáṭí is prepared by macerating it in the juice of the lemon for several hours, and then drying it. It is of use in cases of chronic diarrhœa, and dysentry. It is generally given in combination with other medicines.

CHAPTER III.

Pharmacy, or the preparation of Medicines.

In this Chapter, the weights and measures, with the preparation, and forms, and doses of Medicine will be considered.

Section I.

Weights and Measures.

Weights and measures were reduced to a more exact form by the celebrated Maadopokoro, who is the author of the work named Paribháshá which treats of this subject. Four of the particles of dust which are seen floating in the sun's rays as it enters a dark room make one likshá;—

6 Liksháś are equal to 1 Sorroko or Mustard-seed.

6 Mustard-seeds make 1 Yava, or Barley-corn ;

3 Barley-corns make 1 Gunja (or seeds of Abrus precatorius.)

3 Gunjas are equal to 1 Tolá.

10 Gunja are equal to 1 Pranaka.
4 Másá are equal to 1 Saanoo.
2 Saanoos equal to 1 Tolá or Weight of a Rupee.
2 Tolás ,, 1 Karsha or Aksha.
2 Karsha ,, 1 Shukti.
2 Shuktis or 8 Tolás equal to 1 Pal.
2 Tolás* ,, 1 Karsha or Aksha.
2 Palas ,, 1 Prasrita (handful.)
4 Palas ,, 1 Kuḍava or $\frac{1}{2}$ a Ser.
8 Palas ,, 2 Kuḍavas=1 Mansko or Sharáva or a Ser.
6 Palas ,, 1 Prastha or 2 Sers.
4 Prasthas ,, 1 Pátra or 8 Sers equal to 1 Aḍhaka, and 4 Aḍhaka make 2 Dronas equal to 1 Shúrpa or 64 Sers 2 Shúrpas make 1 Ghonee or 128 Sers ; and 16 Chonies make 1 Kharee ; and 100 Palas are equal to 1 Tolá*.

Some authors say that there are 5 Rattis in 1 Másha (Sursutoh) others that there are 8 or 10 Tolás in 1 Másha. In general Practice 5 Ratis are equal to 1 Másha in making pills, extracts, and powders. In decoctions and infusions 10 Rattis are equal to 1 Másha, 8 Másha are equal to 1 Tottah or 64 Jungahs, is equal to and 8 Tolás are equal to 1 Pala. These are the weights which are used for dry medicines. Several other varieties of weights are given in other books.

Double the weight of moist medicines should be taken beyond the dose of dry articles ; until the weight exceeds a Khoorubo, 32 tolás, or half a seer in weight, when the dose in both should be the same. Should the juice of the vegetables be very strong, half the dose of the dry medicine should be given. Lists of medicines are then given in the medical works, with the dose of each variety.

The Fluid measure consists of a pot made of bamboo, wood, or iron, four fingers breath in depth, and one in circumference. It is called korobo or fluid measure.

Before a medicine is exhibited to a sick person, the physician should examine the state of the air, bile, and phlegm, the internal heat, the individual's strength, the age of the person, the cause producing the disease, and lastly the ingredients of which the medicine is composed. He is next to note whether or not the intestines have been cleared out, and after the best consideration the medicine is then to be administered.

* A Tolá in the Sanscrit MSS. is equal to $\frac{1}{2}$ Tolá of the modern weights in Medical works.

Section II.

Preparations of Medicines.

Pharmacy, or the preparation of Medicines, is treated of in four Books, stated to have been derived from the great God, *I'shwara.*

The compound internal medicines are usually stimulants, such as infusions of pepper, ginger, &c. Limes are the common acids which are used.

The Hindu physicians participated largely in the error of employing medicines without examining sufficiently the properties of simple medicines and their application in different diseases; they supposed they augmented efficacy by multiplying ingredients, and have crowded their works with numerous compounds, without a consideration of the different ingredients. The exhibition of internal remedies is generally made without a sufficient reference to the circumstances of the case, their comparative efficacy in particular cures, and the stages and modifications of diseases in which they are employed. They often do not specify exactly the proportion of the ingredients, but a large number are used in equal proportions, although the dose is not always exactly specified. It will not be necessary to add many of the preparations. A specimen of each will afterwards be given.

These preparations are varied according to the peculiar purpose which they are intended to serve. They are usually exhibited mixed together, without any proper consideration as to their nature. Their receipts are often carefully retained, and handed down in families as useful remedies, not in extensive classes of diseases, but in many cases as certain cures for all sorts of diseases. It being supposed that the value of the simple medicines was increased, and their action rendered more salutary by a proper mixture, it was this that led the practitioners at an early period to investigate the nature of these substances, and to study chemistry. Thus they knew the stages of vinous and acetous fermentations. They also performed various manipulations with that useful instrument the mortar, which was used either hot or cold. They also used the Pharmaceutical forms of infusions, decoctions, extracts, mixtures, &c., which improved the qualities of these medicines.

All kinds of medicines are best recent, with the exception of honey, ghi, ginger, long-pepper, and belongo. These medicines should be kept some time before they are used as medicine. All other medicines should be used fresh, and have the proper smell, and when they are a year old they are to be thrown away. Plants obtained from the Himalaya Mountains are the best, and the juice of plants is usually the strongest; cowherds, hunters, &c., may be employed to collect medicinal plants. A Brahmin, however, is preferred, who is poor, and has performed the necessary ablutions and prayers.

Medicines from the animal kingdom are to be taken for young subjects—and secretions, such as milk, urine, &c., are to be taken after the digestion of the food of the animal.

The effect of these remedies is either to increase, diminish or cure deranged air, bile, and phlegm; of these diseases, or those of the compound parts (dhâtu) of the body. The simple forms of medicines are sometimes applied externally, but they are very seldom administered internally. When a medicine was discovered to possess some property its effects were not tried, but it was usually combined with numerous other remedies of the same kind, in the hope of augmenting the efficiency of the remedy by multiplying the ingredients. On this account the individual articles of the Materia Medica were rarely employed singly!

Medicines should be prepared in a good house, and in a retired situation. If prepared in open situations, in boats, in bazars, and by the sides of roads, their qualities are liable to be injured by unfavorable influences. Should a bad woman, or one menstruating, touch a medicine it will lose its qualities.

Medicines given in too small doses will be like throwing a little water upon a large fire that rather increases than diminishes it. In like manner too large doses of medicine will increase the diseases, and will be liable to produce other diseases.

There is no medicine with one quality, so there is no disease in which there is only one humour affected; medicines, should therefore be mixed according to the state of the patient, the term, and the virulence of the disease. If a medicine consisting of one or two ingredients is not found useful, other ingredients should be mixed with it; and in other cases some of the ingredients should be removed from the prescription.

Section III.

Forms of Medicines.

The Hindu Physicians arrange Medicine, in the following order:

1. *Jivaníya*, or that form which gives longevity.
2. *Vrihaníya*, those which give strength, and corpulency to the body.

3. *Kshinakar*, those which make the body thin.
4. *Rechaniya*, those which produce a laxative effect.
5. *Sandániya*, sedatives.
6. *Dipaníya*, stimulants, increasing the internal fire, appetite, &c.
7. *Valíya*, tonics, or those which increase strength.
8. *Varníya*, that improve the colour of the body.
9. *Kanṭhya*, expectorants, or those which clear the throat.
10. *Hṛidya*, that give a good relish.
11. *Triptighna*, those which diminish appetite.
12. *Arshaghna*, those which cure piles.
13. *Kushṭhaghna*, those which cure leprosy.
14. *Kandúghna*, which cure itchiness.
15. *Krimighna*, anthelmintics.
16. *Vishaghna*, antidotes for poison.
17. *Stanyajanana*, which increase the secretion of milk.
18. *Stanyashodhana*, which purify the milk.
19. *Shukrajanana*, which increase the secretion of semen.
20. *Shukrashodhana*, that purify the semen.
21. *Snehopáya*, that produce smoothness and softness of the skin.
22. *Swedopáya*, which produce sweating.
23. *Vamanopáya*, emetics.
24. *Berasjanopáya*, purgatives.
25. *Hasthápanupáya*, enemas of oil, ghee, &c.
26. *Anuvásanapáya*, oily do.
27. *Surabhirachana*, errhines.
28. *Chardanigrahana*, those which stop vomiting.
29. *Trishnánigrahana*, those which quench thirst.
30. *Hikkánigranaha*, those which cure hiccough.
31. *Puríshanigrahana*, those which stop looseness.
32. *Mútrakrichraníya*, diuretics.
33. *Káshahara*, those which cure cough.
34. *Shwásahara*, those which cure asthma.
35. *Sotahara*, those which cure swelling or dropsy.
36. *Juarahara*, febrifuge remedies.
37. *Shramahara*, those which produce tranquility of the humours and remove fatigue.
38. *Dáhaprashamana*, which diminish the burning of the body.
39. *Shiaprashamana*, which stop shivering.
40. *Udoodoprashamana*, those which remove temporary swelling, as urticaria.
41. *Angamarshaprashamana*, that remove pain as rheumatism, &c.
42. *Shúlaprashamana*, which cure colicky pains.
43. *Shonitásthápana*, that stop hemorrhage.

44. *Sangasthápana*, those which restore the senses.

45. *Bedanásthápana*, those which remove pains produced by external causes, as injuries, &c.

This is the division which is followed in Charaka, and under each class simple medicines are arranged. They are all given in the form of decoction.

Sursutra again divides medicines into two classes, the *Sangshodhana*, or those which evacuate bad humours from the body; and *Sangshamana* those which diminish the exalted action of the humours and restore them to the healthy state.

The Sangshodhana are divided into two classes, viz., purgatives and emetics.

1.—*Powders* (*chúrnáh.*) Powders, or dry medicines, are often used instead of green herbs on account of their scarcity.

For preparing such medicines, dry the vegetable in the sun or over the fire, powder it in a pestle and mortar, and clean the powder by passing it through a sieve.

The usual dose of such powders is from one másha to half a tolá, and it is usually administered with water. They are usually employed in diarrhœa and dysentery, and as a purgative, emetic, &c.

2.—*The fresh juice of Plants.* (Swarasa.) This is a frequent form of exhibiting medicines. The juice, generally of the leaves, is obtained by boiling and then straining.

3.—*Pastes.* (Kalka) These are prepared by grinding the medicine between two stones.

Forms of Medicines.

The manipulations are performed with that useful instrument the mortar, which is used either hot or cold. The qualities of the different medicines are modified by exhibiting them in the Pharmaceutical forms of infusions, extracts and mixtures, &c.

These preparations are divided into medicines used externally, and those which are used internally. Of the former class are ointments composed of oil, ghee or the like, with the juice of the leaves of trees, &c.

The internal preparations are formed of various ingredients, and are administered without any reference to the circumstances of their administration, their comparative efficacy and proportions, or the stages and modifications of diseases in which they are to be employed. Some of the simple medicines are very powerful and their action is too little known.

Internal Medicines are usually given in the form of 1 powders, 2 fresh juices (swarasa); 3 pastes (kalka); 4 Decoctions, &c. (kwátha, shíta) infusions (phánṭa); 5 Extracts (phanita); 6 Roasting (Pátrapáka); 7 Spirituous mixtures (Arishṭa, A'sava and Surá) 8 Pills (Vaṭiká); and 9 Electuaries (Avaleha); 10 Oils (taila)

4.—*Infusions and Decoctions, &c. Infusions* are prepared by mixing one part of the medicine with four parts of boiling water. They are to be infused four hours and the water strained for use.

For *decoctions* (phánṭa, kwátha, shíta kwátha) take two tolás of medicines to half a seer of water, or one part to sixteen parts of water; boil down to one quarter; strain and take this quantity twice a day. Some recommend eight parts of water to one of the medicine, which is to be boiled down to one quarter. These decoctions are made fresh as required and a little honey is usually added. Weak decoctions are prepared by adding to two tolás two sers of water, which is to be boiled to one half the quantity. This is to be taken several times a day. Sometimes medicinal powders are added to the decoction.

Páníya, is a weaker form of decoction, which is frequently administered to afford immediate relief, seven symptoms suca as Sha,anga Páníya which is prepared in the following manner:—

Take of Musta (Cyperus rotundus)
Parpaṭíka (Oldenlandia biflora)
Chandana (Sandal wood)
Kuskus (cuscus grass)
Bhala Shunthí (dry ginger)

of each an equal quantity. Two tolás of this to be mixed with two sers of water and boiled down to one ser; *dose*, a chhaṭák occasionally. This is an excellent drink to check thirst.

Panchana is another form of decoction. It is formed by decocting two tolás of certain drugs in a pint of water, and reducing it to one quarter; *dose*, a chhaṭák twice a day in cases of fever, dysentery, &c.

Prakapah is another form of decoction in which medicines are added in powder to increase the strength of the decoction.

Sometimes the medicine is recommended to be prepared for use by *Maceration* (shítakwátha) for a night in cold water. The water is then strained for use.

The fresh juice of plants is considered the strongest form of medicine. The decoction is next, and those obtained by maceration and by infusion are the weakest.

5.—*Extracts* (*phánita*). Make a decoction of medicine, mix it with jagree, boil until it becomes thick, or until a small portion when thrown into water does not mix for some time, nor swim in the water; or when a piece of it sticks upon a board when thrown upon it. The extract is then prepared for use. Too much boiling should be avoided, as it by this means loses its peculiar qualities.

Bhávana is made by reducing the medicine to powder and mixing it with a decoction of the same drug, and then exposing it from time to time to the influence of the sun.

6.—*Roasting* (*Pútrapáka*). These medicine sare prepared by crushing them between two stones with the addition of water. When in a state of pulp, wrap them in the leaves of the black-berry or Indian fig-tree, tie it tight with a string and cover it with a coating of clay an inch thick. It is then to be exposed to the fire of cow dung until the clay is red. It is then ready for use, and may be exhibited in the form of powders or pills.

7.—*Spirituous Mixtures or Wines* (Arishṭa, Ásava, and Surá) are often recommended by the other writers on medicine.

8.—*Pills* (*Vatiká.*) Pills are prepared in different ways; some are made by rubbing the medicine between stones, others by macerating or grinding to powder. The powder is then to be mixed with water or syrup, and then placed in a open place at night. Other pills are formed by boiling and allowing the mixture to stand in the air or in the sun, and then forming it into balls or pills, which are called Modaka and Guṭiká. Each should weigh from one half to one quarter of a tolá. They have different names and measures for preparing them according to the nature of the medicine and the manner in which it is to be used.

9.—*Electuaries to be swallowed* (*Kavaliya*). These preparations are made by boiling down the decoction of the medicine to one quarter, mix sugar with it and again boil for some minutes, and when it has arrived at the consistence of congealing quickly on being removed from the fire, add the usual powders.

Electuaries to be sucked (*Lehya*). These medicines are made with syrups, powders and certain other medicines. They are very useful in curing dysentery, cough, hœmoptysis, &c.

10.—*Oils* (*ghi*). Oils are usually prepared by mixing four times the quantity of milk, whey, cow's urine, &c.; boil, and when the watery part is evaporated, certain fragrant medicines are added, and it is then strained through cloth. These oils are used as external applications. Several such preparations of oils are used, as errhines.

rain continually fall upon it. Consequently medicine should be administered according to the strength and age, to the stage and nature of the sickness, and to the kind of medicine as specified in the shástras. It is also very necessary in preparing medicine that the exact proportion of the different ingredients be observed; for if more or less of any one of the ingredients be used than specified, it will have a tendency to increase rather than cure the disease.

Should the sick person be strong, and not too young, a whole dose of the medicine may be given. Thus, with such a person, when oil decoctions and the like are to be given, one *pala* is the dose. To a moderately strong person three fourths of a dose are to be given, or 3 *akshas* or 6 *tolás*. Should the sick person be in a state of weak health, or be old, or an infant, half a dose should be given or five *ratis*, or one *máshá*, whether it be made of oil, ghee, a decoction, or any other medicine. Of electuaries and syrups one or two *karshás* may be given, according to circumstances. The dose is afterwards to be increased or diminished according to the circumstances of the case, such as the frequency and consistence of the dejections, &c.

Section V.

Administration of Medicines.

The Hindus used either iron or stone mortars, warmed or cold. The hot mortar was prepared by exposing it to a fire made with the dry litter of goats and the husks of rice. The Pestle was made of iron or earthenware. It requires to be quite clean and of a sufficient size to hold by the hand. A prayer should always be said over the mortar before the medicines are mixed in it.

The Hindus, like the other ancient nations, fell into the error of endeavouring to accomplish too much without examining sufficiently the properties of simple remedies, and their application in different diseases. By thus supposing that they augmented the efficacy by multiplying the ingredients, they have been led to crowd their books with numerous unsuitable medicines.

The *Menstruum* in which medicine is to be given is water, honey, sugar, &c.; or such substances as speedily act on all the body. When *Váyu* (air) is deranged, cooling and heating things are to be mixed with the medicine; for deranged phlegm, warm and dry things—and for deranged bile, sweet and cooling substances.

In diseases of the chest, such as difficult breathing, cough, ulcers of the thorax, of the nose, affections of the voice, the above menstruums are not proper; as the medicines, such as expectorants, &c., must be taken frequently so as to keep up their action.

The time for administering medicines is important, some requiring to be given before, others during, and a third kind after eating. The general opinion is that medicine should be taken on an empty stomach as it is then soon digested; and like a drop of oil let fall upon water is taken into the system and diffused quickly over it. The following precepts should be recollected in the administration of medicines :—

1. In short and acute diseases the medicine is to be taken without food.

2. The medicine may be taken in some cases with advantage before eating.

3. One half of the medicine should be taken before, and another after food.

4. By the old and weak the medicine should be taken with the food.

5. By others after the food.

6. Another kind should be taken with a covering.

7. When the disease is in the middle of the body, the medicine is to be taken between the two periods of eating.

8. Another kind is to be taken with each morsel of food.

9. Another kind is to be taken after each morsel of food.

10. For asthma, cough, thirst, a vomiting medicine is to be administered frequently.

In treating some diseases, rice is sometimes excluded; and in other diseases, rice alone is allowed after the medicine—in other cases more rice than usual is to be taken; in another form the rice is mixed with the medicine when the person is strong, with powerful internal heat. Medicine should not be given after drinking water, after long fasting, nor in great weakness.

When no liquid for drink is mentioned, water is intended; when no part of the vegetable is stated, the root is to used; and when no time is stated, the medicine is intended to be taken in the morning.

Before administering medicine the following prayer is to be offered up :

" Oh! Bramhá! Daksha[1] Ashwiní Kumára[2]—Shiva, Indra,

---

1 Son of Bramhá to whom he first gave the Ayurveda.

2 The Physician of the gods.

Prithiví,[1] Chandra,[2] Súrya[3]—Oh! Dhanwantari,[4] Divyadása,[5] Káshi Ráj,[6] Nakula,[7] and Sahadeva[8]—Oh! Váyu,[9] Mala,[10] and all sages and indigenous situations of medicines, and every kind of devil! cure this disease: and Oh! prophets, like *Rasáyana,*[11] and Mriti which cure weakness and all diseases, may the present prove such: and Oh! Vásuki,[12] endue this medicine with the property of restoring health."

To the medicine the person says—"You are Bramhá and Vishnu, and like Shiva and Durgá, may you cure diseases! May the energy of the east (Indra) and that of the south-east (Agni), the south (Yama[13]), of the north-west (Marut[14]), of the west Varuna[15]), of the north-west (Nairit), of the north (Kuvera[16],) and of the south-east (Ishána) approach to bestow the qualities for the cure of diseases."

The patient must carefully avoid making faces when he takes a medicine, as this is like Bramhá and Shiva; and it is sinful so to act. As soon as the medicine is taken the vessel which contained it should be turned upside down. The patient is then to wash his mouth and a little sweatmeat is to be taken to remove the taste.

When the medicine is digested, it produces languor, heat, and weakness, giddiness and faintness, diminishes memory, &c. It sometimes produces intoxication and thirst.[17]

Care should always be taken, that a second medicine is not

---

1 Earth.
2 The moon.
3 The Sun.
4 One of the first great Physicians among mortals.
5 Ditto.
6 Ditto.
7 Son of the Physician of heaven.
8 Ditto.
9 Air.
10 Fire.
11 Water of immortality.
12 The great serpent and author of a medical work.
13 The judge of men after death.
14 God of air,
15 Of waters.
16 God of wealth.

17 A medicine is known to be properly digested when it acts in the usual manner, and appears in the motions—while the body feels cold and light, with appetite and thirst, and occasional belching, when the person is in good spirits and the senses are acute.

given until the one previously taken has been properly digested otherwise it will not cure the disease.

Section VI.

Uses of Medicines.

Charaka arranges simple medicines under the following heads. They were all exhibited in the form of decoction :

1. *Jívaníya,* or that form which gives longevity.
2. *Vrihaníya,* those which give strength, and corpulency to the body.
3. *Kshínakar,* those which make the body thin.
4. *Rechaníya,* those which produce a laxative effect.
5. *Sandáníya,* sedatives.
6. *Dípaníya,* stimulants, increasing the internal fire, appetite, &c.
7. *Valíya,* tonics, or those which increase strength.
8. *Varníya,* that improve the colour of the body.
9. *Kanthya,* expectorants, or those which clear the throat.
10. *Hridya,* that give a good relish.
11. *Triptighna,* those which diminish appetite.
12. *Arshaghna,* those which cure piles.
13. *Kushthaghna,* those which cure leprosy.
14. *Kandúghna,* which cure itchiness.
15. *Krimighna,* anthelmintics.
16. *Vishaghna,* antidotes for poison.
17. *Stanyajanana,* which increase the secretion of milk.
18. *Stanyashodhana,* which purify the milk.
19. *Shukrajanana,* which increase the secretion of semen.
20. *Shukrashodhana,* that purify the semen.
21. *Snehopáya,* that produce smoothness and softness of the skin.
22. *Swedopáya,* which produce sweating.
23. *Vamanopáya,* emetics.
24. *Berasjanopáya,* purgatives.
25. *Hasthápanapáya,* enemas of oil, ghee, &c.
26. *Anuvásanapáya,* oily enemas.
27. *Surabhirachana,* errhines.
28. *Chardanigrahana,* those which stop vomiting.

29. *Trishnánigrahana,* those which quench thirst.
30. *Hikkánigranaha,* those which cure hiccough.
31. *Puríshanigrahana,* those which stop looseness.
32. *Mútrakrichraníya,* diuretics.
33. *Káshahara,* those which cure cough.
34. *Shwásahara,* those which cure asthma.
35. *Sotahara,* those which cure swelling or dropsy.
36. *Juarahara,* febrifuge remedies.
37. *Shramahara,* those which produce tranquillity of the humors and remove fatigue.
38. *Dáhaprashamana,* which diminish the burning of the body.
39. *Shiaprashamana,* which stop shivering.
40. *Udoodoprashamana,* those which remove temporary swelling as urticaria.
41. *Angamarsha prashamana,* that remove pain as rheumatism, &c.
42. *Shúlaprashamana,* which cure colicky pains.
43. *Shonitásthápana,* that stop hemorrhage.
44. *Sangasthápana,* those which restore the senses.
45. *Bedanásthápana,* those which remove pains produced by external causes, as injuries, &c.

Sushruta again divides medicines into two classes, the *Sangshodhana,* or those which evacuate bad humors from the body, as purgatives and emetics; and *Sangshamana* those which diminish the exalted action of the humors and restore them to the healthy state.

Medicines may be arranged according as they are supposed to cure air, bile or phlegm, or according to their action on certain organs. I shall now give a list of the principal simple remedies in each class, according to their supposed effects.

The following are the principal simple medicines which are employed for the cure of deranged air, phlegm, and bile :—

1. *List of Simple Medicines used for the Cure of deranged váyu, (air.)*

	Sanskrit.	*Scientific Names, &c.*
1.	*Badará,*	Zizyphus jujuba or scandens.
2.	*Dáru,*	Pinus Devadaru.
3.	*Kushtha,*	Costus speciosus.
4.	*Haridrá,*	Turmerick.
5.	*Varuna,*	Capparis trifoliata.
6.	*Másha,*	Phaseolus radiatus.

7.	*(Másha Kalai ?)*	(Dolichos pilosus ?)
8.	*Shringára, Bhojapatra,*	Betula Bhoorja.
9.	*Balá,*	Sida cordifolio.
10.	*(White) Balá,*	
11.	*Dási,*	Barleria cœrulea.
12.	*Kachchhura,*	Dolichos carpopogon.
13.	*Shonaka,*	Bignonia Indica.
14.	*Virataru,*	Pentaptero Arjuna.
15.	*Shana,*	Crotolaria juncea.
16.	*Agnimantha,*	Premna spinosa.
17.	*Vatsádaní,*	Menispermum glabrum.
18.	*Eranda,*	Ricinus communis.
19.	*Ashmabhed,*	Plectranthus scultellaroides.
20.	*Shatamúli,*	Asparagus racemosus.
21.	*Punarnava,*	Boerhavia diffusa v. alata.
22.	*Vasuka,*	Asclepias gigantea.
23.	*Vasira,*	Pothos officinalis.
24.	*Kánchanaka,*	Michelia champaca.
25.	*Vardhaka,*	Siphonanthus Indica.
26.	*Kárpási,*	Gossypium hirsutum.
27.	*Brischíkáli,*	Tragia involucrata.
28.	*Patúra,*	Pterocarpus santolinus.
29.	*Badará,*	Mimosa octandra.
30.	*Yava,*	Hordeum hexastichon.
31.	*Kola,*	Piper chuvya.
32.	*Kulattha,*	Dolichos biflorus.
33.	*Vidári,*	Hedysarum gangeticum.
34.	*Kuverákshí,*	Bignonia suave-olens.

2. *Simple Medicines used for the Cure of deranged Phlegm.*

1.	*Kaliyaka,*	Curcuma xanthorrhiza.
2.	*Aguru,*	Aquilaria agallocha.
3.	*Tilaparní,*	Pterocarpus santolinus.
4.	*Kushtha,*	Costus speciosus.
5.	*Haridra,*	Turmerick.
6.	*Shita,*	Marsilea quadrifolia.
7.	*Shiva,*	Mimosa suma.
8.	*Shatapushpa,*	Anethum sowa.
9.	*Sarala,*	Pinus longifolia.
10.	*Rásna,*	Mimosa octandra.
11.	*Prakírjya,*	Cœsalpinia bonducella.
12.	*Udakírjya,*	Galedupa arborea.

13. *Ingoodi*, The name of a plant commonly called Inguä.
14. *Suvarna, Dhattúra*, Datura Metel.
15. *Kákadúní*, Cannabis sativa.
16. *Lángalika*, Gloriosa superba.
17. *Hastikarna*, The castor oil tree.
18. *Munjátaka*, Munja grass.
19. *Lámajjaka*, The root of the Andropogon muricatum.
20. *Vrihati*, Solanum melongena.
21. *Mushka*, Cyperus rotundus ?
22. *Surasa*, Vitex trifolia.
23. *Arakvadha*, Cassia fistula.

3. *List of Simple Medicines used for the cure of deranged Bile.*

1. *Chandana*, Sirium myrtifolium.
2. *Kuchandana*, Pterocarpus santolinus.
3. *Hhrívera*, A drug and perfume commonly called *Bála*.
4. *Ushíra*, Andropogon muricatum.
5. *Manjishthá*, Rubia manjith, Bengal madder.
6. *Payasya*, Asclepias rosea.
7. *Vidárí*, Hedysarum gangeticum.
8. *Shatávari*, Asparagus racemosus.
9. *Gundra*, Saccharum sara.
10. *Shaivála*, Vallisneria octandra.
11. *Kalára*, Nymphæa lotus.
12. *Kumuda*, Nymphæa esculenta.
13. *Utpala*, Nymphæa cerulea.
14. *Kadali*, Musa sapientum.
15. *Kandalí*, Banana or Plantain.
16. *Dúrvá*, Panicum dactylon.
17. *Múrvá*, Sanseviera zeylanica.
18. *Kakola*, Cocculus Indicus.
19. *Nyagrodha*, Ficus Indica.
20. *Panchamúla*, This is preparad by the mixture of five roots, the Bel, Premna longifolia, Cassia, Gmelina arborea, and the Trumpet-flower.

Actions of Medicines.

There are five principal actions of medicines; or *diaphoretics, emetics, purgatives, (enemata) errhines*, or *stimulants*.—Before any of these medicines are given, the body should be relaxed by rubbing oil upon it externally, and giving some oleaginous mixture internally.

I. *Diaphoretics.*—There are four kinds of them :—

1.—*Tápasweda,* or the application of heat.

2.—*Ushásweda,* or the steam of hot water.

3.—*Upanahasweda,* or the application of certain warm poultices or plasters made of different medicines ; and,

4.—*Dravasweda,* or fomentations with various decoctions.

Of the medicines for relaxing the body ; ghee, oil, charbi, marrow, and such like are to be used ; of these ghee is the best, as it is produced from milk, which is obtained from the cow. This milk first yields curdled milk, then butter, and with the assistance of fire ghee is produced. Nothing else can be obtained from ghee, so that it may be considered as pure. For diseases of the bile, ghee only is to be given ; of air, ghee and salt mixed : and for diseases of phlegm, ghee, long-pepper, pepper, dry ginger and nitre mixed together. A weak person with a bad memory and digestion, should use ghee to cure them. In certain cutaneous diseases, for open boils, and for worms, oil is useful, particularly when the phlegm is deranged. To fat people, particularly when the air is deranged, oil should first be given, particularly when the dejections are not natural. Lard (charbi) is most useful for diseases of the joints, bones and sensible parts.

Perspiration should not be promoted in the scrotum, throat, or eye.

When air and phlegm are deranged in a place, or when only air or cough is deranged, perspiration alone is to be invited to such places. When air and phlegm are deranged, medicines that contain the qualities of coldness and heat, are to be used. When air is deranged, cooling medicines alone are to be used.

Perspiration is not to be encouraged in very fat, very thin, or debilitated persons, when affected with diseases of the blood or air, when the diseases are incurable, in dysentery, or when the person is afflicted with large sores over the body (*Kotha*). Nor will perspiration be proper after poisons, or drinking ; when given to the blind, when the abdomen is swelled, or in Erysipelas (*visarpa*), or Leprosy, or in a bad state of the blood. In such cases milk, ghee, curdled milk, and honey should be given after purgatives.

It is improper to give diaphoretics when the body is burnt ; in diseases of the anus, in grief or fear-producing diseases ; in passions, in hunger, in thirst, in weakness, in jaundice, in gonorrhœa, in hemoptysis, pulmonary consumption, dysentery, during the flow of the menses, or after taking much wine ; in pregnancy, particularly near its termination, in diseases of air, or in fatal diseases. When diaphoretics are used under such circumstances they will do harm, or their peculiar effects will not be produced.

In general, emetics are recommended when the stomach is surcharged with phlegm, and purgatives when the intestines and bile are deranged.

Emetics. After the oleaginous or relaxing remedies, and the exhibition of diaphoretics, the five varieties of the other remedies are to be used. The first of these are *emetics.*

When the practitioner has decided on the necessity of giving an emetic, the preliminary relaxing medicines with honey and *Sainphal* (an impure kind of salt,) are to be exhibited. This is usually done the day before the exhibition of the emetic, more particularly when the strength and internal heat of the person are great. A quantity of whey, congee water or the like, should be taken, and the warm hand be applied frequently to the abdomen for an hour to soften it.

The usual emetic is then to be given with the proper prayer. If it cannot be taken for the taste, in the usual way, it may be sucked through the stalk of a hollow reed, so that it may be thrown down the throat. The emetic should be taken in the morning. The person is to place himself upon a stool, with his thigh parallel to the floor, and his head back, and sides supported by friends. He will first feel sick, then saliva will flow from his mouth, and tears and mucus from his eyes and nose, followed by vomiting. The vomiting will be promoted by thrusting a finger or the stalk of a lily down the throat. The vomiting is to be encouraged until the stomach is completely emptied ; this is known not to be the case by the discharge of saliva, by the bad breath, and by the body being itchy.

Emetics are to be used when the air is deranged.

Among emetics, madana fruit is the best—and may be administered in the form of powder or decoction with honey and rock-salt.

Emetics may be given in diseases of phlegm, inflammation or internal abscesses, when the bile is deranged, &c.

If the emetics do not act freely, use warm water internally mixed with long-pepper.

The following emetics are to be used when the phlegm is deranged.

White mustard, rock-salt, and long-pepper ; repeat the dose frequently until the desired effect is produced. There are various emetics which are exhibited in the form of powder or chocolate ; use warm water after these. The dose of the emetic should be varied with the strength of the individual.

When an emetic has acted properly it first produces an evacuation of phlegm and bile without pain ; the breast, neck, and head feel clear, and the body light. The vomiting may be stopped by snuffing sweet smelling mixtures up the nostrils. One kind of emetic acts as a purgative, another restores irregularities of the humours (dhátu), and retains the body soft.

Vomiting should not be excited in cases of sparks being seen, or sudden blindness, or great fatigue, in spleen, or in jaundice, when the abdomen is swelled, for very fat or thin persons, for infants or for very old persons, particularly when afflicted with piles, sores or diarrhœa, in tetanus, for persons with hoarseness, with hemoptysis or after great losses of blood, nor for pregnant women. When emetics act as purgatives and not as emetics, in the same way as purgatives, when they produce emetic effects, they are unfavourable. The kind of emetic must be varied according as the air, bile, or phlegm is deranged; and various diseases are supposed to be produced when the emetic effect is not produced, such as a bad mouth, fœtid breath, &c. In such cases the person is not to eat, and the emetic must not be repeated that day. Should the vomiting be too severe, it will be repressed by anointing the body with ghee, by cold bathing, and by taking internally a decoction of rasins (kismis) with sugar and water, and other agreeable drinks. In the afternoon, a warm bath is to be given, and light and nourishing food, such as ground pulse of different kinds with the broth of wild animals. An aperient is then to be given to act on the bowels, and food is to be taken in small quantities, to renovate the internal fire and thus repress the vomiting.

Emetics are very useful in diseases of the phlegm, in cases in which poison has been taken—in diseases accompanied with much thirst—in diseases of the internal heat—in diseases of the mammœ—in madness, in epilepsy—in elephantiasis—in diseases of the humours—in fevers—in want of appetite—in boils—in diseases of the stomach (ámáshay)—in dysentry—in diseases of the chest—in large secretions of saliva—in sickness—in difficulty of breathing—when the person has lost his sense of smell and taste—in diseases of the lips and mouth—when pus is discharged—in diseases of the throat—and in bloody discharges by stool.

The following is a List of the principal Emetics :—

1. *Madana,*	Vangueria spinosa.
2. *Kuṭaja,*	Echites antidysenterica.
3. *Jímútaka,*	Andropogon serratus.
4. *Ikshyáku,*	A bitter gourd.
5. *Dámurdava,*	Achyranthes aspera.
6. *Ketavádana,*	A plant with white flowers, Pandanus ?
7. *Sarshapa,*	Sinapis dichotoma.

8.	*Garuga,*	A vegetable and medicinal substance.
9.	*Pippali,*	Long pepper.
10.	*Karanja,*	Galedupa arborea.
11.	*Prapunnáḍa, padmáṭa*	Cassia tora.
12.	*Kavidára,*	Hedysarum alhagi.
13.	*Karvudára,*	Barleria cerulea.
14.	*Nimba,*	Melia azadiracta.
15.	*Ashwagandhá,*	Physalis flexuosa.
16.	*Vetasí,*	Calamus rotang.
17.	*Bandhujívaka,*	Pentapetes Phœnicea.
18.	*Sitá,*	Clitoria ternatea.
19.	*Shatapushpiká,*	Anethum sowa.
20.	*Vimbiká,*	Momordica monadelpha.
21.	*Vachera,*	Acorus calamus.
22.	*Mrigahbojaní,*	Colocynth or bitter apple.
23.	*Chitrá,*	Plumbago Zeylanica.

These medicines not only act as emetics, errhines, &c., but cure all the bad humours from the stomach upwards. From *Madana* to *Prapunnáḍa*, the fruits alone are used for producing the above effect, and from *Karvadáru* to *Chitrá* the roots are to be used for the same purpose. Sometimes they are used simply, more commonly in combination.

Purgatives, (*Virechana*) and *Enemas* (unávávana or vastí).

Purgatives.—The day before a purgative is exhibited the patient is to eat light food in combination with warm water, so as to remove any disarrangement of the phlegm ; the next morning the body is to be anointed with oil and exposed to heat, so as to promote perspiration ; after which the purgative is to be given. Should a purgative be given without the preparatory medicines, the person's constitution will be broken, like dry wood at the time it is warping. These will vary according to the intention of the practitioner, and the state of the bowels which are to be evacuated. There are three such situations :—

First ; the *Mridu Kashṭa,* in which there is much bile and a state of looseness ; when if the bile is required to be evacuated, a small quantity of the medicine should be given cold.

The second state is called *Krúrá Kashṭa,* in which the air and phlegm are deranged, producing costiveness, and the medicine acts with difficulty. In this case the medicine should be given warm and in a strong dose.

The third state is named the middle state or *Madhya* kashṭa, in which the air, phlegm and bile are in equal proportions, and accompanied with a state of bowels neither relaxed nor costive. In this case the medicine should be given of a temperate heat and of a middle quantity and quality.

The dose of medicine should vary with the age, &c., of the patient. To infants give sugar with honey. When a purgative has been administered in the above form its action should not be suddenly stopped. The patient should stay in a closed room, and he should not take cold water, nor use force in the evacuation.

When the purgative has not produced the desired effect, it will produce derangement in the bile and phlegm. The body is hot, there is no appetite—and there is a heaviness in the belly, uneasiness in the breast, itchiness of the arms, and there is not a free evacuation of the urine.

When purgatives act too powerfully, they produce fainting, frequent mucous stools, prolapsus ani, and pain in the belly.

When the purgatives act properly, the patient feels easy ; and air, phlegm and bile pass freely, and he feels happy and light ; air passes by the anus in the usual manner. After the action of purgatives, the patient should take thin and light food—as congee, and sometimes broths.

If purgatives are taken from time to time in a proper form, they clear the understanding and senses, improve the strength of the organs, and of the body. They also improve the appetite and retain the humours in a healthy state, and retard the approach of age.

In infancy a mixture of honey, sugar and trivrit (teori-Convolvulus turpethum) is to be given, in the form of a powder.

When a purgative acts too strongly with a discharge of blood ; in such cases pour cold water upon the body, and give an emetic, with congee and honey ; or give the oily or mucilaginous liquids. The enema should be prepared with honey and ghee ; animal and vegetable broths should likewise be given.

Purgatives should not be given during the beginning of fever ; that is while the patient feels a slight appetite, and his bowels are not very costive. For infants and old or very fat people, purgatives are to be avoided, especially when the body is very hot or much fatigued—in bloody stools, and immediately after labour ; also when the appetite is bad, in derangements of the blood, bile and air, when there are sores on the body, or internally, when there is great thirst, after loss of blood—and in diseases of the lungs. Should a quack give purgatives at an improper time he will kill the person.

Purgatives should be used in fevers, in diseases from poisons, in piles, in swelling of the glands, in jaundice, in epilepsy, in diseases of the heart, in fistula in ano, in vomiting, in diseases of the vagina, in colicky pains, as costiveness, and in cholera (vishúchiká) in disease of the belly (alasaka), in leprosy, in eruptions, in gonorrhœa, in the enlargement of the spleen, in hydrocele, in ophthalmia, and in general in diseases of the eye, especially in purulent ophthalmia, in diseases of the head, ear and nose—in those of the anus and penis, in worms, in diseases of the bile, and involuntary discharges of semen, &c.

The discharges produced by purgatives are first, urine, fœces, bile, the medicine, and lastly phlegm.

Of the purgatives the *Trivrit*, or as it is usually called Teori (Convolvolus turpethum), and Harítakí (Chebulic mirobalan) are considered the best. Of the oily purgatives, the castor oil is the best. In diseases of air, give Teorí in powder (6 annas weight for a dose) with the juice of the sugar cane.

In diseases of the bile, the medicine is administered with milk, and in diseases of phlegm, the same medicine is given with the decoction of long and black pepper and dry ginger.

The covering of the Harítakí, is to be used like the teorí, in the same form and dose—and to cure the same diseases.

Castor oil is prepared by gathering the seed at the proper season, drying it for seven days, and taking the kernels and boiling them in water—the oil is to be removed for use—in other cases the oil is got by pressing the seeds between weights. This oil is to be given to children from birth to the tenth year. It is also given to old and weak and delicate persons.

Purgatives may be prepared and exhibited with ghee, oil, milk wine, cow's urine, broths and certain forms of food.

The action of purgative medicines will be increased by using warm water with some infusion, the warm or vapor bath, and friction with the warm hand. When the laxative effect is not sufficient, it is not to be repeated till the next day ; but when a sufficient effect has been produced the purgatives should not be repeated for ten days.

The internal fire is diminished by purgatives, and as soon as the action is produced, light food is to be given, and a little mango bark mixed with congee water is to be used internally, and externally friction so as to increase the internal fire.

The efforts of nature should not be resisted ; but when the person is weak, and the bowels loose, the medicine is to be given in small quantities and frequently repeated. When the bowels are loose, and the patient either weak or strong, purgatives are to be given, and when in that state if the bowels are not freely evacuated the collection of the bad humours, if retained, will produce other diseases*.

A small dose of the purgative should be first given, and when the individual's constitution is better known, a stronger one may be given.

The following are examples of purgative mixtures : take of Harítakí (yellow myrobalan) salt, and long pepper in equal proportions ; grind them into a paste with water ; dose three drams.

Or take of Harítakí, (Yellow myrobalan), amlakí (emblic myrobalan), vibhítakí (Beleric myrobalan,) in equal parts. Three tolás of this mixture are to be boiled in 48 of water until reduced to 12 tolás. To six tolás of this infusion add three of castor oil.

Or take three tolás (9 drams) of castor oil, with six of milk.

When the purgative is required to be taken for diseased bile ; the following mixture is recommended :—

Take of Garatwak (cassia bark)	$\frac{1}{4}$	tolá.
Tejpátá (cassia leaf)	$\frac{1}{4}$	"
Pepper	$\frac{3}{4}$	"
Teori (convolvulus turpethum),	$\frac{3}{4}$	"
Sugar	$\frac{3}{4}$	"

pound and mix with hot water.

When the phlegm is diseased. Take of Pippalí (long

pepper)	$\frac{3}{4}$	tolá.
Shunthí (ginger)	$\frac{3}{4}$	"
Yavakshára (nitre)	$\frac{3}{4}$	"
Shyámalatá (Echites antidysenterica)	$\frac{3}{4}$	"
Teori (Convolvulus Turpethum),	1	"

pound and form an electuary with honey.

Purgatives, or those medicines which clear the body of diseased humours below the stomach.

1. *Trivrit*, Convolvulus turpethum.
2. *Shyáma*, Panicum frumentaceum.
3. *Dantí*, Croton polyandrum.
4. *Dravantí*, Anthericum tuberosum.
5. *Saptalá*, Abrus precatorius.
6. *Shankhiní*, Cissampelos hexandra.
7. *Vishániká*, Asclepias geminata ?
8. *Vaváka*, Clitoria ternata.
9. *Shavalantarí*, A kind of Convolvulus.
10. *Shatraha*.

* This is known by symptoms of derangements of phlegm and bile, by the loss of appetite, and heaviness and itchiness, heat of the body, and a diminution of the internal fire. The dejections are constipated in such cases.

11. *Suvarnaka,* Çassia fistula.
12. *Chitraka,* Plumbago Zeylanica.
13. *Kinihí,* Achyranthes aspera.
14. *Kushá,* Poa cynosuroides.
15. *Kásha,* Saccharum spontaneum.
16. *Jelaka?*
17. *Kampíluka,* A variety of *teori* (Convolvulus turpethum.)
18. *Ramáká,*
19. *Pátálá,* Bignonia suaveolens.
20. *Haritakí,* Terminalia Chebula.
21. *Nílini,* Indigofera tinctoria.
22. *Eraṇda,* Ricinus communis.
23. *Kuṭhika,* Costus speciousus?
24. *A'ragvada,* Cassia fistula.
25. *Mahávriksha,* Euphorbia.
26. *Saptacheda.*
27. *Arka,* Calotropis gigantea.
28. *Jatísatí,* Halicacabum cardiospermum.

From *Trivrit* to *Kásha*, the roots are used: and from *Jelaka* to *Pátálá* the bark is used, from *Harítákí* to *Eraṇda* the fruits of the tree, the leaves of *Kuṭhika* and *A'ragvada* are used; and the milk of the other medicines of this list is used for producing their purgative effect.

There is another class of medicines which produce both vomiting and purging, they are:—

1. *Kashátakí,* Several sorts of cucurbitaceous plants.
2. *Saptalá,* (Abrus precatorius.)
3. *Shankhiní,* (Cissampelos hexandra.)
4. *Devadálí.*
5. *Ravíliká,* (Momordica Charantica.)

The juices of these plants are used for producing their effects, as the organs of speech for the articulation of vowels and Sibilants.

Enemata (anuvásana). This is considered as the best manner of exhibiting purgative medicines in diseases of the lower part of the abdomen, and lower extremities. Medicines may be mixed with these so as to cure diseases of air, bile and phlegm, as the medicine enters the system like water poured at the root of a tree. These medicines were much used by the ancient practitioners.

The general effect of enemas is to strengthen the muscles, and to lessen fat. They retain the eye and surface in a healthy state—and will retain the body healthy till death, or even lengthen the period of existence.

The bladders of pigs, buffalos, goats, &c., are used for these injections. For this purpose the animal should be healthy and of full age. Should bladders not be found a leather bag may be substituted.

The injecting pipe should be made of gold, silver, copper, iron, hard wood or ivory. It should be smooth, strong and tapering like the tail of a cow, with a slightly tuberculated extremity, six fingers' breadth in length to the cross piece, from the first to the eighth year of age; eight or ten from the 9th to 16th year; and afterwards somewhat longer. During the first years, the tube should be the size of the little finger, afterwards of the ring finger, then of the middle finger; and after the 25th year, the size of the thumb. In administering enemata care must be taken not to introduce it in an oblique direction, nor too far or too short a distance, and not to press it on one side. The cross piece is likewise varied in length at the different periods of life. The size of the injection should also be varied according to the size of the patient's hands.

For the very young two handsfull of the liquid is to be used; for a child of eight years four, and of from 16 upwards eight handsfull.

There are two varieties of glysters, one without (asnehaka) and another with oil (snehaka).

The following is offered as an example of a glyster in costiveness, piles, dyspepsia, intermittent fever, in diseases of the loins, back, and intestines. It should be prepared as follows:—

Take of the decoction of, Suttee.—

Pushkara,	A kind of Costus.
Krishnapáka,	Carissa carondas.
Madana,	Datura metel.
Dubdáru,	Uvaria longifolia.
Kushṭha,	Costus speciosus.
Yashṭi madhu,	Liquorice.
Villa,	Assafoetida

add ten parts of milk and four of oil; mix and administer warm. Various other glysters are prepared in much the same way.

This form of administering medicine is very useful when not too frequently used, in fever, diarrhæa, and dysentry; in diseases of the head and eyes, in tetanus; in convulsions, and in many nervous and other diseases.

Enemata are not proper in madness, in piles, jaundice, in fainting, for the timid or those labouring under grief, in indigestion, in vomiting, leprosy, dropsy, asthma, cough, diseases of the throat, diseases of air, such as swelling of the extremities, before the third or fourth month of pregnancy, and in the very young and old, or when afflicted with nervous diseases.

Two thirds of the usual quantity of food should be taken before the glyster is to be administered ; before or after eating they will produce vomiting.

Before the injection is administered the body is to be cleaned and anointed ; the patient is to rest in the lap of a large man in a clean situation ; where there are no currents of air ; he is to recline on his left side, and in an hour the enema will operate.

If the enema does not operate properly, it will diminish the internal heat, increase the urine, and will not purify the body. It first discharges the dejections, the bile, phlegm and air. In this manner it purifies the body.

Injections by the urethra (uttaravastí).—These should be used by a tube fourteen fingers' breath in length, or the length of the penis, with an opening of the size to allow a mustard seed to pass. For the female the tube should be four fingers' breath in length and the opening capable of allowing the passage of a small pea (mudga). For young girls the tube should be two fingers' breath in length. The tube should be covered with oil and gently introduced, and by pressing the bladder fixed at one extremity ; crosses should be fixed on the tube to prevent its being introduced too far. The injection should be two tolás in size. These injections are used for diseases of the semen, the bladder and the uterus.

When there is a burning in the bladder, an injection of honey, sugar, or a decoction of liquorice and cold water is given. In some cases injections of ghee are used ; and in others astringent injections, such as decoctions of the bark of the vaṭa tree (ficus indica) and banian tree.

After the introduction of the injection the patient should take liquid food such as barley water, congee or animal broths.

After the evacuation by purgatives, emetics, enemata, or blood-letting the patient is left with the internal fire diminished, and on that account heavy food should be diminished still more—and light and nourishing food should be taken.

4.—*Errhines.*

This is a large class of local irritants ; and they are used with the intention of producing sneezing and exciting a discharge from the nostrils, by which the head is supposed to be cleared from the presence of bad humours.

There are five varieties of fumes used as errhines :—

1.—*Prayojika,* or those forms of smoke which are taken by the nostrils at three efforts. For this purpose different spices are made into a powder, and a tube twelve fingers breadth in length, its size of the small finger, and to taper to the end which should be the size of the thumb. The aperture should be the size of a (Kobo) or small pea ; for eight fingers the tube is to be surrounded with silk cloth, over which the medicine is rubbed. The candle thus prepared is to be set fire to, and the fumes are to be drawn into the nostrils.

2.—*Snaihika,* are prepared by oily substances. They are made with wax—different gums, such as gaguli (gum resin) with ghee. This is to be lighted and the fumes are to be introduced into the nostril.

3.—*Varechanika,* those which clear the head. They are made with medicines which irritate the nostrils, such as black pepper, long pepper, and *Aguru* a kind of fragrant wood. They are to be made into a paste, with which the tube is to be covered and then lighted. The fumes produce the effect desired.

4.—*Vámaníya,* which cause vomiting. They are found by burning the skin and hair of animals—dry fish and flesh, and other substances which produce vomiting. The smoke should be taken in first by the mouth and evacuated through the nostrils, and when taken by the nostrils it should be passed through the mouth.

These are the usual forms in which expectorants are given for promoting the secretion of the nervous membrane of the glottis, trachea, and air cells of the lungs. These are rarely used. In diseases of the throat and chest the smoke is to be taken by the mouth, and by the nose for those of the head, nose and eyes.

Káshaghna, which cures cough. The usual manner of exhibiting it is prepared with medicines which cure the cough, such as,

Vrihatí (Solanum melongena).
Kanṭakáriká (Solanum jacquini).
Long pepper.
Black pepper.
Dry ginger.

The root of the Kankataka Shringhí.

The proper errhines are five :

1.—*Nasya,* is prepared with ghee, oil, and decoctions of vegetable errhines. It is usually used in diseases above the neck, from derangements of the air and bile.

2.—*Shiroveshaníya,* is prepared with medicines which clear the head of pent up humours—accompanied with weight and pain of the head. This form is likewise used in diseases of the throat particularly swelling—when worms infest the head and nose, in jaundice, in polypus of the nose—when the person can neither distinguish taste nor smell ; oily substances are usually employed. It is used in diseases of the mouth, eye, and ear, caused by derangements of the phlegm.

3.—*Pratimarsha*, is prepared with those errhines which clear the head, and is used in the form of powder. It is used in health in the following cases,—after waking from sleep, after fatigue, eating both in the morning and evening. This medicine cures diseases above the neck and retards the marks of old age.

4.—*Avapira* is prepared with sugar, the juice of the sugar cane, milk, ghee and animal broths, and those errhines which clear the head. It is used for diseases of the heart, as in fainting—for weak and delicate persons.

5.—*Pradamna* is prepared with those medicines which clear the head in the form of powder, and is introduced into the nostrils by means of a tube. It is used in epilepsy, apoplexy and other diseases producing a loss of sense.

When phlegm is deranged the errhines are to be given in the morning ; when bile, at noon ; and when the air is deranged, in the evening.

Errhines should not be employed in Raktapitta, Virakti, after emetics and purgatives, in swelling of the abdomen (Udara) in involuntary discharges of the semen, in sudden blindness and when the air is deranged, after eating much food, or drinking wine, after poisons, wounds or injuries of the head, in jaundice, when the person cannot sleep, and when very thirsty.

Errhines for clearing the head of humours.

The following is the list of medicines used as *errhines* to clear the head :—

Sanscrit.	*Scientific and other names.*
1. *Pippali*,	Long pepper.
2. *Viranga ?*	A vegetable and medicinal substance,
3. *Apangaka*,	Achryanthes aspera.
4. *Shigru*,	Morunga guilandina and hyperanthera.
5. *Siddhárthaka*,	White mustard.
6. *Shirísha*,	Acacia sirisa.
7. *Marícha*,	Pepper.
8. *Karavíra*,	Oleander or Nerium odorum.
9. *Vimbí*,	Momordica monadelpha.

Sanscrit.	*Scientific and other names.*
10. *Girikarniká,*	Hedysarum alhaji.
11. *Kinihí,*	Achyranthes aspera.
12. *Vacha,*	Orris root.
13. *Jalashúli,*	Halicacabum cardiospermum.
14. *Karanja,*	Galedupa arborea.
15. *Lashuna,*	Garlick.
16. *Ativisha,*	Atis or Betula.
17. *Shunṭhí,*	Ginger.
18. *Talísha,*	Flacourtia catáphracta.
29. *Tamála,*	Xanthochymus pictorius.
20. *Surásarjaka,*	
21. *Ingudí,*	Name of a plant called Ingua.
22. *Mesha,*	A sort of small cardamum.
23. *Sangí,*	Betula Bhoorja.
24. *Mátulunga,*	Citrus medica.
25. *Murangí,*	Hyperanthera morunga ?
26. *Phalí,*	Blossom of the Sacharum Sara.
27. *Jati,*	Phyllanthus emblica.
28. *Shála,*	Ophiocephalus ?
39. *Tála,*	Borassus flabelliformis.
30. *Madhuka,*	Bassia latifolia.
31. *Lákshá,*	Shell Lac.
32. *Hingu,*	Assafœtida.

Sores are frequently recommended to be fumigated. For this purpose a tube is used eight fingers' breadth in length and the fumes of the medicine are to be conveyed so as to be brought into contact with the surface of the sores.

Gargles. The quantity should be such as can be moved in the mouth. The patient should stand erect. He should attend to what he is doing, and when it is mixed with the bad humours of the mouth nose or eyes, it is to be evacuated and another portion is to be taken into the mouth. Gargles usually consist of astringent decoctions with honey or urine of cows, or the juice of acid fruits, black pepper, long pepper, dry ginger, vacha, mustard, harítakí raví balm, mixed with oil, vinegar, wine, cow's urine, salt or honey, according to the disease, &c. They may be used either hot or cold, and when properly employed they cure diseases of the mouth, clear it and produce easiness of the part.

6.—*Emmenagogues.* The remedies for restoring or bringing on the menstrual discharge are vinegar and acids, cow's urine, curdled milk, khito (a kind of pea), cow's nrine and wine.

These medicines are not often used, and as the irregularities are often produced by weakness, tonics are frequently given.

7.—*Diuretics*. This class of medicines are used in strangury, in pain of the bladder, in scanty urine and in gravel and stone. The Principal of these medicines are :—

Virataru,	Barleria longifolia.
Sahachara,	Yellow Barleria.
Darbha,	Poa Cynosuroides.
Lavang,	Nutmeg.
Kusha,	Plant called maŭkáṭha
Kásha,	Saccharum spontaneum.
Ashwavedhaka,	Plectranthus sculellaroides.
Agnimantha,	Premna spinosa.
Vasuka,	Sesbana graudiflore.
Vasira,	Pothos officinalis.
Ikshu.	Sugar-cane.

These medicines are either used in decoction or in powder. For this purpose the following decoctions are used with honey and sugar. Take equal quantities of :

Mahásáhá,
Kshudrasáhá,
Madhuka,
Sadanstra.

Two tolás of the mixture are to be infused in a pint of water, which is to be put on the fire until reduced to one quarter, when it is prepared.

Parturifacients.—Medicines for promoting the expulsion of the fœtus from the womb were not known by the Hindu practitioners. In cases of lingering labor, manipulation (mantha) was employed to promote delivery.

Sialogogues. Medicines for increasing the secretion from the mouth when too dry, are often had recourse to for expelling morbid humours from its neighbourhood. They should never be used before the 5th year. The medicines which are considered as belonging to this class are ; calomel, (rasavása) and corrosive sublimate, (rasakarpúra). The other medicines of this class are black and long pepper, dry ginger, rock salt, acid fruits, *Vacha* and other hot spices.

External agents stimulating the vital powers. These act either externally or internally.

The external agents are those that produce a determination of blood to the part ; 2nd, a secretion of semen ; and 3rd the formation of pustules. The following are generally used :—

Chitraka,	Plumbago.
A'khanda,	Asclepias.
Sarshapa,	Mustard.
Pútikíṭa,	A kind of blistering fly.
Shobhanjana,	Hyperanthera Morunga.
A'rdraka,	Fresh ginger.

These substances are made into a paste and applied over the part.

Local and internal stimulants.—Carminatives, or those agents which stimulate the stomach and intestinal tract, and lead to the expulsion of flatulence. This numerous class of medicines have already been enumerated, under the head of Aliments. The medicines (pipaládi) are :

Pippalí,	Long pepper.
Chavi,	A variety of pepper.
Chitraka,	Plumbago.
Shringavera,	Fresh ginger.
Amlavetasa,	Rumex vesicarius.
Maricha.	Black pepper.
A'shwamodaka,	Common canary seeds.
Valátaka,	Seed of Marking-nu plant.
Hingu,	Assafœtida.
Jíraka,	Cardamum seed.

These medicines are used in powder or decoction with or without other articles.

The astringents are used for curing diarrhœa and dysentery, and another kind of astringent tonics are of use for the cure of ulcers and for stopping hœmorrhage ; the principal are :—

Priyanga,	Panicum italicum.
Samagá,	Lycopodium imbricatum.
Dhátakí,	Grislea tomentosa.
Punnága,	Rottlera tinctoria.
Raktachandana,	Red sandlewood.
Matrarasa,	A kind of kino gum.
Rasánjana,	Sulphuret of antimony.
Padmaka,	A kind of fragrant wood.
Rejanavulí,	Menispermum glabrum.

For ulcers and stopping hœmorrhage the following medicines are used :—

Nyagrodha,	Ficus indica.
Uḍumbara,	Ficus glomerata.
Ashwattha,	Ficus religiosa.
Plaksha,	Ficus infectoria.
Madhuka,	Liquorice root.

Kakubh,	Pentaptera Arjuna.
Ámra,	Mangoe tree.
Jambu,	Rose apple.
Madhuka,	Bassia latifolia.
Vanjula,	Dalbergia ougeinensis.
Tinduka,	Diospyros glutinosa.
Rodhra,	Symplocos racemosa.

The barks of other trees are used in the form of decoctions or powders.

13. *Alteratives (Rasáyana),* are medicines which increase strength and remove diseases. These medicines must be varied according as they are to be administered to the young, the adult, and the old. It is only to the two latter that this class of medicine is to be administered; and before giving it, an emetic or a purgative should be administered; as a cloth should first be cleaned before it is dried. There are four kinds of Rasáyana. The first promote pleasure; the second cure diseases; the third increase memory and longevity; and the fourth prevent the usual changes of life, such as age, thirst, hunger, and other wants. 1. Cold water, milk, honey, and ghee may be taken internally, together or separately, to restore a proper degree of strength to the body. 2. Another kind of *Rasáyana* increases the memory, and the person's life. Various remedies are recommended for this purpose, as the fruits of Sítá and Avalguja. They are to be powdered and mixed with sugar, kept in a vessel for seven days, and then used with cold water. During this treatment the person should reside in a close room, and continue this medicine for six months. He should only use rice, milk, and sugar for food, and bathe in cold water towards evening. His memory will thus be improved and he may live for a hundred years. This plan of treatment may be adopted in leprosy and dropsy, with the addition of cow's urine instead of water. With this medicine the juice of the *mandúkaparní* is used, after which milk should be taken, and barley, rice, jesimin, and ghee exhibited for three months. 3. Another kind, retains the person young, prevents the hair turning gray, and the teeth from falling out. If a man use cold water, milk, honey, and ghee separately, or together, he will not soon have the marks of old age. For the same purpose other medicines are recommended. 4. There is a medicine called *Soma* which produces longevity, and removes the marks of age. There are many varieties, but none are now known, as sinful persons are often in sight. Numerous other medicines of this class are used for increasing the pleasure of the society of women. These are nutritious diet, such as ghee

and animal food. Of this class is considered good food and drink, good news, anointing the body, especially towards the full moon, the presence of young women, love songs, clear nights, betel-nut, wine, flowers, such as garlands round the neck, sweet smells, beautiful gardens, and a fine prospect. The powder of *Vidára* with ghee and honey, and also the powder of Ámalaka with sugar, honey and ghee, the flower of barley, &c., with milk and the seeds of Átmagupta increase the person's happiness, and his desires. These desires will be diminished—when they are against the heart, when the inclination is wanting, when much bitter, hot, salt, or sour articles of food are eaten, which diminish the (dhátu) and desire. In like manner desire will be removed by its abuse, certain diseases of the external organs, and the division of the vessels. Some cure their desires through the influence of the mind, as holy fakírs did; and another class of persons are born without such carnal desires.

14. *Oleaginous applications,* (*Sneha,*) such as oil, ghee, fat, &c., may be given by the mouth as a laxative, as an errhine, as an enema, or for anointing the body, or as injections for the ear and urethra, and with food. There are two kinds, vegetable and animal oils. Of the latter cow's ghee is the best—and tel (sesamum seed oil) is the best kind of medicine of the vegetable variety. Some of this class of medicines are digested with difficulty, others with less difficulty, and a third kind easily.

Ghee is good for weak persons who have a bad memory, who are affected with poison, and in diseases of air and bile. Oil is to be used externally, but it may be given internally in cases of worms, and in costiveness. Warm water should be taken after the oleaginous substances.

15. *Agents* acting by depressing the vital powers are *Refrigerants,* such as cold infusions both internally and externally. Fire is also used. *Narcotics.*—Very few narcotics were stated in the ancient works, Sidi, (ganja, bháng) obtained from the hemp, was used, as also Dátura.

16. *Chemical Agents.*—These medicines are 1st, Escharotics and caustics. 2d, *Lithontriptics* or solvents of urinary stones or gravel. The escharotics and caustics will be considered under the next chapter on Surgery.

Lithontriptics are sometimes employed. For this purpose the usual diuretics are exhibited, particularly *Arjuna,* (Pentaptera Arjuna,) and *Ashwavedaka,* (Plectranthus scutellaroides, Roxb.)

When administered by an ignorant person medicine is compared to poison, is like the knife, fire, or lightning; but when administered with the necessary knowledge, medicine is like *Amrita* or the water of immortality. There are said to be two kinds of medicine, one of which gives strength to the body when no disease is present, and another class cures diseases when they are present. In like manner poison may be administered in the proper manner with great advantage in the cure of disease.

CHAPTER IV.

Surgery, (Shala.)*

The frequent accidents which must have occurred among a race of people devoted to hunting and agriculture, and the feuds that were so frequent among them, induced the Hindu sages to pay attention to wounds, fractures, and dislocations. In this manner, we explain the importance which the ancient writers of the Hindú system of medicine give to this branch of the healing art, and the attention which they bestowed upon it. These remarks prove that at a very remote period of their History, the Hindu practitioners were accustomed to perform lithotomy, the extraction of the dead fœtus, paracentesis, thoracis and abdominis, &c. This proves the extent of their practical knowledge, and the energy and boldnesss in executing hazardous operations which distinguished their ancient surgeons, and forms such a remarkable contrast to the present ignorant and timorous Surgeons of Bengal. This is the more remarkable as these treatises were supposed to be written by *munis* or divine sages, who would not compromise their character by recording precepts utterly contrary to the ritual of their law, or at variance with the principles and prejudices of their countrymen. Indeed, these precepts are often completely irreconcileable with their present notions, which must be considered as slowly growing out of the altered state of society, and are unsupported by their venerable ancient, and most remarkable civil and moral as well as medical institutions.

According to the Hindu Shastras diseases are cured by the influence of prayers and medicines; and when these are ineffectual it is necessary to have recourse to the knife or other such means. According to the shastras, surgery, therefore, may be defined to be that branch of Medicine which principally effects the cure of dis-

* To remove rapidly; or the art of removing foreign substances from the body, particularly the arrow.

eases by the application of the hand alone, the employment of instruments, or the the use of topical applications.

At the great battle of the Asuras and Devatás, Jagya was severely wounded in the neck, and the Aswiní Kumára, or the practitioners of heaven, soon cured the wound. This pleased the devatás so much that they were received among them with much respect, and a share of their honors is still bestowed upon them. Bramhá also declared that the art of cutting, healing ulcers, setting bones, and the use of escharotics, was the first branch of the healing art imparted by the deity to mankind; and as the operations of Surgery are rapidly performed, and afford immediate relief, they impart holiness, riches, and a good name to the performer, and will ensure his passage to heaven after death.

In the Ayur Veda, Surgery is considered as the first of the eight departments of the Medical Science; and Dhanwantari was born to teach this as well as the other departments. He declares, indeed, that surgery cannot be practised with success unless the practitioner is familiar with the practice of medicine of which it is only a branch.

The following remarks on Surgery will be considered, under the heads of:—

1st. The structure of the body, and their natural and relative positions, so as to enable the Surgeon successfully to perform operations.

2nd. The nature of surgical diseases; including inflammation, ulceration, and fistula.

3rd. Description of Surgical instruments and bandages.

4th. The means of removing blood from the body, including cupping, leeches, and scarifications.

5th. Styptics.

6th. Caustics, actual and potential.

7th. Burns and scalds.

8th. Directions for performing operations, for removing foreign substances from the body, and for treating wounds.

9th. The means of improving, and of forming new ears and nose.

10th. Of fractures and of their treatment.

11th. Of dislocations and their treatment.

Section I.

The importance of having a knowledge of Anatomy in those who exercise this branch of the healing art, is so evident; and has been already noted so fully, that it will be sufficient to refer to page 42 for the Hindus' knowledge on this interesting subject.

Section II.

Nature of diseases which are to be cured by Surgical means.

Inflammation (Vrana*, shotha, or shopha). Saraswata divides inflammation into two kinds, the one produced by accidents or external injuries; and the other by internal causes. Injuries of the body produce the first kind of inflammation, while derangements of the air, bile, phlegm and blood or their combinations produce the second variety.

Under the class of accidental inflammations, swellings of all kinds will be considered, as they always commence with a certain degree of inflammation.

The essential symptom of Inflammation is pus, and the peculiar symptoms are produced by the humour that is affected. In all cases the inflammation commences in one point, from which it extends on all sides. The varieties of inflammation are produced—

a. By diseased air.

b. By deranged bile.

c. By deranged phlegm.

d. By the derangement of air, bile, and phlegm.

e. By deranged blood, and

f. By external or accidental causes

a. The variety of inflammation produced by derangements in the air, is characterized by the swelling being irregular and soft, by its red or dark colour, and from its being sometimes large and at other times small. The pain of this variety is sometimes severe, and of various kinds, and it swells and ripens in different ways, the discharge being limpid.

b. The second variety of inflammation, produced by deranged Bile, is characterized by the swelling being of a dark red yellowish colour, or the colour of a ripe wild fig. The part feels hot and painful like the application of a hot iron, and it is accompanied with fever. The swelling quickly forms and ripens into a yellow discharge.

c. When the inflammation is produced by diseased phlegm the swelling is elevated with round edges, with a central depression. It is cold and shining, of a pale yellow colour, with itching pain. The swelling slowly forms and ripens. The discharge from the deranged phlegm is white.

d. When the three humours are deranged, the swelling is of

* Vrana differs from shotha by its being accompanied with less inflammation, and by its not suppurating.

different colours and is accompanied with various degrees and kinds of pain, according as the one or other of the humours predominate, and the discharges are of different colours, but generally resembles bile and blood, being red, black and yellow, and of various consistencies. This variety is cured with difficulty ; it is large ; sometimes forms quickly, in other cases slowly. Sometimes it becomes prominent as it ripens, at other times it remains flat.

e. When blood is deranged, producing inflammation, the swelling resembles that produced by deranged bile, but is of a darker red colour. When large it has a dark yellow colour ; and is very hot and painful with much fever.

f. Accidental inflammation, produced by wounds, bruises, &c., resembles the other varieties in the symptoms, and only varies in the treatment, by cold applications being proper in this class, but not in the other. When the blood is deranged in this variety, it resembles bile, but is of a darker red colour. When air, bile and phlegm are much deranged, the swelling will be incurable but will suppurate, as also when the physician does not apply proper medicines. When such a patient does not eat or act in the proper manner the wound will not heal. By the wound of a part the air is deranged producing pain, and the blood of the part becomes mixed with the bile of the part and becomes deranged. In this manner, pain, fever, thirst and heat of the body occurs, followed by the other symptoms of deranged bile.

Inflammation is likewise divided into three stages, the invasion, the acute, and the suppurating stage. In the first there is not much heat nor discoloration, or hardness of the part. The pain and swelling of the part is likewise slight. In this stage the inflammation is said to be, *A'ma* (unripe). In the second stage the pain is lancinating, or like the bites of ants, or as if they were running about. In other cases, the person feels as if the part was burnt, torn, pressed or bound ; the person becomes restless and uneasy, and the swelling is much increased and discoloured, accompanied with much heat, thirst, loss of appetite, and other symptoms of fever. This stage is called *pachamâna* (ripening stage). The third stage is distinguished by the part becoming pale, the swelling diminishing, becoming soft and wrinkled, and the skin becoming rough, scaly and elastic. The pain becomes throbbing, with a feeling of itchiness ; the abscess opens, the fever diminishes and the appetite returns This stage is called *pakwa* or ripe.

This pus is produced by the air, bile, and phlegm, the bile preparing the pus from the blood. In inflammation the air produces the pain, and the bile ripens the swelling.

The inflammation varies with the tissue which is involved in the disease, of which there are eight varieties, according as it affects the skin, flesh, vessels, tendons, bones, joints, abdomen, and sensible parts of the body. When confined to the skin, inflammation is cured quickly ; but when it affects the other tissues, it is cured with more difficulty and passes through the different stages.

The air, bile and phlegm when deranged produce inflammation, which will vary in its effects according to the part which is affected. When it affects the abdomen, it produces gulma, &c., with a puffiness of the abdomen, which resembles the white ant's nest. Such inflammation and swelling may also occur at the anus, pelvis, or penis ; at the navel or sides, in the groin, mammæ, or spleen, in the liver, pancreas, or the organ of thirst. This internal inflammation varies in the same manner as the external does. When the former occurs in the anus it retains the air in the pelvis, and urine is secreted in small quantities and with pain. When it occurs at the navel there is a hiccough, and a gurgling noise. When the sides are so affected, it is from diseased air ; and when the groin is so affected, the loins and back feel very painful. When the breast is so diseased, the person remains doubled up, and respiration is performed with difficulty and pain. When the spleen is diseased, and when the breasts are affected, the whole body is uneasy, and feels painful ; and in the latter disease there is a copious secretion of phlegm. When the liver is affected with inflammation, it produces noise in the breathing, with hiccough ; and when the pancreas is so diseased, the person is continually wanting to drink.

When the inflammation occurs in sensible parts, whether the disease be recent or ripe, whether it be large or small, it gives great pain. When the internal inflammation is above the navel, the pus will be discharged by the mouth ; and when under this, by the lower outlets. In this case the person will live, but in the former he will die.

When the breast, navel, or pelvis is diseased the person will die when it suppurates internally ; but he may recover when the abscess bursts externally. The first five varieties of inflammation may be cured ; but when produced by air, bile, and phlegm the disease is incurable. In all cases of inflammation when it is accompanied with the symptoms of *Shotha,* such as swelling of the abdomen, discharge of pus or blood, vomiting, hiccough, thirst, painful and sonorous respiration, the fatal result may be expected.

It is of much importance that the Surgeon should be able to detect the stage of the inflammation ; as if the opening be made before the swelling is ripe, or if it is not opened when ripe, bad consequences will follow in either case. In such cases the Surgeon will be known from the quack. This fellow by opening the unripe inflammation, cuts into blood vessels, tendons, &c., accompanied with a great discharge of blood, or followed by a great accession of pain : again, if the inflamed swelling is not opened when ripe, the pus buries itself in the neighbouring parts, forming large cavities, or fistulous openings, which are cured with difficulty. In such cases, the pus, like fire, burns the surrounding parts, which like fuel are consumed.

In the generality of cases of inflammation, (Brana, Shotha) the cure will be soon accomplished ; but if injudiciously treated it will be tedious. The inflammation is of an unfavourable kind when large, when not prominent but shrivelled, when hard or when very soft, when very prominent or when very dark, when very cold or very hot, when of a black, yellow, red, or white colour, when it has an unhealthy disagreeable appearance. It is also unfavourable when the pus is in large quantities, when the muscles, vessels and tendons are numerous in the part ; when the discharge has a fœtid smell and has fibrous substances mixed up with it, when the swelling is large, or there are numerous small swellings, when bad blood is evacuated and when the patient is very old.

The general indications to be followed in the cure of common inflammation are, the use of sedatives, local bleeding, poultices, opening the abscess, cleaning it, healing the breach of continuity, and lastly restoring the natural colour to the part. Sushruta describes sixty different indications to be employed in the cure of inflammation and ulcers, such as, rubbing and anointing the part with certain medicines that dry it up*, pouring water upon the part, fomentations, frictions with ghee, poultices with maturating substances, with the observance of spare diet, emetics and purgatives, &c. There are eight kinds of incisions which are to be used for the evacuation of the pus and blood ; also means to promote adhesion, as pressure, stopping the bleeding, diminishing the heat, the application of thick poultices and astringents, the application of lints covered with medicinal pastes, the use of oil, the juice of certain plants, the application of certain powders to the ulcers, fumigation, means to depress elevation, and to increase or diminish the hardness of particular parts, and the application of caustic and cauteries. The last consideration is to restore the natural colour to the

* Medicine supposed to pass internally by the roots of the hair and the perspiring pores.

part, to restore or remove hair, the employment of enemas, of bandages, of certain leaves to the ulcers, the means to destroy worms, the use of tonics, of errhines, of gargles, of fumigations, and of regimen.

A few remarks will now be added on some of the above subjects. For maturing a swelling, the best medicines are several dangerous barks and roots, linseed, carrots, the seeds of (surunga) the morunga tree; of mustard seed, the flowers of surávíjaz, and the sediment or lees of a kind of beer or spirit. These are all to be combined with heat. When the patient objects to the ripe inflammation being opened with the lancet, the following medicines may be applied, the flower of the marking nut (balá); the leaves of the castor poleandrum (dantí), the leaves of the lombago Zeylanica (chitra) or of the Nerium odorum (corbeer). Pigeons or adjutants dung is also recommended, and various escharotic substances.

Old ghee slightly heated is to be applied to the part, and the food should be thin and light with the flesh of wild animals, light boiled vegetables mixed with oil and salt. The drink should consist of boiled water.

The opening of an abscess should be made when the swelling is soft, without pain, is undefined and of the colour of the skin. A lancet should be used, which is immediately to be withdrawn when the pus is seen. In performing such an operation care should be taken to avoid the vital parts, large vessels and tendons. When the abscess is large, the opening should be the length of two fingers breadth. When the abscess is prominent, oblong and large it will soon be cured, and in order that the operation be properly performed the surgeon should possess the following qualities:—boldness, steadiness, presence of mind, quickness, and should possess a good instrument. Should a fistula exist with the inflammation it should be opened. In the following parts of the body the incisions should be oblique, as in the eyebrows, cheeks, temples, forehead, eyelids, lips, gums, axilla, and groins. In the sole of the feet and palms of the hands the incisions should be circular, and in the arms and penis cruciform incisions should be made. It will prevent the wounding of nerves and vessels. After the opening has been made the patients face is to be bathed with cold water, and he should be encouraged by kind language. The abscess is to be evacuated by pressure, and it is to be cleaned with a piece of cloth wet in warm and astringent water. A lint made of a piece of rolled cloth and covered with a paste made of teel seeds, honey and ghee. A pledget of cloth covered with a simple soothing ointment is to be put over the wounded part, with a poultice and bandage. The prescribed prayers are then to be repeated over the patient; and he is then to be removed to a well aired, though sheltered room, and placed in a large bed, with his head turned to the east, the residence of the gods, and is to be surrounded by cheerful friends. Directions are next to be given as to his diet and regimen. Great care is to be taken to keep the patient clean. The wound is to be dressed on the third day, and care is to be taken not to allow the wound to heal too soon. After it has been healed, the patient is to take care not to use indigestible food, he is also to avoid violent exercise, such as running, until the cicatrization is complete. In dangerous cases the abscess will often require to be dressed twice a day, as it in such cases resembles a house on fire that requires prompt assistance.

A person with this disease should avoid new rice, heavy pulse, hot, heavy, bitter salt and sour articles of food, with dried flesh, and vegetables. In all cases the patient should be recommended to avoid spirituous liquids, to eat little and regularly, and sleep at night the usual time.

Ulcers (Bruno.)

Ulcers are either produced from exterior or internal causes. There are fifteen varieties, some say sixteen. Each of the humours or a couple of the humours, then the three humours deranged at the same time, or when combined with deranged blood, produce such ulcers. There is another kind called a healthy ulcer (Sudo Bruno) which is characterized by having a smooth and equal surface, being soft, accompanied with little pain and without any discharge.

When the ulcer is produced by deranged air (biu) it is characterized by its black or red appearance, it is superficial, and discharges a cold, mucilaginous and scanty discharge. The pain is also peculiar, being of a crackling stiff kind. This pain is severe and does not affect the flesh.

When deranged *Bile* produces an ulcer, it is of a yellowish blue colour, and is surrounded by a red colour and yellow eruptions, spreads quickly, and discharges a hot and red matter with a burning pain.

The *Phlegm* ; when it produces an ulcer, there is much itchiness, and it is deep seated. The vessels and nerves of the part are affected, and it is hard and white without much pain, and the discharge is white, cold, mucilaginous and thick. The part feels heavy.

When produced by *Blood* ; the ulcer becomes red and is surrounded by black vessels. The smell is like that of a horse stable ; with much pain, great heat, and it discharges blood and is accompanied with symptoms of bile.

The ulcers which are produced by the combination of the decreased humours partake of the combination of the peculiar symptoms of each.

The ulcers are likewise divided into large extent of ulcer, large deep seated, very hard and soft, much elevated or depressed, very cold or hot, very black, red, yellow or white, or disagreeable looking ulcers, or covered with a slough, with a fœtid discharge, very painful or bloody discharge, or very old ; all these are unfavorable cases of ulcer. When the discharge is yellow, thin and has the smell of raw flesh it is superficial. When the ulcer is situated in the flesh, the discharge is thick, only white and mucilaginous. From vessels, the discharge is with much blood and it is also watery with much purulent matter. When bones are affected ; the discharge is mixed with oily matter and blood, when in the joints they cannot be moved, and the discharge is mucilaginous, frothy and bloody. When any of the viscera are affected ; the discharge may be accompanied with urine or feces, or a watery discharge.

Treatment of ulcers. The cure of ulcers is easy when treated by a skilful practitioner, and when the patient follows the proper regimen. When treated by an ignorant person, or if the patient does not follow the proper regimen, the cure will be much more difficult. The person should live in a large airy and clean house, upon a large bed with his head towards the east ; he should be encouraged by the presence and attention of friends ; he should not sleep during the day, as it will produce much swelling, and a copious discharge with itchiness. He should avoid much walking and the presence of women. He should avoid new wine, different kinds of peas, and fruits, too much salt, pungent articles, jagree, cakes, dry vegetables, and the flesh of fish and amphibious animals, cold water is likewise to be avoided, with curdled milk and indigestable food. He should avoid exposure to wind and dust, smoke, too much eating, and disagreeable sounds or smells. He should avoid watching at night, and eating at unusual hours. He should keep his hair, beard and nails short, wear clean clothes, and perform the usual ceremonies of religion, and his food should be light and nourishing.

The ulcers are to be dressed with a cloth covered with new ointment, and secured by a bandage of silk or cotton. The ulcers are to be cleaned with a watery decoction of cassia fistula and other astringent vegetable medicines. Ghee should be prepared with the sulphate of iron (kaceera), black Hellebore (kotorohunee), turmerick, and the root of the játee. In other cases they add astringent barks or astringents as nimbo, rajbeerka, yellow (Hurrital) and red arsenic (monosillaa), powders prepared with rock salt, the sulphate of iron, and the lees of urine, with boch and turmerick, &c.

Fumigations by means of different rosins, the smoke of which are applied to the ulcers.

Pastes are also applied to the ulcerated surface. They may be made of

Somongaa
Somo
Sorolaa
Somobolko
Chondono
Kaapola, &c.

When the ulcer is much elevated apply the powders of the following substances, sulphate of iron, (*kasus,*) rock salt, red arsenic, mixed with eggshells and the buds of (*jaatee*). These may be combined, or one or two of them may be mixed and applied to the ulcerated surface.

Purgatives, emetics, and fasting are to be occasionally used in ulcers, and the other indications which have been already stated under the head of treatment of inflammation.

Should there be much bleeding from the ulcer it is to be stopped by means of styptics; when accompanied with fever and much burning on the part, apply cold applications; when there is little discharge, the ulcer superficial, and the surface irregular, apply poultices made of seeds containing oil, as linseed, with fomentation. When the appearance is very dark and the smell disagreeable apply astringent decoctions. When sloughing and dry looking, apply medicines to clean the part. When the edges of the ulcer are very hard, local bleeding by scarification or by leeches is to be used with fomentations. When the edges are soft and flabby apply astringents. When the edges are elevated and of long standing apply caustics. When the cicatrix is white it will be made black or of the natural colour by the preparations of the marking nut. For restoring hair to a part apply the ashes of ivory with crude antimony. If worms are generated in ulcers, apply the decoctions of ophiorrhiza mungos (*surubaa*) and Symplocos Alstonia.

When the worms are produced by cows urine and the like, caustic solutions are to be applied. These are obtained from the ashes of certain trees. A piece of recent flesh may also be applied over the ulcer so as to attract the worms to it. When the ulcer is very old and the person emaciated and weak, give him nourishing food, and medicine of a tonic nature. When produced by poison they are to be treated as poisonous wounds.

The intelligent practitioner will vary the local and general treatment according to the peculiarity of each case, and the state of the patients constitution.

The fatal symptoms of ulcers; are, fever, diarrhœa, fainting, hiccough, vomiting, dyspesia, difficulty of breathing, cough and great thirst.

Fistula (*Nulla Bruna*) a fistula is either produced by derangements of the humours, or by external causes. In the latter case the abscess may not be opened when ripe, the pus hurries itself into the neighbouring parts and forms a canal. When derangement of air produces the fistula; the orifice is small, the surface rough, and it is accompanied with much pain. It discharges largely, especially in the night, and the discharge is accompanied with froth. This form is to be treated with poultices.

When the fistula is produced by deranged bile, it is accompanied with thirst, fever, and heat; the discharge is copious particularly during the day. The part is to be carefully rubbed, and when ripe it is to be opened with a knife, it is then to be cleaned, and a hot iron probe is to be introduced into the canal. Several kinds of medicines are to be mixed and thrust into the wound.

When produced by diseased phlegm, the discharge is thick and white, and its edges are hard and shining. It is itchy and slightly painful at night. A mixture of several medicines is made to rub into the part so as to soften it; other medicines are to be employed to wash the fistula with, and a director is to be introduced and the fistula laid open.

When air, bile, and phlegm are deranged, together producing a fistula, it is accompanied with great heat and fever, sonorous breathing and coma. The mouth is dry and the other symptoms peculiar to the diseases produced by the separate humours. In such cases the disease is incurable.

Fistulous openings are usually found in the mammæ of women after abscesses. In such cases the abscess is to be opened and the fistula is to be treated as in Budodu. When the patient is of weak constitution, is emaciated, is fearful, has lost his appetite the cure will be very difficult. When the knife is not allowed to be used; a thread is to be passed through the fistula and is to be strongly tied so as to divide the skin which is contained in it. A lint made of the following medicines will likewise be found very useful. The bark of the *guntafulaa*, rock salt, lac stick, and beetle nut, these are to be mixed with the milk of the euphorbium and introduced into the fistulous opening.

Descriptions of Surgical Instruments and Bandages.

The description of these instruments is neither minute nor precise; and not being illustrated by drawings, or now employed, a few only of each class will be delineated. In general the name of the instrument was derived from the resemblance to certain objects such as certain leaves, &c.

The hand is considered the first, the best, and the most important of all Surgical Instruments, as it is with its assistance that all operations are performed.

There are classes of instruments, one of which are blunt (*jontros*) the second have sharp cutting edges (*sotros*); and the third are named unosustro or substitutes for cutting instruments, such as caustics, fire, horns of animals open at both extremities by which suction is made, and gourds which are used as cupping glasses and are applied before as well as after the scarifications, I shall now add a few remarks on each of those classes.

1st. *Jontros,* or blunt instruments, consist of *Swasteeka, Sandansa, Talajontros, Narujontros, Solaakaa and Upajontros.*

a. *Swusteeka-juntra* are curved or hooked instruments which are used to extract splinters of bones, or foreign bodies, and including pinchers, nippers and the forceps. They are formed of iron, usually eighteen inches long, having heads or points shaped like the heads of animals, the beaks of birds, &c.

b. *Sandansa-juntra,* or tongs, which are of two kinds, one with, and another without a handle, and are used to remove extraneous substances from the soft parts, as the flesh, skin, veins, &c. They are usually sixteen inches in length.

c. *Tala-juntra* resemble, though smaller than the last named instruments; and were employed for removing foreign substances lodged in the outer canals as the ear, nose, &c.

d. *Naru-juntra* consist of twenty varieties of tabular instruments, of different sizes and shapes, according to their intended use, including canulæ, catheters, syringes, &c. They are used for removing extraneous substances from deep seated canals, as the intestines, urethra, &c.; for examining deep seated parts, for the application of other instruments, for drawing off fluids by suction, &c.

e. *Solaakaa* or *Probes* are rods and sounds. There are twenty-eight kinds, varying in size and shape, for extracting foreign matters lodged in parts of difficult access, for clearing internal canals, more particularly the urethra; some have points like a half pea, others like an earth worm or the point of an arrow. Some of them have

See Page 169.

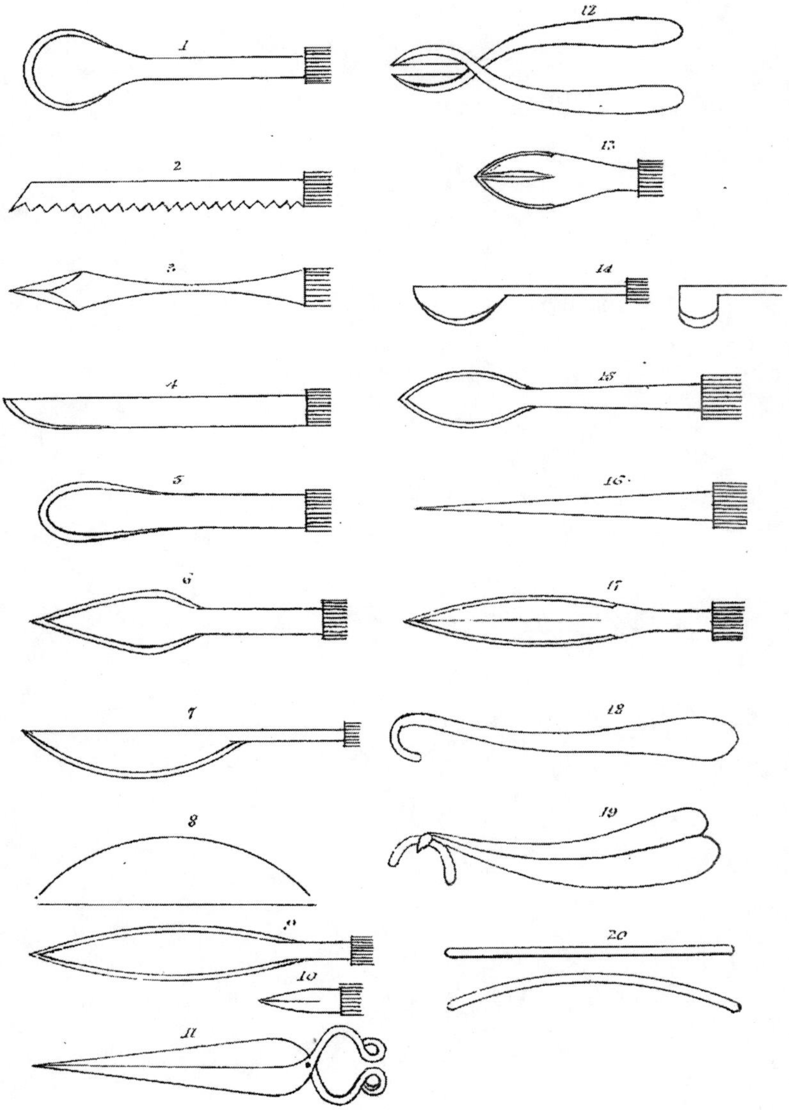

T Black, Asiatic Lith Press. Calcutta.

small cavities at their extremities for applying caustic solutions, &c., to the diseased part. Some of these rods have ends like the rose apple, for applying it heated. There are six varieties of these rods, three resembling the head of a rose apple, and three being hooked. Another instrument, resembles the half of the shell of the plate for eradicating nasal polypi; a frequent and troublesome disease (*nakra*) in many parts of Hindoostan. This disease is alleviated by forcibly extracting the irritating excrescence. Another instrument of this class, has a head like the foot stalk of the *Maleetee* flower. It is used for cleaning the urethra.

f. *Upa-juntros* are accessory instruments, as twine, leather, bark, skin, cloth, loadstone, caustic, fire, finger nails, tongue, teeth, &c.

There are many other instruments which cannot be enumerated, as they are only varieties of the above, modified by experienced surgeons, for particular purposes.

The second class, are cutting instruments (*sotros*), of which there are twenty kinds. These instruments should be formed of good iron, and neither too large, nor too small. They should be well polished, and sufficiently sharp to divide a hair. For this purpose a stone was used. They were in general six inches in length, of which the blade formed a half or a quarter of that length. They should have good handles and firm joints, and be kept quite clean, wrapt in flannel, and kept in a box of sandle wood.

The following are the names of twenty forms of the principle Cutting Instruments used in Surgery:—The supposed forms are represented in the annexed Lithographic Drawing:—

1. *Mondolúgra* or round instrument for scarifying.
2. *Koropotrá*, or Saw.
3. *Beeteeputrá*, or Lancet.
4. *Nokosustrá*, (eight fingers breadth in length.)
5. *Modreeká*, like the first joint of the index finger.
6. *Utpolopotroká*, like the petal of the blue water lily.
7. *Urdodáro*, or Knife.
8. *Suchee*, or Needles.
9. *Kuchápotra*, like the leaves of the kushograss.
10. *Akemoka*, like the beak of a bird.
11. *Soráreemka* or Scissars, (10 fingers breadth in length.)
12. *Untormuko*, to break down (the internal side cutting) parts.
13. *Tricorcoko* (*trocar*), three cutting surfaces.
14. *Kotáreeká*, like a gum lancet or bistoury........ } for tapping.
15. *Breehumoka* or *Trocar*, with a head like a grain of rasi.. } for tapping.

16. *Ará* or *Aul*, a long sharp needle in a handle.... }
17. *Bedusopotraku*, long sharp cutting instrument } for tapping.
like the leaf of the ratan.................................. }

18. *Booreeso*, or hook.

19. *Dontosunku*, pincers for extracting teeth.

20. *Asunee* or *probes*, eight fingers breadth in length.

Those instruments, the length of which is not marked ; are six fingers breadth in length.

Unosustra, are instruments which may be used when cutting instruments are not at hand, or when the patient is too fearful to admit the use of cutting instruments. These are the sharp bark of the bamboos, different kinds of hard stones, or glass, leeches, fire, caustics, nails, rough leaves, such as those of gogee, seefaleeka trees, &c.

Practical Instructions.

After the student has been taught science by books, he is next to be instructed in the practice of the use of the instruments, &c. Without practical skill, theoretical knowledge is of no use. The different surgical operations are to be shown to the student, upon wax spread out upon a board, gourds, cucumbers and other soft fruits. Tapping and puncturing should be practiced on a leather bag of water or soft mud. Scarifications and bleeding may be practiced upon the fresh hides of animals from which the hair has been removed, or upon the dead bodies, and the puncturing or lancing the hollow stalks of water lilies or the vessels of dead animals. The manner of holding and the use of the probe is to be practised upon a piece of hollow bamboo or the like. The removal of substances from cavities, by removing the large seeds of the jack or bêl fruit, and the extraction of teeth is to be practiced upon dead bodies and animals. For sowing he should practice on leather and cloth. The application of bandages and ligatures should be practiced upon flexible models of the human body ; and the means of making noses, ears, &c., be practised upon dead animals ; the application of caustics, and cauteries to be done on animals. The use of injections is to be practised with a water pot having a canal.

There are eight kinds of surgical operations. They are *chedaana* or incision, as in fistula-in-ano.

2. *Bhedno*, opening parts as of large abscesses

3. *Lhekhno*, or drawing lines, by which the parts are nipped, sacrified or innoculated.

4. *Bhedhno,* or puncturing, as opening veins in hydrocele and dropsy.

5. *Eshyno,* to probe or sound parts, as in fistula, to ascertain the presence of foreign substances.

6. *Ahárno,* or the operation of extraction, as of the stone ; of the teeth, and of the fetus.

7. *Vishravâno,* to remove fluids ; as pus, blood, &c., or of bad humours as in Leprous blotches in Elephantiasis, &c.

8. *Seebeeno,* to sow parts together, as in wounds, especially near joints. The substances to be used for sowing are thread, twine, or small ligatures made of the skin of animals, or fibres of vegetable substances, roots, hair, &c. The stitches are to be longer or shorter according to the nature of the wound. Before sowing a wound it should be carefully cleaned, and all extraneous substances should be removed. The needle should be from two fingers breadth in length, to three or more. They are to be long, three edged for deep fleshy wounds, and a third or curved kind should be used in vital parts and in wounds of the scrotum and abdomen. For fixing a torn off ear ! the parts are to be brought together and sown. For practising these operations ; pieces of leather and cloth are to be sewn together. After a wound has been sewn, a mixture of equal parts of the seed of the preunga ; *unguno,* (sulphate of antimony,) *justaabo* (liquorice) and *lodro* (an astringent bark) is to be thickly sprinkled round the wound, which is then to be covered with a piece of lint or silk cloth, and the whole secured with a bandage. The physician is then to give proper directions as to diet, &c.

Besides the above instruments, the surgeon should provide thread, leaves, pledgets, heated metallic plates for erubescents, and a variety of astringent and emollient applications before commencing an operation.

Bandages.

There are fourteen kinds of Bandages :—

1st. *Koosa,* or a hollow cylinder or sheath for the fingers, penis, &c.

2nd. *Dáma,* a large bandage to support parts.

3rd. *Susteeko,* a circular bandage to apply to joints, forehead, chest and under the ears.

4th. *Uneebuluta,* a roller or bandage to encircle the extremities, &c.

5th. *Protobe,* a broad bandage for the neck, and the external organs of generation.

v 2

6th. *Mondola*, a circular bandage for the head.

7th. *Stogheekà*, a bandage enclosing a splint to keep the parts firm, as the joints of the fingers, the penis, &c.

8th. *Gomoka*, a double bandage which is applied to ulcers.

9th. *Kotá*, a four tailed bandage for the cheeks, temples, lower-jaw, &c.

10th. *Cheena*, a bandage for the angles of the eyes.

11th. *Bebonda*, a bandage for the back, abdomen, and chest. It is a firm circular bandage.

12th. *Beetana*, a large bandage for the head.

13th. *Gopaná*, a concave bandage for the chin, eyes, lips, shoulders, scrotum and pelvis.

14th. *Ponchanghu*, a bandage for the clavicle with four tails.

The surgeon is to decide on the kind of bandage in each particular case. Its application varies with the disease. Sometimes the bandage is to be applied above, below, or upon the wound or ulcer according to the effect required. In general the bandage is to be applied after the application of the necessary ointment spread upon linen. There are three degrees of tightness with which the bandage is to be applied, the first being tight, the second loose, and the third moderately tight. When bile and blood are deranged, or when blows and poisons produce the disease, the bandage should be loosely applied ; and when phlegm and air are deranged the tightness may be increased. In other cases bandages may be applied more tightly. To the chest, buttock, belly, loins, axilla, groins, and head, a tight bandage is to be applied. To the extremities, face, ears, throat, penis, scrotum, back, and to the sides of the belly and chest the pressure of the bandage should be moderate. In diseases of the eye and joints loose bandages are to be used. Should the bandage be applied tight, the medicine will not produce the desired effect, and all the symptoms of the disease will be aggravated. This will also be the case when no bandage is applied, by the formation of insects, and by exposure to the influence of heat and cold, which will aggravate the ulcer, and prevent the cure. When accompanied with acute inflammation, and when the part is hot, painful, and sensible, no bandage is to be applied to the part, for the cure of the disease, but to retain the applications to the part. Nor are bandages to be applied when the sore has been produced by fire, or excoriating, when it contains pus ; when sloughing, or if it is near the anus ; when produced by extravasation of urine from Leprosy, &c. If bones are fractured, or joints dislocated, or if the bone is thrust through the flesh, the bandages will be of much use. This is also the case when the tendons and vessels are divided. In the treatment of ulcers ; bandages and all other means that diminish pain will tend towards the cure.

When the ulcer is in the flesh, skin, joints, bone, abdomen : in wounds of vessels and tendons ; when deep, and when superficial, they are cured with bandages. The judicious surgeon will in each particular case, decide on the propriety and kind of bandages, which will vary not only with the nature of the disease, but also with the season of the year, &c.

Section 4.

Means employed to remove Blood from the body. These operations are venesection, cupping, and the use of leeches.

1st. *Venesection.*

Before a patient is bled, he should have his body anointed with oil ; a warm bath is to be used ; and some prepared barley or rice is to be given to eat.

In performing the operation the patient is to be placed either sitting or standing before the Surgeon with his face turned towards the east, with an assistant holding him from behind. The Surgeon is to rub down the blood in the prominent vein which is to be opened, and apply a bandage of the bark of a tree, of cloth or of leather, not very tight, above the part to be opened ; the instrument used for opening the vein ; is the *kutaarekau,* this is to be thrust into the swelled vein while the patient retains his breath ; the wound should be the size of a barleycorn. The blood should flow in a stream. After the required quantity of blood has been obtained, the bandage is to be removed and the wound is to be cleaned with cold water, a few drops of oil are to be let fall upon the wound, and if the bleeding is not stopped a bandage is to be put round the part. Should this not be sufficient to stop the bleeding ; caustics, and even the actual cautery may be used. The quantity of blood which is to be removed, should never be so large as to weaken the person. When the patient is very strong, and the disease very severe, blood to the extent of one seer (Prusto or Hij) may be removed. If much blood is lost, it will produce headache, loss of sight, with pain in the eyes ; will produce thirst, severe pain, insensibility of one side, and of one member, hiccough, cough, difficulty in breathing, jaundice, and the person may die, or it will produce the diseases of air. After bleeding, the body should be anointed with oil, milk, lymph of animals or other remedies which quickly stop the flow of blood. If all the bad blood is not discharged by the first bleeding, another is to be performed on the second or third day after the first. Do not endeavour to remove all the bad blood by the first bleeding, as a little bad blood may be purified by the use of remedies; and thus the danger of bleeding too freely will be avoided. When a swelling requires to be opened; and from the nature of the part, as when near the windpipe; a communicating vein proceeding from the diseased part may be opened.

Bleeding should not be performed when the person is below 16 and above 70 years of age, when the female is pregnant or soon after delivery, nor when the body is dry; when in a state of drunkenness or when there are sores upon the body; when the humours (datu) are diminished; when there is copious perspirations; or when there are diseases of air present. Patients should not be bled in very cold, hot, or stormy cloudy days; when there is no disease present, when the person is weak, after watching, or when digestion has not taken place. When afflicted with general dropsy, in jaundice, during free perspiration, piles, in madness, after vomiting or purging, in severe fevers, in tetanus, in palsy, &c. When venesection is to be performed, the air should be clear and warm. If possible it should be avoided during the rains; but always the abstraction is to take place by degrees, at the intervals of one or more days according to the circumstances of the case. In the cold weather venesection should be performed in the middle of the day. The flow of the blood from the wound in the vessel may be retarded when the person is very fearful, faint, and much fatigued; when he is very thirsty, when the bandage is not properly applied, and when he has much bad blood.

When the person is bled for a disease of the spleen, the vein is to be opened at the bend of the left arm, or the vein between the left ring and little finger in asthma and severe cough; in disease of the penis open the vessels near the middle of the penis. In hepatic diseases open the temporal artery. In madness and epilepsy, and in diseases of the tongue or teeth, open the veins under the tongue. In tertian ague open the veins at the juncture of the sacrum with the spine. In epilepsy the veins of the neck may also be opened.

There are twenty ways of improperly performing venesection:—

1st. *Durdeeda*, when the instrument is too small, and the blood does not flow freely, followed by a painful swelling.

2nd. *Oteebeda*, when an ignorant person opens a large vessel, or makes the wound in the vein large by which the blood passes among the cellular substances of the part.

3rd. *Chuncheetá*, resembles the last.

4th. *Pitcheetá*, when the knife is blunt and tares the parts, which swell.

5th. *Kuteeka*, when several attempts have been made to open the vein.

6th. *Oprorsreetá*, when the person is fearful, the weather very cold, and the blood is not discharged.

7th. *Otudeerá*, when the knife is large, sharp, and a large wound is made.

8th. *Obeedá*, when little blood flows.

9th. *Poreesuská*, when little blood flows from deranged air which dries the wound.

10th. *Kunteetá*, when the wound is too small, and little blood flows.

11th. *Bateetá*, when the arm had been improperly bandaged, and when the hands shake, and no blood flows.

12th. *Onuteetobeená*, like the last.

13th. *Shostropotá*, when there is a great flow of blood from the large wound in the vessel, which cannot be stopped by the usual applications.

14th. *Tirjokbeedá*, when the wound is not direct, and is not sufficiently large.

15th. *Opobeedá*, when the knife is not a proper one, and several attempts are required to open the vein.

16th. *Obiodeeá*, when blood letting is not proper.

17th. *Bidurdá*, when the patient's body is in an unfit state and diseases are consequently produced.

18th. *Denuká*, when the part requires to be rubbed much before the vein can be opened, and when the blood only flows at intervals, like the milk of cows.

19th. *Punopunorbeedá*, when the knife is too small, and several small wounds are made in the vein.

20th. *Seersoodee*, when nerves, tendons, and vital parts have been wounded, it produces severe pain, restlessness and death. When the operation is thus improperly performed, the wound is to be treated by the application of fomentations, and other remedies, which will be stated in the section treating of wounds.

An able Surgeon is therefore required to bleed, as veins are always changing, and if not properly performed, it produces various troublesome diseases of veins; which are not cured by the usual remedies. It is not enough to know the situation of veins; but he must likewise know the time, and the extent to which the bleeding is to be carried. In some diseases, bleeding is half the treatment;

in the same manner as enemas are in many medical diseases. As cutting, fire, &c., give pain; rajahs, rich people, children or old people, and fearful and weak people, when they require to lose blood, may have leeches in preference to venesection; more especially in the cases of bad blood produced by diseased air, bile and cough. When bad blood has been removed from a vein, the person feels happy, the part light, the pain ceases, and the morbid symptoms diminish.

After bleeding avoid anger, violent exercise, too much sitting, walking, exposure to great heat or cold, or improper food, for a month; especially very heating and cooling articles. The patient should live on good and light articles of nourishing food, until his strength is restored. If this is not attended to, bad blood will be generated.

Bad blood in the body, produces itchiness, swelling and pain like that of fire; with a red appearance of the part which suppurates. When deranged air has produced bad blood; it does not flow from the wound in the vein like water; it is covered with foam, is dark, thin, and draws slowly. When deranged by bile, the blood has a yellow blue colour, has a bad smell, and it dries slowly. When the blood is deranged by phlegm the blood is oleaginous, and smooth; it is cold, of a pale yellowish colour, is in large quantities and flows slowly. When bile and blood are deranged in a part; it has a dark colour. When two or three of the humours are deranged in a part; the blood has the peculiarities of the individual, and deranged blood combined. Should severe pain occur in opening a vein, as if fire had been applied, the part is to be rubbed with warm ghee and *gestemodo* (a plant.)

The blood is in a healthy state when it is of a bright red colour like that of red jelly, or of the rainbow; when the senses are perfect with a desire to exercise them; and the person is strong and in high spirits.

2nd. *Scarifications.* By means of a thin and sharp knife; longitudinal or transverse lines at equal distance are to be made neither very deep nor superficial. They should be applied quickly, avoiding vital parts, joints and large vessels.

3rd. *Cupping.* The local accumulation of bad blood may be removed by means of cupping, which is performed by a horn cut smooth, and even, at the large extremity; with a small opening at the narrow end. The large extremity is applied over the scarified part, the air in the horn is sucked out, and the finger is then dexterously placed over the open upper end. An accumulation of blood in the part included in the horn is discharged from the scarification. The horn is repeatedly applied, and the air exhausted in the same manner, until the necessary quantity of blood has been removed. These horns are made of different sizes, to suit the part which is to be operated on. In other cases a hollow gourd is prepared, with a small smooth hole which is placed on the part; the air is then exhausted by burning something in it, before it is applied over the scarified part. The horn is used when the air of the part is particularly affected; and when the phlegm of the part, is much diseased, the gourd is preferred.

4th. *Leeches* (*Jalouká*). Leeches have been employed from time immemorial in Asia, but particularly in Bengal, where they are considered as the best means of removing blood from a part. They are particularly used for Rajahs, for women, and timid persons, and for the very young and very old.

There are twelve varieties of leeches; six of which are venemous, and six useful.

The venemous leeches are:

1. *Indráyudhá*, having longitudinal lines along its back like a rainbow.

2. *Alagarda*, are large with a black head, and hairs on their body.

3. *Krishná*, are large dark leeches with a large head.

4. *Sámudriká* have numerous stripes and spots of various colours upon their bodies.

5. *Gochandaná* have a small head and narrow mouth with a large body and bifurcated tail.

6. *Karbura*, is long like an eel, and moves irregularly.

These deleterious leeches, when they are employed, produce heat, swelling, pain, and itching of the part; followed by excessive irritation and fever, with spasms, sickness and syncope. These effects will be best treated by applying to the bites a mixture of certain medicines, which are considered as antidotes against the poison, other antidotes are given internally, with errhines; the bites of the Indráyunda leeches are considered fatal. These kinds of leeches are found near putrid fish or animals, in foul, stagnant, and putrescent water. Such leeches are consequently to be carefully avoided.

There are six varieties of good Leeches:—

1. *Kapilá*, or tawny leeches. These have a brownish breast, with smooth glossy sides.

2. *Pingulá*, have round bodies, are of a pale red color, and are very active.

3. *Sankumukhí*, have long sharp heads, are of a liver colour, and bite quickly.

4. *Mushiká,* are of a mouse colour and have a bad smell.

5. *Pundurìká-mukhí,* are of a brown hue, and have a mouth like that of a lily.

6. *Shabarìká,* are of a green colour like the leaves of a water lotus, and are ten fingers breadth long. This kind is only proper for removing blood from animals.

These leeches are found in Persia (*Yavana*), ancient Delhi (*Pandu*), at Mutra (*Pautana*), &c. They are found in small numbers in clear and deep pools of water, which contain water lilies, and are surrounded with sweet smelling plants. The middle sized leeches are the best.

These leeches are to be caught in a piece of leather or cloth, and placed in a new water-pot, in which some clay and pure water has been put, some grass or leaves of aquatic plants are to be placed on the pot for them to lie upon, and the roots of water lilies and dry flesh are to be given them for food. The water is to be changed every third day and the water pot every seventh day.

When the leeches grow very large and are very vigorous; when they are weak, or emaciated, when they do not bite, or take little blood, or are of the venemous kind they are not to be used.

When the part is not very sensible it is to be rubbed dry, and it is then to be covered with cow-dung and earth to dry the part. The leech is then to be taken from the water-pot and its body is to be anointed with mustard seed paste. It is then to be put into a bason with fresh water for a short time and then removed and surrounded with a piece of cloth, and the mouth is then to be applied to the part affected. If it does not fix quickly, apply a drop or two of milk or blood to the part, or make one or two very slight scarifications, which will induce them to fix themselves more readily. When the leeches are sucking, sprinkle a few drops of cold water upon their bodies. When the leeches have removed the necessary quantity of blood sprinkle a small quantity of salt upon their heads, to make them drop off. Put the gorged leech upon some dry bran, put a little oil and salt upon its mouth and then strip them. Put them next in fresh water, and if they are lively they will live, and may be used again; but if they are languid, they will soon die and they should therefore be at once thrown away.

The part upon which the leeches have been is to be smeared with honey, cold water, and astringent substances. In other cases poultices may be applied.

Section V.

Styptics.

If all the bad blood is not removed by the bleeding it will leave a swelling, redness, heat, itchiness, and pain in the part. But if too much blood has been removed it produces headache, blindness (*gutta serena*), inflammation of the eye, convulsions, hemiplegia, great thirst, burning sensation of the body, hiccough, difficulty in breathing, jaundice, and death. Avoid abstracting too much blood, particularly when healthy, as it is the root which sustains the body; "for the blood is the life of the body."

There are four ways of arresting hœmorrhages :—

a. By the use of astringents.

b. By the use of ice (*hima.*)

c. By caustics and

d. By the actual cautery; should the other means not prove sufficient.

a. Astringent applications. Different flowers are mixed together, and then powder is to be sprinkled by degrees over the part, and should the blood not stop; the finger is to be placed over the bleeding vessel. The following is one of these mixtures :—take of the flowers of

Lodhra
Madhuka
Gairika
Sarjarassa

in equal quantities. Or take of the flowers of—

Másha
Jaba, barley.
Godhúma, wheat.

These are to be mixed and sprinkled on the part, and if it does not stop; the finger is to be applied to the part for the same purpose.

The barks of different trees, as the Banian tree, Catechu, gum resin, are mixed, reduced to powder, and used as styptics.

The ashes of burnt silk, will also be found useful; over which a tight bandage is to be placed. The patient is to be kept in a cool room, and a cool and antiphlogistic diet and regimen is to be enjoined. Afterwards broths, made from the flesh of deer and other wild animals, are to be used, with light and nourishing food.

b. Cold and ice, by drying the blood, has a strong tendency to stop hœmorrhage, and is often used for this purpose.

c. When the above means have not been sufficient to stop the hœmorrhage, escharotics should next be used. These will be considered in the next section.

Section VI.

Cauteries.

The cauteries used by the Hindu Surgeons, were the actual and potential.

The actual Cautery.

Fire can sometimes be employed ; when neither the knife nor escharotics can be used, as it is the strongest of all the escharotics. It is applied in different ways, sometimes by means of long pepper, goats dung, the tooth of a cow, an arrow point, long circular or hook shaped iron probes ; for superficial purposes ; and straight probes for muscles or deep seated parts. There are three varieties of these irons ; one being small, another large, and a third of a moderate size. After amputations, &c., boiling fluids were used to stop hœmorrhage, as boiling jagree, oil, honey, &c.

The actual cautery is applied in four different ways, according to the nature of the case ; sometimes the application is made in spots ; in other cases in circles, or in parallel and concentric lines.

When the application is properly performed, there is a peculiar noise heard and smell felt, at the moment of the application, and the skin is immediately contracted. When the cautery is applied to the muscles, it changes them to a gray colour ; the swelling of the part diminishes, and it stops the discharge of blood, pus, &c.

Fire is useful in some diseases of the skin, flesh, vessels, ligaments, joints, and bones ; and when there is severe pain or hard swellings of the flesh and insensible parts ; which sometimes occur in carbuncle, piles, boils near the anus, in elephantiasis, and in small swellings ; and in bites of serpents live charcoal is recommended to be applied ; to prevent the dangerous effects of their bites. It is also useful in penetrating wounds and in all cases where it is accompanied with considerable hœmorrhage.

The small sized actual cautery is employed with advantage to the eyebrows, forehead, and temples for headaches and diseases of the head. When applied to the eyelids near the border the eye is to be defended with wet clothes. This is the treatment recommended for intergium. Fire is also applied to remove indurated parts ; to the side, in cases of diseased spleen and liver; and to the abdomen for enlargement of the mesenteric glands. It is also applied to the soles of the feet for the cure of colic; and it is said with the best effects, as it seldom fails to cure the disease.

Fire deranges the blood and bile, and produces severe pain and fever. A mixture of ghee and honey should be applied to the part after the cautery.

The actual cautery should not be used in the cold and hot months, as in September and October, and in May and June; more particularly in the two last months. It should not be used to persons of bilious or sanguineous temperaments; or in whom the blood is diseased; when diarrhœa is present, and external applications have not removed it; when the person is weak and timid; when there are many ulcers on the body; and when the patient is very young or very old.

The diet of a patient to whom the cautery is applied should be very thin, and of the same kind as that recommended for a woman with a dead fœtus in her abdomen. In the more dangerous forms no food is to be allowed.

When the different cauteries have not proved sufficient to stop the hœmorrhage, the vessel may be opened above the bleeding part in order to diminish the flow of blood from the large wound below; and thus give time for the operation of medicines.

When all these means fail to stop the hœmorrhage the physician is to examine the different circumstances of the case, and act accordingly.

Potential Cauteries (*Khára*). These cauteries consist of Potassa more or less pure; it is obtained by burning the bark and branches of the

Muskaka tree,
The Kataja tree,
The Palása,
Asakarna,
Arka,
Sthnuhi,
Apámárga,
Pátala,
Chítraka,

Or the bark and branches of these trees are reduced to ashes, which are thrown into six times their quantity of water or cow's urine. Strain them 21 times, expose them to heat, until they are reduced to the consistence of a mucilage. Again, dissolve them in water, strain, separate, remove the sediment and evaporate to the same consistence as before; some shell lime is then to be mixed with them, and when neither very dry nor moist, they are to be taken off the fire and kept in an iron vessel well closed up.

The Potassa thus prepared, may be used internally or externally. In the first form it is used in solution and is good for removing worms, for curing Leprosy, and as an antidote for certain poisons ; when long taken it produces impotency. As an external application, it is used in three degrees of strength, the concentrated, the mild, and the weak.

The concentrated Potassa is used for opening abscesses and for producing superficial ulcers, in which cases emollients are to be put upon the part after the application, so as to reduce the pain. The solution acts strongly in healing ulcers and in stopping bleeding, and when concentrated it disorganizes the parts. It is applied externally to different cutaneous diseases, to bad ulcers, to fistula-in-ano and other fistula, to piles, to certain diseases of the mouth, as to diseased tubercles, &c. The weak solution may be taken internally in dyspepsia, colic, and indigestion ; and for urinary calculi, gravel, worms, and gumo.

The use of Potassa is not proper in the sanguineous temperament, in internal hœmorrhage, in fever, for children or old people, for weak persons, or for persons with diseases of the eyes, &c. When caustic is to be applied to a part, the patient is to be taken to a room shut up, a portion of the Caustic is then to be applied to the part by means of a Probe. The Surgeon is then to wait for a space of time that will admit of his counting a hundred. If well applied the part becomes black, and the juices of acid fruits are to be applied. Caustics are not to be applied to vital parts, where there are many nerves, blood ligatures, joints, ligaments, *taphu,* to the eye, throat, &c. When used by an ignorant person caustics are like fire, poison, or thunder to the patient whom it quickly kills.

When properly applied by a skilful Surgeon it cures many diseases.

Section VII.

Scalds and Burns.

There are four degrees of burns :—

a. *Plusta,* in which there is severe pain, and change of colour on the part.

b. *Durdogdha,* when accompanied with blisters, with much redness and pain.

c. *Samadogdha,* when it is black, and does not produce much pain.

d. *Atidogdha,* when the part is separated with the destruction of the vessels, &c., with fever, thirst, faintness, and the wound heals slowly.

In *Plusta* hot articles are to be applied ; and in *durdogda* apply cold substances, and sometimes hot, with ghee and fomentations. In *Samadogdha* apply a paste made of *Chandana*, sandlewood ; *Gairika*, yellow earth, and the bark of the wild banian tree. These are to be mixed with ghee ; or apply to the part, animal flesh, chopped. The flesh of domestic animals may be used for this purpose.

In *Atidogha*, separate the loose parts, and apply cold. Then apply the decoction of the cold bark of the Tinduka tree with ghee. In other cases apply wax, liquorice root, ghee, rasin : make into an ointment, and apply to the part. Cold applications are likewise useful.

When a person is struck with lightening, and is not killed, anoint the body with oil, with frictions.

When choaked with smoke, the patient has difficulty in breathing, which is sonorous, attended with coughs burning of the eyes, and redness. This is succeeded by thirst, fever, difficulty in hearing and smelling : the juice of the sugar-cane, and grapes should be given for drink, with water and sugar. The juices of sweet and acid fruits may also be used with an emetic to clean the stomach.

Section VIII.

Directions for performing operations.

When an operation is decided on ; a fortunate moment is to be selected, and the Brahmins and the Surgeons are to be propitiated with gifts. A clean and well lighted room is to be chosen in which the operation is to be performed ; and cloth, the leaves of trees, thread, honey, ghee, the juices of different kinds of trees ; milk, oil, cold and hot water, and strong and steady persons are to be in readiness to hold him, while care is taken not to frighten the patient. Should the patient be very fearful of the knife, or very young, escharotics, the nail or a sharp piece of the bark of the bamboo may be substituted ; and for the mouth or eyelids a kind of grass (*goji*) or other rough leaves may be substituted by rubbing them over the part. The patient is to be placed with his face to the east, and the surgeon before him with his face to the west.

The knife should be wet with water before being used.

The season for operating is when the sky is clear during the rains, and in the hot weather in the evenings and mornings. If possible the operation should be performed near the new moon, as this is the most proper time. Should the person be weak, much diseased, insensible, or when the disease has come on suddenly, the operations should be performed during the evening or morning when the weather is steady and seasonable; a propitious day and hour is to be found out. Curdled milk, corn, &c., are to be offered up to the gods for the success of the operation and Brahmins are to be propitiated.

When a boil is to be opened, or the flesh divided, the part is to have certain escharotics rubbed over it to diminish the pain. When a vessel, joint, or sensible part is to be divided, oil is first to be rubbed over it.

The Surgeon should hold the knife firm in the hand; if thrust into a boil and no pus follows it is to be quickly withdrawn. If there be much pus in the part, it may be opened several times if necessary; boils are not to be considered dangerous if elevated upon a flat surface. Should this not be the case, and the boil does not rise, but extends, the diagnosis is less favourable. The surgeon is a proper person if he be strong and operates quickly; his knife should be good, and he should neither perspire, shake, nor make exclamations. In performing such operations, the sensible parts of the body are to be avoided; as the palms of the hands and soles of the feet, vessels, tendons, joints and bones. When near vital organs the knife should be held so as to cut outwards, and should any such organ be wounded it produces severe pain, and is cured with difficulty.

When the fetus is dead in the uterus, in ascetics, piles, certain excrescences and swellings near the anus, which have existed upwards of a month; the patient is to take his dinner before the operation, and the operation is to be completed while withdrawing the knife. Cold water is then to be applied to the part, the person's spirits are to be kept up, the pus is to be squeezed out, and the part cleaned with tepid water. Lint smeared with honey or ghee is then to be put into the wound to prevent it closing. The wound is to be rubbed with honey or ghee and a bandage is then to be placed round the part.

During the operation, care must be taken to keep a fire in the room near the patient, in which sweet scented substances are to be burnt, in order to prevent the entrance of devils by the wound.

After the operation some holy water is to be sprinkled over his body, and proper prayers repeated; such as the following:—Oh Bramha! Do thou, as well as other Gods, order the serpents, *Pishacha*, *Gandharba*, *Pitri* (spirits), *Jakha*, *Rakhyasa*, who are desirous of acting wickedly to desist from their intention, either on earth, in the sky, or in any direction; and that prophets may cure this wound, Do thou, Oh Bramha! direct the Planets, and rajah prophets, mountains, seas, and rivers, to retain the soul and *bayu* in this body; that they remain healthy by the influence of the rajah of the moon, and *devata* of the clouds; *opana Bayŭ* by the lightning, *odana-bayu*, by thunder, *saman bayu* by Indra; strength by Soloh, sense by Booan. Oh *Samudra* (sea), the navel who know every thing retain thy supplicant; and thou sun retain the eyes and ears healthy. Direct your correct ears, moon retain your pure heat; stars your body fair; night your shadow, and water your semen healthy. May medicine retain your heart, while the sky will retain the elements of the body in health, and the earth the body pure. Thy head oh Bramha (*Parakrama*) will retain energy healthy. *Iswar* the energy of the male. Bramha spirit; *Dhruba* eyebrow; all the Devata will retain the body healthy, and live long, Brumha and other Devata will cure you. The sun and moon will do the same thing, as also *Narada; parbata* prophets, fire, Bayu, Indra and other Devata. Bramha composed this prayer, and will increase the age of the repeater; may it be propitious, and the pain will always disappear.

Bramha preserve you, and the Devata, and Chandra and Surjya preserve you. May you live long, and be quickly restored to health."

The patient is then to be taken to his own apartment, and the physician is to give the necessary directions regarding his diet; which should be very light and spare, and the patient must avoid exercise, laughing, expressions of anger, pleasure or grief, &c. On the third day the bandages are to be opened and clean ones substituted. Should the bandages be opened on the second day, the wound will not be sufficiently united, and it will retard the cure, and increase the patient's suffering; should the pain continue for several days, and be severe, with heat and swelling, the leaves of bitter plants are to be boiled and applied to the part. When tents are used they should be removed every third day, and they are to be continued as long as pus flows from the part.

Means of removing foreign substances from the body.

There are two kinds of such extraneous substances, one of which is firmly fixed in the body, and the other is loose.

The first is the only kind requiring remarks. They are sometimes removed by drawing out, or by thrusting through the part. If at the time of wounding, the person faints; water is first to be thrown upon his face. After the blood has been discharged, from the wound; heat, oil and ghee, and the like are to be applied to the part. Then apply ghee and honey over the wound, bind up the part; and order diet, &c., as usual. If a vessel or tendon be wounded the instrument is to be removed by pincers. If it has disappeared under the swelling it is to be pressed, so as to force out the iron ; or if there be barbs ; enlarge the wound and so remove the arrow. If it has penetrated the bone, it is to be removed with force, and if required a string may be tied to the tooth of an elephant or, neck of a horse and thus forcibly removed, or with a bent branch of a tree. If in the throat, the extraneous matter may be discharged by thrusting down a hot iron to dissolve it or soften it and so remove it. In such cases, the hot iron is passed through a metallic tube. A Probang, for removing fish bones, is usual ; by drinking fluids and emetics it is also dislodged ; this may also be done by beating the person upon the back of the neck.

There are 15 modes of removing extraneous substances :—

1. *Swabhaba.*—When removed by the natural discharges, as by the tears.

2. *Pachana.*—Medicines to promote suppuration, which will be discharged with the pus and blood.

3. *Badhana.*—By a slight incision.

4. *Darana.*—By longer incisions.

5. *Pirana.*—By pressure.

6. *Pramarjana.*—By washing, by warmth, or by a hair cloth or hand.

7. *Bidmapana.*—By blowing, as a substance introduced into the larynx, which produces great irritation and strong efforts of coughing, &c.

8. *Bamana.*—By emetics.

9. *Birachana.*—If the extraneous substances have passed to Pokosio, purgatives are to be given.

10. *Prakhalona.*—If pus or blood be retained in a place, they are removed by warming.

11. *Pramarsa.*—If in the nostrils, errhines are to be used.

12. *Prabahana.*—If air, urine, and dejections are not discharged ; or the fetus is retained ; and are not removed by the efforts of the person, they are to be discharged by manual means.

13. *Achusana.*—When air is deranged, or water, or poison deranges the blood ; or there is bad milk in the mammæ, this milk is to be removed by sucking or cupping, as the poison of serpents are extracted.

14. *Yaskanta.*—A loadstone may be used when the substance is straight, and is not tightly embedded in the flesh.

15. *Harsa.*—When grief is the cause, joy will remove it.

When the foreign substances produce fever, uneasiness, swelling, suppuration and death.

Wounds, Acute Ulcers, (Sodo Bruno.)

Wounds are produced by accidents and are of various shapes and forms. There is one kind which is simple, and another is complicated with the presence of a foreign body. Wounds vary with the part wounded, and the instruments by which they are inflicted. When the *skin* is wounded, it changes its colour, swells, and is hard. If in the *flesh* the swelling is greater, the wound gapes, discharges thick matter like ghee, and does not scab.

When a *vessel* is wounded it is accompanied with much pain, blood flows from the wound which swells, and when it suppurates pus is discharged. When *tendons* are wounded they swell and the discharge is like ghee or phlegm from the nose mixed with blood.

When *bone* is fractured various degrees of pain are produced; the marrow disappears, and the colour of the bone changes to that of a cockle shell. Pus and marrow are discharged from such wounds.

The six varieties of wounds are as follows :—

1st. *Chhinna*, or incised wounds, with a large open surface.

2nd. *Bhinna*, or penetrating wounds, as by pointed instruments, as the horn of a cow, &c.; this wound discharges little externally, when it penetrates a cavity it fills it with blood, and the contents of the organ; this is followed by fever, thirst, loss of appetite, difficult breathing, and the stoppage of the secretions, as urine and sweating. When the stomach is wounded it is accompanied with a vomiting of blood, and a swelling of the abdomen with severe pain. When the small intestines are wounded there is much pain, heaviness of the part, cold extremities, &c.

3rd. *Biddha*, or punctured wound, when the sharp pointed and narrow instrument is removed, or is retained in the wound.

4th. *Khata*, this is composed of the two last, being accompanied with destruction of the superficial parts. Or it is a contused wound.

5th. *Pichíta*, when by pressure, or the weight of a heavy substance fracturing the bones, and injuring the soft parts, the wound is filled with marrow and blood.

6th. *Ghrista*, or bruised by coming in contact with a hard body.

Treatment.

In the four first kinds of wounds, there is a large discharge of blood. If there is severe pain apply poultices made of animal flesh and the like, with fomentations, followed by cold applications; an oily glyster is to be administered internally; and ghee prepared with medicines which correct, or diminish the diseased air.

In the two last kinds of wounds, there is a slight discharge of blood ; and in such cases if there is not a loss of blood from the part, much inflammation and suppuration will be the consequence. In such cases, cold applications are to be used. This is the general treatment of all wounds.

The following is the treatment to be pursued in particular cases :

When the wound is near the head with a flap of skin, it is to be sowed, and a bandage applied to support the part. If the *ear* is separated it is to be restored to its natural position, and by sutures and a bandage it is to be kept there.

When the windpipe is wounded, and the air passes through it, sow the wound closely, put some ghee of the goat, and over it a circular bandage. The person should be kept on his back, and should take only fluid food. If the extremities are severely wounded with fracture of the bone, retain the parts in their natural position, apply oil, and a roller over them. In wounds of the back part of the body, the person is to be supported lying on his back, taking care that no pressure is made upon the wound. If on the breast, he is to be placed upon his breast in the same way. This direction is given in order to avoid the matter collecting within the wound.

When an extremity is separated, immediately pour boiling oil on the surface. Then apply a cap-formed bandage, and remedies to heal the wound. The following oil is recommended for healing wounds :—Take of a decoction of

Chandana, (Sirium myrtifolium.)
Podmoka, (Mentha sativa,)
Ragadhra, (Amaranthus atropurpureus.)
Utpala, (Salvinia verticillata.)
Príungu, (Panicum Italicum.)
Hurdira, (Curcuma longa.)
Mudhuka, (Bassia latifolia.)
Porscea, (Galega purpurea.)

mix, boil, and strain for use.

The unfavourable symptoms of wounds, are great fever and heat of the body, a collection of blood in the part, cold extremities, redness of the eyes, stoppage of the evacuations, delirium, giddiness, convulsions, difficulty of breathing, severe pain, with a serous discharge from the wound. The senses become obtuse.

Severe wounds are sometimes accompanied with erysipelas, tetanus, madness, hectic fever, cough, vomiting, diarrhœa, hiccough, shivering, &c.

If the eye is divided the sight is lost, but if displaced without injuring the nerves, it is to be carefully returned with the assistance of a water-lily, and apply ghee as an errhine.

Means of improving, and forming new Ears and Noses.

A particular ceremony is performed for boring the ears of children, which it is not necessary to describe. As ornaments are hung from the ears, it is of consequence to remove defects from them. Sushruta gives directions for performing fifteeen different operations. However, the experienced Surgeon will vary the operation according to the circumstances of the case, and according to the nature of the defect. Sometimes these are produced by accidents, or by internal causes. If the helix or antihelix are defective the body of the external ear is to be half cut through so as to bind it in the natural position. If there is a deficiency in these parts, a portion of the skin of the same size and figure is to be raised from the cheek, the blood stopped, and a bandage applied so as to keep the parts together of the natural figure and shape. The patient should not sleep during the day, should not eat much, should remain in a cool situation, and avoid fatigue. When the part is properly healed, apply oleaginous ointment, prepared with wax, oil, and fat. When the parts are healed up the lobe may be pierced according to custom.

If not properly performed many bad consequences will follow these operations, as indurated swellings, ulcers, &c.

When the nose is cut off, or destroyed by diseases.—The former is a frequent punishment in the native courts. A fresh leaf is first cut of exactly the size of the nose, it is then to be placed upon the cheek, and the necessary quantity of skin and cellular membrane is to be dissected. The nose is then to be scarified, and after dissecting up the flap it is to be placed upon the raw part of the nose to which it will adhere. Sutures and bandages are applied to keep the parts together. After the bandage has been applied, a couple of wooden canulæ are to be introduced into the nostril to allow breathing, and to support the new nose. A piece of linen cloth previously soaked in oil is to be applied over the bandage. An aperient is then to be given to the patient, and his general health is to be attended to. Should any other deficiency of the nose be present it may be supplied in the usual manner. If the nose should be deformed it may be reduced in size by the knife.

Accidents.

Fractures and *dislocatious* are produced either by falls, pressure, blows, by sudden and violent extension, and other incidents of violence.

Dislocations either lengthen or shorten the joint, or it is turned inwards or outwards, is tender and painful, which is much increased by the least movement. There are six varieties :—

1. *Utpista* when the dislocated joint is crushed and swelled, both above and below, with much pain, which increases at night.

2. *Bislistia* or separated. In this variety there is less swelling, the pain is continued, and the movements of the joint are totally lost.

3. *Bibartita,* when the joint is twisted.

4. *Tirjokhepta,* when one part of the joint is turned outward with severe pain.

5. *Otkhepta,* when one of the bones of a joint are dislocated while the other remains in its usual place.

6. *Abakhepta,* when a bone is forced downward with much pain.

There are twelve varieties of *Fractures* :—

1. *Korkotaka,* when the fracture is in the middle of the bone with swelling.

2. *Aswakurna,* in which the bone protrudes like the ear of a horse.

3. *Churnta,* when accompanied with bruises and the bone is crushed.

4. *Pichchita,* when depressed by a heavy weight without swelling.

5. *Astheechulleta,* when a small part of the bone is elevated.

6. *Kandabhagna,* when a larger bone is fractured and disabled.

7. *Majámugoda,* when the broken part of the bone enters the same bone.

8. *Atipatta,* when the fractured bone is separated.

9. *Bokora,* partial fracture.

10. *Cheena,* when only a small part remains undivided.

11. *Pátta,* when comminuted without pain.

12. *Sphutita,* when the bone is swelled with small openings.

A fracture is distinguished from a simple swelling of the part, by the crepitating noise when moved, by the looseness and pain in the part, and by the great uneasiness.

Treatment.—Fractures do not unite quickly in those persons who eat little, and who are intemperate, or when accompanied with severe diseases. Such patients should not use salt, astringent and acid food, also connexion with women, exposure to the weather, fatigue. They should not take dry food, but use rice, animal broths, milk, ghee, and such like nourishing food. For these fractures use a decoction made of the bark of the *Moduká, Urumbora, Ossoka, Polassa,* and then apply splints of bamboo. A bandage is to be renewed every seventh day in the cold weather, in temperate weather every fifth day, and in hot weather every third day, or according to the individual circumstances of the case. The bandage should neither be too loose, nor too tight. In the first case the apposite of the broken bones is not sufficient, and in the latter case it will produce much pain, swelling and inflammation. Cold astringent decoctions of the barks of different trees are to be applied; such as

Nagrodha, Citrus aurantium.
Batá, Millingtonia pinnata.
Aswatha, Ficus religiosa, &c.

The part should be kept perfectly at rest, and every care should be taken to prevent suppuration.

After a few days warm oil should be applied to the part prepared with different drugs, according as the air, bile, and phlegm are affected.

Compound Fractures.—Apply ghee and honey to the wound, with astringent decoctions; and then follow the same plan of treatment as recommended for simple fractures.

Fractures are easily united in youth, and they require usually one month for the cure; in middle age two months; and in old age three months. In order to reduce a fracture, the bone that overlaps another is to be drawn down.

The following fractures are always dangerous:—

When one or more bones of the head are fractured, when the fracture is comminuted; when the thigh bone or pelvis are fractured; when the fracture extends to joints, when the fracture is produced from a fall from a great height. Fractures are also dangerous when the person is very weak, or very old, has old ulcers, leprosy, and when bad symptoms of deranged bayu are present.

In the Treatment of Dislocations.

First apply fomentations and warm oleaginous applications with frictions so as to soften and relax the parts. The surgeon will then reduce the dislocation by forcing the bone out of its new position, and by pressing and binding the joint in the opposite direction from that in which it has been displaced, so as to allow the bone to slip into its natural position.

When the hip or knee-joint are dislocated, the extension must be made with a kind of pully called *chakra*. The patient should then be placed in a bed and the part kept at rest. When of long standing, fomentations and oily frictions are to be diligently applied before the reduction is to be made.

A dislocated *rib* is to be reduced by pressing with the thumb and second finger, after the soft parts have been well relaxed by being rubbed with ghee. A proper splint and bandage, is then to be applied.

The dislocated *humerus* is to be reduced by pulling the bone strongly downwards, or along the side after a pillow or ball has been put in the axilla; when the bone will slip into its place. The joint is then to be surrounded with a bandage which passes round the axilla and the neck in the form of 8. This bandage is called *Swastíká*.

The dislocated *elbow-joint* is to be reduced by the extension and flection of the fore-arms, while pressure is made by the thumb and fingers upon the displaced head of the bone.

The same means are to be employed in order to reduce the dislocations of the wrist and ancle joints.

When the bones of the neck are dislocated, it is to be reduced by a person placing his thumbs under the angles of the jaw-bone, and fingers upon the side of the neck and drawing the head slowly upwards, while another person retains the body at rest. When the dislocation is reduced, the person is to be kept in an erect position for a week.

The dislocation of the lower jaw is to be reduced by drawing it downwards, when the bone will slip into its place; the part is then to be rubbed with warm ghee, and a four tailled bandage is to be applied over the chin, so that two of the bands are tied behind, and two on the top of the head.

When the bones of the nose are depressed, they are to be raised into their natural position by means of an instrument called *Sháláká;* a hollow wooden tube is kept in the nostrils, so as to retain the bones in their natural position. Ghee is then to be rubbed externally over the part.

After a dislocated bone has been reduced, a plaster is to be applied to the part; consisting of munjista, liquorice, red sandal wood, and rice, and are to be all pounded and mixed together. The plaster is then to be formed by mixing the powder with ghee which has been washed a hundred times in water. This plaster is to be continually applied over the dislocated joint, for a considerable time after it has been reduced. Should there be much pain in the part, a cold infusion of magrodude, pucha, mulie in milk, and chakra oil are to be applied.

Every morning during the treatment some prepared ghee mixed with such medicines as will improve the health, and keep the bowels relaxed, is to be taken.

In sprains and bruises nothing is to be done, except the applications of cold lotions and plasters. In some cases circular bandages wetted with ghee by itself, or mixed with a decoction of *casha* (a kind of grass), is to be applied over the part.

The treatment is said to be proper when no deformity is left in the part, and it has its natural action.

BOOK IV.

—o—

PRACTICE OF PHYSIC.

THIS EXTENSIVE SUBJECT WILL BE CONSIDERED UNDER SOME GENERAL REMARKS ON DISEASE; AND THE DESCRIPTION AND TREATMENT OF PARTICULAR DISEASES.

CHAPTER I.

General Remarks on Disease.

IN this chapter I shall consider the nature, classification, causes, and description of disease, with a few remarks on Pathology as explained in the shasters.

Nature of Disease.

Disease is distinguished in the shasters by the causes, peculiar signs, and effects of certain substances in diminishing or increasing particular sets of symptoms, and lastly by Pathology or more properly morbid anatomy.

The nature of disease was explained by the Hindus on the same principles as their physiology. Nature, which exhibited the highest degree of order in her operations, is liable to occasional irregularities; from the impurities, and the imperfect manner in which the elements, and qualities, are mixed together. In like manner the harmony of the humours of the body are liable to derangement. At one time the disease is owing to an increase of one of the principal humours, at another to its diminution, with regard to the other humours. They thus explained the occurrence, and varieties of disease:—The soul (*jivita*) of the body, like the great soul of the world, tended to retard these derangements, or restore such irregularities. When disorder has been introduced; the soul, (vix medicatrix naturæ) tends to reduce the humours that are increased, and to augment those which are diminished. In like manner certain medicines have peculiar effects in producing these changes, and thus assist the soul in her salutary influences.

As long as the humours remain in due proportion, the individual remains in health, as perfect harmony reigns in the universe while the elements retain their just proportions; but, as soon as the harmony is lost, by the assimilation being imperfectly performed, derangements of the system are the consequence, and the body becomes the prey to disease. Hence, these irregularities in the quantity and quality of the humours, are the proximate cause of diseases. This is rendered more frequent by the body continually undergoing changes by the waste that is going on; which is made up by the supply of aliment.

Disease is therefore the pain (*duhkha*) of the soul, caused by the derangement of the humours.

Classification of Diseases.

The ancient Hindu Medical writers arranged diseases according to their prominent symptoms, and not according to the peculiarity of the symptoms and their combinations, which were influenced by the structure and uses of the part. Thus they gave the name of *shúl*, to diseases accompanied with much pain; when accompanied with local swelling it is considered as *gulma*, while more general swellings were considered under the head of *udara*. They thus lost an important principle in the grouping, and inculcated dangerous principles in the treatment of diseases: for some diseases will assume the peculiarities of the three diseases. Others pass from the one to the other, while the nature of each of the diseases, and the tissue affected, are quite different; and require to be treated by methods quite opposite to each other.

In the Ayur Veda medicine is divided into eight chapters, which require, it is added, to be carefully studied before a person can be successful as a practitioner. But so extensive is the range of the subject, that one person cannot successfully exercise all, and he requires to confine his attention to one department. The classification in Ayur Veda is as follows:—

1st. Injuries, and phlegmoid tumours.
2nd. Diseases of the senses, and head.
3rd. Diseases of the whole body, as fever, leprosy, &c.
4th. Derangement of the faculties, from demoniacal possessions.
5th. Diseases of infants, and of nurses.
6th. Antidotes.
7th. ? Alchemistry; and
8th. The means of increasing the human race. A modification of this division is usually followed in the Hindu medical works.

Diseases are likewise divided into three kinds, one of which is curable, another is cured with difficulty, being of a chronic nature, and the third class is incurable. Each of these diseases is again divided into primitive, and consecutive ; external, or internal ; local, or general. These again are divided into three varieties :—The first is, when one disease has occurred and another follows, which is increased by the first, the medicine for which must cure both diseases, but particularly the chief. A second variety is when a disease has been present without any other ; and a third is when the precursory symptoms are only present. In such cases medicines are to be given, so as to remove the diseased cause.

Another classification is founded on the origin of diseases, into hereditary, and acquired. These, however, are not divided into sporadic, epidemic, and endemic classes ; although this is so natural a division. The contagious, and non-contagious nature of diseases, and their being communicated from one person to another by mediate, and immediate contact, was well known to the Hindu physicians.

In Charaka, and other works of great authority, diseases are considered under four classes :—The first is called *Agantuka,* or accidental diseases, and are produced by external causes, such as accidents and poisons. There are two varieties of these diseases, the first being corporeal, and the second mental. Medicine will cure the one, and management the other.

2d. *Nija (Saurira),* bodily diseases, form the three other classes. They are caused by eating and drinking improper articles of food ; which derange air, bile, and phlegm ; or blood locally, or generally. Both *Ágantuka* and *Nija,* may affect the mind as well as the body.

3d. *Mánasa* (mental diseases), produced by derangements of the mind ; caused by passion, grief, joy, anger, malice, envy, pride, lust, covetousness, delusion, low spirits, &c.

4th. *Swábhábika* (natural diseases), which act on both mind and body in the same manner ; as appetite, thirst, decrepitude, sleep, death, &c.

These four classes of diseases thus act eventually on the soul, as well as the body ; and may be cured by evacuating superfluous humours, and increasing those that are deficient, by diet, and management (*Sushruta*).

Diseases have likewise been divided into two classes :—

I. *Shastrasádhya,* or those cured by manual treatment.

II. *Snehádi Kriyásádhya,* or those cured by medicine (*Sushruta*).

The most usual classification of disease is into the following seven classes :—

1st. *Adibala prabritta* or hereditary diseases. This is explained by the mother's blood, and seminal secretions of the father being affected with certain diseases, which are conveyed to their children; these diseases are hemorrhoides, phthisis, dyspepsia, epilepsy, leprosy, and elephantiases. (Menu, p. 60. chap. 3. s. 7.)

By care and attention these hereditary taints may be retarded in their appearance, and even prevented from developing themselves. In other cases such taints produce other diseases.

2d. *Janmabalprabritta* (disease of the embryo). When the mother does not take care of her food, exercise, &c., this class of disease is produced. From these causes the infant may be born blind, deaf, dumb, dwarfish in size, &c.

3d. *Doshabalprabritta* (diseases of the humours) caused by intemperance. Some are produced from the stomach, some from the intestines, some affect the whole body, others only the mind.

4th. *Sanghátabalprabritta*, or accidental, as when caused by wounds, poison, &c.

5th. *Kalabalprabritta*, diseases caused by cold, heat, rain, storms, &c.

6th. *Daibabalprabritta*. When improper actions are performed, a class of disease of the most loathsome appearance, and incurable nature are supposed to be produced; such as by the abuse of the Deities, or Brahmans, the contempt of spiritual preceptors, and other heinous offences. Such can only be cured by a course of severe and long continued penance, by mysterious performances, and liberality to the sacred Brahmans. In the present day these causes sometimes are so aggravated that the sacrifice of the person's life is not sufficient for its purification, as is leprosy. Among the ignorant the only means of preventing this is supposed to be by sacrificing themselves in the sacred Ganges, and it not unfrequently happens that, instigated by friends, these miserable and deluded persons drown themselves in the sacred stream, as an expiation for their supposed sins.

Another division of this class of disease is produced by contact, by breathing the same air, eating together, sitting upon the same seat, wearing the same clothes, or ornaments, of a person labouring under the disease. In this manner Leprosy may be propagated.

7th. *Swabhababalaprabritta*, or natural diseases, give pain to the soul; such as thirst, appetite, age, sleep, and death. This class is again divided into the timely and untimely.

When the principal humours (*dhátu*) are deranged, the disease is called by the name of the humour affected; such as *rasaja* (chyle diseases), among which are dyspepsia, pain of the body, &c.;

raktaja, or diseases of the blood, such as leprosy, erysipelas, &c.; *mángsaja*, or diseases of the flesh, such as fleshy tumours, &c.

Causes of Disease.

Charaka, as we have seen, divides disease into three classes, mental, bodily, and accidental; which he supposed were situated in the semen, chyle, or blood. The general causes of diseases are also three, proceeding from matter or objects of sense (*ortoh*), such as vision, smell, sound, taste, and touch; the second from improper exercise, and the third from the seasons. Thus diseases are caused by improper exposure to too much, or too little light; to too severe, or too little exercise; to a season of too great heat, or too much or too little rain, cold, &c. These are the three general causes of disease. They act in this manner; when a person is too much exposed to light, as by looking at the sun, blindness will be the result. Dyspepsia will be produced by being exposed to bad odours. As an example of improper exercise, that of carrying heavy weights produces Hemoptysis; and by irregularities of the seasons, Cholera, Fever, Dysentery, &c., are produced.

There are also three sorts of medicines: one sort that cleans the body when taken internally, as emetics, purgatives, &c., another sort purifies the external body when applied externally, as oil, diaphoretics, bathing; and the third kind is the use of knives, or instruments; fire, and escharotics.

Charaka states also that there are three objects of enquiry in this world, the first and chief enquiry being the means of preserving life; the second, the means of acquiring wealth; and lastly the means of obtaining beatitude in the next world.

There are three means of preserving life, proper food, sleep, and proper government of the senses and passions. The means of acquiring wealth are such as are not at variance with virtue and religion, such as mercantile transactions, the service of government, and husbandry. We should not envy the wealth of others, but strive to follow their example. The acquisition of happiness for another world will be obtained by study, by a virtuous marriage, by performing the sacrifices pointed out in the shasters, governing the passions, avoiding envy, evil thoughts, by speaking the truth, by hospitality to strangers, by the society of the learned and the good, and by prayers to God.

The particular causes of disease are those which affect the air, bile, phlegm, and blood.

Another form of disease is produced by sin, which is to be suspected, when a disease is not cured by the means pointed out by the shasters. These diseases are called *karmaja*, and are to be cured by good actions, by prayers, by certain forms of penance, &c. "If the disease is incurable, let the patient advance in a straight path, towards the invisible north-eastern point, feeding on water and air, till his mortal frame totally decay, and his soul become united with the Supreme Being." (Menu. p. 175, ch. vi. s. 31.)

The exciting causes of the diseases of air, are fighting with strong men, too much exercise, venery, much study, especially at night, severe cold and rainy seasons, &c. The exciting causes of the diseases of bile, are anger, grief, fear, fasting, indigestible food, acid, and pungent food, &c. The exciting causes of phlegm diseases are sleeping in the day time, want of exercise, sweet and salt food, drinking too much fluids, eating too much, &c. The causes of the disease of the blood are the same as those producing bilious diseases, also sleeping during the day, exposure to heat, too much exercise, indigestible food, improper mixtures of food, &c.

Another cause of disease is when they proceed from other diseases. In this case the original disease disappears leaving the new one to follow its usual course. The original disease in other cases remains, and may produce a second disease. Thus from enlarged spleen, fever and dropsy are produced; from piles, dyspepsia, and *gulma*.

Description of diseases.

The descriptions of disease in the Hindu writers are generally distinct and satisfactory, though often at variance with some of our theoretical notions; sometimes, however, from the imperfect list of symptoms given, it is difficult to distinguish the disease intended to be described, especially as it sometimes appears that the Physicians mistook an accidental combination of a few symptoms, for a distinct disease; and in other cases, placed under varieties, distinct diseases.

The description of a disease is usually commenced with an enumeration of the supposed causes, situation, and humours deranged, as indicated by the symptoms, and the varieties produced by the humours affected.

Before considering the description of particular diseases, it will be necessary to consider the indications of the morbid changes of the humours, which enter into all the diseases. By these indications, the physician is able to know the increase or diminution of any of the humours, which will regulate the particular treatment which he is to follow.

The seven essential parts of the body *(dhátu)* produce various diseases by a preternatural increase, or diminution of their quantity :—

1st. When chyle *(rasa)* is increased, it produces want of appetite, heaviness of the body, as if too much had been eaten, weakness of digestion, large secretion of saliva and phlegm, languor and lassitude, stretching, giddiness, nausia, vomiting, and fever. When chyle is diminished the person is subject to diseases of the breast, his skin is pale, his body becomes light, weak, the eyes become diseased, &c. In such cases the chyle is thin; the person has a depraved taste, is restless, and grey hairs appear early in life.

2d. When the blood is increased the body feels heavy; the body and the eyes have a red colour, with a burning sensation, eruptions appear over the body; and the person feels giddy, has no appetite, and his urine is red. He is subject to piles, bloody discharges, and baldness. Females in such cases are subject to menorrhagia. Such a state predisposes the person to attacks of inflammation of different viscera, and, the formation of large abscesses; to leprosy, rheumatism, erysipelas *(bisarpa)*, &c. When the blood is diminished preternaturally, the skin appears dry; the person feels a desire for sour things, and the vessels appear empty.

3d. When the *flesh* is morbidly increased, the body feels heavy, the muscular parts increase in size, the abdomen enlarges, and the person is subject to coughs, asthma, &c. When diminished; the loins, cheeks, lips, penis, thighs, breast, axillas, hips, abdomen and neck, become thin, the whole body dries up, with pains; and the large vessels diminish in size.

4th. When the *fat* is increased, the surface of the body has a shining appearance, it produces languor and fatigue after slight exertion, thirst, perspiration of a disagreeable smell, bronchocele, diseases of the lips, gonorrhœa, cough and asthma, and an increase in the size of the belly, buttocks, neck, and breast.

When diminished the part becomes flabby, and the joints lax, the body dries up, and soft food is desired.

As a disease fatness is produced by smearing the body with oil, by eating frequently, by want of exercise, by sleeping during the day; by sweet, or oily urine; and by increased phlegm. Such a state produces difficulty of breathing, thirst, appetite, a desire to sleep, perspiration, and a bad smell of the body, which becomes unwieldy. The person cannot speak distinctly, nor work; there is a diminished desire for women, as the vessels are filled, and the circulation is imperfectly performed. The other essential parts which are produced from the fat are imperfectly formed, and the strength is diminished.

Such a person is liable to attacks of diabetes and gonorrhœa, eruptions, terminating in large abscesses, fistula-in-ano, &c. In such a person, disease is always more dangerous according as the accumulated fat fills the vessels.

The causes of *thinness*, are what increases the air of the body, such as much work, frequent connexion with women, study, fear, grief, sorrow, want of sleep, thirst, and not eating and drinking enough to satisfy the appetite. This state of the body is likewise produced by whatever diminishes the essential parts of the body, and dries up the chyle.

This state of the body produces appetite and thirst, and the person is easily affected with cold, heat, wind, and rain. Such a person is weak, breathes with difficulty, is subject to diseases of air, to attacks of spleen, and dyspepsia, from the diminution of internal heat. In this state of the body, every disease is aggravated, and the causes increasing this state should be avoided. Various vegetable infusions, with nourishing and sweet food, are used to increase the size of the body. In like manner milk, curdled milk, ghee, flesh, sleeping during the day, a happy disposition, and certain laxatives have the same effect.

Both great fatness and leanness should be avoided; and the middle state should be considered the most favourable state of the body.

5th. When *Bone* is increased in the system, it produces additions on old bones, and the teeth become large. When it diminishes the body dries up, the patient complains of pain in the bones, and the teeth and nails become irregular.

6th. When the *marrow* is increased, the body and eyes feel heavy, the person has an increase of semen, and by drying it causes a difficulty in passing the urine, which is increased with pain and swelling of the bladder. When the marrow is diminished the semen diminishes, and there is pain in the bones, which feel empty.

7th. When the semen is increased, there is an increased discharge, and calculi form. Its diminution is accompanied with pain in the penis and testicles, and the person has no inclination for women.

The state of the excretions produce morbid symptoms, and diseases:—

1st. When the *fæces* are increased there is a noise in the belly with pain; and when diminished there is pain in the breast and side, and the air makes a noise in the upper part of the abdomen.

2nd. When *urine* is increased it produces pain in the bladder, there is a frequent desire to perform mictirition, and the evacuation is copious. When diminished there is pain in the bladder, and the urine is scanty. Whatever increases the dejections, removes these symptoms.

3rd. When the *perspiration* is increased, it has a bad smell, and a small eruption appears over the body, which is itchy. When it is diminished the roots of the hair become rough, the skin dries, and the touch is defective, and depraved. Rubbing the skin with oil, and substances which increase perspiration will remove these symptoms.

4th. *Menses.* When morbidly increased, this discharge has a bad smell, and is accompanied with pain, fulness of the breasts, and a copious discharge, with weakness. When diminished, the discharge is scanty, and does not take place at the usual period, and there is pain in the uterus. Those medicines which have the qualities of the sun are to be used, to remedy such deficiencies.

5th. When the *Milk* is increased in quantity, the mammæ are large, with pain, and there is a frequent discharge of milk. When preternaturally diminished, the mammæ are small, with little milk. Such medicines should be used as increase the phlegm.

Diseases of Life (*bala* and *oja*, the place or organ of *bala*) is of an oily appearance like ghee, of a white colour, and cool, while it remains in its own organ (*oja*), and is different from the essential parts of the body, which retain and support life. Life is situated in the breast of the male, and in the abdomen of the female. This is supposed to explain their want of strength and activity, with the softness of the body, their happy disposition, their quickness and vanity, and the fairness of their bodies. Life is the last formed of the humours, and is the chief; for as long as it remains, the muscles continue to perform their offices, and the person's voice, and the colour of his body continues good, and the ten senses continue in a healthy state. When diminished, the body dries, and without it the person dies. Life may be diminished by injuries, by a diminution of the seven datu, by anger, grief, fatigue, low spirits, and fasting. Sometimes life is increased, and at other times it is prostrated. When life changes its usual situation it produces a relaxation of the joints; the person cannot move or work, and air, bile, and phlegm, are diminished. In these diseased states of the body it cannot move, it is heavy, swelled, and the person is languid, depressed, and sleepy. The colour of the body changes, syncopy occurs, the flesh diminishes, the person feels weak, followed by death.

In these cases of diseased life, such articles are to be used, as strengthen and retain it in health. Thus bitter, cold, dry, and constipating articles of food are to be avoided; as also frequent connexion with women, &c. In such cases the body is to be rubbed with ghee, oil, and turmerick, with bathing, &c. The food should consist of very light articles.

From the above remarks it appears that a state of health is that in which the air, bile, and phlegm is in just proportion, in which the abdominal fire is sufficient, the seven essential parts, and the dejections are natural, the semen and mind correct, and the life (soul) happy. It is this equilibrium of all these parts that constitutes health; but it is impossible to distinguish the proper proportion of each of these parts, as they vary in different individuals. It is therefore by the effects of such derangements that we judge of their presence. When the senses are not in a perfect state, we know that the equilibrium of the parts is destroyed. They also act on each other. Thus when the air, bile, and phlegm are diminished, they derange the essential parts of the body, as heat diminishes the water in a vessel put over it.

These theoretical opinions led the Hindu Physicians, in their description of diseases, to follow the natural order, and to confound the accidental, with the pathognomonic symptoms. Hence they arranged diseases in unnatural groups, from a fancied connection between them. Thus fever was considered as a type of a group of diseases, in which dysentery, diarrhœa, indigestion, &c., were arranged, as these diseases are accompanied, in some cases, with fever.

Section II.

Diagnosis.

The nail* of *Vishnu,* like a sun, enlightened *Rishis,* who prepared the shasters. By a knowledge of these, the nature of disease is distinguished by examination, assisted by analogy, thought, and a knowledge of the shasters. By these means the physician first finds out the nature of the disease his patient is labouring under, the medicines ordered by the shasters, and the regimen to be followed.

The nature of the disease is to be ascertained :—

1st. By the appearance, as the countenance, tongue, &c.

2nd. By the feeling, as the pulse, temperature of the body, &c.

3rd. By questions, embracing the country, temperament, and history of the disease.

Other authors state that the disease is known by means of the five senses, and asking questions. Thus:

* That is, so great is Vishnu, that the most insignificant part of him sheds lustre upon the most learned of mankind.

1st. By *hearing* he will distinguish the state of the lungs, by the peculiar noise of the breathing.

2nd. By the *touch* he will mark the state of the body, as to cold and heat; and the state of the skin as to the hardness and softness, roughness and smoothness.

3rd. By the *sight*, the physician will know the largeness and smallness of the body, with its colour, &c.

4th. By *taste*, as in distinguishing diabetic urine, &c.

5th. By the *smell*, as of the different discharges from the body.

Lastly. By questions, the physician will find out the country, and temperament of the sick person, his sex, manner of life, and the history of the disease. The pain felt by the patient, the degree of his strength, and appetite, and the state of his evacuations.

These observations are all most necessary in order to arrive at a true diagnosis; and without knowing the disease, the physician will be unable to employ the proper means for its cure.

Pulse. Nothing is said in Charaka and Susruta regarding the pulse; its condition appeared to be considered of little importance, and the remarks on the subject are given under the head of the description of each disease. It is to more modern books that I am obliged to have recourse for the following description, which is so curious that I am induced to add it here. It is principally derived from the "*Náṛi-parikhyá**."

Modern Hindu Practitioners rely very much on the state of the pulse, in the treatment of disease. In the morning it is cool and slow, in the middle of the day it becomes hot and quick, in the evening its motion becomes rapid and quick, and at night it again becomes cool and slow.

When the person has the temperament of *air* it feels zigzag; in *bile* it is frequent; and in the temperament of *phlegm* it is slow and full. Hindu Physicians suppose that the pulse possesses a peculiar character in every disease. This idea is strengthened by their sacred writings. "The Theory of the pulse is so obscure and mysterious, that in heaven even physicians do not know it thoroughly. When it is to be consulted the patient ought to abstain from food, from occupation, from the bath, and the use of oil; to avoid cold and heat, and to remain at ease and awake, for some time before the physician arrives. It is only then that the pulse can be properly consulted."

The pulse is considered from its incessant movements, as a proof that there is a soul, or life, in the body. It may be felt at eight different parts of the body; at the two wrists, at the two feet, at the

* By an anonymous author stated to be written by Siba.

neck, above the collar bone, and on the two alli of the nose. The seat of the pulse of the foot is near the inside of the heel, where it should be felt by two fingers; in the two hands at the wrist, where it should be examined by three fingers. The pulse should be examined several times, by slightly raising the arm, and extending the fingers, and the right hand of the physician should feel the pulse, while the left should support the elbow joint of the patient. In the neck, above the collar bone and the nose, the pulse should be examined with two fingers. These are the seats of the principal pulse, and by them it is known whether there is life or not, in the body. The Physician will also know, by feeling these pulses, that the person is sick or healthy, and whether he will live or die.

When the physician and sick person have risen in the morning and performed ablutions, and their other prescribed duties, and are seated on a clean mat, and in an agreeable situation, the state of the pulse is then to be examined. A person who is not acquainted with the different pulses will not be able to appreciate them, and such a person ought not to be respected.

The pulse of the women should be felt at the left side of their necks, left hand, and nose; and of men on the right side of these parts. These pulses are over the whole body, and should be considered as the healthy, or sick pulses. The wrist is the best place to examine them. The pulse of the following persons, like a river in a storm, cannot be properly examined until they rest two hours. 1st. Soon after washing or bathing. 2nd. At the usual time of dinner, or just after eating. 3rd. A hungry person. 4th. One who is thirsty. 5th. When heated by walking in the rays of the sun. 6th. After severe exercise, as fighting. 7th. After riding. 8th. After anointing the body with oil, or when sleepy. 9th. A pregnant woman, or soon after child-birth. 10th. One who bears a heavy load; and 11th. After sleeping during the day.

In each disease there are peculiarities of the pulse. In *fever* the pulse becomes very frequent and hot, but when air predominates the pulse vibrates. When Bile predominates the pulse is very rapid, and jumping like a frog, and when Phlegm predominates in fever it becomes very full and slow. When two or three of the humours predominate, the pulse has the peculiarities of the combination.

In *Dysentery* and *Diarrhœa* the pulse becomes cold and weak, in chronic diarrhœa it becomes full, and sometimes rapid and slow.

In *Piles* the pulse becomes depressed in the middle, quick, and zigzag.

In *Dispepsia* it is full.

In *Cholera* it is deep, and very weak.

In *Worms* it is frequent, rapid, and weak.

In *Jaundice* it is frequent, sometimes full, and sometimes slow.

In *Hemorrhage* the pulse is sometimes quick, and sometimes slow, and hard.

In *Phthesis Pulmonalis* it is slow, and very weak.

In *Cough* it is irregular and frequent.

In *Asthma* it is very hard and quick.

In *Hiccough* it is very quick.

In *Vomiting* it is slow and irregular.

In *Syncopy* it is full.

In *Delirium Tremens* (*pánátyaya*) it is very hard and full.

Urine. The remarks on the urine in the ancient shasters are made under each disease. It is recommended to be examined in the morning, and received into a clean vessel. When changed by the increased quantity of air its colour will be gray, and will cause a slight smarting when voided. If changed by an excess of bile its colour will be red, and it will produce pain at the glans penis, at the time of being discharged. When phlegm predominates the urine will be white, thick, and frothy. In such cases the sick person will be of a weak, and melancholy habit of body. When two or three of the humours are diseased, it will take the colour of the peculiar mixture.

Tongue. When the increase of air occurs, the tongue turns to a yellow colour, becomes uneven, rough, and the papillæ prominent, like a cow's tongue. When an increase of bile takes place, the tongue becomes of a red, or brown colour, and becomes rough; and when the increase of phlegm occurs, then the tongue becomes of a white colour, with a thick coating, and moist. When the three are deranged the sick person's tongue becomes black-coloured, and sometimes very rough. When two are deranged two, or when three, the symptoms of three states are observed. When dying the tongue is straight, and becomes dry, pale, and shining. In such a severe disease very few grains of life remain.

Section III.

Prognostics.

As a flower prognosticates the future fruit, smoke the severity of fire, and the clouds the near approach, and the severity of the coming shower, so certain symptoms prognosticate the favourable, or fatal result of a disease. These signs, however, are often but slightly apparent to the general eye, and can only be detected by the eye of an experienced physician. In other cases the death of the patient having fatal symptoms may be everted by the intercessions of holy Brahmans, or by the use of medicines which produce longivity. An accomplished physician should study prognostics, and make allowance for the cure of certain cases. He may otherwise boast that he will cure complicated, or incurable cases ; by which he will lose his credit.

The prognostics of disease are either favourable, or fatal. These depend on various circumstances in each particular case ; which are obtained from the messenger sent, and collateral circumstances, and lastly from the symptoms of each disease. A few remarks on each of these will next be given.

1st. The appearance of the messenger, his dress, and his manner of speaking will influence the prognosis. In like manner his actions, the time of the day he reaches the physician, and other circumstances should influence the physician's prognosis. On calling the physicians, the following signs, or omens, are considered unfavourable. When there are many men or women collected, or following each other, to call the physician. When the messenger sees a man arrive riding on an ass, camel, or in a carriage (*ákú*) ; or if he has a stick, or string, or a sharp instrument, ripe fruit, &c., in his hand. When he is dressed in red, or black, or in wet clothes. When the messenger is very sorry, and expresses his fear. When the messenger is defective in a member, is deformed, or has a disgusting appearance. When the person sent speaks in unfavourable language of the sick person, when he is anointed with oil, &c. When the person, who calls the physician, has a shoe or skin in his hand, or is scratching his feet or other parts of his body with his nails, or is crying : All these occurrences are unfavourably, as to the event of the disease.

It is also considered bad when the physician is called at noon-day, at midnight, early in the morning and evening, when he has his face turned to the south, or when he is eating or naked ; anointing himself, is asleep, or is in an unclean place. Also when doing any thing with fire, is fatigued, is performing the funeral services of his relations, &c.

The kind of disease varies its prognostic ; when the patient is affected with a bilious disease, or when he has arrived in a very hot state, and finds the physician near the fire, it is unfavourable. It will be favourable when the person is affected with phlegm, or cold diseases. When the messenger is dressed in white clothes, is a handsome and fair person, is of the same caste as the patient, comes in a carriage with a cow, and is not impatient, are favourable signs.

When the messenger finds the physician sitting in a clean place, with his face towards the east, and the messenger has in his hands a water-pot full of water with an umbrella, they are favourable signs.

Should the physician on passing to the patient see a woman with her son, or a cow with her calf; or a virgin well dressed and adorned with jewels, or sees fish, or unripe fruit, butter-milk or flowers; or meets a Rájá, sees a strong fire, or a horse running, or a goose walking, or sees and hears peacocks, these prognosticate a favourable result to the patient's disease.

If the physician sitting by the side of his patient, the patient rubs one hand against another, scratches his back, answers questions with his face upwards, draws the bed-clothes, or shakes his hand, or constantly moves his head or puts the physician's hand to his breast or head. These are unfavourable signs.

The prognostics will depend upon the complication and kind of disease which affects the patient, and the peculiar violence of particular symptoms.

The severity and nature of the disease will depend on the nature of the essential parts of the body affected. While the skin, flesh, and blood are affected, the phlegm and air are the humours diseased. When the three humours are not affected, and marrow alone vitiated, the disease admits of relief, if not of cure. When the fat, marrow, or bone is affected, and two or three of the humours are vitiated, one of them being the bile, the disease is incurable. This forms the complicated form of disease, which is always more difficult to cure than when a single humour, or the presence of a single disease exists. The eight most severe forms of disease are, nervous disease, as tetanus, paralysis, &c., gonorrhœa *(prameha)*, leprosy *(kushṭha)*, piles *(arshah)*, fistula-in-ano *(bhagandara)*, stone *(ashmari)*, unnatural presentations of the fœtus, and dropsical swellings of the abdomen *(udara)*. These eight are the most severe diseases, and are cured with great difficulty.

In general the prognosis is to be favourable when the patient's voice remains unaltered, when he awakes from sleep without agitation, when eating rather cools than heats the body, and when the sick person does not forget his God, but prostrates himself daily in prayer with humility and resignation. The unfavourable symptoms are the opposite of the above, with indigestion, irregular and obstructed excretions, head-ache, redness of the eyes, loss of voice, generation of worms in wounds and ulcers; from which bloody, and fœtid discharges proceed.

If in any disease the patient is very thin and weak, with difficulty of breathing, thirst, dryness of the body, vomiting and fever, these are bad symptoms. If fainting, diarrhœa, hiccough, occur in the course of the disease they will not be cured. If swelling of the body occurs in the course of nervous disease without feeling in the skin, with shaking, swelling of the abdomen, with wind accompanied with pain, or other such symptoms, the disease will destroy the person.

If the white part of the body suddenly becomes black, without any previous cause, and the blood changes its colour. When the other internal parts do not remain in the usual condition, whether that be rest or motion; if any large organ diminishes in size, or becomes large; what is long becomes short, or short long; if bodies that should be discharged remain, and if those that should remain are discharged; or if the members naturally hot become cold, shining become dull, moist become dry, they are dangerous signs. When members cannot move, or have an unnatural smell, or cannot perform their office, or are removed from their natural position, if they open, or are discharged outwardly, or inwardly, are heavy, or light, the person will soon die.

If in the morning perspiration occurs on the forehead; or tears always fall without any disease of the eyes; if the dandriff in the hair is of the colour of the powder of the cow's litter: if a pigeon, &c. perches on the head of the person; if, without eating, there is a great discharge of dejections; or when there are no dejections, and the person eats freely, it is deadly. If the chest or mamillæ swell; if the trunk swells, and extremities become thin, or the contrary; or half of the body swells; or half become paralized; if the person cannot speak, or it is diminished, or changed, these are signs of danger. The same is the case if the nails, teeth, mouth, or body, has the smell of putrid flowers; if the sputa, dejections, or semen sink in water; if the person sees objects multiplied, or imperfectly; if the body and hair have a shining appearance, as if covered with oil; if the person is very weak, without appetite, or with Dysentery with cough, with much appetite and thirst, or if weak with vomiting, especially if the sputa be mixed with blood, and the patient has no appetite. Should the feet, hands, and lips be swelled, with weakness, and want of appetite, while the buttocks, hands, feet and shoulders are diminished in size, and the person is weak with fever and cough; if they vomit their breakfast in the evening, are dejected; have gnawing pain, fever and cough, if the person falls, producing a sound like that of a goat, has no strength or feeling in the testicles; and if the head falls on the shoulder, the danger is great. If the chest dries first after bathing, and the person is always biting his under lip or the tongue; is pulling his ears or hair, or considers the gods, bráhmans, and his master, friend, and Physician as his enemies, they are fatal signs. If the aspect of the planets are unfavourable; if the stars fall, thunder occurs on the day of the ascent of the star under which the person was born, it is unfavourable.

If the physician has examined properly the person, and finds the disease increasing, and the person feeble, he will not recover. In the course of gonorrhœa *(prameha)*, if any considerable morbid discharge from the *urethra* takes place with fever, and a great flow of urine, it will be fatal.

The dangerous symptoms of leprosy *(kushṭha)* are, when the body is covered with sores, from which pus, blood, &c., are discharged; the members drop off, and the eyes are of a red colour, with hoarseness of the voice. When such patients are not able to bear the five forms of treatment, as purgatives, emetics, diaphoretics, injections, and blood-letting, the disease will be fatal.

If in the course of piles *(arsha)* the patient has dispepsia, pain of the abdomen, with much hemorrhage, dysentery, and swelling of the extremities, the disease will be fatal.

If in the course of fistula-in-ano *(bhagandara)* air, urine, dejections, worms or semen are discharged from the fistula, the patient will die of the disease.

The fatal symptoms of stone in the bladder *(osmarica)* are swelling of the umbiliacus, and of the scrotum, with great pain in passing the urine, which is mixed with gravel.

The fatal signs of complex labour *(múragarbha)* are tumours, or polipi in the vagina, which prevents the passage of the child; unnatural contraction of the vagina, &c.

The fatal symptoms of a dropsical swelling of the abdomen *(udora)* are as follows:—having no feeling in the sides, loss of appetite, and the body swelling, with dysentery. If after purgatives the abdomen again swells, the person should be considered as incurable.

If a person with *Fever* does not see, is insensible, sleeps without any movement, is internally hot, with an external feeling of cold, he will die. When the hairs become prominent upon the body, the eyes red, the breast very painful, and the breathing by the mouth, such a fever will be fatal. If there be hiccough, much thirst, insensibility, eyes fixed, or move involuntary, difficult and noisy breathing, with weakness, the fever will be fatal. If the eyes become muddy, and the person cannot see; sleeps much, with great weakness, and loss of strength and flesh, the fever will be fatal.

When there is with dysentery, difficulty of breathing, great pain, thirst, weakness and fever, the person will die, particularly when old.

Phthesis *(yakhmá)*, with cough and bloody expectoration, the eyes white, no appetite, and difficulty of drawing in the breath, diarrhœa, and a copious flow of urine with pain, will be fatal.

When *gulma,* or colicky pains, from a collection of wind in the abdomen, which feels like a moving ball, and is accompanied with difficulty in breathing, thirst, no appetite, and weakness, the disease will be fatal.

Internal abscesses of the abdomen *(bidradhi)* if accompanied with swelling, without any discharge, and if the person vomits, has hiccough, thirst, pain, and difficulty in breathing, he will die.

Jaundice *(pandu)*. If the teeth, nails, and eyes are yellow, and every thing seems so, in such case the disease will be fatal.

In hemorrhagea (*roktopeto)*. When the person vomits blood, has his eyes red, and every thing appears so, the disease will be fatal.

Madness (*unmáda*). If such a patient always either stoops or keeps his head raised, is thin, weak, gets no sleep, has no fear, he will die.

Epilepsy (*apasmára, mrigi*). If the fits occur frequently with weakness, the eyelids always move about, and the eyes become unnatural, the disease will be fatal.

The signs of death are as follows :—

Sight. When the person imagines he sees red, black, or yellow colours before his eyes, when he has lost all shame, strength, memory, and his natural appearance. It is also a fatal sign when the eyes become small, sunk, and unequal ; and when they are of a red colour, and cannot move ; under such circumstances a flow of tears is also a fatal sign.

Mouth. When there is a falling of the under, and rising of the upper lip ; when they are crooked, and are of a dark blue colour, the person will die. When the teeth become reddish or dark coloured, or fall out, or are of a grayish colour, the person will soon die.

Tongue. When the tongue is of a black colour, and extraneous matter appears upon it, or it cannot be moved, or is dirty and swollen, or its papulæ are very prominent, with fetor of the breath, the patient will soon die.

Nose. When it becomes pale, dry, and shining, and is turned to one side ; the nostrils extended, dry, and dirty, and the passage of the air produces a noise ; or when the point of the nose retracts, and is flattened, with weakness and depression, the person will soon die.

When therefore the eyes, by which we see ; the ears, by which we hear ; the tongue, by which we taste ; and the skin, by which the sense of heat, and cold is performed are defective, or differ from the state of health, the patient should be considered in a dangerous state.

Hair. If it falls naturally in a line on each side (as in women), and the eyebrows become contracted and repressed, and the patient pulls his eyelashes, the person will soon die. If such a person have no disease, he will die within six, and if diseased within three days.

If the person cannot swallow, if he cannot move his head, and remains at rest, and is insensible, he will soon die. Whether strong or weak, should he faint on being raised up, the person will die.

If a person diseased sleeps with his face turned upwards, and he is continually stretching, and bending his legs, he will soon die.

When the feet and hands are cold, and the person breathes quickly and irregularly, or retains his mouth open, like a crow in hot weather; such a person is not to be treated by the physician, as he will die. If a person always sleeps, or he is always watching and cannot speak, the physician is not to give medicine.

When the tongue is always moving along the upper lip, with continual hiccough; or if a person speaks incoherently to another person previously dead, he will not live. If blood flows from the pores of the hair, and the natural openings of the body, without poison, the person will soon die. When the hysterical ball (*astila*) from air, occurs in the breast, and prevents the swallowing of food, and the pain extends, and there is no appetite, the person will die. If an unusual swelling in the feet occur in the course of a disease in a man, or in the face of a female, it will destroy the person.

If in consumption, dysentery, asthma, fever, hiccough, vomiting, and swelling of the external urinary organs occur, the person will die. If such a sick person has much burning over the body, or much perspiration, hiccough, difficulty in breathing, even a strong person will die. If with the yellow or black tongue, the left eye be sunk, with bad breath, the person will die. If the mouth be filled with tears, the hands and feet perspire, and the eyes lose their shining appearance, and become dull, it is a sign of death. If the person swells or becomes thin very quickly, he will die. If the smell of the body resembles clay, fish, fat, oil, or other unnatural scents; or when lice leave the hair, and come to the forehead, or animals will not eat the food the patient has left; or when the patient is very restless he will die. When fever, dysentery, and swelling of feet, or hands, occur alternately, it is unfavourable; should the person lose his strength suddenly, he will not live. When the patient has no appetite, has frequent stools, with severe pain in the head, and thirst, the person will die, when combined with other bad symptoms.

It is also a bad sign when the patient is very weak, with thirst and hunger, which is not appeased by the usual quantity of food or drink; and should a practitioner cure any patients with the above indications, he deserves to be Physician to a king.

As death approaches, various kinds of devils are supposed to collect near the patient, and destroy the good qualities of the medicines which are administered to him. In such cases the treatment, and the care of the physician are alike unavailing.

Some of these remarks are just, and some of them are too much neglected by European Physicians. The *Cabiráj* often remarks with justice the errors which they sometimes fall into in consequence of their neglecting the study of the prognosis of diseases.

Section IV.

General Treatment of Diseases.

As the generality of diseases are supposed to be produced by derangements in the humors. One or more of which are morbidly increased or changed in quantity, the indications of treatment are to promote the just balance of the elements and humors, by a judicious choice of aliment, and by such means as assist the vital principle in the completion of the assimilation. The management of diet was supposed to be the great means of accomplishing this end; and was regulated in point of quality, quantity, and time of administering it, by the nature of the disease. Should the judicious selection of food not succeed in curing the disease, or when severe, the person was directed to observe an entire abstinence of food, for a certain time, and if this failed, the corrupted humors were ejected from the body. This was accomplished either by emetics, purgatives, or blood-letting. In like manner, when the disease was subdued, it was supposed to be necessary to expel all the vitiated humors; which, if allowed to remain, accumulate, and a relapse of the disease will be the consequence. To prevent this, strong drastic purgatives, which produced from five to eight evacuations, were repeated daily, until the physician was satisfied that the whole corrupted humors were expelled. To prevent such a recurrence of disease, the same evacuating means were employed. But these humors are not to be dislodged indiscriminately, but at certain seasons, and diurnal periods of the disease. Health was thus supposed to be promoted by the exhibition of an emetic once a fortnight, a drastic purgative once a month, and blood-letting twice a year, at the change of the seasons. The vital principle was supposed to give warning when the corrupted humors were ripe for being evacuated ; and the physician was directed to observe carefully, so as to be able to assist, and not disturb the spontaneous efforts of nature. The seasons in which she exhibited these beneficial influences, were supposed to be determined by the known cause of the disease, which led to the belief of the definite course, and the mystical powers of numbers ; by which nature may be invariably observed to arrive at certain determinate results, which were supposed to be regulated by an arithmetical progression. This led to the belief of the maturation of the diseased humors, and of the existence of a period, in which the perfect state of mixture takes place. These were called critical days, which have long held a place in the pathological belief of physicians. These days were recognised by the Egyptian priests, as related by Pythagoras and others, and denoted the time at which the due admixture of the elements had taken place. The same term κρασις was employed by Hippocratus and adopted in Europe, when the humoral pathology was the fashion. So plausible were the opinions of the humoral pathology, that they seem to have been at one time believed, and the most pernicious preventive means followed, over a great part of the globe ; and among nations so separated from each other, as to preclude the possibility of their having derived them from each other. Among the Hindus the humoral pathology appears to have originated without any assistance from other nations, and became as generally believed, and carried to the same consequences as it was in Europe.

Another equally plausible opinion was, that all diseases divide themselves into two great classes, of sthenic or asthenic disease. The one being an increase, and the other a diminution of excitement ; between the extremities of which health was supposed to be placed. This appears to have been an early opinion among the Hindus, is now generally believed over all the Asiatic nations ; and has led them to the division of remedies into stimulating, and cooling, which were employed according to the nature of the disease. For the hot or sthenic diseases cooling remedies were used ; while hot medicines were exhibited to remove cold, or asthenic diseases. To the class of stimulants belonged pepper, bitters, purgatives, &c. ; and to the cooling remedies cold, pawn mixed with lime, bathing, with several excellent stomachics ; as *chiraitá*, &c.

CHAPTER II.

Description and Treatment of Particular Diseases.

CLASS I.

Diseases of the Humors.

The apparent actions and changes of the fluids, or humors of the human body, attracted the attention of the bráhmans at an early period, and upon these changes they founded their theoretical speculations regarding the nature, and production of disease. These opinions seemed to be confirmed by the occurrences of hemorrhage from wounds, the appearance of certain eruptions, and the discharge from abscesses and ulcers ; while the solids in these cases seemed passive, with no indications of change beyond what the fluids seemed to produce upon them. Hence the general principles of Pathology were based, by the bráhmans, on alterations of the fluids only, and they supposed that while their elements and qualities remained in due proportion health was sustained ; while disease was produced by an undue proportion of these humors.

The diseases of air, bile and phlegm may proceed from the semen of the father, from the menstrual blood of the mother, from the state of the mother's body during utero-gestation, from certain food acting in the same way, from the habits of exercise, from the state of the parts in which the fetus is retained in the abdomen, and from the state of the menses at the time of conception. These causes derange the humors and produce the individuals' habit of body, and the kind of disease to which they are subject.

The derangement of these humors are the root of all diseases, and require to be carefully examined by the physician. All diseases are considered as being produced : 1st, by the derangements of the humors of the part, and 2ndly, by the peculiar diseases of the part.

The different seasons predispose to different diseases : the air of the body is liable to be deranged in the two rainy and two hot months ; in the two months before the cold weather bile is liable to be deranged ; and during the cold months, the bile remains in health, while the diseases of phlegm are common, and increase in spring.

The diseases of the humors may be arranged according as they affect the air, bile, and phlegm, and their combinations. There are eighty diseases produced by derangements of the air (*báyu*) ; forty of bile (*pitta*) ; twenty of phlegm (*kapha*) ; and sixteen by the combination of the derangements of these humors.

In the embryo state, the humors are in such a state that they do not interfere with the action of each other, as the serpents poison does not injure the animal itself. But in the course of life various causes interrupt this harmony; and various changes regulate and determine, at all times and seasons, the health, and morbid condition of the human body.

Air (báyu). The causes which derange air are fighting, abstinence in eating and drinking; the use of dry food, falls, watching when the body is wounded, great discharges, as of blood, semen, &c. The same effects are produced by constipation of air, urine, and dejections; or when they are not evacuated at the proper time. Bathing, great grief, fear, and exposure to cold, produce this class of diseases. The air is also increased when the food is digested, and in the evening.

The indications of derangement of the air, are a swelling of the abdomen, with stiffness of the body; the surface of which is dry, rough, and cracked. The person feels pain in different parts of the body, more especially of the arms, testicles, fat, &c.; is low-spirited, languid, and fatigued, has shivering fits and spasms; the hair drops off, and the person's head is always bowing backwards and forwards, with other irregular movements of the body. The voice becomes altered, and the person speaks much, and dreams in his sleep. When awake he speaks often without thought, he feels a singing in has ears, loses the power of vision, has no memory, with paralysis of one or more ot the members. There is a dryness of the mouth with thirst; the body becomes of a red or green colour, and he complains of an astringent taste in the mouth.

Sometimes the person has severe cutting pains in the stomach *(sul)* and over the body. Parts of the body feel hard, with noise in the ears, dimness of sight, obtuseness of the senses, thirst, dozing, irregular movements of the body, watching, and uncomfortable dreams, with a feeling of doing impossibilities, yawning, and roughness of the skin.

Diseases of Air will vary according to its situation and use. The vital air for the mouth *(práná)*, which assists in swallowing, produces when disordered, hiccough, vomiting, &c. The air we breathe *(udáná)* produces asthma, consumption, &c. when diseased. The *(sámáná)* or vital air in the stomach produces vomiting, anxiety, fainting, thirst, and pain in the chest and side. In the *intestines* it produces noise along their course, pain in the navel, with costiveness, scanty urine, and flatulence, &c.; in the *ear* it produces deafness; in the *integuments*, a discoloration, roughness, and sometimes there is a diminished sensation, and eruption over the skin. When deranged in the *blood*, it produces different painful eruptions, and tumors. When deranged with *fat* it produces tumors, without pain. In *vessels*, it produces a contraction of their size, with pain and fullness. In *tendons*, it produces paralysis, with shaking pain and spasm. In *joints*, it produces stiffness, pain, swelling, and emaciation ; in the *bones* it produces pain and emaciation ; in the *marrow* it causes acute pain ; in the *semen* it produces a morbid discharge, or a diminution of the secretion ; and when deranged over the body it produces a bluntness of sense, paralysis, spasm, swelling, and pain in many parts of the body. Besides these it produces various other classes of symptoms, according to the parts of the body which are principally affected.

The principal diseases produced by deranged air are fainting, *bato rukta, pitta rukta,* and *kapha rukta,* and leprosy. This last disease commences in the limbs, with dark blotches, and insensibility of the part. It produces rigidity of parts (*apotanoka*) by which the body is drawn to a side, or backwards and forwards ; and there is another form of the disease called *dhumus stamb* (Tetanus, Trismus.) It affects particularly the lower jaw, and face, by drawing the neighbouring parts to one side or another. *Choria* (kalaia khunj) is according to the *Nedan* and *Susruta* produced by derangements of air. This disease is characterized by the person first feeling a trembling or shivering over the body, with dimness of sight, and pain in the neck, jaw, and teeth, or any other part about to be affected. These symptoms are followed by convulsive twitchings of the head, neck, and face ; and of one side of the body, particularly of one leg. These parts are pulled to the side affected, and shake involuntary. These movements extend to all the voluntary muscles of progression, producing a dancing motion. The muscles of the upper or lower extremities may thus be affected, of one or both sides, and when it has extended over the body and continued long, it is considered incurable. It is supposed to be produced by irregularity of the bowels, from having eaten indigestable food ; which produces costiveness and indigestion. Much talking and laughing, carrying heavy loads, and other causes deranging air, are supposed to produce this disease.*

When the *air* is superabundant it will be diminished by cold, and articles of food having this property ; by strengthening food, which, on being digested remains long in the vessels, such as ghee, the flesh of goats, &c., masculi, salt, or sweet or sour food, shampoo-

* Some Sanscrit books apply the term Ardita to Choria, others, apply it to Tetanus or Trismus which they describe, and not the true Choria.

ing, anointing the body with oil, or taking it internally, by drinking sherbuts, by bathing, by medicines which increase the secretion of semen, alvine secretions, urine, and perspiration; which remove thirst and appetite, and render the body more active.

When air is diminished the person cannot work, he speaks little, is unhappy, and his judgment is impaired.

The best means of curing these derangements of *air* is by exhibiting oleaginous, salt, sweet, and acid food, by bathing, by the use of wine, by shampooing, by exhibiting enemas, &c.

Bile (pitta) is increased by sour, hot, salt, or bitter articles of food, by eating the shoots of young bamboos, and other such indigestible articles of food. When the appetite is not satisfied with the quantity eaten, or by eating before the food previously eaten has not been digested; when old curries are used; curdled milk, wine, or conjee are drunk; when exposed to anger, to hot weather, especially during the months of September and October, and the middle of the day, or middle watch of the night the bile is increased.

When bile is in unusual quantity it produces a disagreeable breath, hot and sour eructations, with boils over the body. The person is subject to fits of anger, his bowels are open, the skin distended, and he staggers as if drunk; his body is hot, the perspiration copious, and although he eats he has no appetite, is thirsty, and has no memory, but is otherwise intelligent. He does not see distinctly, has a dislike to particular kinds of food, which become sour, bitter, and sweet, in the stomach. The colour of the body is unnatural, being pale, with pain over the body.

Bile is diminished by eating sweet, and bitter articles of food; by remaining in cool shaded places, by night air, and moon light; by sitting upon the ground, in water, or exposed to mists. It is also diminished by the use of ghee, and milk; by those medicines which increase the discharge from the mouth, nose and eyes; by blood-letting, and whatever diminishes thirst and appetite. When so diminished the internal heat is weakened, and the body has an unhealthy appearance. The twitchings produced by increased bile in a part are best removed by rubbing it with milk, and exhibiting cooling articles of food.

When air is deranged with bile it produces inflammation and fainting; with phlegm coldness and swelling of the affected part; with blood it produces a degree of pain like the penetration of a needle, sometimes deprivation of healthy sensation, and other symptoms of deranged bile. When the *prán báyu* is deranged with bile, it produces vomiting, a burning heat of the body; with cough, weakness, idleness, drowsiness, and discoloration of the skin. When the *udána báyu* is deranged with bile, fainting, a burning heat of the body, want of memory, cough, want of perspiration, anxiety, indigestion, and shivering are produced. Deranged *apána báyu* with bile produces perspiration, heat, and inflammation; with cough, mucous stools, urine of a pale colour, with shivering. *Samána báyu* deranged with bile produces inflammation and heat of the body, and in the female a retention of the menses, cough, and heaviness of the lower part of the abdomen. *Biána báyu* deranged with bile produces a burning heat and restlessness of the body, with cough, heaviness of the body, and pain, so that the person cannot move as he wishes.

Phlegm (kapha), is deranged by indigestible articles of food, and sweet, or very cool things; such as milk, sugar-cane, liquid food, curdled milk, sleeping during the day; or by the cakes made of rice, coconuts, ghee, &c. These derangements are more liable to occur in the dewy, cold, and spring months, during the first third of the day, and after eating.

The derangements of phlegm produce a fulness of the abdomen, and the food the person eats is not properly digested; he has no appetite, and his body is pale, heavy, cold, and hard. He has frequent dejections; his skin is smooth, oily, and itchy. There is a discharge of mucus from the nose, eyes, and mouth. Such a person is very languid, is always dozing, and sleeps much; the part where the phlegm is deranged swells, and his mouth has a pungent and sweet taste.

The cure of these derangements is accompanied by the use of dry food, alkalies (salts), astringents, exercise, and the use of bitter, and pungent articles of food; by the exhibition of emetics, by connexion with women, long pedestrian journies, gymnastic exercises, watching at night, smoking, and the use of cathartics, and diaphoretics.

Should two or three of these humors be deranged at the same time, the particular symptoms of each will be present; and the degree of derangement of the one compared with that of the other will be observed, by the prominence of the particular class of symptoms. Their treatment must likewise be varied according to the violence of the symptoms present.

When the body is weak the most peculiar symptoms of the deranged humor do not appear, and the person seems in health.

The diseases of air, bile and phlegm, are also produced by sin, which leads the person to perform wicked actions from ignorance. Such diseases of the humors produce not only diseases of the body, but also those of the mind, and heart; as melancholy, pride, foolishness, &c. These were the diseases in which internal evacuant medicines were used, after which the treatment was to be regulated by the part affected: thus when the skin was affected, external applications were used, as ointments, plasters, &c. While the diseases of the body are cured by medicines, which diminish the humors that are too abundant; those of the mind are cured by perusing the Shásters, by abstinence, by leading a religious life, and by various mortifications of the body.

The blood is supposed to be more generally affected with the deranged humors, than with any other of the essential parts of the body. When so diseased its local, or general abstraction is recommended, and numerous medicines are administered, to purify it.

It is consequently the duty of the practitioner to find out the nature of the disease; to decide on the best remedies; to diminish the air, bile, or phlegm, the seven essential parts of the body, and the dejections (*mala*) which may be preternaturally increased, and if any of them are diminished he should endeavour to increase them so as to restore, and retain the parts, in that state of equanimity, which constitutes health. These effects may be produced by the frequent exhibition of purgatives, emetics, and food which has these peculiar effects.

When a disease is produced by the sins committed in a former state of existence; by the derangements of air, bile, and phlegm at birth, or by any cause producing very dangerous diseases, especially in very old people; it will be cured by medicines and penances. Diseases of the poor will generally be incurable, as they are not able to pay for their medicines.

Section II.

Class II.—*Diseases affecting the General System.*

Order I.

Fevers, (Jwara.)

Fevers are first considered because it is said that man is born and dies with fever; because it affects the whole body, the organs of senses, and the mind; and is so severe that only man and gods can survive it, and by which various other diseases are produced.

The following mythological description of the origin of fever is given in some of their more recent medical works:—*Dakshya* the father-in-law of *Shiva* did not invite him to a feast given to the gods, and spoke disrespectfully of him. His wife *Durgá* was present, and was so enraged, at the disrespect, that she considered it better to die than live under such a disgrace; and while sitting, her spirit left her body. *Nundi* the servant of *Durgá* seeing her die, went and informed *Shiva* of the event. He in grief for his loss, tore off one of his locks, and it fell into the fire, and a great devil named *Birabhadra* was produced from it. Others say that in his anger he heaved a deep sigh, and from his mouth the devil was produced. *Birabhadra* asked *Shiva* to be allowed to destroy his father-in-law. This was permitted, and after polluting the sacred fire of *Dakshya*, destroying many of his guests, and tearing his hair, he wrenched his head from his body. It was during the paroxysm of grief and rage of *Shiva* for the death of *Durgá* that the breath which proceeded from his nostrils, hot, and destructive, gave origin to fevers, which attack all persons, of all ages, and in all conditions.

The *cause* of all the principal varieties of fever, with the exception of five from accidents *(ágantuka)*, is using improper mixtures of food; as eating fish and milk; the want of seasoning in food; sleeping at improper hours; fighting with a strong man; exposure to the morning sun while fasting; eating voraciously of food of a very hot nature, when the body has been previously weakened by extreme hunger; and by fatigue, fear, grief, and watching. Fevers are also produced by poisons, drinking stagnant water, in which withered leaves have fallen; taking a full meal without any appetite, or after delivery, especially if improperly treated. In other cases the first secretion of milk in the breast, produces fever, exposure to unseasonable weather, or to sudden vicissitudes of temperature; checked perspiration, long continued constipation; and living in wooded, ill ventilated valleys. Other causes of fever are the influence of bad stars, neglected adoration of saints or gods; visiting a new climate; the malign influence of evil spirits, and severe local diseases, or injuries. By such causes the air, bile, and phlegm are deranged, pass into the stomach *(ámáshay)*, and thus expel the internal heat. The humors stop also the chyle vessels, and derange the heat, which digests the food: in other words, whatever exposes our moral qualities, or bodily frame, to deviations from their natural and accustomed movements, produces fevers; and it requires remedies to drive back the heat, to its natural position, when the person is restored to health.

General symptoms of Fever.

The attack of fever commences with the person complaining of lassitude and fatigue; he is continually yawning, and stretching;

his skin loses its natural colour, and there is a bad taste in his mouth; his eyes are watery, and he alternately wants the application of heat, and cold to his body. Little, and much food distresses the person, as it is not digested; he has no appetite, the body is chilly and heavy, with dejection of mind; and he is quarrelsome, and ready to fight with a much stronger person than himself.

These precursory symptoms are followed by heat of the surface, cessation of perspiration, and pain affecting the whole body, but particularly the members. There is also pain in the chest, languor and drowsiness, loss of appetite, restlessness, heaviness of the abdomen with costiveness, and a copious flow of urine. These symptoms are always present in fevers; but, when *air* is deranged, there is also much gaping; when *bile* is affected the eyes feel hot, and when *phlegm* is deranged there is no appetite.

General Treatment of Fever.

The treatment of fever varies according as it is new, or has not lasted seven days; is recent, or has not affected the individual more than twelve days; or is old, having continued twenty-one days, or upwards.

When the fever is *new* the patient should only take conjee water for food; and when the internal heat is diminished, dry ginger and long pepper may be boiled in it. When with fever there is a disease in the side, or lower part of the head or abdomen, the red rice should be used for making the conjee. Should phlegm be diseased conjee should not be given; nor when the new fever is very strong. When these acute symptoms are diminished and when *bile* is deranged the use of conjee water is proper. The drink should be boiled water again warmed. Should the patient complain of nausia, and fulness of the stomach, on an accession of fever, the treatment should commence with the exhibition of an emetic, and during the continuance of an attack of fever all heavy food should be carefully avoided; particularly when there is no appetite.

In other MSS. it is stated that the fasting is to be continued for three, five, or ten days, according to the improvement of the symptoms which takes place. By this means the practitioner will discover the state of the air, bile, and phlegm.

During the continuance of a *new* fever the patient should reside in a room shut up, in which a *panká* may be used. He should be clad in warm clothes; should neither sleep during the day, bathe, nor anoint his body with oil. He should also be removed from his wife, avoid all oily and indigestable articles of food, especially astringent articles, anger, violent exercise, and exposure to strong wind. By these means the morbid matter is allowed to ripen, and is then to be discharged by evacuant medicines. It will increase the disease, and render it probably fatal, if these evacuant remedies are used before the morbid matter is matured.

Should in any case the fasting produce weakness, it is to be stopped as improper; and means to strengthen the body substituted. Fasting is not to be employed in fevers which attacks infants or old people, in pregnancy, when the body is light, or in cases in which air, urine, and dejections have been discharged, in large quantities, by medicine.

In recent fever the patient is to be allowed a decoction of bitter herbs, &c. so as to restore the derangement of the humors. He may now be allowed a little more food than during the first stage. Milk, which during the first stage is like poison, may now be taken with advantage.

Should the disease continue and pass on to the third period, when the fever is said to be *old*, it is to be treated by emetics, purgatives, and different febrifuge decoctions. The diet should be in larger quantities and of a more nourishing quality, than during the two first periods of the disease; such as broths, prepared with animal flesh, milk, and the like.

In all such cases of fever it is necessary to recollect that the treatment will vary according as the air, bile, and phlegm are more or less affected.

The fever is said to have disappeared when the appetite returns; the body feels light, and the person is not easily fatigued. When the acuteness of his senses, memory, and understanding is restored, the unnatural heat of the body disappears, and he has no pain; when he moans, is forgetful, when small pimples form round the mouth, and when the warmth, smell, and perspiration, sneezing, and the alvine evacuations are natural.

Should there occur, after the seventh day, sonorous breathing, listlessness and torpor, with thirst, constipation, hiccough, coughing, and vomiting with no appetite, the patient is in eminent danger. In such cases the person usually becomes very weak, and dies.

The most unfavourable prognostic symptoms of fever, when the patient should not be taken charge of by the physician, are when the senses are not in their natural state, or no longer act; when the person is weak, with sudden and severe attacks of fever; when the patient is decrepid, his extremities swell, and the fever remains during a greater part of the night; when affected with strabismus, and when his mouth remains open, and he is delirious. When he cannot be roused from his sleep, with the feeling of cold on the outside of the body, while he is hot inside, the patient is in great danger. In such cases the person generally dies.

Varieties of Fevers.

These are divided into continued, mixed, accidental, and intermittent fevers; which will be considered under the following nine genera:

Continued fever	1 Fever produced by deranged *Air*.
	2 Fever produced by deranged *Bile*.
	3 Fever produced by deranged *Phlegm*.
	4 Fever produced by deranged *Air* and *Phlegm*.
	5 Fever produced by deranged *Air* and *Bile*.
	6 Fever produced by deranged *Bile* and *Phlegm*.
Mixed remittent or synochus fever.	7 Fever produced by deranged *Air*, *Phlegm* and *Bile*.
Accidental fever.	8 Fever produced by derangement of the humors.
Intermittent fever.	9 Fever produced by derangement of humors.

All these fevers are produced by derangements of air, bile, or phlegm, and fasting is one of the chief means of restoring the balance, while the fever is advancing, or when unripe. This is known by a peculiar pain in the chest, by drowsiness, and listlessness, by the yellow colour of the saliva, by the want of appetite, by the constipated state of the bowels, and by secretion of urine; by the body feeling heavy, by the absence of perspiration, by the bad taste in the mouth, and by a constant and severe fever. *Dhanwantari* says that medicine should not be given in this stage of fever, and not until the seventh day; others say, not until the tenth day after its commencement. However, should the bowels have been constipated before the fever, and the humors are ripe, they should be removed either by emetics, purgatives, or errhines, or a severe disease will be the consequence by the pent up impurities. Should fever be produced by derangements of air, ghee should be freely used; if phlegm is particularly deranged, give first an emetic; if bile, purgatives, which will be varied with the peculiar symptoms. When the phlegm is ripe, errhines are recommended. A suppository is also recommended for these cases of constipation. It should be composed of long-pepper, *jubdán*, *clivé*, *medream*.

If the fever does not completely disappear by these means it proves that some of the diseased humors still remain, which should be removed by the exhibition of hot ghee. The cure is accomplished by increasing the strength, promoting the appetite, which is known by a lightness and elasticity of the body. The next indication is to discharge the deranged air, bile, or phlegm, by means of errhines and purgatives ; and during the continuance of the fever the usual food and drink are to be avoided, until the natural excretions are restored, the senses act naturally, and the patient feels hungry, and thirsty, at the same time.

1*st Variety of Fever*. *Bátik-jwara* is that variety which is produced by a derangement of the air *(báyu.)*

This fever commences with shivering, there is sometimes much at other times little heat ; the throat, mouth, and lips are dry. The patient has no sleep, does not sneeze, his skin is dry, with head-ache, and pain in the chest, as well as over the body. Whatever is taken into the stomach feels heavy, and creates uneasiness ; the stools are very hard ; pain in the abdomen ; flatulence as if much food had been eaten, and he is frequently yawning.

The treatment of this form of fever will depend on the stage at which it is examined. In the shivering fit, hot remedies are to be exhibited. According to *Sushruta* it is treated by enemas, the employment of errhines, composed of different medicines for removing the head-ache, and humors from the head, and by exhibiting the following infusion :

Cassia fistula	*(A'bashwash.)*
Ruellea strepens	*(Granthika.)*
Cyperus juncifoliao	*(Musta.)*
Black hellibore	*(Tikta.)*
Myrobalan	*(Haritaki.)*

Take 40 *raktika* of each, boil in one pint of water till a quarter remains, and strain. This quantity is for one dose, and is usually given in the morning and repeated for two days ; various infusions of herbs, and barks of trees, are used in the same way. Prepared ghee with febrifuge medicines are used, when the above remedies do not cure the disease. In all cases the particular treatment will vary with the symptoms present.

The food to be taken in this fever is, first kidney beans (*Phaseolus mungo*) boiled, bruised, and eat with spice ; conjee with the juice of lemon, and warm water for drink. Long-pepper, hemidismus (*Sarura*), raisins (kismis), dill (sataspispa), (ranuka), of each 40 *rati*, to a pint of water ; boiled down to a fourth, and taken twice a day.

Should this sort of fever be produced by severe exercise, or if the patient is very hungry, he may take broth with boiled rice, fish, conjee, and other such light food.

Should a strong evacuant medicine be given in the first stage of this, or any other fever, it will produce severe intermittent fevers.

2nd form of Fever. When Bile is deranged, producing fever, it is called *(Paittika Jwara.)* This form of fever commences with a shivering fit, followed by a severe hot stage ; a frequent desire to go to stool, vomiting, a bitter taste in the mouth, and restlessness. Aphthæ form in the throat, lips, mouth, and nose ; the patient perspires freely, often speaks nonsense, and has sometimes fainting fits, and attacks of giddiness. Such a patient is very listless, his body is pale, with a burning sensation over the surface, he has great thirst, the stools and urine have a yellow colour, as well as the eye, which is often also red.

Treatment. This fever, like the last, has three stages. In the first stage give laxatives, with cooling and bitter food. The paltá leaves *(Paṭolpatra)* 1 tolá ; with half a pint of simple water, or barley water boiled, and a little honey, for the taste, is given once a day, and is considered very cooling. The following cooling medicine is also given in this fever :—Take of

Parpaṭaka, the bitter leaves of the Oldenlandea biflora,
Basaka, (Justitia ganderussa,)
Kaṭutiktá, (black helebore,)
Kirátatikta, (Chiraita,)
Dhányaka, (coriander seed,)
Priyangu, (Panicum italicum,)

15 ratis of each, or one sicca weight. A tolá to be infused in a pint of water until it is reduced to $\frac{1}{4}$ which is to be taken twice daily.

There are various other bitter remedies, all of which are said to cure this fever. It is also treated by covering the forehead with several cooling medicines mixed with water. When pain in the head is severe, with great heat, the person is recommended to sleep on lily, nim, and plantain leaves, to cool the body. They also recommend free ventilation, and residing in a cool situation. The house may be sprinkled with sandal-wood, and water. By a purgative you may prevent the recurrence of the disease, when only the preliminary symptoms are present.

In this fever the diet should consist of fried gram, or peas boiled in water, and strained. This is mixed with sugar and honey : the juice of acid fruits is also given.

3rd form of Fever. Derangement of phlegm *(Kapha),* produces a fever named *shlaishmik-jwara,* or *kapha-jwara.* This fever is ushered in by loss of appetite, and the symptoms of the hot stage is less marked than in the last form of fever. The person feels languid, and listless, with a sweet taste in his mouth. In this fever the body feels cold, as if wrapped in a wet cloth, and the stools and urine are white. Such a person remains quiet and silent, does not eat; but feels as if he had eaten too much, his body is very heavy, eyes white, with nausea attended with cough. He is very sleepy, and there is a discharge of mucus from the eyes, mouth, and nose.

Treatment. For seven days the person should not eat his usual food in this fever; but should live on prepared peas, and the like. The stomach in the first stage of this fever should be cleared by an emetic, which will often cut the fever short, but this remedy is not to be used when the patient is very weak: after the emetic the juice of the leaves of Vitex negundo (*Incha* or *Sindubára)* is to be administered, with the powder of long-pepper. Heating medicines of all kinds are also used in this fever, as the diet should be light as well as heating.

4th. Báta-paittika Jwara. This fever commences with giddiness, fainting and thirst: the body feels cold to another person, although he complains of his body being hot and burning; loss of memory, no sleep, pain in all the joints, head-ache, cough, throat and mouth dry, vomiting, goose-skin, no perspiration, low spirits, and yawning.

To remove this form of fever take of
Shunṭhí, dry ginger,
Gulancha, (Minispermum glabrum,)
Muthá, (Cyperus rotundus,)
Chirátá, (Chiraita,)
Shálpání, (Hedysarum gangeticum,)
Chákulyá, (Hemionites cordifolia,)
Byákuṛ, (Solanum Jaquini,) a variety of prickly nightshade,
Kanṭikárí, (Solanum melongena,) prickly nightshade,
Ganirí, (Premna spinosa,)

18 ratís each, mix in water, boil to $\frac{1}{4}$, and take twice a day.

Diet. The decoction of *mudga,* a sort of pea, and the juice of *ámlaka* is often used. When there is much heat in the body we may give a decoction of gram, with the juice of the fruit of pomegranate for diet.

5th. Báta-shlaishmik Jwara. This form of fever is not very severe in its accession. The body feels cold, with slight shivering and pain in the bones; the person sleeps much, has pain in the head, with much saliva in the mouth, and running at the nose, with cough, a dry skin, and body hot.

The treatment consists in exhibiting the root of long-pepper, *chabya,* (Piper chavya or Orris root, *Roxb.,)* and root of *chitraka,* (Plumbago zeylanica,) and dried ginger: 32 ratís of each are put into a pint of water, and boiled down to one-fourth. Take this twice a day. Heating medicines may also be used in this fever, as chiraita, dry ginger, *gulancha,* (Minispermum glabrum,) *básaka,* (Justicia ganderussa,) long-pepper, *lashun,* (garlick,) and *sindubára,* (Vitex negunda,) 20 ratís each. Boil in a pint of water, till reduced to one-fourth, and take this twice daily. When the pain in the joints is severe, the vapour bath may be used; and should there be great dryness of the mouth, in order to increase this secretion take salt, the powder of black-pepper, and the juice of lemons.

Diet. Boil in water the following medicines:—the bark of

Bilwa, (Ægle marmelos,)
Shonáka, (Bignonia indica,)
Gambhárí, (Gmelina arborea,)
Páṭalá, (Bignonia suave-olens,) and
Ganikáriká (Premna spinosa:)

of each 32 ratís, mix in two seers of water, and reduce it to one seer. This is again boiled with some rice, and when cool strained.

6*th. Bile and Phlegm, (Pitta-shlaishmik Jwara.)* The mouth is clammy and sour, with much saliva, in this form of fever. The person is always dozing, complains of faintness, and coughs; has no appetite, thirst, and is at one time hot, and at another time cold.

Cure. Abstinence in eating and drinking is to be enjoined; the medicines that cure the diseases of bile and phlegm are to be given, such as

Gulancha, (Minispermum glabrum,)
Nimba, neem bark,
Dhanyáka, coriander,
Chandana, red sandal-wood,
Caṭurohiní, helebore,

ratís 32 each, boil in a pint of water, till reduced to one-fourth; take this dose twice a day.

Perspiration is also to be encouraged, as phlegm shuts up the perspirable pores, and restores the internal heat to its proper place; and water promotes the movements of the body, and cures the fever. Hot sand in a bag may be applied to the body, and by changing continually its position, it soon produces perspiration. Long-pepper with its stem, dry-ginger, each 23 ratís, mixed and boiled together may be given twice daily.

7*th. Mixed Remittent or Synochus Fever, (Sannipát Jwara Bikára.)* In this form of fever the air, bile, and phlegm, are deranged; and it is always dangerous. At one time the patient is hot, at other times cold, with pains in the bones, and joints ; the eyes are watery, of a dirty yellow colour, and hollow ; the patient complains of ringing, and pain in the ears, with pain in the head, neck, and thorax ; is always dozing, but cannot sleep at night ; has no memory, and is often delirious. Bodies seem to turn round, and sometimes he is laughing, crying, performs unnatural actions, is always coughing, has quick breathing, no appetite, the tongue is black like charcoal, and irregular like that of a cow, with pain. Blood, phlegm, air and bile flow from the mouth, the patient moves his head about continually, with thirst, watching, and pain in the breast. The urine is secreted in small quantities, with costiveness and no perspiration ; great thirst, noises in the throat, so that there is a difficulty in comprehending what the sick person says ; with round elevations, and central depressions of a blue and red colour, over the surface of the body. The person vomits blood, mixed with phlegm, and his abdomen diminishes in size. His body does not become thin, but his belly is heavy and enlarged. This kind of fever remains long, and much care and proper medicines are required for its cure. After the first stage, should the fever continue severe, it will be generally fatal ; and at the last stage of the fever the lower part of the ear (the parotid gland) swells. This is supposed to be a fatal sign.

The 7th, 10th, 12th days, are always the days on which the fever is severe, or from these periods the symptoms diminish in severity.

In other books it is stated that the critical days are the 7th, 9th, 11th, 14th, 18th, 22nd ; from which period the disease is diminished or increased. Those who live till the 22nd day generally recover.

There are thirteen kinds of mixed fever. In three kinds one of humours, that is the air, bile, or phlegm, are morbidly increased, or diminished beyond the others. In a second form two are increased or diminished. The thirteenth variety is that in which the three humours are morbidly increased.

1. *Bisfaraka Bátulbana.* When the air is increased, the usual symptoms of this form of fever will be accompanied with a bad taste in the mouth, difficulty of breathing, shivering, cough, yawning, giddiness, syncope, delirium, and pain in the sides of the belly.

2. *Pittulbana* or *Asukari.* The peculiar symptoms of this form are looseness, giddiness, fainting, aphthæ in the mouth, red spots, and a burning sensation, over the body.

3. *Korupono* or *Kaphulbana,* is distinguished by a feeling of languor, a difficulty in speaking, sleeping much, eyes cloudy, and a sweet taste in the mouth.

4. *Pobru Bobru. Bátapittulbana.* When bile is increased the person feels as if he had taken narcotic medicines, complaining of thirst, dry mouth, drowsiness, flatulence, loss of appetite, cough, difficult of breathing, giddiness, and languor.

5. *Bato Soleso, Ulbono,* or *Sigrokarí.* When the air and phlegm around the neck is stopped, fever comes on with shivering, fainting, sneezing, thirst, pains in the sides of the body and in the abdomen, and difficulty in breathing.

6. *Petu Soleso Bono Bolu.* Is distinguished by a burning sensation in the body with chilliness, much thirst, pain in the right side of the chest, head-ache, pain in the breast and throat, vomiting phlegm and bile, looseness, difficulty of breathing, hiccough, and drowsiness.

7. *Bato-Peto-Soliso-Ulbono* or *Kutopákolo.* In this form the three air, bile and phlegm are morbidly increased, and like thunder, fire and the sword, it kills quickly. The peculiar symptoms of this form of fever are, the patient breathes slowly and imperfectly, he is motionless, his eyes are fixed, and after three days he dies.

8. *Songonohohoko.* The peculiar symptoms of this variety are delirium, languor, faintness, shivering, giddiness, and paralysis of half the body. This is a very dangerous disease.

9. *Pákolo.* Faintness, delirium, stiffness of the neck, head-ache, cough, difficulty of breathing, giddiness, drowsiness, severe pain in the chest, hemorrhage from the mouth, and nose, and the eyes being fixed characterise this form of fever. The patient generally dies within three days.

10. *Jammo.* In this variety severe pain in the chest, and abscesses form in the liver, spleen and lungs; and both the patient's stools, and the matter vomited contain blood and pus.

11. *Korkotoko.* Is accompanied with a burning sensation internally, the person cannot speak, his face and eyes become red, he cannot expectorate the phlegm from his throat, has severe lancinating pains in the breast, with drowsiness, difficulty of breathing, and hiccough. These symptoms increase daily; the patient's tongue becomes black and rough, his throat becomes covered with prickles, involuntary evacuations follow; he moans much, like the cooing of a pigeon; his mouth, lips, and palate are dry, he sleeps much, and he cannot speak, with convulsions, or nausea and vomiting.

12. *Boidáríko.* In this fever there is pain in the loins, the body is cool, and during the accession the body feels cold, with diarrhœa, giddiness, languor, head-ache, drowsiness, pain in the neck and chest, cough, difficulty of breathing, and insensibility.

13. *Abhinyása Jwara.* Is characterized by dryness of the mouth, by the patient being always sleepy, and his body feels as if it belonged to another person; he speaks very little, and with great pain, is stupid, and breathes with difficulty. His internal heat is diminished, he feels an internal burning sensation accompanied with weakness, and a dead-like feeling of the skin.

Treatment of Mixed fever. In this fever the patient must abstain from food; he must be put into a sand-bath, and errhines, emetics, and expectorates administered to him. Should the person be drowsy several colyria are recommended. During this fever he should drink boiled water, which has been cooled.

8th. Accidental fever, (Ágantuka.) The causes of this order of fevers are injuries; such as wounds, &c. They may also be produced by the evil designs of an enemy, or a devil; by the passions; by the curses of a guru, a bráhman, or a prophet; by poison, or by the effects of air mixed with deleterious matter, as that proceeding from a kind of poisonous trees which are supposed to come from the east. These causes derange the air, bile, and phlegm, and thus produce fever.

Adultery, grief for parents, friends, &c. derange also the air, anger deranges bile, and devils derange both air, bile, and phlegm.

When a man wants to kill another, or to remove an obnoxious individual to another country; or to have command of him, certain *mantras,* and directions are given in the *Tantra Shástra* for accomplishing these. But should he err in any of the injunctions enjoined, the person himelf will be attacked with the fever, and he will not have power to injure the other. In some such cases the two front teeth are extracted to prevent the person blundering in pronouncing *mantras.*

When the fever is produced by poisons the tongue is white, or black in the middle, the person has frequent stools, and fainting fits, and has no appetite, or memory, and complains of thirst, and pain over the body. By improper medicines this fever is sometimes produced with swooning, head-ache, and vomiting.

Making offerings of fire, &c., to bráhmans will cure this species of fever. When produced by a bad conjunction of planets, gifts will cure it. By giving shelter to the traveller, setting him in a clean place, washing his feet, giving him food, will prevent the consequence. Another form of cure is going to the principal sacred temples, and making offerings through the bráhmans.

When it is produced by the passion of love there is no memory, the person dozes, is lazy, and delirious. In this variety every thing cooling is to be given; if *cough* is deranged, bitter things are to be given; if *air*, cooling things; if *bile*, sweet things. This fever is cured, when produced by poison, by the usual antidotes. When produced by grief, remedies for curing bile are to be used; when from lust, the person is to be comforted, and his purpose promised. If from fear, causes producing joy will perform a cure.

When produced by the curses of a good man, or by the sorcery of another, want of memory and thirst are the peculiar symptoms present; and when an evil spirit produces it, the person alternately is sorrowful and laughing; and at other times he cries and laughs. These are to be cured by proper prayers, stated in the *shástras*, by binding the person, and beating him, by which the fever will be cured, as by these means the devil suffers, and is expelled.

9th. Intermittent fevers (*Bishama Jwara*). This is another form of fever, which occurs before and after attacks of other kinds of fever; by the derangements of the humours of the body. The essential parts of the body such as chyle, blood, muscles, fat, bone, semen, and marrow, in the order now mentioned may be affected. One or more are sometimes deranged, and form so many types of fever.

These are *Santata, Satata, Anyejyuka, Tritíyaka, Cháturthaka.* The general symptoms of intermittent fever are as follows: when the paroxysm occurs at uncertain periods the patient feels first cold, then hot, and afterwards perspires.

The following five varieties are described:

1. *Santata* continues for several days without an intermission.
2. *Satata* has two paroxysms daily.
3. *Anyejyuka* occurs daily, at the same hour.
4. *Tritíyaka* occurs on alternate days.
5. *Cháturthaka* occurs every fourth day.

At the time of the accession of the fever the paroxysm may be prevented by frightening the patient, by brandishing a naked sword before him, by advancing poisonous snakes near him, with the poisoned fangs removed, by the approach of dangerous elephants, and by the alarm of thieves. For a like purpose on the day of the return of the fever, emetics, purgatives, diaphoretics, or strong liquors are to be exhibited. These are to be given before the paroxysm is expected.

The following varieties of this class of fevers are described by Hindu Medical writers.

1. *Santata-jwara* affects the chyle and blood; and it continues for 7, 10, or 12 days; followed by an interval and again occurs, and remains for several days.

2. *Satata* has two paroxysms daily, one at night and another during the day.

When the person is weak and the fever is old, he is to live on light food, such as broths prepared with certain kinds of pulse, the flesh of birds and animals, which have been fed with gram. Others say there are two kinds of this fever, one of which commences with a cold fit, and another with a hot fit. The first gives much uneasiness, and is cured with difficulty.

3. If the paroxysm of fever recurs at the same hour daily, it is called *Anyejyuka*. In this form use the following medicine :

Take of bark of the *nimba* tree,
Paṭolapatra,
Drákshyá,
Ámlaka,
Bibhítaka,
Harítakí,
The flowers of the *mutá*,
Kurchi bark,

two máshás of each, add a pint of water, and reduce the mixture to a half by boiling. Several medicines are also recommended to be mixed, and the steam from the mixture is allowed to come in contact with the body, which has been covered, so as to be exposed to the vapours.

4. When the fever returns at an interval of one day it is called *Tritíyaka*. These are the following three varieties of this fever :

a. When *phlegm* and *bile* are deranged in this fever, before the accession, pain is felt at the nape of the neck.

b. When *spirit* and *phlegm* are deranged, the patient first feels pain in the loins.

c. When *air* and *bile* are deranged, the fever is introduced with head-ache. For the cure of such fevers, various *mantras* are employed.

5. In *Cháturthaka*, the paroxysms of this fever occur every fourth day. When the paroxysm continues for two days, there is no paroxysm on the first and fourth day, the fever is that called *Cháturthaka Biparjyaya*.

This fever presents the following symptoms. It commences with shivering, dryness, and swelling. The patient has no strength, so as not to be able to walk. He evacuates much bile, air, and phlegm which are particularly affected.

Errhines are used for the cure of this fever. Certain roots are used for the same purpose, gathered on the nights of lucky days, and are sometimes tied to the hair of the head, and other parts of the body. When the body is heavy, with perspiration, and little fever and stools, it is called *Proapiko*.

When half the body is hot, and the other cold; when what is eaten is not digested, and does harm; the deranged bile and phlegm have produced these morbid symptoms. When the bile of the body is deranged, and the phlegm of the arms and legs, the body is hot and the hands and feet cold. When the phlegm of the body is deranged, and the bile of the hands and feet, the body is cold, and the hands and feet are hot.

The fever is also modified, as the essential parts are deranged. Thus the air may be deranged in the blood, flesh, bone, marrow and semen; and the supposed danger increasing in the order above stated, until the last, the semen, when the fever is considered always fatal.

The type of the fever varies also according to the season of the year. Each of them forms two lunar months; during June and July, the rainy season *(Barshá)*, air predominates, and the fevers takes on the characters of deranged air. The season called *Sharata,* autumn, or sultry months (Sept. and Oct.), the bile and the phlegm predominate; *Basanta* or spring (Feb. March and April), the phlegm is in excess, and is succeeded by derangement of the air and bile, followed by fever.

Áhaka-jwara, (Nakra or *Násá-jwara.)* The natives of Bengal are subject to this peculiar form of intermittent fever. The description of it is not contained in the more ancient medical works. It is produced by a swelling of the Schniderian membrane, and is said to be caused by the air and phlegm deranging the blood of the part. It is accompanied with pain over the body, but particularly in the neck and back, and other symptoms of fever.

It is of frequent occurrence in Bengal; attacks adults alone, between the age of 20 and 40 years of age. It is treated by the natives by abstracting a little blood from the nose by the point of a needle, or by rubbing a little rough grass over the diseased part. Errhines are also of use, and those who take snuff daily are free from the disease.

ORDER II.

*Small-pox, Masúriká.**

Stimulating and heating substances produce this disease; as also pungent, acid, or saline substances, and improper mixtures of food; eating before the former food has been digested; unwholesome meats, and certain roots or fruits; bad air or water; and the influ-

* In Persian it is styled *Chechak;* in Sanskrit *Guṭí* and *Masúri* or *Masúriká,* resembling a pill or lentil *masúra,* (Ervum hirsutum and Cicer lens.)

ence of a bad planet. These causes derange air, bile, and phlegm, &c., which with the bad blood produces an eruption like the *masúra*.

Before small-pox appears, fever occurs, with pain over the body, but particularly in the back; and itching, lassitude, stretching, restlessness, redness of the face and eyes, with cough. The skin swells slightly, and is of an unusually red colour.

When air is much deranged in this disease the pustules are of a dark-green, and red colour; or dull, hard, and rough, and are accompanied with severe pain. This variety ripens slowly.

When bile is deranged, in this disease, severe pain is felt in the large and small joints, with cough, shaking, listlessness and languor; the palate, lips and tongue are dry with thirst, and no appetite. The pustules are red, yellow, and white, and they are accompanied with burning pain. This form soon ripens.

When produced by diseased *phlegm* the pustules are large, white, and shining, with much itching, and less pain than the former kind. They ripen slowly. In this form, some of the general symptoms of small-pox are aggravated. There is catarrh with chilliness, head-ache, fever, heaviness of the body, nausea, loss of the appetite, languor, drowsiness, and the patient sleeps much.

When blood is deranged diarrhœa, lassitude, and stretching occur; with thirst, laziness, want of appetite, burning over the surface, and the mouth becomes ulcerated. The eyes are red, strong fever is present, with the symptoms already enumerated under deranged bile.

When air, bile and phlegm are deranged, in this disease the body has a blue colour, and the skin seems studded with rice. The pustules become black and flat, are depressed in the centre, with much pain. They ripen slowly, and the discharge is copious, and very fœtid.

When air, bile and phlegm are thus deranged the patient is always dozing, he has no appetite, breathes with difficulty, and is drowsy, restless and delirious. This form is cured with much difficulty, and it is called *Charmo* or fatal form.

The following are other varieties of Small-pox:—

1. *Measles* (*Romántiká, Hám, B.*) is produced by vitiated phlegm and bile, and the symptoms are fever followed by an eruption of small red papellæ, like the roots of hairs; these appear over the body, accompanied with loss of appetite and cough.

2. *Water-pox* (*Togotoh, Masúriká, Páni Basanta, B.*) The pustules are large, and full of water. In this form the skin is alone affected.

When the blood is particularly affected in small-pox, the pustules are of a redder colour, have a thinner cuticle than usual, and quickly ripen. They may generally be cured, but on being opened, should blood be discharged, the disease is incurable.

When the pustules proceed from *flesh* they are hard and shining, they ripen slowly, and the skin covering the part is thick. The pain over the body is severe, with listlessness, itchiness of the skin, thirst, and fever.

When the disease is produced by diseased *fat,* the pustules are large, soft, round, and slightly elevated, with severe fever and pain. This form is very dangerous, and is accompanied with loss of sense, laziness and stupor. Some strong persons maybe cured of this disease.

When the *marrow* is particularly diseased, the pustules are very small, flat, and slightly elevated and dry. The person is insensible, with severe pain of a gnawing kind in the vital parts. This form quickly destroys the person.

When the *bones* are particularly affected in this disease; they feel pained, as if bored by an insect. The pustules appear as if ripe, small, shining and very tender. The person feels chilly, restless, and delirium occurs, with a burning feeling.

When *semen* is affected in this disease, the symptoms are the same as when the bones are affected; and this form is so fatal that as soon as a person is affected with it he dies, so that there is no time for the pustules appearing.

These different forms will be known by an experienced physician. When small-pox is caused by derangements in the skin, blood, bile, or phlegm; or phlegm and bile, it will be quickly cured. When air or bile; or phlegm and air; and when the air, bile, and phlegm are deranged the disease is incurable. Of the latter kind the eruptions are sometimes like coral, or like rose-apple (*Jám*), oval, like the iron weight of a fishing net, or like a grain of linseed. The colour of this dangerous form of small-pox varies according to the strength of the individual. The other bad symptoms are cough, hiccough, coma, fever of a severe kind, delirium, listlessness, and thirst. The body remains very hot, blood flows from the mouth, eyes and nose, and there is a gurgling (*ghaṛghaṛí*) noise in the throat, with difficult and sonorous respiration. Such cases of small-pox are incurable; as also those in which great thirst is accompanied with difficulty in breathing, which is performed through the mouth.

Should the elbow, wrists, or axilla swell after the small-pox, the person will be cured with difficulty.

In *Bhábaprakásha,* a modern compilation, another form of small-pox is related. It is called *Shitalá.**

* The name of the goddess of small-pox, from *shita,* cold, and *la;* which indicates the cold treatment, which is most favourable for the

It commences with fever, and the eruptions appear before the 7th day, and they maturate before the 14th day. In another week they begin to dry. In this compilation, antiphlogistic remedies are recommended to be used from the beginning; and the ashes of cowdung is to be rubbed over the body. When the pustules have been broken, the person is to drink cold water, and he should remain in a cool room. Such a cool regimen, with an airy and clean place to reside in, is all that is required. Febrifuge decoctions are also used to diminish the fever, and various religious ceremonies, with prayers and offerings, are used.

In the other Manuscripts the manner of treating small-pox varies according to its nature. In general, the treatment commences with rubbing ghee made hot, or warm water over the body, before the eruption appears; an emetic should also be given.

When the eruption makes its appearance the pustules are rubbed over with turmerick, mixed with ghee. Cooling food is recommended, particularly the powder of fried rice and gram, boiled with sugar and water. Broths made of the birds, which pick with their bills, such as pigeons, &c., are to be used towards the termination of the disease. Nothing is said about a hot room, so that we may infer that the patient is to reside in an open airy place. Few people are allowed to visit the sick person; dirty people are particularly excluded, and no one is allowed to touch the person. It is said to be contagious, but as it is generally considered as produced by sin, and the Hindus being predestinarians, this property of the disease is only casually stated in a few MSS. The treatment of small-pox is varied according to the humour particularly deranged.

The air pox (*Báyu Masúriká*) is to be treated by exhibiting the decoction of the powder *helamochee* with red sandal-wood. In other cases a decoction of

Gulancha,
Coriander seed,
Panchamúlí,
Rásná,
Rátri,
Ushíra, and
Durálabhá is recommended.

Two tolá of each medicine is boiled in a pint of water to $\frac{1}{4}$; this is given for a dose. The body is rubbed with ghee, mixed with a paste made of the bark of

cure of the disease. When attacked with the disease, the patient often vows to make an offering at the shrine of *Shitalá*, and as an earnest of that puts some pice into a vessel of water, as she loves every thing cold.

Madder, (Manjista,)
Bata,
Shirísha,
Urumborroh, mixed together.

Kodeero (the leaves of Cakekim) and the leaves of *Nim*, are to be mixed, formed into a paste, and rubbed over the body.

When the small-pox is situated in the mouth and throat, gargles made of

Subarnamákshyik, and
Dátrífala, Emblic myrabalan,

are formed into a decoction and taken with honey.

When affecting the eye, the vapour of a decoction of wheat and licquorice is to be used.

When the pustules are broken and drying up, the powder of the ashes of cow-dung, and the ashes of astringent trees, as the bark of the *catechu* tree and *bata*, &c. are applied.

The diet in this variety of small-pox should consist of sweet articles of food with rice, and broth made of a decoction of peas.

The treatment of small-pox produced by bile (*Pitta Masúriká*) is at the commencement, the decoction of

Nim bark,
Porpotoka,
Páta, *Patol*,
The red and white sandal-wood,
Ushíra, Hellebore,
Bássá, *Durálabhá*,

two tollah of each medicine, to two pints of water, which are to be boiled down to one pint. The decoction is to be taken in small quantities sweetened.

In small-pox produced by deranged blood (*Raktaja Masúriká*) blood-letting, and the above decoction are required.

Small-pox produced by deranged phlegm (*Kapha Masúriká*) is to be treated by a decoction of bitter plants; and the body is to be rubbed with the bark of *shirísha* and *urumborroh*.

The treatment of Measles consist in administering the juice of the leaves of *sushabí* with the powder of *haridrá*.

The preventative means to be employed in this disease* are admi-

* This small-pox is an example of a disease existing for a long period in one country, without penetrating into another. It is on this account that neither the Greeks nor the Roman authors were acquainted with this peculiar, and virulent disease; while the account given above proves that it was well known at a very early period in Hindustan. It was its frequency which induced the Hindu physicians to attend to the

nistering the powder of tamarind seeds with the powder of turmerick daily in cold water, by which means the person will not be attacked with the disease. The juice of plantain tree with white sandal-wood and water; or the juice of *Passo* with licquorice will have the same effect. These are to be given likewise when the fever comes to check, or diminish the violence of the disease.

It appears that the Chinese as well as the Hindus were familiar with small-pox many centuries before the Arabian physicians described it. It was probably conveyed westward by the Persian conquerors of Hindustan; which seems to be a further confirmation of the country from which it originally came, and the manner in which it gradually approached and eventually reached Europe. The distance and the hot deserts through which the only intercourse for so long a period was held, prevented for a time its progress westward; but, as navigation extended, ships from India would frequently touch at the Arabian ports of the Persian Gulph, and Red Sea, where it seems first to have appeared, A. D. 900.

The description of the small-pox by Rhazes,* the distinguished Arabian physician, first drew the attention of the European physicians to the disease.

Some say it was introduced into Arabia in 572, the year that gave birth to Mohammad; other testimonies seem to accord with the statement that it was at the siege of Mecca (A. D. 569), by Abraham that the Arabians were first affected with the disease.

The conquests of the followers of Mohammad conveyed the disease to Persia, Syria, and Egypt; and the successful stand made by the inhabitants of Constantinople, for some time prevented the spread of the disease beyond the Hellespont. So completely does this appear to have been the case, that Honus, a resident physician in that city in the tenth century, states that neither the small-pox nor measles were known in his time in Constantinople.

The whole of the southern coast of the Mediterranean sea had been subdued by the Arabians; but, it was not till the commencement of the eighth century that the disease was introduced into Spain by the Moors. The victorious Saracens overran Spain, cross-

disease; and its danger afterwards led them to erect a goddess which they now propitiate to prevent, as well as to mitigate, the attack of the disease.

* The translation was printed in England by Dr. Meade, in 1747: see his Works, page 297.

ed the Pyrenese mountains, and inundated the southern provinces of France. They were driven back by Charles Martel; but they left the small-pox and measles with the conquerors. From this source the diseases quickly spread over Europe.

The Spaniards in their invasion of Hispaniola and Mexico conveyed the same diseases to these countries, where it committed the most extensive ravages. It would thus appear that the small-pox as well as the measles commenced in Asia, and extended to Africa, Europe, and the new World.

The ignorance, however, of the European nations, of the middle ages, was such, that they did not record any description of the first appearance of this peculiar and fatal disease in their different countries. It was under the vague name of "plague" or of "consuming fire," which was applied to eruptive pestilences in general, that it may have been described; we may easily suppose that the great mortality which took place on the first introduction of the disease must have led the inhabitants to believe that the new disease proceeded from the anger of an offended deity, inscrutible in his nature, and only to be prevented or cured by humiliation and prayers.

Order III.

Acute Rheumatism (A'mbát).

This disease is produced in dispeptic patients who lead a sedentary life, taking improper food, or are intemperate. All indigestable food has this effect; such as oleaginous articles, particularly when the person, at the same time, takes much exercise. By such causes the chyle is not properly prepared, and indigested food *(A'm)* is formed in the stomach. This *A'm* is carried into the great abdominal vessels. The deranged chyle produced in this manner, by the morbid condition of air, bile, or phlegm is like mucilage, and deranges all the abdomen. This *(A'mras)* morbid chyle is the cause of all the varieties of this disease. The deranged phlegm and air are accumulated in the loins producing pain and rigidity of the body, and hence it is called *A'mbát,* (air mixed with morbid chyle.) From the loins it extends over all the body.

The general symptoms are pain over the body, loss of appetite, thirst, want of appetite, languor, heaviness, fever, and there is a deadened sensation of the parts. When this disease is in such an aggravated form, it is most difficult to cure.

When the deranged phlegm and air with the morbid chyle passes to the wrist, ankle, neck, hip, knee, loins, it produces a burning sensation, much pain, like the bite of the centipede, with swelling.

The person feels great lassitude with a copious flow of urine; he cannot sleep, and complains of pain in the abdomen; and is distressed with thirst, vomiting, giddiness, fainting, pain in the chest, costiveness, &c.

When bile is much deranged in this disease there is a burning sensation and redness of the part;—and when air is principally deranged, the pain is very severe. When phlegm is much deranged, the itching and rigidity of the part is considerable, and it feels as if it was covered with a wet cloth. When one humour is alone affected, it is curable, when two it is difficult to cure, and when three, and the whole body is affected the cure is very difficult, tedious, and the disease is even fatal in some cases.

Treatment. This should be commenced with fasting, diaphoretics, and bitters, tonics, and stomachics. Heating medicines with purgatives and enemas are also of much use in this disease. The sand-bath is also used, and on the leaves of the castor-oil plant hot sand is to be placed, and this is to be applied to the pained parts. The following vapour-bath is also recommended. Steep old rice in water until it ferments, the water is then poured off, and the following medicines are put into it:

The seeds of Dolichos biflorus, *(kulattha,)*
Teel seed, (*til,*)
The root of the castor-oil shrub,
Barley,
Linseed,
Boerhavia diffusa alater, (*punarnabá.*)

To four seers of water, take a tolah of each of these medicines; boil, and in this state place the vessel with the mouth partly closed under the chair in which the patient sits, his whole person being covered with a thick cloth. Several pots are to be prepared in the above manner. He will thus remain for twenty minutes to half an hour.

Several kinds of plasters are likewise used. The following is a specimen of this class of medicines. Take of the roots of the

Abrus precatorius, (*Hingshirá,*)
Kebuka,
The Morunga. Guilandina sigrua,

to be mixed with cow's urine, and the earth of ant-hills so as to form a paste, which is to be applied hot to the affected part.

For purgatives take half a tolá of

Convolvulus turpethum, (*Teuṛí,*)
Sixteen ratís of rock salt,
And a little ginger,

with two ounces of conjee water. These are mixed and exhibited as a purgative.

Take of *dashamúla,* (already explained,)
Minispermum glabrum, (*gulancha,*)
Castor-oil seeds,
Erundo and Mimosa octandra, (*rásná,*)
Ginger and Pinus debdaru, (*debdáru,*)

of each 32 ratis, mix in a pint of water, which is to be boiled down to a quarter of a pint. Take this twice a day for seven days. The tonic and stimulating decoction is prepared by mixing together the roots and seeds of long-pepper, the roots of Piper chavya (*chabya*), Plumbago, and dry ginger ; of each 32 ratis. They are to be put into a pint of water, and boiled down to a quarter of a pint. Take this twice a day.*

Diet. In this disease the *patola,* the fruit of the Trichosanthes dioica, old rice, barley, and a kind of pea (*mugh*), is also used, (*Charaka*). *Sushruta* recommends the patient to wear a warm dress, and to reside in a warm close room.

Order IV.

Swellings, (*Shotha.*)

Under this head is considered swellings of different kinds. When air is deranged, and mixes with the diseased blood, bile, and phlegm, it conveys them to the external parts of the body, stops the air-vessels, and their contents, which accumulate, and produce swellings.

This disease is caused by great fatigue in walking, with fasting ; by eating much indigestable cakes, sour articles of food, vegetables, or clay ; by salt, which debilitates the humours, and by other indigestable, or unhealthy articles of food and mixtures. In other cases it is produced by leading a sedentary life, personal neglect of medicines, uncleanness, injuries to vital parts, untimely parturition, the improper use of emetics and purgatives, and piles. These cause a swelling of the body, which is accompanied with pain and heaviness, restlessness, heat, and discolouration of the body.

According to *Charaka* there are nine varieties of *Sothah,* three being produced by air, bile, and phlegm, when affected separately ;

* *Charaka.*

three when two humours are deranged ; one when three are deranged at the same time ; one when caused by an injury, and one by poison. *Sushruta* does not allow that three varieties are produced by the combination of two diseased humours ; and consequently considers this disease as having only five varieties produced by general, and one by a local, or accidental cause.

1. When *air* is deranged the swelling passes from one part to another, the skin is thin, the surface dry and soft, of a red or black colour, with dullness of feeling. The parts when pressed pit, but they recover the level on the pressure being removed. The symptoms increase in the day time.

2. When the swelling is produced by deranged *bile* the swelling is moist, and has a bad smell, is of a yellow, red, and black colour, produces various kinds of pain, and ripens soon. In such cases the body is soon fatigued, the patient is feverish, perspires much, complains of thirst, and dullness, the pulse is very frequent, his eyes of a red colour, and the pain is severe.

3. *Phlegm. Dropsy* is characterized by always remaining in one place, is of a yellowish pale, and shining colour, is cold and hard, and painfully itchy. The patient has no appetite, and cough is discharged from the mouth and nose, the person is always sleepy, the swelling and the internal heat are diminished, and when the disease occurs it causes much uneasiness to the person, and is cured slowly. Pressure does not diminish this variety, the symptoms of which increase at night.

4, 5, 6, 7. When two of the above humours are deranged, the symptoms of both forms of the two humours, stated above, are present ; and when three are deranged, all the symptoms are present in the separate varieties.

8. *Accidental Swellings (Abhighátaja shotha)*, when the body is wounded by a cutting instrument, by injuries ; or when bruised by an accident, breathing cold air, and the air of the ocean is of much use. The vapour or juice of the marking-nut *(bhallátaka)* applied to the body, or rubbing the part with cowach *(kapikachchhú)* will be of use. These produce swelling, heat, and redness, accompanied with the other symptoms of diseased bile. Bad water, either drank, or with which the body is washed, produces such swellings of parts.

9. *Bishaja-shotha.* When the poison of any animal is taken by the mouth, is introduced into the system by a wound, or by contact ; when urine is applied to a wound, or the person wears a cloth that is dirty, is covered with excrement, or he breathes air coming from a poisonous tree it produces this form of swelling. The application

of the powder of different poisonous articles, or of certain animals walking over the body, produce the same effect: Thus if frogs, &c. discharge their urine upon a part, it swells. The poison is either discharged from the trunk, teeth, or nails of the animal into the wound. By such causes the part swells, becomes pendulous, and is accompanied with pain. These swellings are soft, rise quickly, and are not fixed in one place, but move about. Sometimes they are quickly produced, and increase downwards *(distid)*; and are very hot, and painful. When air, bile, and phlegm are deranged in the stomach *(ámásiya)*, the swelling occurs in the head and upper extremities, when deranged in the small intestines *(pankashaya)*, the swelling will occur in the trunk, and when in the rectum *(andaka)*, the swelling will occur in the lower extremities. When air, bile, and phlegm are deranged over the body, it will swell the whole body, and pass from one part to another.
to another.

When the swelling occurs in the trunk of the body it will be cured with difficulty, and also when the swelling is over the body. When the upper or lower half of the body is affected the disease is dangerous, or when the swelling proceeds proximated from the part first affected.

The swelling will not be cured when the person breathes with noise and difficulty, when accompanied with thirst, vomiting, weakness, hiccough and fever, and when he has no appetite, and is affected with diarrhœa and severe pain *(súl)*. Such a diseased person will die. When the swelling commences in the feet of the male, or in the face of the female, both are very dangerous. It is also very dangerous in both sexes, when the swelling is about the anus.

When the swelling is recent, with no bad symptoms, it will be cured. When the throat and vital parts are swelled with much pain; or when it attack infants, or old persons, or very weak persons, the disease will be fatal.

Treatment. In this disease sour and salt food are to be avoided; curdled milk, jagary, fat, milk, wine, oil, ghee, unleavened bread, and all indigestable kinds of food are to be avoided; the person should also avoid sleeping during the day, as also broths made of the flesh of domestic animals, and venery. When the deranged air produces this disease, medicines for curing air are to be exhibited; such as castor oil, or the powder of the bark of the root of *Teurí* (Convolvulus turpethum). These purgatives are to be repeated at intervals for a fortnight, or a month.

When bile is deranged, ghee prepared with a decoction of astringent medicines, such as the bark of *nyagrodha* (Ficus Indica), and other such medicines are to be used. When phlegm is much deranged take prepared ghee in a decoction of the Cassia fistula, and medicines with the like qualities.

Besides the above remedies the following general indications of treatment are followed:—Different preparations of Iron are used. In like manner equal quantities of marabuline and jagary are exhibited daily; or dry-ginger, black and long pepper, with saltpetre, and the oxide of iron, in equal parts, are to be mixed with cow's urine, and are to be exhibited daily.

Diet. The diet is to consist of barley, with the decoction of *mudga* (a kind of pea), and flour; no salt nor ghee is to be used.

The warm bath, with a decoction of *nim* leaves, (Melia azadirachta,) *arka* (Calotropis gigantea), the leaves of hog-weed *(barshábhú)*, is to be applied to the swelled parts.

Various kinds of external medicines are applied to dry up the swelling. Such as mustard powder, rock salt, (Lea hirta) *sánguṣṭa.* For the same reason strong purgatives and emetics are occasionally used. General bleeding is useful when the disease occurs without the presence of any other disease.

The juices of several roots mixed with recent cow-dung are recommended to be rubbed over the swelled part. In the same manner irritating substances are applied to the swelled part to disperse it.

In other cases milk is heated, and the mouth of the pot with the hot milk is applied over the swelled part.

It is always proper to give oliaginous substances internally, to promote perspiration, and to rub the above mixtures externally over the part.

ORDER V.

Great Fatness, (Medah.)

Cause. When persons remain without exercise, sleep during the day, take too much ghee, milk, and preparations of sweetmeats, rice, and different kinds of indigestable cakes, the chyle becomes oily, and sweeter than natural, and as it circulates it produces fatness. It is accompanied by the following symptoms:—The person feels a difficulty of breathing, thirst, is not sensitive, is always sleepy and uneasy, and cannot excite the body or work; such a person has always a good appetite, his perspiration has a disagreeable smell, he has less inclination for women. He speaks indistinctly; and the other essential parts of the body are not nourished. The fat is alone inflamed, and such a person usually dies of diabetis, carbuncle, fever, fistula-in-ano, or large internal abscesses. He is also subject to disease of the air (*báyu*), and the diseases he may contract are always severe. When such a disease occurs, he should avoid the causes of fatness; and should also take different preparations of iron with cow's urine.

The powder of bitumen with cow's urine is exhibited in this disease. *Guguli* (Amyris agallochum) and the sulphurate of antimony is recommended internally, with honey and water, barley, *mugh* (a kind of pea), and other kinds of dry tonic food. Exercise, enemas, with tonics, and those medicines which make the body thin should be used.

ORDER VI.

Emaciation, (Kársa.)

If a person takes dry food which does not contain much nourishment, as astringent and pungent kinds of food, much exercise, and venery, they produce emaciation; if he indulges in too much study, fear, grief, thinking, watching at night, or food in small quantities, the chyle is formed and absorbed in small quantities, does not circulate and nourish all parts of the body, and produces emaciation. In such a state the person becomes weak and cannot bear hunger or thirst, heat or cold, currents of air, or rain. Such a person is liable to the attacks of nervous diseases, or diseases of air; and will die of asthma, consumption, acitis, despepsia, *gúlma* hæmatemesis, or hæmopysis.—Such a person has severe attacks of diseases.

Treatment. Such a person should use milk, ghee, animal and sweet articles of food, with barley, and flour. He should sleep in the day time, avoid venery, and not work much. The powder of *poischia, asuganda, bidárí, shatábarí, balla,* and *nágaballa,* are used as tonics, with alteratives.

ORDER VII.

Burning of the Body, (Dáha.)

This is generally a symptomatic disease attended with fever. The blood of the whole body is affected in this disease, the body becomes hot, and the patient complains of a burning sensation over the body, as if hot charcoal was applied to the surface which becomes of a red colour like copper. The eyes of such a person are red, and his breath is like hot iron.

There are seven forms of this disease, one being produced by bile, another by blood, the third by external injury of the trunk, the fourth by not quenching thirst, the fifth by the injury of vital parts, the sixth by excess in drinking, and the seventh by the loss of the essential parts of the body, as chyle, blood, &c.

1 and 2. When produced by *bile* it is accompanied with fever. When *blood* is affected the body, eyes, &c. become red, and he complains of a burning sensation over the body.

3. When any viscus is injured, and is filled up with blood, and affects a *dáha* which is difficult to cure.

4. When produced by excessive drinking the internal heat comes out externally, and is increased by the derangement of bile and blood. It then produces great burning of the body.

5. If a foolish person does not drink water, when he is very thirsty, the watery part of the body is diminished ; and the internal heat is increased, producing a burning of the external and internal parts of the body ;—his throat, palate, tongue and lips, become dry, and the tongue protrudes, with shaking of the body.

6. When the essential fluids of the body are diminished by any cause, as an excess in venery, too much exercise, copious evacuation of any of the fluids, the body feels very hot, and the patient faints, has much thirst, his voice becomes low and altered, he cannot move his body, and soon dies.

7. When any vital part is injured, as the bladder, heart, or brain, it produces a burning sensation over the body which is incurable.

When the body feels cold to another while the patient is suffering from an internal burning, it is always a very unfavourable symptom in this kind of disease.

Treatment. Take clarified old ghee and the flowers of barley, mix them well together, and rub it over the body. In old cases, water with vinegar should be applied to the body. Cloths wet in old and fermenting rice-water. In other cases sandal-wood reduced to a paste between two stones, with which the root of the Andropogon muricatum, a fragrant grass, is to be mixed and applied over the body.

The free use of the *panká* is likewise recommended, and the patient should sleep or lie upon the leaves of the water-lily or plantain, and use the cold bath. He should take internally the juice of the sugar-cane, and different kinds of *sharbats*, the decoction of the stalk of the water-lily, a sort of fennel (Anethum panmorium), coriander seed, Emblice, myrabolan, and the fragrant wood of the *padmakáṣhṭha,* of each 32 ratis: boil in a pint of water so as to reduce it to half a pint, which is to be taken two or three times a day. Other antiphlogistic means are likewise recommended.

Burning of the feet (*páda-dáha*) is a variety of this order; and is a peculiar, severe and very untractable disease of India. In the treatment it is recommended that leeches should be applied to the feet, with the continued application of the mixture* of *masúra* (Ervum hirsutum). This is rubbed between two stones with water and applied to the feet. Butter is likewise recommended to be rubbed on the feet, which are then to be brought near the fire. With these means the usual treatment of *báta-rakta* (slight leprosy) is to be followed.

Order VIII.

Jaundice, (Páṇḍu.)

This disease is produced by excesses in venery, eating earth, sour or salt food, or drinking much wine. It is likewise produced by sleeping during the day, and eating very hot things, which derange the air, bile, and phlegm.

There are five kinds of this disease produced by deranged air, bile, or phlegm; when these three are deranged together, and when produced by eating earth, especially chalk. When the air, bile, or phlegm are diseased, they derange the blood; and produce the pale or yellowish white colour of the skin. Before the disease appears the skin feels as if pinched, the sputa is red, the person cannot do any work, and has a desire to eat earth; his eyelids swell, the dejections and urine are yellow, and whatever is eaten is not digested.

1. When air is deranged producing this disease, the skin, urine, and eyes, or other parts, are rough, dark-coloured, and brownish with shaking, pain over the body, and the dejections and urine are constipated, with giddiness.

2. When the *bile* is deranged, the urine, dejections, and eyes are of a yellow colour, the body is hot, with thirst, and fever, there are frequent dejections, and the surface of the body is very yellow.

3. *Phlegm.* In this form the phlegm proceeds from the mouth and nose, the person often dozes and complains of lassitude and heaviness of the body; the skin, eyes, and face are of a whitish colour; the urine is also pale.

* Rather plaster, as it is thick, is spread over the part and allowed to remain.

4. When the *air*, *bile* and *phlegm* are at the same time deranged, there is fever, no appetite, retching and vomiting, the person complains of thirst, and the body feels painful and tired. When such a person is very weak and insensible the person will die.

5. When produced by eating *earth* there are three kinds; one deranging the *air*, another the *bile*, and a third the *phlegm*. Astringent earth (*kasáya mritiká*) also deranges *air;* salt-earth (*usara*), deranges *bile;* and sweet-earth (*madhura*), deranges the *phlegm*. When earth deranges the elements of the body, and whatever is eaten remains undigested, the blood which is formed stops the mouths of the vessels of the intestines that carry the chyle, blood, &c., and they derange the senses. The strength of the body is impaired, and the surface becomes pale and yellow, and it produces dispepsia. In this form of *Jaundice* the person feels drowsiness, languor, cough, has difficulty in breathing, pain in the belly, and feels no appetite : his cheeks and eyelids swell, also the legs, umbilicus, and penis; *diarrhœa* occurs, and the dejections are as if they consisted of a mixture of blood and phlegm, with worms.

Prognosis. When there is much fever with dispepsia, nausia, vomiting, thirst, and languor occur; when the person is very weak and insensible, or when caused by the derangement of the three humours, or when very chronic, with rough skin and swelling over the body the prognosis will be unfavourable. Should the patient see every thing yellow he will not soon get well. When constipated, when the dejections are yellow and mixed with bile, when accompanied with diarrhœa and much fever, restless and thirst, and when the eyes, teeth and nails become yellow, the prognosis must be unfavourable. In like manner, when the extremities are swollen, and the trunk is thin, or when the trunk is swollen and the extremities are small; or when there is much swelling about the anus, penis and scrotum, the prognosis must be guarded. When the patient suffers much, when senseless, or when attacked at the same time with dysentery and fever, such patients the physician should not treat.

A variety of Jaundice is named *kámalá*, which is produced by eating much sour, salt, and other indigestable articles of food after an attack of Jaundice. In this case the bile is much affected, and produces yellowness, particularly of the face, accompanied with drowsiness, loss of strength, and the other symptoms above stated.

If in *kámalá* there is swelling and pain in the joints, then it is called *kumbha-kámalá* (from *kumbha*, a water-pot, and *kámalá*, Jaundice). In this case the dejections and urine are of a dark or yellow colour; the body is swelled, and the eyes and mouth are of a red colour. When vomiting takes place the matter vomited is of a red colour, as also the dejections and urine.

In some cases the patient is delirious, his body is hot, he has no appetite, is thirsty, and the dejections and urine become constipated: such cases are unfavourable. In other cases the person dozes, and the internal fire and the understanding, are much affected. Such persons will soon die; as will be the case when there is vomiting with no appetite, fever, debility, noise in breathing, cough, and frequent dejections.

Another form of Jaundice is called *Halímaka* or *Lácorokaka*. This variety is produced by air and bile, and is characterized by fever, pain over the body, giddiness, languor, drowsiness, emaciation of the body, with the symptoms of the from of Jaundice produced by *air* and *bile*.

The *Treatment* of Jaundice should be commenced by exhibiting several doses of mild purgatives, and emetics. The purgatives usually consist of Cassia fistula, or myrobalan with sugar. Before taking these he is to eat freely of ghee, which has been boiled in turmerick. The patient's body should be anointed with oil, after he has taken the above mixture for several days, and it has acted freely; the next object is to discharge impurities from the head by means of errhines with glysters: such as the powder of the oxide of iron, with ginger, black and long pepper, with *biranga*. It is also recommended to give the fœces of the goat, mixed with black salt (*bitlavan*), and turmerick. These are made into a powder with honey, and taken frequently, for several days. A quarter or half a *tolá* of the powder of the bark of Convolvulus turpethum (*teuri*) may also be exhibited in sugar, as a purgative. A wine produced by fermented sugar is also to be used in this disease. Butter-milk and rice must be taken for a long time, as they will improve the appetite, and cure the disease. The patient should also take broths prepared with venison and prunes.

If air, bile, and phlegm are much deranged, medicines to cure these are to be given with the other remedies. If the patient, along with the above symptoms, has swelling of the anus, penis, and scrotum, and is senseless, with dysentery and fever, he is not to be treated.

In the form of Jaundice, called *kumbha káláma*, the rust of iron is recommended to be heated to a white heat, eight times, and each time it is to be thrown into the urine of the cow. This is then powdered, and taken with honey in doses of about half a dram.

In the variety of Jaundice called *Halímaka* prepared ghee with the juice of raisins, Minispermum glabrum *(gulancha)*, and myrobalan (*ámlakí*), is often used with advantage.

2 F

Order IX.

Nervous Diseases, (Báta Byádhi.)

These diseases are produced by the continued use of dry, cold, or light articles of food, taken in unusually small quantities; excessive venery, and watching; improper and violent exercise; fasting; and copious discharges of blood, or other evacuations. They are also produced by much jumping, swimming, or fighting, wearing wet cloths, or wanting to do impossibilities, as raising weights, &c. Any cause producing the absorption of parts by which the individual is weakened, and swoons; too much thinking, sorrow, grief, fear, and other diseases producing emaciations; sleeping uncomfortably during the day, or in an unusual position; anger, or not attending to the calls of nature; the accumulation of indigestable food, or certain injuries of vital parts, produce these diseases. They are also caused by the person falling from a height, by riding very fast on an elephant, horse, or camel, or whatever goes very fast. These causes derange air, filling the empty vessels in one part, or over all the body, and thus produce the symptoms of the disease.

When air is so deranged it produces the following symptoms: the muscles of the small joints are contracted with rigidity, and cannot be moved. These symptoms are accompanied with so much pain, that they seem as if broken by force. The skin becomes rough, the person speaks nonsense, and complains of pain in the joints of the hand, back, and head; he cannot sleep, nor walk with vigour, and is deformed, and the members become thin. When women are so affected, they have miscarriages, and it diminishes the semen, and stops menstruation. The parts affected shake, there is no feeling in the part, the person has severe pain in the head, and no smell; the eyes become dry and dull, and a painful weight is felt in the pit of the stomach, and stiffness of the nape of the neck. These symptoms are accompanied with spasm of different parts, with loss of sense and great fatigue.

These different causes, and the different parts of the body affected, produce various forms of the disease. When the air is deranged in the abdomen, the dejections and urine are constipated, pain is felt in the abdomen and its sides, and diseases of the heart, hysteria (*gulma*), and piles (*arsha*), are produced. When air is deranged generally there is much pain over the body, which shakes with pain in the joints. They feel as if broken. When situated in the pelvis it stops the usual evacuations, with great pain, and flatulency, and produces gravel, and the stone. In women it produces deformities in the fœtus, and the plurality of children. When air is deranged in the anus, the legs, thighs, *os coccygus*, hands, and breast are painful, and the body is thin. When deranged air is situated in the *stomach*, the sides, back, scrobiculus cordis, and navel are painful, with thirst, belching, and cholera; the person complains of cough, and the throat and mouth are dry, with asthma. When air is deranged in the small intestines (*pankáshay*), they make a noise, with scanty dejections, and little urine. Such a person has uneasy choliky pains in the abdomen, with pain in the lower part of the back.

When air is deranged in the *organs* of *sense* it destroys their functions. When deranged in the *skin* it becomes dry, rough, and has no feeling; has a black colour, and is painful. In some cases it is stretched over the body without wrinkles, and is of a red colour, accompanied with pains in the joints, and slight chops in the skin over the body.

When air is deranged in the *blood*, great pain is felt in the body which is hot, and the colour of the skin is unnatural. The body is thin, the person has no appetite, and the skin has red eruptions over it, and after eating the body is unwieldy, and the person cannot work. When air is deranged in the *flesh* or *fat* the body is heavy, with pain, as if beaten with a stick, and the person is much fatigued.

When air is deranged in the *bones* and *marrow* the long bones and joints are very painful; his strength and flesh become diminished; the person has no sleep, and pain is very severe and continued.

When air is deranged in the *semen* it is quickly discharged, or is constipated, and in women it retains the fœtus long in the uterus, or abortions are produced. The semen in such cases has an unusual colour, and produces twins.

When air is deranged in the *vessels* it produces painful contraction, or fulness of the vessel.

When air is deranged in the *nerves* (tendons?) the whole body may be diseased, or it may be confined to one situation. It produces episthotonos, with lameness, spasm, and cramps of the leg, with hemiplegia.

When in the *joints* it produces swellings, and pain in the joints.

When the vital air (*prán báyu*), which is situated in the thorax, is deranged with bile, it produces vomiting with a burning sensation of the parts. When this air is mixed with phlegm it produces weakness, debility, langour, and drowsiness; and the taste for food is deranged.

Vital air in the throat (*udán báyu*), when mixed with *bile* produces great heat in the body, swooning, fainting, and languor.

When mixed with *phlegm* there is no perspiration, horripilation is felt over the body; the person becomes melancholy, has little internal heat in the stomach, and the body feels cold.

Vital air in the umbilical region (*samána báyu*), when mixed with bile, produces much perspiration, a burning sensation of the body, fainting, and swooning. When mixed with phlegm constipation of the dejections and urine, and a state of goose-skin over the surface may be remarked.

Vital air in the anus (*apána báyu*). When mixed with bile the body is very hot, or is only slightly warm, and the urine is bloody. When mixed with phlegm the person has a sense of heaviness in the lower part of the trunk, and the body feels cold.

Vital air over the body (*byán báyu*), when mixed with bile the body is very hot, and there are convulsions of the extremities, with great fatigue. When mixed with phlegm the person remains stupid, and rigid, and he feels pain, and swelling of the body.

Different varieties of nervous diseases are thus supposed to be produced by the derangements of the air (*báyu*). In *Bhábaprakásha* eighty varieties are described. The following may be considered the most important:—

1. When air is much deranged, and passes into the different vessels of the body it produces contractions of the body. This form is called *akhyepaka*, or spasmodic convulsions.

2. When air is deranged, and rises from its situation, it produces pain in the chest, head, and temples. The body and members are bent like a bow; and it produces convulsions. The person has difficulty in breathing, the eyes are fixed and shut. The person moans, and has little sense. This form is called *apatantraka* or rigid spasms. In this disease the body is drawn up either backwards or forwards, or to either side.

3. When the eye remains fixed, with loss of sense, the person makes a peculiar noise, the air is dislodged from the chest with relief, and is followed by weakness of the senses: it is called *dáruna* or *apantánaka*.

4. When air is mixed with phlegm, and is situated in the vessels, the person is rigid like a stick, hence its name is *dandápatánaka*.

5. When the body is bent like a bow it is called *dhanustambha*.

6. When the air is deranged in the fingers, ankles, belly, chest, or neck, the air contracts the nerves of these parts, and forces the body forward, accompanied with Tetanus, and vomiting of phlegm; the eyes are fixed, and severe pain is felt in the sides: this form is called *ámbotreama*.

7. When the air affects the veins of the back it produces *apostrotonas* (*bájhyá-áma*); this form is incurable, as the breast and back joints are broken by the violence of the symptoms. This variety of the disease is produced by external injuries, in miscarriages, and great hemorrhages.

8. *Pakhyághúta* (paralysis, *hemiplegia.*) There are two varieties of this disease, one affecting one side of the body, and another affecting one half of the body taken transversely. When air affects the vessels and nerves of one side, it produces this disease; when the person loses the power of that part, which is without feeling, and with loseness of the joints. When deranged air alone produces *hemiplegia,* the disease will be cured with difficulty. When air and bile, or air and phlegm produce this disease it may be cured; but when there is great weakness of the essential parts of the body, as after hemorrhagia in parturition or injuries, the disease is incurable.

9. When all the body is palsied it is called *sarbánga-rog.* When air and bile are both deranged, it produces great heat of the body, and fainting. When air is deranged with phlegm, the body is cold, is swelled, and heavy.

10. *Árddata,* or *hanustambha,* (Tetanus and Trismus ?) When the air is deranged by a person speaking very loud, or by eating large mouthfuls of meat, or hard things, or laughing much, or gaping or sleeping uncomfortably, or bearing heavy weights, it affects the lower jaw or half the face and neck, which it draws laterally, and the head shakes. The person cannot speak, there is a deformity of the eye, nose, mouth, and neck, with pain in these parts, as also in the chin and teeth, and the senses are in an unhealthy state. The dangerous symptoms of this disease are when the person is weak, the pain severe, and he cannot move his eyelids, nor speak distinctly; when the mouth is turned to one side, and with the shaking of the part of the body, as the head, has continued for three or more years. In all these spasmodic diseases the symptoms for a time disappear, and again recur.

11. Sometimes while cleaning the tongue with the tongue-scraper, when eating dry and hard food, or by external injury, the air is deranged in the joints of the jaw, and are sometimes dislocated, when the mouth remains open. In other cases the jaw is locked, when the patient is unable to speak or eat.

12. When sleeping in the day time, especially in an unnatural attitude, or when regarding intensely an object above the person, *air* may be so deranged, and mixed with phlegm as to produce the stiffness of the neck, which remains straight and rigid. This is called *manyástambha.*

13. When the air affects the nerve of the tongue, it becomes rigid and immoveable, and the person cannot speak, eat, or drink. This disease is named *jihwástambha.*

14. When air enters the blood-vessels of the head, the vessels becomes dry, black, and painful, producing head-ache or the disease called *shirograha.*

15. When air attacks the buttocks, back, loins, hip, thigh, knees, legs, and feet, it produces pain in these parts; passes from one to the other, often without the pain being properly defined. In other cases the affected parts shake; sometimes when air is mixed with phlegm it produces heaviness of the part, dispepsia and drowsiness. This variety is called *gridhrasí.*

16. *Bishwáchi.* When air affects the tendons of the back of the hand and arm, it produces this disease, in which there is no motion in the hand or arm.

17. When air and blood are changed in a part, it swells with severe pain. In this manner the knee-joint may be affected, and become large, like a jackal's head. This disease is called *kustaka-shirsha.*

18. When air is deranged in the sides of the thighs, it draws the tendons of these parts, which contract, and the person walks feebly. This disease is called *khanja.*

19. If both sides are affected the person cannot walk, this disease is called *pangu.*

20. When in walking the person limps, his body shakes, or as if the person was walking over *kalái,* a kind of pea, and is feeble, it is called *kaláskhanja* (chorea sanctir viti).* In this disease the parts seem as if loosened from their natural binding. The disease is characterized by the person feeling in the commencement a trembling or shivering sensation through his body, accompanied with a dimness of sight, and a pain in the neck, jaw, or teeth, or of the part affected. These symptoms are followed by involuntary twitching of the head, neck, and jaw, often of one side, especially of one leg. The patient speaks indistinctly, and then the involuntary motions extend to the whole voluntary muscles of progression, producing a dancing motion. When the disease extends over the body, and has continued long, it is considered incurable. Its existing cause is considered to be irregularity in the bowels from eating indigestable food, too much walking or laughing, carrying great loads, &c.

* In some Sanskrit works the term *Ardita* is given to this disease, and others apply the term *Ardita* to Tetanus and Trismus.

21. When the ankle joint is strained in walking it produces pain in the ankle with stiffness, it is called *bátakantaka.* The pain resembling that of a thorn piercing the flesh.

22. Air, bile, and blood accumulated in the feet produce a burning sensation of the part, particularly when the person is walking, it is called *pádadáha.* This is one of the most distressing and intractable diseases peculiar to this country. It is called "Fever in the feet."

23. When *phlegm* and *air* are deranged in the two feet they become cold, with insensibility, as when sitting very long in a particular position, when the leg feels dead with a disagreeable numb feeling. It is called *pádaharsha* (foot numbness) ; and is a frequent complaint among the natives, from their sitting on the ground, in often constrained positions.

24. When air is deranged in the shoulder-joint, it dries the ligaments and tendons of the part. They are contracted, and the arm becomes fixed. It is called *apabáhuka,* or stiff arm.

25. When the air is mixed with phlegm, and enters into the air-vessels (*dhamaní*) the person cannot speak, or speaks slowly, and indistinctly. This disease is called *múka* (dumbness), and *minmina* and *gadgada* (indistinct speech).

26. When pain commences from the bowels and bladder, and passes to the anus and urinary passages, producing great pain in these parts, which feel as if torn asunder, the disease is called *tunie.*

27. When it commences from the anus and urinary passages, and passes up to the intestines with great violence, it is called *pratunie.*

28. Swelling and pain, with a rumbling noise of the abdomen, produced by the air being confined in the abdomen, is called *ádhyána,* or drumb-belly.

29. When the swelling is confined to the stomach with pain and noise, it is called *pratyádhyána ;* and is produced by the air being mixed with phlegm.

30. When a hard oblong swelling is felt under the navel, which passes from one part to another, or rests stationary, and becomes prominent, and air, urine, and dejections are constipated, it is called *ashthilá* or *bátashthilá.*

31. When the hard swelling is longitudinal, and is accompanied with much pain, and the urine and dejections are constipated, it is called *pratashthilá.* These derangements of air produce diseases in various situations; when deranged in the bladder, it causes the stoppage of urine, &c.

32. When air is deranged in the head, it is always shaking. The disease is called *bapati.*

33. When air is affected in the feet, legs, thighs, and wrist, it produces spasm and is called *kuli*. The other diseases of air are named according to the part particularly affected. In all these nervous diseases it is of importance that the Physician observe whether the symptoms of bile and phlegm, &c. are present, as they will affect his prognosis, and treatment. In *hanugraha* (lock-jaw), *ardito* (or paralysis of the face), *akhepoká* (spasmodic diseases), *pakhyághâta* (hemiplegia), *apatánaka* (epilepsy), our prognosis may be rather favourable, when the person is strong, the disease is recent, and is not accompanied with any bad symptoms. This is particularly the case when the patient is rich, as the treatment will generally be tedious.

The unfavourable symptoms are when the disease is accompanied with erysepelas (*bisarpa*), or with severe burning sensations, with great heat and pain, as if the body was torn, and with constipation, fainting, and loss of appetite, or when the digestion is very weak. In such cases the patient will die. This disease is also dangerous when the person is swollen, when the parts are without feeling, and are accompanied with flatulency and shaking of the body, with great pain and weakness.

Should the air not be deranged, and be confined to its usual situation, the person will live for a hundred years free from disease.

Treatment of Nervous diseases.

After distinguishing the disease, the next object is to find out the proper remedies for it, and how to exhibit them. When this is not attended to, the practitioner's reputation, and his income will be diminished; and if he does not use remedies on the discovery of the disease, it will be like a plant, which at first was easily removed, but when allowed to enlarge, and take deep root, it is removed with great difficulty. In nervous diseases oily enemas are to be used several times a day, and the body is to be frequently anointed with a mixture of

Kumkuma, saffron,
Agura, Acquilaria agallocha,
Kushtha, (Costus speciosus,)
Tagara, (Tabernæmontana coronaria,)

and other stimulants. Preparations of milk are also much used in this class of disease. The following mixture is often used. Take equal parts of *panchamula*, or (*bilwa*), *shonáka*, *gámbhári*, *pátalá*, and *ganikáriká*, form a decoction; or take with a decoction a decoction of Coriander seed, or *Kakalaidi;* a mixture of various vegetable stimulants and antispasmodic medicines ; such as—

Kákolí, (berry of the Calculus Indicus,)
Kshíra kákolí, (resembles squill, and is often sold as such,)
Mudgaparní, (Phaseolus Trilobus,)
Másaparní, (Glycine debilis,)
Chinrahá, (Minispermum glabrum,)
Carkatashringí, (the root of the Momordica mixta, (?) &c.)

When the joint is contracted mix together oil, ghee, the fat of animals, and the flesh of the crocodile, and turtle. Boil together for some time, and then let it be frequently applied warm to the parts. When there is much spasm, apply the mixture with a piece of cloth. Hot baths with hot douches, and shampooing are also of much use. Oily purgatives are useful, and hot oil in bladders is to be applied to the head, when there is head-ache. Emetics, and leeches to the part, are also recommended. Several aromatic, and anodyne substances with ghee are to be smoked or inhaled. Errhines of different kinds, made with prepared oil and ghee, are also used.

In this class of diseases the *diet* should consist of milk, with broth and meat, and sweet and acid fruits.

The person should wear warm woollen or cotton clothes, and the room should be in the centre of the house, cool, without any currents of air. The bed should be comfortable, and have soft cushions ; and the person must avoid intemperance in eating and drinking, and intercourse with females.

When the *air* is deranged in the stomach, he should take equal parts (half a *tolá*) of the powder of

Chitraka, (the root of Plumbago zeylanica,)
Indrajaba, (seed of the Wrightea antedysenterica,)
Pátá, (Cissampelos hexandra,)
Katuká, (Hellebore,)
Atibishá, (Atesor betula,) and
Abhayá, (Myrobalan.)

Repeat this medicine several times a day, and continue to take it for seven days. When deranged in the small intestines, oily purgatives, enemas, and food with salt are to be used. When deranged in the bladder, diuretics should be given. When affecting the senses, prepared oil and ghee, are to be applied to the parts. When affecting the skin, flesh, and blood, venesection is recommended. When deranged in the large tendons, joints, and bones, pressure is to be used, as by shampooing and rubbing the part frequently with prepared oils, bandages, and the application of hot irons over the affected part.*

When the whole or half the body is affected, heat is applied in various ways to produce perspiration. The patient embraces hot stones, and is put into a hot room. In other cases they dig a hole which they heat, put leaves in it, and the person lies down in it, and when he is in a free perspiration he is removed to his bed. Venesection is recommended when the whole body is affected, and cupping is used in the variety which is local. When there is no feeling in the part; the application of the actual cautery, and of a mixture of oil, salt, and soot is recommended to be rubbed into the part.

The treatment of dislocation of the lower jaw consists in surrounding it with a cloth, and reducing the dislocation (*bapuskas*). When the jaw is fixed by tetanus, they apply prepared oil or ghee externally, so as to keep it well moist during the treatment, and then endeavour to open the mouth by force. When open a mixture of medicines to produce a free discharge of saliva is recommended; such a mixture is formed by the powder of long-pepper and ginger. At the same time the mouth should be frequently gargled with warm water. He should also eat garlic, with salt. Numerous other oils and medicines are likewise recommended in this dangerous class of diseases.

Order X.

Leprosy, (Kushtha or Kuth.)

This disease is the most aggravated of all that afflict the body, and when a person dies with it the Hindus believe that the person will be afflicted with it in the next life, unless he performs the *práschitta*, penance. This penance consists of abstinence for a day, shaving the whole hair off the head, presents of a certain number of cowries and other articles to the bráhmans, who perform certain prayers, and to whom the person confesses his sins. This ceremony is now generally performed before entering upon the treatment of any supposed dangerous disease.

The Hindus distinguish three kinds of Leprosy, the black, white, and red varieties, which are produced by various causes. Sometimes the disease is caused by bad air, and drink; eating substances which do not assimilate, as milk and fish, food of a rancid, salt, and indigestable nature; or thin oleaginous food: when the

* Rhumatism is a frequent disease among cows, and the actual cautery is freely applied by the natives, with the best effects. Such cows are frequently to be seen marked all over the joints with these applications of the red hot iron.

person eats immoderately of such food, for some time, it will produce this disease. In other cases irregularity in eating and fasting, mental agitation, violent exercise, exposure to fatigue, or too great heat, especially after a full meal; night watching with exposure to the night air, using new rice, milk, curds, fish, and the too frequent use of pulse, radishes, sesaman and treacle, produce leprosy. In others it is produced by checking natural evacuations, or suppressing them when artificially excited; such as vomiting or the expulsion of air, urine or dejections, or the irregularity and alternate use of hot and cold applications. Sometimes it is produced from eating hot or cold articles of food, first at dinner, or after fasting, when the usual food is not eaten, after much perspiration, fatigue, or fear, or when the person bathes or drinks cold water at improper times. In other cases the disease is produced when the food is not digested, or when time has not been given for this purpose, before more is taken into the stomach; when after the use of emetics and purgatives, the usual simple food, &c. is not employed; when the person sleeps during the day with a loaded stomach; or when he visits his wife before the food is digested. The blood and seminal secretions of parents when tainted by leprosy, affects their offspring. Lepers in one life, are born again with the complaint; and the disease is supposed to be communicable by contact, by breathing the same air, by eating together, by wearing the clothes, or ornaments, of a person labouring under the disease. Whoever speaks disrespectfully or does any other improper action, or commits sins against his *guru* or *bipra* (pandit bráhman); such as, committing adultery with a bráhman's wife, killing a good man, and robbing a person of his estate, will be liable to be afflicted with this disease. Such causes derange air, bile, and phlegm, by which the skin, blood, flesh, and watery parts of the blood (*ambu*) are deranged, and produce the eighteen forms of leprosy: of these seven are severe, and eleven are mild.

Before leprosy appears the skin becomes glossy, thin, and rough, and of an unnatural colour; there is much perspiration, or a suppression of it, itchiness and occasional horripilation; the body feels hot, parts of the surface become insensible, and the blood in the veins becomes blacker than usual, while other parts of the surface become discoloured, painful, swell quickly, remain so for a long time, and slowly heal. In such a person any injury turns to a sore, is very painful, heals with great difficulty, and a rough cicatrix is left. The person has fits of giddiness, with impaired, or an irregular state of the appetite. The seven severe forms of leprosy are produced by deranged air, bile, or phlegm: they are thus described.

1. *Sidhma,* is produced by deranged phlegm and air, and is characterized by small, white, coppery, or red spots, which spread over large surfaces accompanied with a thin mealy dust. This is the Lepra Vulgaris, or L. Alphos.

2. *Audumbará.* In this form the blotches are livid, and resemble the ripe fig, or Ficus glomerata. This form is accompanied with much pain, and a burning on the surface. The hair becomes tawny; and the morbid humor is bile.

3. *Rishwajihwa;* the patches of tubercles, are shaped like the tongue of a bear; hard and red round their edges, dark in the centre and are accompanied with severe pain. This form is produced by a derangement of the air, and bile.

4. *Kapala;* is covered with black and purplish patches resembling the broken pieces of a black earthen vessel. These blotches are irregular, hard, and dry, and are accompanied with pricking and pain. The *air* is the humor principally affected.

5. *Kákanaka,* resembles the seed of *kunch* (Abrus precatorius), with red and black spots in the centre. The blotches are extremely painful, and often terminate in suppuration. The three humors are deranged in this variety; which is incurable.

6. *Pundaríka.* The patches in this variety are pale red in the centre, with dark dull red edges, and resemble the petals of the lotus, when exposod to the sun. This variety is produced by derangements of the phlegm and bile.

7. *Dadrukushtha.* The patches in this variety are elevated, black, round, and spreading; there are many sorts, which are accompanied with much itching, burning, and pain; and are produced by derangements of the phlegm, and bile. These are the general symptoms of the severe forms of leprosy.

The slighter varieties of leprosy, *Kshudra,* are according to *Sushruta* as follows:

1. *Sthaláruska.*
2. *Mahákushtha.*
3. *Ekshyukushtha.*
4. *Charmadala.*
5. *Bisarpa.*
6. *Parisarpa.*
7. *Sidhma.*
8. *Bicharchiká.*
9. *Kitima.*
10. *Pámá.*
11. *Rakashá.*

Charaka has the following arrangement.

1. When there is no perspiration, and the patches are very large, and of a dark brown colour, and oblong, like the scales of fish, and rough like an elephant's skin, it is called *ekakushtha,* (Ichthyasis.)

2. When it has patches of a dark yellow colour, like the cicatrices of healed ulcers, with a hardness and roughness of the part, it is called *kitíma.*

3. When sores and chaps form in the hands and feet, about the nails, accompanied with small tubercles of a red colour, much pain, and itching, it is called *vaipádíká.*

4. When the tubercles are large, of a red colour, and very itchy, they are called *álásaka.*

5. Should the patches be of a slightly dark redish colour, itchy, spreading, and elevated into tubercles, it is called *dadrumanala.*

6. When the spots are of a red colour, with severe pain, and itchiness, the blotches are very sensible, ripen soon, and much matter is discharged, it is called *charmadala.*

7. Small tubercles in great numbers, of a black or purplish hue, with a copious bloody discharge, accompanied with burning, and itching, it is called *pámá.*

8. When the eruptions are merely larger than the last, and are accompanied with much pain in the palms of the hands, or buttocks, it is called *kachchhú.*

9. When the eruptions are of a dark yellow or red colour, and the skin is dry and thin, the variety is called *bishphotha.*

10. Another form has yellow, or dark redish coloured blotches, accompanied with much heat and pain, and numerous itchy tubercles : it is called *sotárush.*

11. When the tubercles are small numerous and itchy, of a dark yellow colour, and discharge much ichor, blood, &c., the variety is called *bicharchíká.* The four first varieties are supposed to be produced by derangements of the *air* and *phlegm ;* and the seven last by derangements of the *bile* and *phlegm.*

When leprosy is in the *skin,* its colour is unnatural, rough, dry, and insensible ; and the hairs on the body are generally erected, and the person perspires freely. When *blood* is deranged the body becomes itchy with fetor, and the skin is hard, and pus is discharged.

When *flesh* is diseased it is called *gajacharma* (Ichthyasis Simplex) ; the mouth is often parched, perspiration is defective, the surface of the body is rough, is like the scales of fish, and eruptions form over the body, with pain. Patches of vesicles sometimes form, and terminate in ulcers, which remain for long periods.

When *fat* is affected the hands and feet become stiff, immoveable, and ulcerated, and drop off, with severe pain ; the sores pass from one part of the body to another, and the symptoms of diseased flesh appear also in this form.

When the *bones* and *marrow* are leprous, the nose falls in, the eyes become red, and worms breed in the sores. The voice becomes unnatural, and hoarse. When the leprosy is in the skin, blood, or flesh, or in the air or phlegm, it may be cured. When in the fat, with two of the humors deranged, as air and phlegm, or air and bile, the person will not be cured, nor will it soon destroy the individual. When the bones and marrow are affected and two or three humors are viciated, one of them being the bile, it is incurable.

Fatal symptoms of leprosy occur with worms in the sores, or with the painful disease of the heart (Angina pectoris); with dispepsia, or with symptoms of diseased air, bile, and phlegm; with sores which discharge copiously; with inflamed eyes, the voice hoarse, and altered, and with weakness so that the person is not able to bear the employment of the five forms of medicine, as purgatives, emetics, &c.

The white, and the red leprosy *(shitra* and *kilása)*, are distinguished from the black leprosy by their not being accompanied with any discharge, and only affecting the skin. *Charaka* adds, that they sometimes affect the *skin, blood, phlegm,* and *fat.*

When the white leprosy is not produced by burns, and when the hair is not white but remains of the natural colour over the white patches; when the patches are not large and do not join each other, and when recent, the disease may be cured. When produced by burns, and the above symptoms are absent, these kinds of white leprosy are incurable.

When situated about the external genitals, palms of the hands, or lips, the white leprosy is incurable although recent.

The leprosy, with fever, and the drying up or emaciation of the body, and other symptoms of pulmonary consumption (*shosha*); a variety of Ophthalmia (*Netrábhishyanda*), and those diseases produced by the influence of the planets, such as small-pox, &c. are contagious.

Treatment.

Leprosy commences first in the skin, and gradually extends deeper and deeper affecting the different essential parts, as flesh, blood, fat, &c. Thus like the small shoots of the Banian tree, which are at first confined to the surface, they advance deeper and deeper, until they extend over the whole body. In the first stage, when it is superficial, the use of proper diet and medicines may cure it; but when it has extended to a greater distance, the difficulty of curing it becomes much greater.

Diet. In leprosy, flesh, with the exception of that of wild animals, and oleaginous articles of food are not to be used; as also hard food, milk, curdled milk, certain kinds of pulse; sour articles, or sweet, prepared from sugar-cane. Improper and indigestable articles of food, or eating too often of roasted or heating food are to be avoided, and also sleeping in the day time, and connexion with woman. Good and old rice is to be used with barley, flour, and peas (*mugh*) boiled in water, and mixed with the leaves of *nimba*. Such vegetables as contain a bitter principle are useful. In other cases, barley is recommended to be steeped in cow's urine for a night and then dried in the sun. This is to be repeated seven days; then fry it, and some of it is to be taken every morning with a decoction of the following bitters,

Kantikári, (Solanum Jacquini,) and
Nimba, (Melia Azadirachta, &c.)

Prepared oils are to be used to anoint the body with.

The ulcers are to be cleaned with astringent decoctions; with an oily preparation called Vajraka, and a paste or liniment of the aragbadha (Cassia fistula). The water with which the person washes or bathes should be impregnated with *khayar*, catechu, which also should be mixed with the drinking water.

In the beginning of the disease purgatives and emetics are first to be administered. If the leprosy is confined to the skin evacuant medicines, and smearing the body with different sorts of medicines are of use. If confined to the blood it is to be purified by evacuants, smearing the body with proper medicines, drinking bitter and astringent decoctions, and venesection. When confined to the flesh the remedies are the same as those of blood, with tonic tinctures, of various kinds. When confined to the fat it is incurable; but the progress of the disease may be checked by proper diet and medicines, especially tonics. When the bones are affected it is incurable, and should not be treated.

When marrow is diseased the man will soon die. In the seven severe forms of leprosy, besides emetics and purgatives, glysters, supposotories, with errhines are to be used. If these five forms of medicines have been employed without effect, the case may be considered as hopeless.

When *air* produces leprosy, prepared ghee, with astringent tonics are to be used; when *phlegm*, emetics; when *bile*, blood is to be removed from the person, and purgatives are to be administered.

The following mixtures are much recommended in leprosy. Take equal parts of

Meshashringí, (Asclepias geminata, &c.)
Shwadangshtrá, (Flacourtia catafracta,)

Gulancha, (Minispermum glabrum,)
Shángashthá, (Leea hirta,)

mix with *Panchamuli.* This mixture consists of equal parts of the bark of

Bilwa, (Æglę marmelos,)
Sanáka, (Bignonia indica,)
Gámbhári, (Gmelina arborea,)
Pátalá, (Bignonia suaveolens,) and
Ganikáriká, (Premna spinosa.)

These medicines are to be boiled in water, shaken, mixed with ghee, and boiled down till the watery part is dissipated. This to be taken internally, mixed with oil, and rubbed over the body. In other cases the ghee is prepared in the same way with

Bhallátaka, (Marking Nut,)
Abhayá, (Myrobalan,)

and a vermifuge plant called *biranga.* It resembles black-pepper, is prepared as above, and used for the cure of all the different forms of leprosy.

Blood-letting is used frequently in the cure of leprosy, and is abstracted from different veins. When prominent patches form, scarifications, leeches or caustics, are to be used.

Various medicines are recommended for rubbing over the body. They are usually of a stimulating nature. The following is one of these. Take of

Haritála, (Yellow arsenic,)
Manahshilá, (Red arsenic,)
the juice of the Madar, (*Arka,*)
a kind of horse-raddish called *Sigru* or *Shobhánjana,*
black-pepper, and the seeds of Sesamum, (*Til,*)

mix together, in equal parts. These are to be rubbed with water, and applied to the surface affected. There are seven other varieties of such mixtures. The following is recommended. Take of the leaves of Cassia fistula (*sondál*), and mix them with butter-milk, and rub it over the diseased part, particularly where there are tubercles. Others recommend the froth of the sea (*samudra phena*), after it has been dried, to be rubbed over the diseased parts.

The following may therefore be considered as the best means of curing leprosy. Use freely catechu by mixing it with the water of the patient's bath, in his drinks, food and medicine, while he avoids animal food, wine, and intercourse with women. When the disease is subdued, use purgatives freely to prevent a relapse.

With these means, certain diet, wearing clean clothing, and a proper degree of exercise is to be used. Such treatment will generally cure the disease: especially if emetics are given every fortnight, purgatives every month, and venesection twice a year. Two tolás of the powder of turmerick in cow's urine are to be taken at the same time, every day for one month; and every third night an errhine is to be exhibited.

The following mixture is also much recommended. Take of the bark of the *nimba* tree, the leaves of a kind of cucumber commonly called Palwal, (*Paltá,*) the leaves of Solanum Jacquini, (*Kantikárí,*) Minispermum glabrum, (*Gulancha,*) with the bark of Justicia ganderussa, (*Básaka,*) of each ten polls (about ℥iv.) mix them with 64 seers of water; and boil to 16 seers. Remove it from the fire, and add four seers of ghee by degrees, and again put it on the fire until the water is dissipated. To this medicine add the

Harítakí, (Paste of Myrobalan,)
Bibhítakí, (Terminalia belerica,) and
A'mlakí, (Phylanthus emblica;)

of each two pals,* 5 tolás, and 2 másás, and 7 ratis, are to be added. The whole is to be mixed in a mortar, to which ghee is to be added; it is again to be placed over the fire for a short time, and when mixed, it is then to be strained through cloth. This, taken internally, is said to cure leprosy, the 80 diseases produced by deranged air, the 40 diseases of bile, and the 20 diseases of phlegm. It is also useful in bad boils, worms, piles, and the five kinds of cough. Other mixtures equally efficacious in curing numerous diseases, are recommended. These vaunted qualities of certain mixtures is to encourage the patient, as well as the practitioner; and their inefficiency explains the numerous other mixtures which are recommended as substitutes.

Should worms form in leprous ulcers, a paste made of the bark of Nerium odorum (*Assamára*), and the seeds of a vermifuge plant called *biṛanga,* with cow's urine, is to be applied to the sore.

Treatment of White Leprosy.

The diet in the white leprosy is the same as in the black.

The treatment of white leprosy consists in the exhibition of external, and internal medicines.

External Medicines.

Take of the flowers and leaves of

Pútika, (Cæsalpinia bonducella,)
Akun, (Calotropis gigantea,)
Sthahí, (Euphorbium,)
Baruna, (Tapia cratæva,)

* Eight tolás make one pal.

in equal proportions. Mix to the consistence of paste, with the urine of the cow, and apply to the part affected. The ashes of the skin of elephants and tigers; and the powder of the flying bug (*pádapoká*), is also used. Another remedy is the fæces of a fowl which has been kept fasting for three days; during which time it is only to receive a mixture of the seed of Cassia tora (*prepunára*), and licquorice root. The fæces is to be rubbed over the part; and repeat the application daily for a month, during which time the same mixture is occasionally to be given to the fowl. Another external application is prepared as follows: The juice of the mango tree is to be mixed with the bark and leaves of the murabuli, the mixture is to be put into a copper vessel, and mixed with the juice of the Ficus Indica (*bot* tree). It is then burnt, and the ashes are to be mixed with a decoction of myrobalan, and mustard oil. This medicine is to be rubbed over the affected part.

The *Internal Medicines* employed for white leprosy are very numerous. The following mixture may be taken as an example: Take of the powder of the root of Plumbago Zeylenica (*Chitrakah*), black pepper, dry-ginger, and long-pepper; macerate them in cow's urine in an earthen water-pot, in which ghee had been kept, and some honey; keep the mixture for a fortnight, strain, and give one tolá for a dose.

Order XI.

*A kind of Leprosy,** (*Báta-rakta.*)

This disease is produced by the blood being diseased with *air* (*báyu*). Its exciting causes are using sour food, and alkaline salts. In like manner spices, or other hot articles, indigestable articles of food, putrified, or dry meats, as the flesh of crocodiles, of the buffalo, of the rhinoceros, or the like. Tíl oil-cake, and other indigestable articles of food, curdled or butter-milk, bad wines, and excess in eating and drinking, the passions, unhealthy and improper mixtures of food, eating too often, or sleeping during the day produce this disease. Delicate constitutions, and fat people, who lead a sedentary life are predisposed to this disease. Long continued riding on horses, elephants, or camels, and whatever produces great heat of the body; by these causes the blood is diseased, and is conveyed by the air to the feet, where it accumulates, and produces this disease, first in the feet, and then in other parts

* Under this head several diseases are described; such as certain forms of rheumatism, abscesses; and such cachectic states as may, they say, terminate in true leprosy.

of the body. *Báta-rakta* is ushered in sometimes by free, at other times by a cessation of perspirations; the body becomes of a dark hue, and parts have no feeling. If there are sores they are very painful; the joints are loose, the person feels languid, and cannot work; and small pimples appear over the body, with pain of a gnawing or lancinating kind, as if ants were eating the flesh, or needles thrust into the skin. The knees, legs, thighs, loins, shoulders, hands, and arms, are so affected. The pain intermits, and these parts become heavy, without feeling, and the skin has patches of an unusual colour.

When air is much deranged there is severe pain of the body, as if ants were eating the flesh, and the vessels, nails, fingers, and joints are contracted. The patient has no appetite, and if not treated the symptoms increase. The person cannot work, and the body shakes, with rigidity of the joints.

When blood is much deranged swellings appears over the body, with much pain. The skin is of a copperish colour with slight stinging pain (*chin chin*). If the patient take oil and dry food, in small quantities, he feels better.

When bile is deranged the body feels hot, with a burning sensation, and dulness of intellect. He perspires much, has fainting fits, with an appearance of drunkenness and thirst; pressure of the part produces great pain, with redness, heat, swelling, and sometimes abscesses are formed.

When *phlegm* is deranged the body is very cold, as if a cold wet cloth was applied over the body, which feels heavy, and without feeling. The skin is smooth, shining and itchy, and feels cold, with slight pain.

When two or three of the above humors are affected the symptoms resemble the two or three forms, as above enumerated.

In some cases the ankles and wrists are first affected, and then it extends over the body like the poison of certain animals.

The disease is incurable, when accompanied with a sore from the ankle to the knee, or when it is opened and pus escapes in large quantities. When the person is very weak and reduced the disease will be fatal; but if the person lives for a year, or it is chronic, he will live. When the disease is severe the person cannot obtain sleep, has no appetite, has a difficulty in breathing, parts of the body slough, he complains of head-ache, fainting, delirium, pain in the body, thirst, fever, has no sense, with shaking, hiccough, contraction of the fingers and toes, so that he cannot walk nor work, and erysipelas appears with vascular eruptions. Severe pain is felt in the vital parts, tumors appear over the body, want of memory, fatigue, and delirium follow, and precede death. When all the symptoms of this severe form of the disease are not present, the disease may not be fatal. If none of the severe symptoms are present, the disease may be cured. When only one of the humors is deranged; as air, bile, &c. and the disease is recent, it may be cured; but, if two of the humors are deranged, the disease will remain, when three are affected the disease is incurable, and when all the severe symptoms are present the disease will be fatal.

The treatment of this disease is to be commenced by general and local bleeding; when the patient is not weak, or much reduced in flesh. Emetics and purgatives are then to be used. If the air is much deranged old ghee is to be administered, with the milk of goats, prepared with liquorice, honey, and sugar. In other cases equal quantities of the following medicines are recommended:

Sunt, (dry ginger,) mixed with
Singataka, (Trapa bispinosa,)
Kaserika, (Scirpus kysoor.)

In other cases a decoction prepared with milk and the five following medicines, is recommended:

Sálparní, (Hedysarum gangetic,)
Prisniparní, (Hemionites cordiflora,)
Kantikárí, (Solanum jacquini,)
Bherhotí, (Solanum melongena,)
Kokurá, (Ruellia longifolia,)

equal parts of these plants, are mixed together, to form the decoction. This mixture is called *panchamulí*, and may be used as follows. Take of

Panchamulí, and
Mahá panchamulí, with liquorice,
Meshasringí, (Asclepias geminata,)
Sahala, (Pinus longifolia,)
Básaka, (Justicia ganderussa,)
Debdáru, (Ovaria longifolia,) and
Kantikárí, (Solanum jacquini.)

These are to be mixed and formed into a decoction in the usual way. Tíl oil may also be prepared in the same way as the above. These mixtures are to be administered internally and applied externally. In other cases the powder of myrobalan with sugar is administered. A powder composed of five corns of long pepper, is to be taken daily for ten days, and is to be decreased by degrees for a fortnight, during which time the patient should live on rice and milk.

The diet in this disease should consist of the simplest food in small quantities; as old rice, barley, flour, milk, broth of wild animals, and the decoction of a kind of pea (*mudga*). When the disease is violent, bleedings should be repeated several times, and emetics, purgatives, and enemas are to be given ; such persons should live in a shut-up room, avoid currents of air, during the treatment ; and he should sleep on a long comfortable bed, with soft pillows. The body should be shampooed, and he should avoid fatigue, sleeping during the day time, connexion with woman, anger, heating, salt, sour food.

Order XII.

Urticaria? (Sitapita.)

This disease is called *Sitapita* or *Udordah,* and another form is named *Khatah.* The disease is produced by cold air applied to the body, which deranges the *phlegm, air,* and *bile.* These move about on the surface, and within the body, producing thirst, redness of the eyes, nausea, and cause loss of appetite. The body becomes heavy, and the person incapable of work. The disease appears with slight swellings in different parts of the body ; like the sting of the wasp. The part is at first itchy and then very painful, with vomiting, fever, and heat of the body. When the air is much diseased, beyond the other humors it is called *Sitapita ;* and when phlegm is much deranged, producing red circles, accompanied with itching, it is called *Udordah.*

It is called *Khata,* when the stomach is deranged. This is more liable to occur if at the commencement the stomach has not been properly cleared by emetics, and when bile and phlegm are deranged. If in such a case an ignorant person does not promote vomiting, but endeavours to cure the deranged *bile* and *phlegm,* the disease will be aggravated. In such cases the body is covered with large and small circular patches which are itchy, elevated, and have a red colour. They appear and disappear on different parts of the body. This form of the disease will also be produced by repressing vomiting when nature is endeavouring to relieve herself of the contents of the stomach.

Treatment. In *Udordah,* mustard oil is to be rubbed over the body ; in other cases turmerick, *dub* grass (Panicum dactylon), and the urine of the cow, are to be mixed and rubbed over the body. The warm bath is of great use ; and a decoction of *nimba* leaves, as an emetic and purgative, with one tolá of *trifalá,** and half a tolá of *teori* or Convolvulus turpethum, and *tribrit,* or castor oil. If for seve-

* Which consists of myrobalan, Emblici myrobalan, and Beleric myrobalan, mixed in equal proportions, or one tolá.

ral days the person takes the powder of myrobalan (*ámlaki*), liquorice root with sugar; or Legusticum ajwaen (*jawáni*) with sugar, and uses the proper diet he will be cured of the disease. The juice of fresh ginger, with old impure sugar (*jagary*), is also used. In *Sitapita*, the same treatment is to be employed; in *Khata*, tonic medicines are to be given with blood letting. The powder of the *nimba* leaves, and Emblic myrobalan (*ámlaki*), are to be taken internally. He should also take rice prepared with horse raddish, and the gravy of birds. Cooling diet is to be used in the two last forms; and in *Sitapita*, heating food is to be employed, and every thing cooling avoided.

Order XIII.

Erysipelas, carbuncle? (*Bisharpa*).

When *air*, *bile* and *phlegm* are all deranged in the skin, flesh, or blood, they produce a slight swelling of the whole body, which passes from one part to another. When produced by air, the part becomes black, soft, and unequal; accompanied with pain, as if needles were thrust into the part, and the fever produced by deranged air. When surrounded with vesications it is incurable.

When the disease is produced by bile it spreads quickly, and is accompanied with inflammatory fever. This form is accompanied with redness, and vesications. When the inflammation is deep, the flesh and vessels are destroyed, and it discharges a matter like a mixture of water and clay. Such cases are incurable.

When produced by *phlegm* it spreads slowly, has an oily appearance, and is white. There is little pain in such cases, with considerable itching. When produced by the derangement of the three humors the symptoms are of a mixed nature. When this disease passes to suppuration it is incurable. When produced by sharp instruments, or such like injuries, the bile and blood are deranged and produces a swelling of the part; which becomes black and red, and is accompanied with violent inflammatory fever. The affected part is surrounded by a black edge, and eruptions like peas.

The first three forms of this disease are curable, and the two last are incurable.

Treatment. When produced by air different preparations of ghee, and decoctions, and plasters are applied to the part. The medicines used are the same in all the above forms as follows: take equal parts of

Musta, (Cyperus rotundus,)
Sotáobha, (Anethum sowa,)

Debdáru, (Pinus debdaru,)
Kusta, (Costus speciosus,)
Kustumbru, (Coriander seeds,)
Cigruh, (Hyperanthera morunga,)

mix them with water and ghee, the mixture is then to be boiled, strained, and applied to the part. It is sometimes used as a decoction.

Stimulating medicines are likewise applied to the part, when the disease is produced by bile. The application in this form should be used cold. Thus take equal parts of

Bibera,
Lámojaka,
Chandana,
Rasanjana, (Sulphurate of Antimony,)
Guerika,

mix them together with milk, and apply it to the part. In some cases cold water, or water mixed with honey or sugar, or the juice of the sugar-cane may be used with advantage.

When erysipelas is produced by phlegm the following medicines should be used. Take of

Ajagandá, (Ocymum gratissimum,)
Ashwaganda, (Physalis flexuosa,)
Sahala, (Pinus longifolia,)
Tribrit, (Convolvulus turpethum,)
Ajasringí,

mix them with cow's urine to the thickness of cream, and apply it to the part. Another application is as follows. Take of

Kaláner sarga,
Agura, (Aquilaria agallocha,)
Kachu, (Arum colocasia,)
Gunghá, (Morunga hyperanthera,)
Rásaná,
Bássau, (Panicum italicum,)
Sítasiba,
Indraparní,
Mahíkadamba,
Pralendu,
Munjáta, (Saccharum munja,)

these medicines are to be mixed with cow's urine to the consistence of cream, and then applied to the part.

Besides these external applications, purgatives, and blood-letting are recommended. When abscesses are formed, or the part ulcerates, the usual plan of treatment for abscesses, and ulcers is to be followed.

Order XIV.

Boils, pustules, Erysipelas? (*Bishphotaka*)

The causes of this form of disease are using too much heating, sour, or acid substances ;—heavy and indigestable or salt food ;—eating too freely, and exposure to the sun—or to too sudden alterations of the weather. By such cause, *air, bile,* and *phlegm* are deranged, which affect the blood, flesh, bones, and skin ; and produce large bullæ, accompanied with fever. This part appears as if burnt. Sometimes these bullæ appear over all the body, and in other cases they are confined to particular parts. When the air is much deranged in this disease it is accompanied with head-ache, fever, thirst, pain in the joints, and the bullæ become black, accompanied with much pain. When produced by deranged bile there is much fever, burning of the body, and a large discharge of fluid from the bullæ. They then become red, or yellow.

When produced by deranged phlegm it is accompanied with vomiting, dispepsia, languor, and the affected parts become itchy, hard, and white, without pain. Suppuration often takes place, and continues for a long time.

When the three humors are deranged the disease is incurable ; and also when the bullæ are depressed in the centre and hard. The patient in such cases complains of a burning sensation, thirst, fainting, vomiting, fever, delirium, rigors, and drowsiness. These are unfavourable symptoms, as also when the bullæ become red.

When the disease is produced by blood, the tubercles are like the seed of the *gunja ;* (that is red with a black spot.) This form is incurable (*Charaka*).

The treatment of this disease is the same as that described under the head of *(Bisharpa)*. The bark and leaves of the (*Sabanjana*) tree (*Morunga*) is to make into a paste with old conjee, and applied to the parts with salt ; bitters are also of much use, such as the decoction of *neemba* bark and of *gulancha*.

Order XV.

Hæmorrhagia, (*Raktapitta.*)

This order of disease is divided into those which occur from the mouth, nose, ears, eyes ; from the anus, urethra or vagina ; or from the skin.

Hemorrhage is caused by anger, grief, fear, wrestling, and other severe exercises ; too much intercourse with women ; or too free use of hot things, as pepper and salt, or sour articles, when taken in considerable quantities. The improper mixtures of food, or exposure to the heat of the sun, or to fire. By these means the chyle is deranged, which irritates the bile, and this mixing with the blood produces *Raktapitta*. It may thus occur from above downwards, or from the surface of the body. This blood usually proceeds from the spleen or liver.

Immediately before the disease occurs the patient is languid, the body is weak, cold, and cool things are desired. His throat is burning hot, as if he had swallowed smoke, with vomiting. The breathing has the smell of quenched iron. When produced by deranged *air*, *bile*, and *phlegm*, it is known from the blood discharged being very thick, of a yellow colour, shining, and slippery, and mixed with phlegm of a grey colour, of a thick consistence, and with a yellow froth. In other cases it is thin. When bile is deranged in this disease, the blood has an astringent taste, and is of a dark colour, or of the colour of cow's urine, and as if mixed with different colours, as of the colour of smoke, or of a dark colour.

The symptoms which terminate this order of diseases are weakness, difficult breathing, cough, fever, vomiting, and slight head-ache; sometimes the patient faints, and his skin is yellow, hot, and after eating, the pit of the stomach burns. He is restless, and has severe pain in the chest, with hoarseness, head-ache, and the discharge of fecal matter from the mouth; he has no appetite, is languid, and what is eaten is not digested.

The unfavourable symptoms in this disease are when the hemorrhage is like the water in which flesh had been washed, or like a vegetable decoction; is of a liver colour, or like water mixed with mud. When it resembles pus mixed with blood, when it is dark like the fruit of the *Jambu* tree (black-berry), or of a variegated colour, like the rain-bow, such cases are fatal.

When there is a frequent vomiting of blood; when eructations have the taste of blood, when the eyes are red, and every thing appears the colour of blood, the case is hopeless.

When *phlegm* is deranged the blood is evacuated by the mouth; when *air* is deranged it is by the anus; and when the two are deranged, the blood is evacuated above and below. When the blood passes above, the person may be cured; but not so when below. When evacuated both ways, it is incurable. When the person is strong, the disease recent, and not severe, and only occurs one way; and when the person in general feels well, with no other bad disease, it will be cured.

Treatment. The hemorrhage from a stout person is not to be stopped at the beginning; as it otherwise will produce jaundice, dispepsia, leprosy, enlargement of the spleen, fever, and *gulmah.* When the blood is evacuated from the urethra or anus, emetics are to be administered; and when from the mouth or nose, purgatives are to be used. If the person is very weak, the discharge of blood may be stopped by administering astringent articles.

When air, bile, and phlegm are much deranged, and the person strong, such a person should fast for some days, after which he is to drink conjee with a little rice, with sugar, lemon juice, and the juice of grapes.

Several decoctions and electuaries are recommended with preparations of ghee, to cure this complaint. The purgatives are to be mixed with the juice of grapes and liquorice root, sugar, and the juice of other sweet fruits. Emetics are always to be used with honey, water, and the decoction of liquorice.

The diet should be cold water, and the flesh of wild animals, boiled rice, broths made of gram (*mung*), potatoes, and different other vegetables, seasoned with ghee, and mixed with the juice of the pomegranate, (*umlika*) myrobalan, with the broth of pigeons, turtles, and shell-fish. Different preparations of rice as conjee with ghee may also be used.

The body should be anointed with cold oil, and cold applications are to be made to the body. In this disease the juice of the rose-apple leaves, or mangoe leaves, or *orgono ;* and the juice of the fruit of figs may be used with rice water, and the root of cucumber *(triposí.)* In other cases half a tolá of liquorice root in water; the pulp of the seeds of *ingodah* with liquorice root, and sugar-cane bruised, are to be kept in a new earthen pot for one night steeped in cold water, with the flower of water-lily, and taken with honey.

If the blood proceeds from the nose he should snuff the powder of myrobalan. After a great loss of blood, the patient may drink the blood of animals with honey, or he may eat the flesh and unprepared liver of a goat with the bile. The juice of horse-dung with honey and sugar is also recommended. The powder of fried rice with honey, sugar, and the white concretion *(tobashia)* of the bamboo is also used. A decoction of the bark of rose-apple, mangoe, and *orgono* trees, are to be taken with honey; and cold and sweet applications, both internally and externally are recommended.

Section III.

Diseases of the regions of the Body.

Class III.

Diseases affecting the mind.

The diseases of the mind are swooning, epilepsy, madness, and devil madness.

Order I.

1.—*Swooning, (Múrchhá.)*

When the person is weak, or when the *air, bile,* and *phlegm* are very much deranged, by eating improper mixtures of food, such as milk and fish, or flesh, &c., by constipation, &c., this disease is produced ; in which the organs of sense, both external and internal are deranged, with faintness.

When the derangements of *air, bile* and *phlegm* close the passages of the vessels, the person cannot see, and falls down as a piece of wood : this disease is called *múrchhá* or *moha.*

There are six varieties of this disease, but in all the bile is deranged. The six are produced by derangements of *air, bile,* or *phlegm,* by blood, by drinking spirits, and by poison.

The approach of this disease is known by pain in the breast, gaping, languor, loss of sense, and strength. These symptoms are the same in all the varieties.

When produced by derangements of *air,* every thing appears of a dark-blue or red colour, or like the sky. The person cannot see, and faints, but the senses soon return. There is shivering, pain of the body and breast, weakness, and the skin becomes dirty, and of a reddish, or green colour.

Bile. The person sees every thing of a yellow, or green colour : he cannot see, and faints. He is soon restored to his senses, with perspiration. When he recovers, the skin becomes yellow, the body becomes hot, eyes red, and dejections yellow.

Phlegm. He sees every thing of the colour of clouds ; the sky appears misty and dark, followed by fainting, in which sensation remains long absent. The body feels like as if a piece of soaked leather had been put upon it : and phlegm is discharged from the mouth and nose, followed by nausea and vomiting.

4. When these three humors are deranged at the same time, they produce all the symptoms of the three separate diseases ; but

without the symptoms of Epilepsy. When these diseases occur, and the person does not feel when needles are thrust into his flesh, red hot irons put upon the surface, or hot substances put into his mouth, the person will soon die.

5. Seeing *blood* often produces swooning from its containing earth and water, which possess the properties of *tamoguna*, the cause of darkness. In this manner the Hindus explain the occurrence of fainting, on seeing blood, by the quality of darkness which it possesses.

6. When swooning is produced by *poison* there is shivering, drowsiness, thirst, followed by weakness and insensibility. There are various kinds of this variety, but all produce these symptoms. Fainting is generally produced by deranged bile, when mixed with *tamoguna*, or darkness. When bile and air are mixed with *rajoguna*, it produces swooning, and drowsiness; coma is produced when air and phlegm are mixed with *tamoguna;* and phlegm and *tamoguna* when mixed together produce sleep. Drinking spirits derange the *air*, *bile* and *phlegm*, and produce swooning, which continues until the effects of the spirits cease.

Another form of this disease is called *sangnyása* (apoplexy). It is produced by the deranged air, bile, and phlegm, which pass to the place in which life is retained, and overpowers all the functions of both mind and body, and the person suddenly falls down, and remains as if dead, or like a piece of wood. If not immediately, and properly treated, such a person will die.

Treatment. In general all the symptoms of swooning will disappear in a few minutes, with the exception of *sangnyása*, which requires immediate treatment. In all forms of swooning throw cold water upon the face and body, rub the body with the hand, allow a free circulation of air, and assist this by means of the *pankhá*. Wet the mouth with cold water, and approach sweet smelling substances to the nose. Such as the juice of sweet fruits, as of grapes, pomegranates, dates, (*khurma*,) the juice of wild animals, barley, and good rice; in like manner prepared ghee with a decoction of *myrobalan*, or a decoction of *Imblic myrobalan;* or a mixture of fried rice, grapes, honey, sugar, and the juice of the pomegranate, with the petals of the water-lily. The treatment followed in bilious fever is also recommended.

The treatment of *sangnyása* is difficult, and requires promptitude. Should the person not soon recover from the swoon, needles are to be thrust under the nails, and remedies which produce strong irritation, are to be applied, such as sweet music; and when the person is restored to sensibility, he is to have an emetic, and a purgative followed by the exhibition of *siláj atu*. If these means do not succeed, the case is to be considered as hopeless. When the disease is produced by poisons, the person is to be treated as recommended under the head of poisons.

Order II.

Epilepsy, (Apasmara or Mrighi.)

Generic character. Sudden loss of sense, loss of sight, and the person falls down with convulsions. These symptoms are preceded by palpitation of the heart, lightness and hollowness of the chest and body, perspiration, inaccurate thinking, dullness of sense, and loss of sleep.

When air, bile, and phlegm are deranged by grief, sorrow, or the like, they pass into the vessels immediately communicating with the heart, and produce this disease, with the loss of sense and memory.

Exciting causes. This disease is produced by the improper use and indulgence of the senses; as too much, or too little listening, seeing, tasting, smelling, &c.; the improper mixtures of food, or putrified articles of food; the neglect of the calls of nature, connection with women during the flow of the menses, and by such passions, as sorrow, grief, and anger. By these causes the mind is so effected as to produce epilepsy.

There are four kinds of disease, one being produced by the derangement of each of the three humors, and the fourth by the combination of the three.

When *air* is deranged, the symptoms of epilepsy are followed by shivering, grinding of the teeth, foaming at the mouth, hurried respiration, and to the patient every object appears obscured, red, and confused. The treatment best adapted for this form of disease are enemas, the following decoction of *Jotela.*—Take equal parts of

Pamjamulí,
Haritakí, and
Goat's urine.

Prepare the decoction in the usual manner with ghee.

When *bile* is deranged the symptoms are accompanied with a yellowness of the body and countenance. To the patient every thing appears of a yellowish colour, the sputa is of the same colour, and the eyes appear red. The patient has great thirst, and every thing feels hot, and as if enveloped in flames. In treating this form the ghee should be prepared with the bile of

Goda,
Nokana,

Nága,
Pirśoto, and
Cow's urine.

This preparation is to be taken internally, and applied externally over the body.—The ghee may also be prepared in a decoction of

Tribrit, (Convolbulus turpethum,)
Páṭhá,
Haridra,
Dár-haridra, (Zanthorrhizon,)
Anantamúl, (Periploca Indica,)
Pushkara,
Kataka, (Strychnos potatorum,)
Bacha, (Acorus calamus,)
Sulence,
Biṛanga ;

with cow's urine and milk, and some of its dung and curdled milk. This may be used for all kinds of epilepsy. Venesection is also recommended. Another remedy is, giving a wild boar purgatives for three days, then rice and milk; when this has been digested, he is to be destroyed, and the chyle in the vessels removed, and mixed with thin parts. It is to be put in a new pot, and when it has arrived at the vinous fermentation, it is to be given to the patient.

When phlegm is deranged the symptoms are whiteness of the countenance and body, the saliva and foam are of the same colour, the body is cold, and the patient shivers. The person sees every thing white, and as it appears to approach near him, he faints. These fits cease very slowly.

The general indications of cure are to give enemas in derangements of air, purgatives in bile, and emetics in the form produced by deranged phlegm.

When air, bile, and phlegm are deranged together, all the symptoms of the separate forms are present. This disease is incurable if not recent, as the person becomes weak and emaciated, and the fits are frequent, and accompanied with severe convulsive movements of the body. The eye-brows contract frequently with the eyelids, and the eyes move rapidly. In such cases the patient will die. The fits come after ten days, a fortnight, or monthly. In other cases they occur very often. As some seeds thrown in the ground during the rains do not germinate for a long time after, so in this disease the deranged air, bile, and phlegm produce the disease after long intervals. In the form of epilepsy the body should be anointed with *átuk,* which is to be taken internally, and at the same time administer strong errhines, emetics, and purgatives.

Order III.

Madness, (Unmáda.)

The causes producing this disease are improper food, endeavouring to perform impossibilities, strong passions of the mind, cursing the gods, bráhmans, and spiritual guides; eating poison, &c.

The *air, bile,* and *phlegm* are affected by the above causes, which deranged knowledge *(satwagun)*, affects the seat of understanding and the heart, and pass through the vessels conveying sense *(mana)* when the person becomes mad, speaks foolishly, is restless, and his eyes are continually moving about.

There are six kinds of madness. Three being produced by derangements of air, bile, and phlegm; one by the combination of these; another by the violent actions of the passions; and the last by poison.

Air is deranged and the mind is thus affected by the use of dry, cooling, articles of food; by food in small quantities; by strong purgatives; by the causes diminishing the humors *(dhátu)*, or by fasting. By these causes the air is deranged, producing madness; in which the man laughs, dances, and sings unreasonably, and moves his limbs about. At other times he cries without cause; the skin of his body becomes dry, rough, and of a dark-red colour. These symptoms are more violent after the digestion of food; and the patient becomes greatly emaciated.

When *bile* is generally deranged by the use of indigestible food, and the use of pungent and heating substances, the symptoms it produces are impatience of control, and anger; the person wishes to use violence to others; he remains naked, prefers cooling food, and wishes to live under the shade, or in water. The body is yellow, and hot.

When *phlegm* is deranged by the usual causes, as a too sedentary life, and taking too much nourishing food; by which the phlegm is deranged, affecting the functions of the heart, and producing the following symptoms: A love of solitude, taciturnity, and loss of appetite; the person has a desire for women, enjoys deep sleep, and has vomiting, or expectoration. After eating any thing the symptoms are very violent, and the body as well as the nails and countenance are whitish.

When *air, bile,* and *phlegm* are deranged together, all the separate symptoms are produced, and the disease becomes of very difficult cure.

When the disease is produced by the passions; as when frightened by a robber, a tyrannical official, &c.; by the loss of wealth, and friends, or by the love of particular women, the symptoms are characterized by talking, laughing, singing, and sometimes crying. This variety terminates in Idiocy.

The *treatment* of the above five forms of madness should consist of cleaning, and anointing the body with mustard oil: of eating ghee for some days, and then strong purgatives and emetics are to be given, with errhines, and mustard oil. Curious, or wonderful exhibitions are to be made before the patient; and he should be informed of the death of relatives, and friends. He should also be frightened by the alarm of robbers, by the approach of elephants, and harmless serpents. The person should be beat with a whip, when he acts improperly; and he should live on light food, such as barley, and conjee water, made agreeable by the addition of carminatives. Ghee should be prepared, with a decoction of the following medicine: take of

Samap,
Elabáluka,
Elá, (Cardamoms,)
Chandana,
Debdáru, (Erythroxylon siduoxylloides,)
Haridra, (Turmerick,)
Kuṣhṭha, (Costus speciosus,)
Parminí,
Lariha,
Haranuka,
Tribrit, (Convolvulus turpethum,)
Dantí,
Bacha,
Tálísa, (Corypha,)
Nabupisara.

These are to be prepared, in the usual way, with ghee and milk.

During the cure the person should be treated, as much as possible, with kindness, and consideration.

6. When madness is produced by poison, the person becomes faint, from the sudden loss of strength; his eyes becomes red, and the countenance and the body become yellow or blue. The unfavourable symptoms are when the person is weak and emaciated, remains in one position, and is always looking downwards, or upwards. When the patient has no sleep, and is so courageous that he will throw himself from a height, the disease will be fatal.

The treatment in this variety is the same as that for poisons in general.

Order IV.

Possessed persons, or Devil-Madness, (Bhútonmáda.)

There are two kinds of spiritual beings, a good and a bad spirit, which are supposed to enter the body, and to produce disease. These are called *Bhútonmáda*, (*Devil-Madness*;) and *Debonmáda*, (madness produced by good spirits.)

When produced by attack of devils, the person shews his aversion to every thing divine, is very strong, and has much knowledge; and when from the entrance of good spirit or *(Debtá)* the person has a pleasure in flowers and good smells, becomes pure and holy, and is inclined to speak Sanskrit. He obeys bráhmans with strictness, and looks courageous. There are no intermissions in these forms of madness.

Devils know the present, the future, and what is hid or unknown. They are never at rest; and they are employed in different kinds of business. An unclean or wounded person, or those who do not perform their ceremonies, may be injured by devils. They are very numerous and powerful, and are usually considered as the attendants, or servants of *Shiva*. This explains how the energy, and work of the affected person, is much beyond that of man; his mind is now powerful, his knowledge extensive, and he understands the shástras. Sometimes the person appears sane, and at another time is mad. Such madness is produced by a devil, which is known by the unnatural motion of the person's eyelids.

There are eight principal devils that torment the human species.

1. When *Debagraha*, or good spirit, enters a body, the person is always happy and contented, remains clean in his person, and wears garlands of the sacred flowers, &c.; his person has a pleasant smell, and he has no sleep. He speaks Sanskrit correctly. The person is strong, his eyes remain fixed, and he blesses those who approach him. He has a great love for bráhmans, and performs the prescribed ceremonies, and attends to old customs of his ancestry.

2. *Asuragraha*. They are the enemies of the *Debtás*. When the person is possessed with them, he perspires much, speaks of the bad conduct of bráhmans, and the *Debtás*. His eyes are turned and fixed, he has no fear, and is always performing bad actions. He is a glutton, is not pleased with his food and drink, and is always mischievous.

3. *Gandarbagraha*. The person possessed with this devil is always happy, prefers living in an island, near the bank of a river, or in the jungle; and his conduct is good. He is fond of singing, of sweet smells, and of looking at flowers. He is fond of dan-

cing, and laughing. These are the choristers of heaven (demigods) who wear sacred flowers, put marks on their person, and have a great love for adorning their persons. They speak little but properly, and agreeably.

4. *Jakshyagraha.* This class of demigods are fabled to superintend the treasures, and gardens of heaven. When he enters the body, the person's eyes become yellowish red like copper. They wear thin red clothes, talk little, but are profoundly intelligent, and have much patience ; such a person walks fast, is never revengeful, though very strong, and is always wanting to bestow his means upon others.

5. *Pitrigraha.* These are spirits which are separated after death from the bodies of mankind. When an ancestor thus enters the body, the person is always preparing prayers for them, and performing the different ceremonies *(shráddha)* for ancestors. Such a patient is quiet and peaceable, and is fond of animal food, and sweetmeats.

6. *Sarpagraha.* When the serpent-devil enters the body, the person walks irregularly, or from one side to another, like a serpent ; his tongue is thrust from one side of the mouth to the other ; and he is passionate, and is fond of treacle, honey, and sweetmeats.

7. *Rákshyasagraha,* or cannibal-devil. When one of these devils enters the body of a person, he is fond of eating flesh, blood, and wine. He has no shame, his appearance is disagreeable, and he is very strong, and passionate. Such a person walks about at night, is unclean, and is always performing bad actions.

8. *Pishácha,* or fiend, is known to have entered the body, by the person always stretching out his hands. His body is thin, and is disagreeable to look upon, and he speaks fast, and without meaning. His body has a disagreeable smell, and he is unclean, restless, and covetous. Such a person eats much, prefers living in jungles and retired places ; he walks with an unnatural motion of the limbs and is sorrowful, and frequently cries.

The unfavourable symptoms of such persons possessed with devils are ; his eyes are swollen, he walks fast, and his tongue is passed rapidly, and continually, from one side of the mouth to the other ; he is always sleepy and sometimes falls down ; and at other times he is affected with severe shivering. When the madness is produced by falls from high places, such as from elephants, or trees, they are more difficult to cure. It is also dangerous in old age, and when hereditary. When the disease has continued 13 years it will not be cured.

The devils invade the body of persons on different days according to the species. *Debtá* invade at full moon, and devils (*Asur*), enter in the morning and evening. The *Gandarba* enters on the eighth, and *Jakshya* on the first day of the moon. *Sarpagraha*, or serpent-devils, enter on the fifth day after new and full moon. *Rákshyasa* enter at night. *Pishácha* enter on the 15th day after new and full moon. We cannot see when a spirit enters the body, in the same manner as the soul enters, and leaves the body without being seen; as light enters the water in a glass, or as heat or cold enters a body, without our being aware how it takes place. *Unmáda*, and *Bhútonmáda*, are said to be cured when the functions of the sense, judgment, and heart, are restored to a perfect state, and the tissues are natural.

Treatment. During the cure the patient should be treated kindly. A physician should commence the cure of a person possessed with a devil, by cleaning and anointing his body with mustard oil, he should be dressed in new clothes, and he should repeat the proper prayers, and act agreeably to the *shástras;* so as to satisfy the devil (*graha*) who is the cause of the madness. The usual red and white pigments are to be applied over the forehead, red clothing and garlands of red shoe-flower are to be worn, and honey, ghee, flesh, wine, milk, and articles of food are to be presented, for performing the *pújá* with. Some *graha* are satisfied with wine, some with goat's milk, &c., as stated in the *shástras*.

From the day of the invasion, find out when the devil will destroy the person, as each has a day particularly consecrated to him, and on that day use the proper means for removing the devil. The *pújá* is to be performed at the temple of one of the gods, by the physician, who if possible conveys there the person diseased; a fire is prepared, and flesh, &c., are thrown upon it, with suitable prayers. Some *kusa* grass (used for funerals) is to be sprinkled over the ground, a preparation of coloured ground rice, a cake of unleavened bread, ghee, and an umbrella is to be given to the devil. A mixture of sugar, milk, and rice boiled, is also to be presented.

When devils (*Asur*) afflict a person, the above remedies are to be administered in the square of the house. The removal of *Rákshyasa* devils is to be accomplished at the meeting of four roads, and in deep jungles. The *pújá* of *Pishácha* devils is to be performed in empty houses. When the devil has not been expelled by these means, with the prescribed prayers, other remedies are to be used. The smoke from leather, and hair, from the skin of a bear, or goat, from asafœtida, with goat's urine, are to be burnt, when even strong devils will be removed.

The other remedies are long-pepper, black-pepper, dry-ginger, rock-salt, asafœtida, myrobalan, and bach, with the urine of goats, and the bile of fishes. These are to be used as errhines. Ghee and oil should be prepared, with the fæces, skin, hair, fat, urine, blood, bile and nails of the following animals: a lion, tiger, bear, cat, leopard, elephant, horse, and cow. These are to be mixed and used for anointing the body with, as errhines, or cold cream is to be mixed with these. Numerous other mixtures of the same kind are also used in this disease.

Persons not liable to be afflicted by devils are, prophets, charitable persons, those who speak the truth, and those who attend to the orders of the *shástras,* and perform particular duties, and employ proper terms in addressing holy men. Those who have the eight qualities of the body, are always pure, humble, and wise, visit holy places, always govern their passions, and speak the truth; and those who pray, and attend to the prescribed ceremonies and are charitable, over such persons devils have no power. Devils only go about at night, and they live, under their eight chiefs, on blood, fat, flesh, and disgusting animals.

Class IV.

Disease of the Head and Neck.

Order I.

Diseases of the Head, (*Síraroga.*)

Under this order will be arranged the varieties of Head-ache, and the diseases of the organs of sense.

Head-ache.—There are eleven varieties of head-ache; which are produced by derangements of the air, bile, and phlegm; by the mixture of the three; by diseased blood; by a deranged or diminished state of the humors, by worms, the eighth is named *Súrjyábartta,* the ninth, *Anantabáta,* tenth, *Ardháyabhedaka,* and the eleventh *Sankhaka.*

1. When *air* is diseased in the head, it is suddenly affected with pain, which is severe at night; but it is diminished by hot applications, and bandages. To cure this variety of head-ache, take ghee, milk, and *mudga* (a kind of pea), and boil them in water: *máskalái* at night will also be useful. Avoid bitters, hot milk, warm baths and *douches* applied to the head. A hot poultice composed of fish, and the expressed oil of sesamum will be of use.

The smoke produced by oleaginous substances is to be applied, and the person is to anoint his body with prepared oil, and have errhines and purgatives exhibited. The juice of *oleaginous* substances mixed with the food, and with medicines useful for curing deranged *air*. Throwing warm water upon the head is often used, and sometimes the water is mixed with other medicines.

2. *Bile*. In this variety, the head is hot, as if burning charcoal was placed over it, and there is an appearance of smoke proceeding from the mouth. The pain is diminished when the head is kept cool, and during the night. Medicines are to be given with cold water, milk, ghee, oil, and the like, and applications are to be made to the head; as vinegar, the juice of the sugar-cane, of acid fruits, or whey. The paste of aqueous plants, purgatives, enemas made with oil, and broths made of wild animals are also to be used.

3. *Phlegm*. In this variety the head is heavy and dull, and it cannot be turned about. The head feels cool, and the eyelids and mouth are swollen. In this form the medicines which cure diseased phlegm are to be used, such as strong emetics, errhines, and gargles. The head should be rubbed with a paste made of liquorice root and ghee. The bark of *inquido* is also useful; and snuff made of the bark of *kaṭfala*. He should likewise take the decoction of those medicines which cure phlegm, and live on rice and barley, mixed with long and black pepper and ginger. The decoction of *mudga* (a kind of pea) may also be used.

4. When the above three *dhátu* are diseased, the different symptoms are combined. In this form the treatment is the same as that above described, as being applicable when one only of the humors are diseased; particularly the use of old ghee internally.

5. When the blood is deranged, producing this disease, the symptoms are the same as when bile is deranged. The pain in this variety is so severe, that the head cannot be touched, or bent forward.

6. When the disease is produced by a diminution of brain, or fat, phlegm, or blood, in the head, it produces great uneasiness and pain. This pain is increased by hot applications, by smoke, by errhines, and by blood-letting. In this form nourishing food is to be used, with prepared ghee applied internally and externally. The prepared ghee recommended in pulmonary consumption is also to be used.

7. Worms sometimes produce severe pain in the head, of a kind as if an animal was eating, or tearing the head. A watery red or bloody discharge flows from the nose, and the patient's life is to be considered as in danger. The treatment consists in using medicines to discharge the worms; as blood, when used as an errhine,

it will cause the worms to become stupid. Stimulating snuffs are of use, such as the powder of the seeds of *shringi*, and *biranga*, mixed with cow's urine, and other vermifuge medicines. By these means the worms will be expelled.

8. *Súrjyábartta*. In this variety, when the sun rises the eyes and brow feel painful; and it continues, and increases, while the sun is above the horizon. It diminishes in the evening, and towards night. It is produced by derangement in the air, phlegm, and bile. For curing it use old ghee, and other medicines, as above mentioned; and the food is to consist of milk and rice, with broths made of wild animals.

9. *Anantabáta*. When air, bile, and phlegm are deranged in the vessels of the neck, they produce great pain, particularly in the eyebrows, temples, and cheeks. It also produces shaking of the head, pain in the lower jaw, and diseases of the eyes (*neuralgia*).

This variety is to be treated in the same manner as *Súrjyábartta*, but particularly by the puncture of the diseased vessel. The diet should be sweetmeats prepared with ghee, honey, sugar, and flour, with the remedies which cure bile and air.

10. *Ardháyabhedaka*, (*hemiplegia*.) When much dry food is taken it produces this disease; or eating without an appetite, or too frequent; exposure to the easterly wind, or to dew, and the abuse of venery. When the urine and bowels are constipated, and the person has been subjected to much grief, or severe exertion, he is liable to the attacks of this disease; as also by derangements of air, bile, and phlegm. The attack occurs sometimes every fortnight, in other cases every tenth day, or in other cases every day. The half of the neck, brow, temples, ears, eyes, are very painful. When severe, as it often is, like that of poison, or as if burnt, and the sight and hearing become imperfect. This disease is very obstinate, and most distressing; so that a thousand physicians cannot sometimes cure it. In this form errhines prepared with the powder of the seeds of *Sirisa*,
Mulaká, camphor,
Pipala, long-pepper, and
Bacha, are to be exhibited. An external application is made by mixing together the paste of
Sáliba,
Kusta,
Pipala and *Madhuka*, liquorice,
with the juice of acid fruits, ghee, and oil. This is applied over the head. The broths of wild animals, with ghee, and cold applications, are also useful. The head should, in this disease, be always kept

well anointed with mustard oil. If by the above means the head-ache is not checked, blood-letting should be performed.

11. *Sank haka.* When air, bile, and phlegm, with blood are deranged, it produces severe pain in the temples and head, which becomes hot. This form is dangerous, like poison. When the person cannot swallow, he will die in three days. But if he lives beyond this time, medicines may then be given for the cure. The treatment is the same as of the last variety.

Order II.

Diseases of the Ears, (Karnaroga.)

The more copious secretion from the external ears, and the most changes of temperature of the air, render diseases of this organ of frequent occurrence in this country. They produce much suffering, and much attention seems to have been paid by the Hindus to their nature and cure.

There are twenty-eight diseases of the ear. The corporeal *air* is the cause of all these diseases. When it is deranged in the ear, and is confined in its passage by the other humors, it produces severe pain in the organ, which is called *karnashúla,* and is very difficult to cure. When air is deranged in the passages of the ear, several kinds of sounds are heard, like those of certain instruments called *karnanáda.* When *air* is deranged with phlegm in the ear passages, and if not treated it will produce deafness called *bádhirjya.*

Fatigue, or eating hot or astringent substances, or the frequent use of errhines produce a derangement of the air in the ear passages called *karnakshyera,* which consist in a peculiar ringing noise. In others the disease is produced by blows on the ear, by bathing in water during which water enters the ears, or by a boil in the part which suppurates. This disease is called *karnasangsrába.*

When *air* and *phlegm* are deranged in the ear it produces itchiness; and bile being deranged dries up the phlegm, and wax in the ear. This disease is named *karnagúthaka.* When the wax melts it passes out of the nose (*sursuta*), or mouth (*nidan*), and the disease is called *pratináha,* and is accompanied with much pain in the head.

If worms form in the ear by flies depositing their eggs in the ear, the disease is called *krimikarnaka.*

When the ear is wounded or otherwise injured it is called *bidradhi.* In other cases there is great pain, burning, and tightness in the part, with a discharge of yellow pus or blood; it is then called *karṇabidradhi.* By the derangements of bile abscesses are formed, which is called *karṉapáka.*

When *phlegm* is deranged and dried up by the heat of the bile, it melts, and then is discharged from the ear, with a disagreeable smell. It is called *pritikarṉaka.* There are also four kinds of bloody tumors, seven varieties of other tumors, and four kinds of swellings to which the ear is liable.

In defects of the external ear, *Susruta* recommends the surgeon to prepare a new ear, by removing skin from the neighbouring part, leaving a connection to keep up its vitality. Cutting off ears was a frequent method of punishment and the formation of a new ear removed the deformity, which was the more striking in the Hindu, as the ear was the place for hanging ornaments, especially among the rich.

Treatment. In these diseases ghee is to be used with the diet, with rest, and bathing, not including the head, while intercourse with women is avoided. In *karṉashúla, praṉáda, bádhirjya,* and *kara* the treatment is the same. Give oleaginous purgatives, and apply steam of water impregnated with different herbs which cure air diseases. This is conveyed to the external ear by means of a tube. Fish, cock's flesh, and that of a bird called *lába* are to be mixed, and applied hot to the ear. The leaves of the banian tree, are to be made in the form of a cup, which is to be heated over a fire, and the drops of juice which ooze through the leaf, are to be applied hot to the ear. The juice of garlic and ginger is also to be applied to the external ear. Other stimulating and narcotic medicines, and different oils, are recommended for these diseases of the ear. Strong errhines are also to be used.

In deafness the oil is to be prepared with cow's urine mixed with a decoction of *billah,* and applied to the ear. Milk and water are also of use. For curing the diseases named *karṇashrába, pútikarṉa* and *krímikarṉaka* are the same remedies as above enumerated. Strong errhines and fumigations, washing, oils dropped into the ear, and various astringent decoctions will be found of use. Gum, raisin, frankincense (*dhuná*), powdered with the juice of the wild cotton tree, are to be applied to the ear. Worms are to be removed by the application of such medicines as expel them. The sulphurate of arsenic, with cow's urine, is found of use. For removing the bad smell from the ear, use fragrant fumigations. Mustard oil will remove the ringing of the ears. Inflammations of the ear are to be treated as in other local inflammations. For the morbid secretion of wax remove it by instruments, and fomentations; and emetics and errhines are to be administered for the itching of the ear. For removing external substances from the ear exhaust the air in a cow's horn, and apply it tightly upon the part.

Order III.

Diseases of the Nose.

There are thirty-one diseases of the nose. When the nostrils are closed, when one is dry, very dirty, and hot, when matter has formed, and when the patient can neither smell nor taste, the disease is called *Pínasa,* and is produced by a derangement of air and phlegm. When the *air* is stopped in the palate and nostrils, and there is a bad smell which proceeds from the mouth and nose, the disease is called *Putinaska.* In these diseases the treatment should consist in anointing, and heating the body. Then an emetic and purgative are to be given, and errhines exhibited. Hot food is to be used in small quantities, and of a kind easily digested. Boiling water is to be taken as soon as possible, and the part exposed to steam impregnated with aromatic substances. The powder of pepper, dry ginger, &c. may be mixed with mustard oil and the urine of cows, to be boiled together, and used as an errhine.

Bile when deranged in the nose produces small pimples, which quickly suppurate, and are called *Násikápáka.* In this disease a disagreeable discharge often proceeds from the nose and umbiliacous, for which blood-letting is to be used. When blood flows from the nose it is called *Násа-raktapitta,* in which case *air, bile,* and *phlegm* are deranged. When the vital part of the nose is wounded, deranged air, &c. passes through the nostrils producing a bad smelling secretion mixed with blood, it is called *Pueraktа.* When stimulating substances are applied to the nostrils, or by regarding the fire, the air is mixed with phlegm and passes from the nostrils with a noise, this is called *Kabuti* or sneezing. If phlegm thickens, as if prepared by fire, and has a saltish taste, it is called *Bransuti.* If hot air proceeds from the nostrils, and *air* is discharged like smoke or is very hot, it is called *Dipta.* Phlegm when deranged with air so as to close the nostrils is called *Pratinaha.* When *air, bile* and *phlegm* are deranged in the nostrils it dries. When the discharge is thin like water, and passes from the nostrils, particularly at night, it is called *Pásáparsisrábah.*

When the nose is very hot and dry, and the passage of air gives great uneasiness, it is called *Násáparisasah.*

Polypi of the nose, (*Násársah,*) and tumors of the nostrils (*Násárbuda*) are described under the head of surgery.

Pínasa has an acute and chronic form. In the first the head is heavy, the patient has no appetite, and the discharge from the nose is thin. The voice becomes altered, with occasional vomiting and weakness of the body. When chronic, the phlegm as it is discharged from the nose, thickens, and the voice becomes natural. The colour of the skin is natural, and the discharged phlegm is thick, and very adhesive.

Pritisyaiah resembles *Apinnasa* and is sometimes produced by the neglect in the calls of nature, by eating indigestable food, and allowing the accumulation of dust in the nostrils; speaking or crying much; frequent fits of anger, unusual and sudden alteration in the seasons, such as want of the accustomed rain, and exposure to the sun, watching or sleeping during the day, being wet with very cold water or dew, and excessive venery produce the diseases of the nose; as also hot tears passing into the nostrils. By these causes the humors are deranged in the head, producing the usual symptoms of catarrh; the general symptoms of which are sneezing, heaviness of the head, languor and pain, and stiffness over the body (*Guseska*).

When produced by *air* the nostrils become filled up, there is a thin discharge with dryness of the throat, palate, and lips, with severe throbbing pain of the temples, and hoarseness.

When *bile* is deranged the symptoms are a hot discharge of a yellow colour, the body is weak, of a gray colour, and hot. There is much thirst, and what is vomited is hot, and like smoke.

When *phlegm* is deranged the discharge is white or grayish, and is copious and cold. The body becomes pale, eyelids swollen, head very heavy, and the throat, palate, lips, and head, are itchy.

When *air, bile* and *phlegm* are deranged the symptoms occur rapidly, disappear, and recur again, whether they be acute or chronic. At one time the nose is clean but it again becomes dirty, dry, and closes with fœtid breath, and loss of smell. This is the bad form of the disease, and is cured with difficulty. If neglected this disease passes into *Pínasa.* When it has continued for a long time it produces deafness, blindness, loss of smell, cough, and dispepsia.

When *blood* is deranged, and is discharged from the nostrils, the eyes are reddish. This form is produced by injuries of the chest, and both the mouth and nostrils have a bad smell. He loses the sense of smell, and worms are produced in the nostrils. These worms are small and of a black and white colour. The different forms of *Prahsiáka,* if not seen by the practitioner early, are not curable.

There are five forms of *Arbuda,* or tumors attacking the nose, and four of *Sota* (swellings), four kinds of *Arsa* (Polypus), and *Raktapitta* (hemorrhage): all these form so many diseases of the nose. They have already, or will be hereafter described under the head of Surgery.

Treatment. In *Putinaska* ghee is to be introduced into the nostrils with fomentations. Emetics and errhines are also to be used, with light food, and warm water as drink. Smoking with aromatic herbs is also recommended. In this disease mustard oil is to be used ; it should be prepared with the following medicines :—

Hingu, (asafœtida,) black and long pepper, and dry ginger,
Bachaka,
Shibati,
Katphala,
Lákshyá, (Butea frondosa,)
Bacha, (Acorus calamus,)
Kusta, (Costus speciosus,) and
Biranga.

These are mixed, and used as an errhine.

Násíkápáka. In this case antiphlogistic means are to be used, as the application of leeches, and the paste made of the bark of the trees which produce a milky juice, as the banian tree.

In *Puerakta,* when pus and blood are discharged, it is to be treated as fistulæ in other parts of the body.

In *Pínasa* hot substances are to be eaten, as ginger with salt, so as to thicken the mucus, and when chronic ghee is to be taken internally with emetics. When the mucus becomes thick it is to be discharged by means of errhines, purgatives, gargles, and smoking with aromatic substances. The person should remain in a shut up place. His head should be kept warm, and he should avoid cold water and venery. He should also avoid grief, dry food and new wine ; when accompanied with fever, vomiting, languor, and diarrhœa, fasting is recommended with tonics and carminatives.

Order IV.

Diseases of the Eyes, (*Akírogah.*)

It is related that *Janaka,* rájá of Mithilá or Tirhoot, did not perform the usual ceremonies and prayers to the sun, for which he was afflicted with the diseases of the eye. By abstinence and humiliation before the sun, however he was cured of the disease ; and since then, by proper offerings he obtained the favor of, and was instructed by, *Surya* concerning these diseases. He afterwards wrote a *Shástra* on the subject, called *Sáláka Tantra,* which is stated to be "in profundity like the ocean."

There are 76 diseases of the eye, of these 10 are air diseases,

10 bile, 13 phlegm, 25 are produced by the derangement of the three humors, 16 by blood, and 2 external diseases. These diseases are again subdivided into 9 of the joinings of the eye, 21 of the eyelids, 11 of the white part of the eye, 4 of the black part, 17 of the eye in general, 12 diseases of the true organs of vision *(Dristi)*, and two external diseases from injuries.

1. *Description of the Eye.* After a description of the size of the eye it is stated that it is formed by a combination of all the elements. The flesh being produced by the earth, blood from the fire, the black part from the air, the white part from the water, and the different canals for the tears are produced by ether or sky. The black part extends over one-third of the eye, and the pupil about one-seventh part of the black part. The tunics are the two eyelids, and of the globe of the eye. The first surrounds the vitreous humor (*Tezajala*, or glistening water), the second is covered with flesh, the third with fat, and the fourth with bone. They distinguish five circles, the eyelashes, eyelids, the white sclerotic coat, the iris, and the pupil. There are five joinings, the eyelashes with the eyelids, the eyelids and white of the eye (sclerotic), the white with the transparent cornea, and this with the pupil, and the corunculo lachrymalis. The humors are carried into the eye by the vessels, and produce many diseases.

The causes of these diseases are bathing when the body is very hot, intensely regarding minute objects, or those at a great distance, or sleeping at irregular periods, frequent crying, grief, anger, external injuries, excessive venery, constipated or sour articles of food, or a kind of pea *(Máskalái.)* Irregularities of seasons produce them, retaining the tears in the eye, smoke and dust, profuse vomiting, or stopping it suddenly. These causes with derangements of air, bile and phlegm or blood, produce diseases of the eye. The deranged humors are conveyed into the eye by the vessels, and produce the different diseases in the different parts of the eye. The general symptoms of diseases of the eye are its changing its natural colour, pain, redness, a discharge of tears, and there is a burning sensation in the eye as if there was an external body in it. The eyelids feel painful, as if thorns were under the eyelid, and there is intollerance of light.

2. *Inflammation.* There are four varieties of inflammation of the eye, produced by derangement in the air, bile, phlegm, and blood. The ten diseases of the air are characterized by severe pain in the eye, which remains immoveable, a feeling of sand in the eye, which is dry, with an inclination to rub it. The patient complains of head-ache, and the tears are cold.

Bile produces inflammation of the eye, which is characterized by burning, with the discharge of blood and pus, and cold applications are grateful. The eye seems to be covered with a haze, feels hot, and has a yellow colour. There is likewise a discharge of warm tears.

Cough, when it produces inflammation it is characterized by hot applications being grateful to the eye, which feels heavy, swelled, itchy, and cold. There is also a copious discharge of tears, which are of an oily nature.

Blood produces inflammation which is characterized by the discharge of a copper colour, the eye is red, and the small vessels of the eye become turgid. Before this appears the peculiar symptoms of bile are present. When this inflammation is neglected, or improperly treated, it produces one of the four varieties of severe ophthalmia *(Adimanta)*. This aggravated form has the following symptoms: severe pain, as if the eyes were torn; throbbing, which extends to half of the head, and is characterized by the above symptoms of each variety. When this is produced by phlegm it will destroy the eye in seven days; if blood is diseased it will destroy the organ in five days, if air in six days, and if bile in one day. In the acute stage of this ophthalmia the pain is severe, as if a foreign body was in it, with redness and swelling, and a copious discharge of tears from the eye. When merely chronic the pain is less, with itchiness in the part, the discharge of tears is slight, and the eyelids can be opened, and the globe appears healthy. When the inflammation produced by air is neglected, the accessions recur at intervals, and produce pain of different kinds. The eye swells, suppurates, and is red like a wild fig. It suppurates without swelling, when the other symptoms are the same. The eye in such cases is very painful, and the disease is incurable.

Another form of the disease is named *Bátaparjiya*, in which air is deranged, and the eyebrow and eye are painful, so that the person winks, and brings the eyelids forcibly together.

Suskákipáka. When the eyelids are dry, and suppurate, the eye is very painful, the sight is troubled, and the patient cannot shut the eyelids.

Anutáyabáta. When the air of the neck and head, ears, cheeks, or vessels of the back of the neck are deranged, and in other situations, the eyebrow and eye are very painful.

In *Amládhasita*, the eye is of a green colour with a red circumference, from the colour of the blood in the part. It extends over the eye which is hot, swelled, and tears continually flow. This is produced by sour articles of food.

Sirotpáta. It is accompanied with more or less pain in the eye, which becomes red. When neglected this form is called *Siráharsa*, when the discharge is of a copper colour, and the person cannot see. These are the general diseases of the eye.

2. *The diseases of the black part of the Eye.*

Ulcers of the Cornea, (Bruna-sukra.) In this disease the black part appears spotted, the discharge is very hot, and if it is not near the pupil and there is only one spot, which is without pain and any discharge, it may sometimes be cured.

When the ulcer is of long standing, extensive, and deep-seated, it is difficult to cure. When depressed in the middle and the margin elevated it will destroy vision. When both coats (cornea and iris) are destroyed by the ulcer, which has a red margin, and has been of long standing, it is incurable.

Abruna-sukra. When the inflammation is in the black part of the eye with a burning sensation, it is very white like the moon, it is curable. If of old standing, is white, large, and deep-seated, it will be cured with difficulty.

Pákátiya, or opacity of the cornea following inflammation.

Ajakúyáta, small tumors like the litter of goats, slightly red, which protrudes through the cornea, from which a bloody discharge proceeds mixed with pus.

The *Dristi* (crystalline lens) is the principal part of the organ of vision. It is like the form of a pea *(masuri)*, and is produced by a mixture of the essential parts of the five elements. It resembles the firefly, and it is largely supplied with the eternal fire (*Abaytazi*). It is covered by the external tunic of the eye, and has externally an opening (pupil ?). By cold it is kept in a healthy state. The diseases of this part of the eye are very tedious in their cure.

3. *Diseases of the membranes of the Eye.*

When the first tunic *(Pratarnapatala)* is deranged, the vision is indistinct. When the second tunic is affected the sight is very imperfect, and the person sees an appearance of motes, musquitoes, hairs, and nets. In other cases it is in the form of a circle like spectres, rays, and as every thing were indistinct and immersed in water, or like rain, clouds, and darkness. The person cannot distinguish distance, so that near objects seem at a distance.

When the third membrane is deranged he can neither see above nor below; large objects appear covered, and he cannot distinguish the features of a person placed before him. Such a person has often double vision.

Linganása. In this form the whole crystalline lens *(Dristi)* is affected, and if not very deep the person can see the moon, star, and lightning. When *air* is much increased the patient sees every object red ; and when *bile* is affected, he can see the sun, the rainbow, and lightning. In other cases every thing appears black, variegated, and like the feather of a peacock. When affected by *phlegm* every object appears as if covered with oil and white. When the three humors are deranged, every thing appears spotted as of a mixture of different colours. When blood is deranged every object appears red and dark. In *Linganása* the colour is made of six different tints.

When the eye is affected with deranged *bile* it is called *Pittabidagdha dristi*, which is characterized by the yellowness, and images appearing yellow. If it affects the third membrane he cannot see during the day, but can see at night.

When *phlegm* is affected it is called *Sleshmabidagdha dristí* which is characterized by the white appearance, and every thing seems white. When deranged in the three membranes of the eye it is called *Nyctalopia*, or night blindness. He can see during the day. Grief, fever, vexation, severe diseases of the head, cause this disease of the eye, in which every object appears enveloped in smoke ; hence it is called *Samadarsher*. In other cases the person cannot see small objects during the day, but sees every thing at night. This is called *Rasajáta*.

When air, bile, and phlegm are deranged, and produce a change in the iris like the mungoose eye (which is very red) every thing appears of a mottled appearance during the day. It is named *Nakuländha*.

Gambiraká. When *air* is deranged it produces the disease in which the pupil of the eye is contracted, and it diminishes the size of the eye, and is accompanied with great pain.

Linganása is of two kinds. The first is called *Sanimita* and the second *Animita :* the first is produced by inflammation of the eye, and the second by the sight of holy sages, by regarding a kind of large snake (*Maharaza*), or luminous objects by which vision is destroyed. The eye in this disease does not lose its natural appearance.

Abigáta hatadristí is produced by accidents or injuries to the eye, by which the person cannot see ; the organ becomes red like coral, and severe pain is felt as if a person was tearing the eye out.

4. *Diseases of the white part of the Eye.*

Prastárijarma. In this disease there is a thin red or dark-coloured membrane covering the white part of the eye.

Suklárma. The enlargements in this disease are white and soft, and it advances slowly.

Raktárma is characterized by fleshy growths of a red colour.

Adimánsarma (Ptergium) is a liver-coloured thickening of the white part of the eye. It is stationary. Another form is thick, and fleshy, and of a white colour.

Stárjarma is fleshy swelling of the white of the eye.

Sukti, when there are many small spots of a green flesh colour.

Arjana is when there is a red spot.

Pistaka is a round white elevation of the white of the eye like a drop of water.

Jála. The white part in this case is like a net-work, with hard small vessels of a red colour.

Sirája, in which white pimples appear in the white of the eye, surrounded by enlarged vessels.

Balásaka is a silvery copper-coloured spot surrounded by vessels.

5. *Diseases of the joinings of the eyes :—of the eyeball, cornea and sclerotica, eyelids, eyelashes, &c.*

These diseases are nine in number. The parts sometimes swell, suppurate and are painful ; the disease is called *Puyalisa.* Blood and thick pus are discharged in these cases. Another form swells much, but does not suppurate ; is itchy, but without pain. It is called *Upanáha.*

When air, bile, and phlegm are deranged at the joints, and the passage of the tears are discharged over the eyelids in the form of tears, it is called *Netranári* (Fistula Lachrymalis), of which there are four varieties according to the nature of their discharges. When pus alone is discharged it is called *Parsásarba.* When phlegm is alone diseased, and the joint suppurates without pain, the discharge is of a white colour, thick, and shining like oil : it is then called *Sleshmásrába.* Diseased blood sometimes produces this disease, and when there is a hot discharge mixed with much blood it is called *Raktasrába.* When bile is diseased, the discharge has a yellow colour, and it is called *Pittasrába.*

When small pimples appear at the joints of the eye, of a red colour, they burn and are painful. They are called *Parbaniká.* Sometimes this occurs at the juncture of the cornea and sclerotica, and are accompanied by the same symptoms as the last. They are of a red colour, and are called *Alaghi.*

Krimágranti. Sometimes worms are produced at the juncture of the eyelids, and eyelashes. They produce much itching ; and sometimes they form between the eyelid and the white part of the eye. They are of different colours and forms, and destroy the eye.

Diseases of the Eyelids.

There are twenty-one diseases of the eyelids. In this class of diseases, air, bile, and phlegm may be diseased in a combined or separate form. In other cases these derangements affect the vessels of the eye, and the blood and flesh, &c. may separately, or when combined, produce diseases of the eyelids.

Atsangani are small eruptions on the external part of the lower eyelids, they often open internally; and are produced by diseases of the blood.

Kambiká are swellings at the borders of the upper eyelid. When they break, pus and blood are evacuated; and they are like small castor oil seeds.

Another form of swelling is of the colour of blood; of the size of a mustard seed, hard, and itchy; and water, pus, and blood are evacuated from them. When painful they are called *Pataki*. When numerous clusters of small eruptions, are rough, elevated, and situated on the inner side of the lid, they are called *Bartasarkará*. Another form are small like melon seeds; have little pain, are situated in the eyelids, are rough to the feel, and are called *Arsabarta* or *Bartársi*. When like the new shining germ of a plant, the eyelids are long, hard, rough, indolent and irregular, and the patient cannot open the lid, the disease is called *Saskársa*, or dry hemorrhoidal tumors of the eyelid.

Another form is very hot, painful, and of a copper colour; and is soft, and small, with little pain: it is called *Angannanámika*.

Sometimes the eyelids are covered with small irruptions, and all the small swellings have the same appearance and colour, and are stationary. They are called *Bahalabarta*.

Another form of swelling is when the lids are swollen, itchy, and painful, the lids being tight over the eye, and the eyelids do not completely cover the globe of the eye. This disease is called *Bartabanda*.

When the internal part of the eyelid is spungy, hot, painful, of a copper colour, and changes quickly to a red colour, it is called *Klistahbarta*.

If in this disease bile is deranged and affects the blood, much dirty matter is discharged called *Bartahkardama*.

When the swelling of the lids is both external and internal, with burning and itchy pain of a dark yellow colour with a discharge, it is called *Sábabarta*.

When the upper lid is externally swollen, of a red colour, and much matter is discharged in its inner surface, it is called *Práknimabarta*..

When the eyelids are shut, and they cannot be opened without their being previously soaked in water, on account of the secretion, the disease is called *Akhnabarta*.

When the joints of the eyelids become immoveable, and everted it is called *Bátahattabarta* (Entropium.)

When a pendulous swelling forms in the inside of the eyelid without pain, and is caused by blood, it is named *Arbuda*.

When the vessels which move the eyelids are deranged they produce winking, or a continual movement of the eyes, when it is called *Nimassa*.

When the small fleshy excrescences, situated in the eyelids, are of a red colour, soft, painful, and grow again when removed by the knife, they are produced by diseased blood, and are called *Sunitársa*. Another form of tumor forms on the eyelids like a plum, hard, soft, moist, and does not suppurate, but becomes large and knotted it is called *Lagannah*.

When air, bile and phlegm are deranged the swelling appears above the eyelid, breaks, and blood, water and pus are discharged through many openings. The pain is so severe as to resemble poison, and is called *Bishabarta*. In other cases these derangements contract the eyelids so that the person cannot see distinctly. This disease is called *Kuncharna*.

When air is deranged the eyelashes are turned inwards, and inflame the eye, and the person is always rubbing them. It is called *Pakakapat*, (Entropeon,) and is a difficult disease to cure.

Bile when deranged in the eye produces the falling off of the eyelashes ; when the eyelids are itchy and hot, the disease is called *Pakaksáta*.

Treatment of the diseases of the eye. Eleven of these diseases are cured by the excision of the diseased part ; nine by scarifications ; five by incisions ; fifteen by punctures ; twelve by the use of different instruments ; seven are cured with difficulty ; and fifteen diseases are incurable. The two general diseases of the eyes are considered incurable.

In treating Ophthalmia *(Abisanda)*, the patient is to have his body anointed, and fomented according to custom ; and in both *Adimanta* and *Adisanda* venesection is to be employed, followed by oleaginous glysters and purgatives. Cooling washes, and the vapour of certain medicines, with errhines, are to be applied to the diseased eye. It is then to be covered with a yellow-coloured cloth. Warm fomentations, and boiled hot flesh is to be applied to the eye, with poultices made of milk and rice. The patient should drink milk boiled with the decoction of those plants which cure diseased air.

Goat's milk, boiled with the decoction of the root and leaves of the castor oil shrub is to be applied to the eye while warm.

When the ophthalmia is produced by derangement of the bile, blood-letting, purgatives, and the applications recommended in other inflammations are to be used. In other cases ghee and goat's milk are to be prepared with the following medicines. Take of

Gundrá, (Cyperus pertenuis,)
Sháli,
Shaibala, (Vallisneria octandra,)
Loclobido,
Dárbi, (Zanthorrizon,)
Elá, (Cardamoms,)
Udpoloh,
Rodhra,
Mustaka, (Cyperus rotundus,)

and the leaves of the water-lily and other cooling medicines. Ghee is to be used as an external application. The other parts of the antibilious treatment is to be followed; and gold rubbed in the milk of a woman, and mixed with honey, may also be applied. Liquorice root, mixed with woman's milk or sugar and water; or a piece of cloth made of the wild silk is to be first moistened with water, and then applied to the eye.

When ophthalmia is produced by phlegm, blood-letting, fomentations, errhines, and colleria, with the application of vapour are to be used. Different gargles, and irritants for the discharge of mucus from the nose are recommended. The colleria, &c. are to be prepared with medicines which cure phlegm. The patient should eat of such substances as do not increase phlegm, the ghee should be prepared with bitter plants. This should be repeated daily. The fomentations should be prepared with the decoctions of

Bálá, (Hibiscus tortuosus,)
Suntí, (Dry ginger,)
Debdáru, (Erythroxylon sideroxcylloides,)
Kushta, (Costus speciosus.)

The vapour of these medicines is to be applied to the eye. At other times various medicines are formed into a mixture, and applied externally to the eye: such as myrobalan, *haridrá,* (turmerick,) *maduka,* (liquorice,) *anjana,* and antimony. These medicines are dried in the sun, and when the mixture is to be used, moisten it and apply it upon the eyelids.

When blood produces diseases of the eye, it is recommended to use general and local bleeding, strong and frequent purgatives, errhines, cold applications, and to apply a mixture of different medicines upon the eyelids. When there is much pain use soothing fomentations, leeches, and the usual treatment for bile. The juice of *nimba* leaves mixed with iron and copper are also recommended. The juice of sugar-cane, honey, sugar, woman's milk, *darbia,* and *maduka,* (liquorice,) are to be applied externally, with the juice of the pomegranate. Water and sugar, rock-salt, and whey are also used as external applications.

Besides the seventy-six diseases, which are common both to children and to the adult, there is another which is peculiar to the former. This is called *Kukunáka* or purulent ophthalmia. It is caused by the bad milk of the mother, and also by the derangement of phlegm, air, bile, or blood, singly, or collectively. It affects the eyelids. The symptoms are the continual rubbing the eye, as well as the nose and forehead; great intollerance of light, and a copious discharge.

In the *treatment* bleeding is first recommended with scarifications of the eyelids. Then apply stimulating substances mixed with honey, in order to discharge the bad humors. With this the usual medicines recommended for the mother and child, for purifying the humors and improving health are to be given; such as emetics, &c. are to be used. A decoction of the young leaves of *jumbu* (rose apple), *ámra* (mangoe), datree mulica, and myrobalan trees, are also recommended. The eyes are to be washed with this, as well as with other astringent medicines. The following mixture is also recommended. Take of—

Nipálaja, (red sulph. of Arsenic,) *maricha,* (black pepper,) burnt *kunch,* (a shell,) *rasánjana,* (sulph. of Antimony,) and *saindhaba,* (rock-salt,) with jagary and honey. These medicines are mixed with the honey and treacle, and applied with a probe to the eye.

There are many peculiarities in the diseases of the eyes, that cannot be described in a book; but by these general precepts an intelligent person will be able to vary his treatment according to the circumstance of each particular case.

The diseases of the eye in which the use of instruments is required are:

Utsinjiní,
Bahalabárta,
Hurdamabárta,
Shábabárta,
Bandabasta,
Klistabárta,
Pataka,
Kambíkíni, and
Bátasarkárá.

Scarifications. Before performing this operation the person should take an emetic and purgative. He should be placed in a closed cool room without much light, the eyelids separated by the thumb and forefinger of the left hand. Moisten the eye with a piece of soft cloth which has been dipped in warm water; and with the point of a knife on the rough leaf, as of the wild fig-tree, &c. the scarifications are to be made. Continue the application of the warm water as a fomentation; after which the following mixture is recommended. Take of—

Manageh, (red Sulphurate of Arsenic,)
Káses, (Sulphurate of Iron,)
Baso, (long and black pepper and dry ginger,) and
Saindhaba, (rock-salt.)

Mix with honey, and apply a small portion with the probe to the inside of the eye-lid. This is to evacuate more completely the bad humors. After these have been discharged the medicine is to be removed by bathing the eye with warm water. Ghee is to be applied to the eye. These applications are to be used, with the exception of the scarifications, every third day.

The effect of these scarifications on the inside of the eyelids is to stop the morbid discharge, to diminish the swelling and itching as the eyelid becomes smooth. Such results prove that the eyelid has been properly scarified. If not performed well, the following are the symptoms; the redness, swelling, and discharge, continue, and the symptoms of the disease are not removed. The eyelid becomes black, heavy, and is moved with difficulty. There is much itching and irritation in the eyelid; and sometimes it produces suppuration of the eye.

The nine diseases in which scarifications are to be used, are—

Bortábabandá,
Clestabártang,
Bálabártang,
Pataki,
Sáhabarta,
Cardamaburta,
Cambikíni,
Súkárá, and
Utsanjaní.

The characteristic symptoms of these diseases of the eyelids are mentioned above.

Incision of the eye should be employed in

Bishagrentí. In this disease fomentations are first to be used; when matter forms, open the abscess, and then apply powdered rock-salt with the sulphate of zinc, (*kásís,*) long-pepper, red sulphurate of arsenic with honey, to the part, and put on a bandage.

In *Lágana* divide the parts and then apply the powder of *Ráchanás* (supposed to be the concrete bile of the cow), saltpetre, sulphate of copper, and honey. In other cases the actual cautery must be applied. Treatment of *Unjánámeká,* (styr,) consists in fomenting the abscess, and then applying the sulphurate of antimony with honey.

For the cure of *Bishagrenta,* first foment, open the part, and then apply the powder of the three kinds of *matabah, tuto,* (sulphate of copper,) *kásís,* (sulphate of iron,) and rock-salt. These medicines irritate, and increase the secretion of tears, and clear the organ. Then use astringent applications.

In *Upanáha* cut off the diseased part, and then apply fomentations; and a mixture of long-pepper, rock-salt, and honey.

Excision. In *Udemánsarniá,* (Pterygium,) excision is to be used for the cure of this disease. First mix ghee with the patient's food; then apply stimulating powder to the part, followed by fomentations. The eye is then to be rubbed with the finger, and when the eye-lids are somewhat loosened apply a hook, and draw the fleshy growth; slightly outwards. Then pass a needle under the diseased growth; tie it, and then separate the diseased part from the cornea and sclerotica with a round formed knife. Then apply fomentations and a bandage.

The only diseases in which excision is employed, are:

Sírájála,
Sorbanícá,
Ursa,
Sarskársa Urbada, small tumors.

In *Pakakapat,* (Intropeon.) In this distressing disease it is recommended that from the inner to the outer canthus of the eye a portion of the skin is to be removed, about three lines in breadth, in the lower third of the upper eyelid. This operation is particularly described by *Susruto,* who states the kind of room which should be used as an operating room, that in which the patient is to be placed, his diet, &c. After the operation apply honey and ghee to the wound, which should be brought together by hair sutors. These are removed on union taking place. If this operation is not successful, destroy the roots of the hair by the actual or potential cauteries.

Amaurosis, (*timra* or darkness.) The patient is first to get oleaginous purgatives prepared with old ghee which has been kept for some time in an iron vessel. The ghee is also recommended to be prepared from amphibious animals. It is to be rubbed up with water and applied to the eye; different preparations of antimony are likewise recommended, such as antimony, honey, sugar, red sulphurate of arsenic, mixed together, and applied to the eye. Different colleria, fomentations, errhines and other external applications are also to be used. These preparations of antimony with other stimulants are to be used. Bleeding is not recommended, but errhines are highly extolled. Various other remedies with nutritive diet is recommended, as barley with much ghee, the juice of myrobalan, and the flesh of wild animals and birds.

Cataract, (linganása.) In treatment of this and other diseases the patient should first take ghee, as it is supposed to cure the diseases of *air*, which are supposed to derange the other humors. The weather should neither be very hot nor very cold in which the operation is to be performed. The eyelids are to be kept properly separated by an expert assistant; the patient is then to be directed to look to his nose, and a knife with a point shaped like a grain of barley is to be held between the fore and middle fingers, and thumb of the right hand if the left eye is to be operated on, and in the left hand, if the right eye. The knife is then to be carried forward near the junction of the sclerotica with the cornea, neither high nor low in the eye, (near the transverse axis) and pass it on until water escapes. Then introduce a probe with a hook at its extremity, which is to detach and remove the cataract. When the person sees well, immediately after the operation, it has been properly done, particularly when the pupil appears clear like the other eye. After the operation apply the milk of a woman to the eye, with fomentations. Then cover the eye with a bandage. For ten days after the operation he must remain perfectly quiet in a dark room. During this time his food should be light.

In the treatment of the following diseases of the eye, the knife is not to be used:—

Sukákípáka,
Kaphabidagdhadristí,
Pittabidagdhadristi,
Sakra,
Urjana,
Pishtaka,
Ámlakí,
Ákilnabarta,
Damadarsí,
Suktí,
Príkelnabarta,
Balásabasta.

In external injuries, and their consequences, the following diseases are cured by bleeding:—

Strágála,
Siráharsa,
Nainapáka,
Pabanunátah,
Pueálása,

Also in acute and purulent Ophthalmia.

ORDER V.

Diseases of the Mouth, (Mukharoga.)

The diseases of the mouth are sixty-five: viz. eight diseases of ths lips; fifteen of the gums; eight of the teeth; four of the tongue; nine of the palate; seventeen of the throat; and three general diseases.

Diseases of the Lips. By using too much food, such as fish, the flesh of buffaloes, milk, curdled milk, &c. the three humors are deranged producing diseases of the Lips. They become rough, hard, and stiff. When the bile is much deranged they are very painful, and small eruptions appear upon the surface. When bile is deranged, there is much inflammation, the lips become yellow, and the eruptions are painful, and of a yellow colour. When phlegm is deranged the lips are covered with a thin oleaginous looking matter, are cold, stiff, and of a dark yellow, white, or mixed colour. The eruptions are likewise of different colours.

When blood is deranged in the lips they become red, swollen, and very painful. They often bleed. When the flesh is affected they become swollen, heavy, sometimes ulceration takes place, and worms form in it. When fat is affected the lips become glistening, like the surface of ghee. They are also itchy and heavy, and the discharge is like pure water. These ulcers do not heal easily.

Treatment. When air produces diseases in the lips the treatment is to apply equal parts of goat's fat, sesamum oil, ghee, and wax, to the diseased part. Fomentations are also to be used to the lips. When ulceration takes place, apply frankincense, green rosin, (*dhuná*), a kind of gum (*gugulí*), and powdered liquorice. Mix and apply them to the ulcers in the form of powder. When the disease is produced by diseased bile, apply leeches and other local and general antiphlogistic remedies. When phlegm is diseased after local bleeding, use fomentations, gargles, and errhines, with fumigations. Powder of long and black pepper, ginger, impure soda (*sargí ká kára*), nitre and black salt, mix them together with honey, and apply to the part.

When fat is diseased in the lips, foment, and if the lips ulcerate apply the actual cautery, after which apply powdered *pringí, ladra* and the three kinds of myrobalan: mix them together with honey. Such are the means of curing those diseases of the lips, which admit of being cured.

When the blood is derauged in the lips, the same treatment is to be followed, as when the bile is deranged.

6. *Diseases of the Gums.*

There are fifteen diseases described under this head.

Sitáda is when the gums are black and blood is discharged without any external cause. In such cases the gums are separated from the teeth, soft, and putrid. In other cases they slough. This disease is produced by derangements of phlegm, and blood.

Treatment. Remove blood by scarifications; then use gargles made by decoctions of dry ginger, mustard seed, and the three kinds of myrobalan. This mixture is to be used frequently.

Dantapapataka. This disease is produced by derangements of phlegm and blood; and is characterized by painful swelling of the gums, covering two or three of the alveolar processes.

Treatment. In the acute stage use scarifications; after which mix rock, black, and common salts, *sachulla,* and *samberi,* with nitre and honey. Errhines should also be used, and food prepared with ghee.

Dantabeshta is produced by deranged blood, and is characterized by a discharge of pus mixed with blood. In this disease the teeth become loose.

Treatment. After scarifications use the following gargles: mix equal parts of the decoction of

Lodhra, (Symplocos racemosa,)
Patanga, (a kind of Sandal,)
Jastimadhu, (liquorice,) and
Lákshyá, (lac,) or take honey, ghee, and

sugar, mix and apply to the part.

Sawesara is characterized by a painful swelling of the gums, which are itchy, and are accompanied with a copious discharge of saliva. This disease is caused by a derangement of phlegm, and blood.

Treatment. After scarification apply a mixture made of the bark of

Lodhra, (Symplocos racemosa,)
Mustá, (Cyperus rotundus,) and
Rasanjana, (Sulphurate of antimony) with

honey. Other astringent barks may also be used in the form of decoction.

Mahásansira is produced by the derangement of air, bile, and phlegm. In this variety the teeth become loose, with severe pain about the palate. Matter is formed in the gums, and the inside of the mouth is inflamed. This form is to be treated as the last.

Parídarah is produced by derangement of bile, blood, and phlegm ; and is characterized by blood being discharged from the gums ; which are flabby, and separate from the teeth. This form is to be treated as *Sítáda*.

Apakusa is produced by derangement of bile and blood. In this disease, abscesses form in the gums with little pain ; the teeth become loose, and when the gums are touched, they bleed. There is fætor of the mouth, and after the discharge of blood from the gums, they again swell.

In the treatment use purgatives, emetics, and errhines. Scarify the part by rubbing the rough border of the fig, or other such leaves. Then mix the powder of long and black pepper, ginger, salt, and honey together, and apply it to the part. As a wash use the powder of long-pepper, mustard, dry ginger with tepid water. Prepared ghee with sweet and astringent medicines are to be used as a detergent.

Baidurba. This disease is caused by external injury, as by cleaning the teeth with too hard a tooth-brush. In this disease the teeth become loose.

Treatment. Any sloughing parts are to be removed with the knife, and the use of the caustic prepared from potassa. After which the antiphlogistic form of treatment is to be used.

Adídanta. When the air is deranged it produces irregularity in the growth of the teeth, with much pain ; such teeth should be extracted, apply the actual cautery, and then treat it as of a caries of the tooth.

Adímánsika is the swelling round the wisdom-teeth, producing much pain and swelling, with the discharge of saliva. It is produced by diseased phlegm.

Treatment. Scarify the swelled part, then apply powdered

Bacha, (Acorus calamus,)
Tejobatí, (Pothos officinalis,)
Páṭhá, (a sort of plant,) and
Sarjeká, (impure soda and nitre.)

Mix them with honey, and apply to the part. A powder of long-pepper mixed with honey may be used, and the wash of astringent and bitter decoctions is to be used frequently.

Susruta also states that there are five different fistulas connected with the gums.

In the treatment scarify the fistulous openings, and then use astringent and bitter gargles. Actual and potential cauteries are also to be used. Should such fistulæ be neglected they will extend to the bone, and the teeth should be extracted, and the part treated as a fractured bone.

If on removing the last molar tooth there occurs much hemorrhage, pain, and paralysis of part of the face, they prove that the tooth should not be extracted. When this has been done, use a decoction of

Játí, (Grandiflorum,)
Madana, (Mimosa catechu,)
Swádukantaka, and
Khadira, (Catechu.)

7. *Diseases of the Teeth.**

Tooth-ache (Dálana), in which the tooth becomes very painful. This is caused by the derangement of air. When there is a small black decayed part of the tooth which is painful, and discharges matter with swelling, and much pain, it is called *Krimídantaka*, or worm-eaten tooth. The treatment of this disease should consist of stimulant applications, and oleaginous mixtures. If the tooth is loose it should be extracted. After the above medicine the actual cautery is to be applied to the diseased part.

When the mouth is turned to a side, and the teeth broken, as in spasms, it is produced by phlegm, and is called *Bangana*.

Sensible teeth, (Dantaharsa.) In this disease the person cannot bear cold, or hot applications; cool air, and sour articles produce much pain. Diseased bile and air produce this form of disease. For the cure of this disease apply hot ghee, and a decoction of

* It is curious to compare the opinions of the ancient European authors on the nature and diseases of the teeth. Homer calls them "Barriers opposed by nature to slips of the tongue, and the abuse of speech." In the temple of Apollo a tooth-instrument made of lead was suspended to shew that only those teeth should be pulled out which could be removed by so weak an instrument. Aristotle asserts that men have more teeth than women, and that this is the case with several animals, as sheep, goats, and pigs! Aretæus declares, "God alone knows the cause of tooth-ache." Pliny assures us that human teeth contain a pernicious virus, and that a bite from them will destroy weak animals. Sylvius having copied the anatomical errors of Galen, and the discoveries of Vesalius, which exposed those errors; objections having been made to them, he replied that "Galen could not have been wrong, and that the human organization must have changed since his time." Thomas Bartholm saw a man in whose jaw there grew an iron tooth; and he enters into an argument to show how such a thing may be.

medicines which cure diseased air. The application of the usual fumigations will be useful. The food should be animal broths, milk, ghee, and different preparations of rice, with oil to the head. When the teeth are dirty, and phlegm and air are diseased, dried up and deformed, like the scale of fishes, or a piece of broken pot, it is called *Dantasarkará.* In this disease remove the tartar, and apply powdered stick-lac (*laka*), with honey. This tartar increases, and the teeth become loose, and eventually drop out. It is then called *Kapáliká,* which is cured by following the same treatment as the other varieties.

When bile and blood are deranged, the teeth become of a dark colour, as if burnt in the fire, and the disease is named *Siábadantaka.*

Air when deranged, may produce dislocation of the lower jaw, which is called *Hanamaka,* and the symptoms and treatment are the same as the form of the disease named *Ardíta.*

The following articles of food are to be avoided in diseases of the teeth ; acid fruits, cold water, hot, dry, and hard food, cleaning the teeth with a hard piece of wood, and not the soft recent branch of a tree as usually employed.

8. *Diseases of the Tongue.*

When *air* is deranged in the tongue the person has no sense of feeling or taste in the organ, which is rough and divided into fissures. This form should be treated like the disease of the lip produced by diseased air. *Bile.* In this variety there is great heat, long and red papillæ spread over its surface. The part is to be rubbed hard to discharge blood, and when the bad blood has been removed, sweet applications are to be used with collyria and washes for the mouth. When *Phlegm* is deranged the tongue becomes heavy, thick, and the papillæ, over the surface of the tongue enlarge.

The *treatment* should consist in rubbing the tongue with the rough leaves of certain trees, or by scarifications, and then applying to the part, the powder of long and black pepper with honey. Water, in which the powder of mustard seed and salt have been mixed, is to be used for cleaning the mouth.

Alása. This form of disease is produced by deranged phlegm and blood, and is characterized by swelling on the upper surface of the tongue, particularly near its root. In this disease the tongue cannot be moved, and sometimes abscesses form.

Apasíbá is produced by diseased phlegm and blood, under the tongue. It is like a second tongue. In this disease there is a profuse discharge of saliva, accompanied with itchiness and burning pain.

In this disease the tongue is to be rubbed with rough leaves to discharge the bad blood, and followed by the application of caustics, long-pepper, &c. mixed with honey. The powder of yellow mustard-seed and white salt are to be boiled in water, and used as a wash for the mouth. Errhines and fumigations, will also be of great use in this disease.

9. *Diseases of the Palate.*

1. When the phlegm and blood are deranged in the soft palate, it becomes large, like a full bladder, and is accompanied with thirst, cough and difficulty in breathing. This disease is called *Kantasunda* (enlarged tonsils.) When they have become troublesome they are to be seized between the blades of a forceps and drawn forward; and by means of a semi-circular knife the third of the swelled part is to be removed. If all be removed so much blood may be discharged as to destroy the individual. If too little is removed it will produce an increase in the swelling, with fainting; a red secretion from its surface will be produced with sleepiness, an indistinctness of sight, swimming of the head, &c. After the operation, the part is to be rubbed with powdered black-pepper,

Alibissá,
Páṭhá, (a sort of plant,)
Bacha, (Acorus calamus,)
Kushṭa, (Costus speciosus,)
Labana, (salt,)

mixed with honey. The infusion of several astringent herbs may likewise be used as a gargle.

In other cases the swelling is accompanied with much pain and heat; suppuration being produced by phlegm, and blood. It is called *Tundíkarí.*

2. When the part is much swelled, hard, and of a red colour, and is produced by diseased blood it is called *Adussah,* which is accompanied with fever and severe pain. When the swelling is of the shape of a turtle, is without pain, is produced slowly, being caused by diseased phlegm, it is called *Kachhapa.*

3. Sometimes the swelling is like a water-lily, and in the soft palate is called *Raktabuda,* and is produced by a disease of the blood.

4. When flesh is swelled in the palate, there is no pain; when produced by phlegm, it is called *Mánsasangáhta.*

5. When swelled like a plum, without pain, and remains in one spot, being produced by phlegm, and mixed with fat it is called *Puputah.*

6. *Tálupáka* is produced by deranged bile, and is characterized by suppuration in the soft palate.

7. *Tálushosh.* In this disease the palate is very dry, and is accompanied with difficulty in breathing, and much pain. These six last diseases are to be treated by the use of the same medicines as the first. Fumigations are used for two days in the disease produced by deranged phlegm. The operations to be performed in the different forms of the swelling vary according to their nature. Sometimes a part of the diseased part is excised; others require to be opened, others scarified, &c. The diet in all these forms of disease should be milk, and a decoction of *mudga* or pulse. In all these forms of disease sigars are made of those aromatic substances which are best suited to the nature of the disease, and smoked by the patient.

Order III.

Diseases of the Neck.

These diseases consist of 1. Diseases of the throat; 2. Hoarseness; 3. Goitre; 4. Scrofulous swellings; and 5. Tumors of the neck.

1. *Throat.*

There are five forms of diseases of the throat.

When air, bile and phlegm are deranged in the throat separately or combined, or when the blood is diseased they form the five varieties of this disease. These produce a swelling in the throat, which shuts up the wind-pipe, and produces sudden death. It is called *Rahíní.* In such cases the treatment is to bleed the patient generally and locally; give an emetic, apply fumigations, and use gargles and errhines.

When the *air* is deranged, in the severe forms all the symptoms of deranged air are produced. After the discharge of blood, apply rock salt over the wounds, and warm ghee; fat, and marrow warmed are to be used as a gargle and retained in the mouth. This is to be repeated frequently.

Bile. In this form papillæ of flesh quickly enlarge, become hot, and ripen, with severe fever. After bleeding, sugar, red sandal-wood, and honey are to be applied to the part, with a decoction of grapes and *Parusaka.*

Phlegm. The passage of the throat is closed, and the swelling remains long and at length suppurates. Fleshy elevations are formed. After bleeding, soot, mixed with hot articles, as long and black pepper, &c. is to be applied to the part. Oil prepared with

Siyatá, (Arabian jasmine,)
Biranga, and
Danti, (Croton polyandrum,)

to be used as a gargle.

When air, bile and phlegm are deranged at the same time, the swelling suppurates to a great depth in the tongue. It is incurable, and the three forms of symptoms of diseased air, bile, and phlegm appear. The treatment is the same as for the separate form. When blood is deranged many small swellings form upon the tongue, and near its root, accompanied with symptoms of deranged bile. This form may be cured. The treatment is the same as the last form.

When a swelling like a plum is situated in the throat, and produces difficulty in breathing, and a hard and rough swelling, it is caused by phlegm, and is named *Kantasáluka*. In this form scarifications are to be made on the swelling. The treatment should be the same as that of *Tantukará*, or disease of the palate. *Adijíba* is a swelling at the root of the tongue like a second tongue, (this is probably a swelling of the epiglottis,) and is produced by the phlegm and blood. When it suppurates it is incurable. The treatment is the same as that of *Apazíbika* one of the diseases of the mouth. Various other swellings of the throat are also mentioned, such as *Balása*, a swelling of the throat which prevents swallowing, and is produced by phlegm. It is incurable. Phelgm and air produce the swelling in the throat, which is accompanied with severe pain, and difficulty in breathing. This is also a very dangerous form of disease.

Diseased phlegm and blood produce a swelling in the throat accompanied with itchiness, and a burning sensation. It is soft, heavy, and does not suppurate. It is called *Ekabrinda*. In this form scarifications are to be made, and astringent gargles are to be used. When it is accompanied with fever, it is called *Brinda*. This is an incurable disease.

A thick swelling of the throat, causing difficulty in breathing, and surrounded by small papulæ like piles with much pain, is produced by air, bile and phlegm; it is called *Satagní*, (or it is like the instrument of this name which at once kills 100 persons:) it is incurable.

Gilin. The swelling in this disease is like the stone of a plum, not painful, but hard; and is produced by diseased phlegm, and blood. It is cured by being removed by a knife.

Sarungna (Croup?) When phleghm stops the passage of air, this produces dryness of the throat, hoarseness, difficulty in breathing and great uneasiness. It is incurable.*

Mánsatána, is a swelling in the throat which produces suffocation. It is always dangerous.

Bidárí. The swelling is accompanied with great pain, redness, followed by sloughing. This is an incurable disease.

Gullagha, is a large swelling in the throat extending over the throat with great pain, and high fever. The patient cannot swallow food nor drink water. It is produced by phlegm and blood, and is considered incurable. In general the forms of disease produced by bile should be treated by the antiphlogistic treatment, and those by phlegm by astringent and hot applications. When produced by air the applications should be of ghee, oil, and other medicines for the cure of air.

2. *Hoarseness, (Swarabheda.)*

The causes of this disease are loud speaking, poison, long continued reading, external injuries, exposure to cold, &c. When air, bile, and phlegm are deranged in the air-passages they produce the six varieties of hoarseness. One is produced by derangements of the air, bile, or phlegm; by the combination of the three; by fatness; and by weakness.

1st. *Air* when deranged produces this disease, when the person's eyes, mouth, urine, and dejections become black, and his tone of speaking is slow, and like an ass braying.

2nd. When *bile* is deranged, the eyes, mouth, urine, and dejections are of a yellowish colour, and the patient speaking from the throat, with a sense of burning pain in the part.

3rd. *Phlegm* when deranged, the throat is filled with mucus, and the person speaks little and that slowly and with difficulty, particularly at night.

When air, bile, and phlegm are deranged, the combined symptoms of the three varieties are present; and the patient speaks so indistinctly that he cannot be understood. This form is incurable.

4th. When weakness or diminution of the essential parts (*dhátu*) produce the disease, the patient cannot speak, and when he tries, smoke appears to proceed from the mouth, with pain. He speaks very little. This form is also incurable.

5th. When it is produced by *fatness* the person speaking is indistinct, and he thinks his throat and palate are covered with something. Such disease will not be cured when the person is weak, old,

* Croup is not unfrequent in Hindustán but it is less dangerous, being of a more chronic nature than in Europe.

thin; when it has been of long continuance, and is congenital. In fat people, and when produced by the combination of the three humors it is also incurable.

In treating this disease the body is first to be anointed with oil, and the bowels cleared by emetics, purgatives, and enemas. This is to be followed by the application of different kinds of errhines, gargles, and fumigations to the throat. When these remedies have been used without the desired effect the medicines recommended for asthma and cough are to be tried. When air is deranged, the patient should take ghee after dinner. The ghee is to be mixed with a decoction of

Kásamarda, (Cassia or Senna esculenta,)
Bútaka,
Márkaba.

When bile is deranged, the ghee is to be prepared with the juice of

A'rttagala,
Jabakshar, (Saltpetre,)
Asmadá,
A'r,
Chritsak,
A'mlaka, (Emblic myrobalan.)

For diet he should use milk, rice, and molasses, with ghee.

When phlegm is deranged use rice, milk, and powdered liquorice-root with ghee; and other expectorant and heating substances, with cow's urine, are also to be used.

The variety produced by fatness, is to be treated as in the form produced by diseased phlegm.

3. *Goitre, (Galaganda.)*

The swelling of the throat, whether it be small or large, is called by this name. It is of an oblong form like the scrotum. It is produced when air and phlegm are diseased in the throat, and diseased fat slowly produces it.

When *air* is diseased there is pain in the throat, and black veins spread over it. The swelling is of a green or red colour, dull and irregular. This form increases slowly and rarely suppurates; but, when it does it is without any apparent cause. The person has a bad taste in his mouth, with dryness of the palate and throat.

Phlegm. In this variety the swelling is hard, fixed, cold, and the colour is not altered. It increases slowly, is heavy, itchy, and large, and sometimes suppurates. The taste of the mouth is sweetish, and the palate and throat is as if covered with some matter.

When produced by diseased *fat* it is slow in its increase, and suppurates with little pain, and is of the shape of a pumpkin (*Kadu*), with a small root. The swelling increases, and diminishes with changes in the size of the body. The face is shining as if anointed. The swelling is heavy, of a yellowish colour, and of a bad smell. It is itchy and painful, accompanied with a peculiar change in the voice. The unfavourable symptoms are difficulty in breathing, softness of the part, and after it has continued for one year, it is accompanied with dispepsia, and hoarseness. When the person is thin and weak he will die.

Treatment. Foment the parts with steam, by means of a tube proceeding from a vessel, in which those vegetable remedies are boiling which cure diseased air. When air is deranged, the steam of warm milk is used; and warm poultices prepared with flesh and oil are to be applied, and an opening made into it, and it is then to be treated like a common inflammation. The following external applications are also recommended. The seeds of

Sana,
Atasí, (Linum usitatissinum,)
Múlaka, (Raphanus sativus,)
Sigru, the pulp of the
Pilu, and
Tíla, Sesamun seed, are made into a poultice

and applied to the swelling. A paste made with urine, and the juice of acid fruits, such as

Aquiseka,
Brikshaka, (Wrightea antidysenterica,) and
Tilaka, are recommended.

Oil prepared with

Bala, (Sida cordifolia,)
Shwetbalá, (Vallisneria octandra,) and
Pítabalá; or with
Amartabalá,
Nimba, (Melia azadirachta,)
Hansiabia,
Trikaka,

and long pepper; is used internally.

When produced by phlegm, fomentations are to be applied as above; open the swelling, and oil prepared with different salts, and with the ashes of long pepper, and other heating medicines is to be exhibited internally. Use also externally, paste made of *gunja* with the water of the ashes of *palása,* and applied to the part hot.

Diet—use barley, a decoction of *mudga* with cow's urine, or with powdered long and black pepper, ginger, and honey.

When caused by fat apply a paste made of

Simá,
Sudda,
Mandura,
Danti, (Croton polyandrum,) and
Rasánjana, (Sulphurate of antimony.)

The gum rosin of the *sál* tree, with cow's urine may be used daily: or make an incision, remove the fat, and sow up the wound; then apply ghee and honey to the part, or hot oil. The patient is to live on a preparation of barley, and apply a tight bandage to the part. The decoction of the three kinds of myrobalan is also recommended.

4. *Scrofulous swellings,* (*Gandamálá.*)

When many small tumors like plums appear in the axilla, neck, back, and groins, they are produced by diseased fat, and phlegm. They suppurate slowly, and continue to appear and suppurate for a long period, when it is called *Apachí.* When not attended by any bad constitutional disease it is curable, but when accompanied with *Coriza,* with pain in the sides, cough, fever, and vomiting, it is incurable.

Treatment. When indolent and recent, follow the same treatment as of local inflammation, support his strength; ghee, fat and marrow, are to be prepared with a decoction of

Apehibatí, and
Dasamula,

and applied to the part. Different fomentations, fumigations, and poultices are to be applied, and when they suppurate, open and discharge the matter; wash the wound with a decoction of

Bilwa, (Ægle marmelos,)
Arka, (Calotropis gigantea,) and
Arjuna, (Pentaptera arjuna.)

A poultice made of *Tila,* and the leaves of the Castor-oil tree mixed with salt, and applied to the part. Then apply oil which has been prepared with a decoction of

Rásná, (Mimosa octandra,) and
Sarala, (Pinus longifolia.)

When the disease is produced by bile, apply leeches, with milk and water, and other cold applications. Aperients are likewise to be given, and a paste made of

Madhuka, (Bassia latifolia,)
Jambi, or
Juna, and
Betasa, with
Sugar.

When it suppurates open, and wash with a decoction of astringent barks. Then apply a poultice, and ghee prepared with liquorice, and other sweet medicines ; as

Kákolí, (Coclus Indicus,)
Kshárakákolí, &c.

When produced by *phlegm* use rubbing with the finger, or with iron, stone, or a piece of bamboo : make also a paste of

Bekantaká,
Arikbuda,
Gunja, (Abrus precatorius,)
Kakádmi, and
Tapasabirka,

and apply to the part. If not situated in a vital part remove the tumor with the knife, and when the blood is stopped treat it as a simple wound.

5. *Tumors of the Neck, (Manskunder.)*

Is a variety of the *Gandamúlá* or scrofulous swellings. They are hard and large, and when they suppurate they should be opened. After which the cavity is to be cleaned with astringent washes. Detergent medicines are also to be used, as honey, ghee, and caustic preparations. Then apply oil prepared with a decoction of

Biranga,
Páṭhá, a plant called *Aknadi*, and
Rasaní, (or turmerick.)

When the tumors are produced by fat apply a paste made of Sesamum seed. Then two folds of cloth are to be placed over the part, and a hot iron is to be applied frequently over the part. If the tumor is not removed in this way, the knife must be had recourse to. In this and in all scrofulous affections, emetics and purgatives are to be occasionally exhibited. Errhines are also of use. The actual cautery is to be applied across the arm immediately above the wrist leaving an interval of the breadth of a finger between each application.

Class V.

Diseases of the Chest.

Order I.

Asthma, (Swása.)

This disease is produced by the same causes as produce hiccough. It is by the *Prán-báyu* changing its place, and being confined in its passage by phlegm, which produces the difficulty in breathing. There are the following five varieties of asthma :—

1. *Swása* is a severe disease, and has only slight varieties. It is ushered in with pain in the chest and sides, loss of appetite, restlessness, tightness of the abdomen, a bad taste in the mouth, and a constipation of the bowels and bladder.

1. *Mahá-swása*. The air is confined in the air passages by the phlegm, and thus produces Asthma. The patient respires with difficulty, and with a noise like that of a wild bullock. He becomes low-spirited, his eyes are always moving about ; his mouth open, with constipation of urine and fæces ; he speaks with difficulty, and his distress may be observed from a distance.

2. *Urdha-swása*. The patient in this disease respires with difficulty and with an effort ; the air passages being closed by phlegm, and the air trying to escape gives much pain. His eyes are directed upwards, he cannot see, and different objects appear before the eyes ; sometimes he faints, his mouth remains dry with restlessness and severe pain over the body. The respiration becomes more difficult, and he dies.

3. *China-swása*. This form occurs in fits at irregular intervals. In these cases he is sometimes still, and cannot breathe. The vital parts are much affected, and very painful. He is constipated in his bowels, with much perspiration and drowsiness. He complains of much pain in the bladder, which is very hot, his eyes are always rolling about, and red ; great debility, low spirits, mouth dry, bad colour of the skin, and delirium. Such persons quickly die.

4. *Tamaka-swása*. In this variety the air passes in, but is not discharged easily. The vessels of the neck and air passages are affected, with a collection of mucus in the air passages. Catarrh is produced, as indicated by yellow sputa from the mouth, and snoring, with great uneasiness and difficulty in breathing. When he coughs he often faints, but on mucus being discharged he feels easier. At times he cannot speak, does not sleep, and when he does he complains of much pain in the sides and chest. He is easiest in the sitting position, and likes hot things. His eyes are turned upwards, he perspires much in the forehead, his mouth is dry, and the body swings about as if he was riding upon an elephant. From time to time his breathing is difficult. This disease is increased in cloudy, rainy, and cold weather ; especially during the prevalence of easterly winds. Whatever increases phlegm, is liable to increase the disease. This form of disease may bê cured if recent, but in the old, or when it has continued for some time, it is not curable. When this form is combined with fever, and dozing, it

forms *Pratamaka.* When produced or increased by *Udabarta,* (constipation,) *Ajirna,* (dyspepsia,) *Rajah,* (or dust) and darkness. In this form cold things give relief, and the person sees imperfectly like one in darkness. This is called *Sangtamaka.*

5. *Khudra-swása.* It is produced by dry food and exercise. In this form there is less difficulty in breathing, and there is no pain or uneasiness. It does not prevent diglutition, nor the action of the senses, and only produces difficulty in breathing on running, &c. No other disease is produced by this one, and it is curable unless when combined with some other disease.

Treatment. In Asthma mild purgatives and emetics are to be given. Old ghee prepared with myrobalan, black salt, and asafœtida, with powder of long pepper. Ghee prepared with the five salts, as rock, black, common salt,

Sabaritulla, and
Sambari.

In other cases the ghee is to be prepared with the decoction of
Básaka, (Justicia ganderussa,)

or ghee prepared with Turmerick, Liquorice,

Sringí,
Madurikú, (Anithum sowa,)
Byághrí, (Solanum jacquini,)
Shunṭhí, (Dry ginger,)
Rasánjana, (Sulphurate of antimony,)
Banlochana, and
Mustaka, (Cyperus rotundus.)

Acid fruits are recommended, with broths made of the flesh of birds which pick their food, as fowls, pigeons, &c. The heads of deer prepared with peas, and mixed with ghee are also used.

The following electuary is recommended. Take of the powder of the bark of

Byághri, (Solanum jacquini,)
Sringabira, (Ginger,)
Sarkara, (Sugar,)

The ashes of the quills of the porcupine, and the seeds of *Trikantaka.* These are to be mixed with the juice of the litter of the cow, honey, and the powder of long pepper, and administered in the usual manner.

Order II.

Cough, (Kása.)

This disease is produced, by smoke or dust entering the mouth and nostrils, by fighting, by great fatigue, by dry food, by articles of food entering the air passages, by sneezing, or by resisting the calls of nature. These causes derange the vital air *(Prán-báyu)* in the chest, and the *Udán-báyu* which is situated in the trachea, by which the air which passes through the air passages to the mouth, produces a peculiar noise, like a broken metallic vessel.

The disease may likewise be produced by air, bile, and phlegm, by ruptures of the respiratory organs, or by the loss of particular humors. All these varieties of cough, pass to consumption if neglected. The disease commences with a feeling in the mouth and throat as if it was covered with some irritating substance. It feels itchy, or there is a stinging which prevents the passage of the food into the stomach.

The symptoms of cough are produced by deranged *air,* the change of voice, the dry and frequent cough, distresses the patient, with pain in the temples, head, stomach, and chest. The face becomes sallow, and the person becomes weak.

When *bile* is deranged the mouth is dry and bitter, and the breath is hot with fever ; the person complains of thirst, and severe pain over the body ; the expectoration is sour, and of a yellowish colour, and the skin becomes yellow and hot.

When *phlegm* is deranged, the mouth is full of mucus with headache, loss of appetite, languor, frequent cough, with thick mucous expectoration. The person cannot labour, has frequent fits of coughing, the body is heavy and weak, he has no appetite, the frequency of coughing increases, and much phlegm is expectorated.

Katazoá Kása is caused by excessive venery, fatigue, carrying heavy weights, going great distances when unaccustomed, and violent exercise upon horseback or elephants. By these causes the air passages are injured or ulcerated, when the patient is first affected with dry cough followed by spitting of blood, much pain in the throat and chest, which is increased by pressure. The joints and other parts of the body are painful, as if pins were penetrating it ; pain in the muscles, fever, difficulty of breathing, thirst, hoarseness, and change in the voice, so that it resembles that of wild pigeon.

Khyá Kása (Pneumonia ?) This form of the disease is produced by taking improper food, at improper, or unusual times ; excessive venery, and neglect of the calls of nature. In other cases the disease is produced by grief, by food which has a bad taste, or produces disgust by which the internal heat is diminished and deranged, with the air, bile, and phlegm. This disease is characterized by the person being affected with severe pain and emaciation of the body, fever, and a burning sensation of the body. His intellect becomes affected, and the person loses his strength. The cough is at first dry, is accompanied with vomiting, and is followed by purulent and bloody expectoration. When these symptoms are present they are rarely cured; and in weak persons the disease is generally fatal, unless when recent. In old age the cough (*Jará Kása)* will remain, and not be removed.

When *Katazoa* and *Khyá Kása* are recent, with the assistance of a good physician, and proper remedies, a cure may be obtained. When air, bile and phlegm produce these diseases separately, it may be cured.

The *Treatment* of *Khyá Kása* is the same as that of *Jakháh.* The treatment of *Katazoa Kása* is as follows:—When the cough is produced by deranged air it is first to be treated by oleaginous medicines, such as prepared ghee, glysters, different animal broths, milk, and fruit. The patient may also take the decoction of—

Shálparní, (Hedysarum gangeticum,)
Prishniparní,
Brihatí, (Solanum melongena,) and
Kantikárí, (Flacourtia sapida,)

with the powder of long pepper.

Another electuary is prepared of powder of

Shunṭhı, (Dry ginger,)
Shringí,
Kaná,
Long pepper,
Barghul,
Jagry, with *Tila* oil.

When produced by bile give a purgative with sweet substances, as—

Tiorí
Tribrit, (Convolvulus Turpethum,) and
Sugar.

He should likewise take a decoction of—

Sarádí,
Panchamula,

with long pepper and raisins. His food should be the broth of wild animals, good rice, and bitter vegetables. His drink should be prepared with

Bala, (Sida cordifolia,)
Brihatí, (Solanum melongena,)
Básaka, (Justicia ganderussa,) and
Drákshá, (Grapes.)

These are to be mixed with two seers of water, which are to be reduced by boiling to one: take this frequently. Milk with sugar is also recommended. When the disease is severe, and is produced by *phlegm* give first an emetic, with fried barley, and hot spices; such as long-pepper, saltpetre, and light and dry food, with stimulating medicines. For this purpose take a decoction of horseraddish,

Patkala,
Pushkara, (Costus speciosus,)
Bhárgí,
Pipuli, (long-pepper,) and
Súnṭhí, (dry ginger,) or the juice of fresh ginger with honey. Form these into a decoction, in the usual manner, and use it occasionally.

3. *Phthisis Pulmonalis,* (*Consumption.*)

Ráj Jakshyá, (the prince of disease;) *Shoṣha, Kshyá, Khina,* (emaciation;) *Kshata,* (rupture or ulcer of the respiratory organs.)

The mythological origin of this disease is that the moon married seven sisters, but attaching himself to one, the others complained to their father, who punished the moon, by declaring that he should be afflicted with consumption. This origin; and the precepts in the treatment, proclaim its frequent, and fatal nature. It is characterized by coughing accompanied with bloody expectoration.

It is produced by grief; by the evacuations being retained, when nature endeavours to expell them; by great loss of the humors of the body; by performing unusual and unnatural actions, as ineffectually endeavouring to raise heavy weights; and by running, swimming, or other violent exercise. Consumption, by eating bad food, or at unusual times, and in unusual quantities, by fasting, by boils and sores in the chest, and by old age. Is also supposed to be produced by diminishing the mental and bodily strength, by blunting the senses, by producing difficulty in breathing, by altering the voice, by producing vomiting with expectoration, by a discharge from the eyes, nose, and mouth. In such cases the body dries, and the surface appears dirty.

When the air, phlegm, and bile, are deranged in the above disease; the chyle vessels are stopped by the humors, but particularly phlegm, and the other parts of the body are not nourished. Another form is produced by excessive venery, from the great discharge of semen, by which all the other elements are deranged. The disease commences by the person becoming emaciated and debilitated; difficult breathing and pain over the body comes on, with cough, and a discharge of mucus, from the mouth and nose. The palate is dry, vomiting, and loss of appetite takes place, from the internal heat being diminished. There is also derangement of the mind, jaundice, cough with expectoration, and the loss of taste, and smell. The patient sleeps continually, and the eyes become of a pearl white colour. The person is fond of animal food, and is desirous of intercourse with women. The following symptoms indicate the presence of this disease; when the patient's voice changes, he sees in his dream crows, parrots, porcupines, peacocks, vultures, monkeys, and lizards; and he supposes he is mounted upon these animals. He sees also dry beds of rivers, dry trees, as if destroyed by storms, and by fire.

The characteristic symptoms are pain in the shoulders, and sides of the chest. A burning feverish feel of the palms of the hands and soles of the feet is felt, which extends over the body.

Consumption is sometimes produced by derangements of one of the three humors. The symptoms produced by derangement of the air are hoarseness; pain, particularly in the shoulders and sides of the chest, and a bent form of the body. The symptoms of bile are fever, the body burning, diarrhœa, and hemoptisis. The symptoms of phlegm are a fulness and heaviness of the head, no appetite, cough, and the windpipe is painful as if bruised, with a change in the voice. When all the above symptoms are present at the same time, and in the same person; or when there is cough, diarrhœa, pain of the chest and sides, hoarseness, loss of appetite and fever, or when cough, asthma, and the discharge of blood is present, with emaciation, the person will die. When these bad symptoms are absent the physician may attend the person, but when the person has a strong appetite, the food does not produce strength, flesh, or diarrhœa; or when the testicles or stomach swell, the person will not recover. When the person is strong, the disease recent, and he has slight fever; when he can work, has a good appetite, is equal to the treatment, and follows the judicious instructions of the physician, such a person may recover.

When the eye is white, when there is no appetite, with great derangement of breathing; when there is a great secretion of urine, with pain, the person will not recover. The other form of consumption is produced by excessive venery, grief, old age, great fatigue, by taking long journies on foot, by the debility produced by old ulcers, and by the rupture of the organs of respiration, by which the body will become thin, and the disease declare itself. By excessive venery the body becomes emaciated, debilitated, with the other symptoms of diminished semen, such as pain in the scrotum and penis, impotency, or a slight discharge of semen, mixed with blood, when the body becomes yellow, and the other humors are diminished.

When consumption is produced by *grief* the person remains complaining, with the other symptoms of the last form ; but without the evacuation and the symptoms of deranged semen. When the disease is produced by old age the body becomes very thin, the person cannot labour, his organs of sense and strength are diminished, his body shakes, he has no appetite, and his voice is like a broken pewter-plate when struck. There is always a flow of saliva from the mouth, weakness, and heaviness ; and his eyes, nose, and mouth discharge mucus. The dejections, and surface of the body are in these patients dry and rough. When the body is thin from great fatigue, or walking ; the person cannot get up, his body changes in colour, is painful and some parts lose their sensibility. The palate, throat, and mouth are dry. When produced by other kinds of violent exercise or by a rupture of the lungs, the symptoms are the same as above.

When old ulcers debilitate the body, by the great loss of blood, when there is much pain, and there is little nourishment in the food which is taken, the disease is incurable. When consumption is produced by a rupture of the respiratory organs, as by the frequent use of the bow and arrow, by carrying great weights, when a weak person fights with a strong man, when jumping from a great height, or when a person attempts to run after and seize an ox, a horse, or a dacoit, or pull at a bow, or throw pieces of wood or stone, the disease is dangerous. In like manner, loud reading, walking quickly and to a great distance, or swimming much, much horse exercise, or running up a height or to a great distance, dancing quickly, or other bad customs, eating very dry articles, or very little food, or only one kind of food, will produce the disease. When this disease is present there is great pain in the breast as if it was wounded, pain in the sides, and the body dries up, and shakes. By degrees the spirit and strength fail, and the colour of the skin is diminished or unnatural, there is no appetite, with fever, pain, dejection of mind, diarrhœa and loss of appetite. The sputa is of a light blue or yellow colour, with a bad smell, and like the knot of a piece of rope, being unequal. At other times the sputa is mixed with blood. These symptoms increase daily, with pain in the chest, more blood is vomited, and the cough becomes more severe. When the body is much emaciated from the drying up of the juices, indicated by the parched dry mouth, &c., the urine has the colour of blood, and the sides, back and thighs are painful. Consumption often occurs in the progress of other diseases, and is always accompanied with danger, being cured with much difficulty. When the internal heat is natural, and the symptoms not severe, and remain but a few days, the person will be cured. If it continues one year the cure will not be accomplished, and when the severe symptoms above enumerated are present the person will die.

Treatment. When the appetite is good, and the person is not very thin, and is careful, the physician may treat him. Ghee is to be taken internally, which had been prepared with *Stiran,* and other sweet, and nourishing medicines. This is to be followed by the use of mild purgatives, and emetics. Enemas are also to be given, and errhines to clean the head. The diet should consist of prepared barley, flour, rice, with animal broths ; when his appetite is good, give nourishing food, particularly the flesh of crows, owls, brahmany kites, rats, mongooses, wild-cats, earth-worms, and all animals that burrow under the earth. These are to be boiled with oil, salt, and peas. The bodies of the animals are to be cut and bruised, and juice extracted. Wine made of grapes is to be given, with flesh of asses, mules, horses, camels, elephants, prepared in the usual way. The ghee of goats and sheep, with preparations of barley, are very proper. A mixture of ghee, honey, long-pepper, black pepper, with *chubbo* (a pungent bulbous root), and *Biranga* (a vermifuge kind of seed), mixed with honey is also of use. The *Tubushin* (or salt of *balum,* or carbonate of allumina) is mixed with honey and *Til* oil. Another mixture is made by the powder of

A'suganda, (Physalis flexuosa,)
Tila, (Sesamum orientale,) and
Mása, (Phaseolus radiatus,)

with ghee of goats and honey. Garlick, pepper, &c., are given in gradually increased doses, and continued as alternative medicines. There are various mixtures recommended to nourish and give tone to the body, none of which it is necessary to enumerate.

It is recommended to eat the flesh, dejections, and blood, and live in the same house and in the same room with goats. The patient should carefully abstain from venery, avoid grief, anger, fatigue, and the other causes which produce the disease. He should also court the society of bráhmans, physicians, gurus, and study the sacred writings. This is recommended in consequence of the danger of the disease.

4. *Hiccup, (Hikka.)*

This disease is produced by nearly the same causes as *Swása* (asthma), and *Kása* (cough). Such as heavy and indigestable food, or roasted, hot, and dry food ; or much food, or an improper mixture of food, or articles that increase cough, &c., so as to produce constipation. In other cases very dry things, cold things, or situations, exposure to dust, smoke entering the mouth or nostrils ;

or much heat, as exposure to the sun, and hot air. Violent exercise, as shooting arrows, carrying heavy loads, walking great distances, not attending to the calls of nature, or long fasting produce this disease. It is called *hikka,* because the air comes to the mouth frequently, with a peculiar noise, and the spleen, liver, and intestines seem to be coming up to the mouth. This disease quickly debilitates, and destroys the *prána* (life).

The precursory symptoms are a heaviness of the throat and chest, an astringent taste in the mouth, and a rumbling noise in the belly. There are five kinds of hiccup, in all of which air and phlegm are deranged.

1. *Unnugá.* This form is produced by taking too much food and drink, which deranges the air, and produces the disease.

2. *Jumulá.* In this form the passage of air proceeds, after a considerable time, with eructations of air, and the head and neck shake at the moment; hence the name.

3. *Khudrá* (hiccup) takes place slowly, is not strong, and proceeds from the scrobiculus cordis.

4. *Gambirá.* In this form the hiccup commences from the navel, is strong, and very noisy, and is always accompanied with other severe or fatal symptoms.

5. *Mahatí.* There is frequent hiccup, which produces pain in the vital parts, and shakes the whole body. The unfavourable symptoms are when hiccup is accompanied with fixed eyes, as if drawn up by some one; when there is great weakness, and the patient's arms and legs are thrown out, with frequent sneezing. When the person is very weak, and old, or becomes weak after excessive venery, with no appetite, and a cough, it will soon prove fatal. When combined with other diseases, as delirium, fainting, great thirst, &c., it will be fatal. When the person is strong, has a good constitution, hiccup may be cured. Thus when the patient is not thin, when his memory is good, his tissues and senses are healthy, the person will recover. In the treatments prayers are first to be offered up to all the gods, on which occasion one nostril is shut up by the finger, and by the other nostril the air is taken into the lungs. Fear of all kinds cures it; and when a child is attacked if he be accused of having stolen something, or if he is threatened to be beaten, the sudden charge will cure the disease. Needles suddenly thurst into the skin, to produce a sudden surprise, will also cure it. Liquorice-root, mixed with honey, and taken in the nostrils as an errhine, or powdered long-pepper, with sugar and warm ghee, milk, and the juice of the sugar-cane will be of much use in curing the disease. If the person is not very weak give him a purgative and

emetic; and use fumigations with gram, raisin, and other fragrant medicines. The ashes of the bones of animals, with honey, are also used for the same purpose; or the ashes of the feathers of peacocks, with honey and ghee. Impure soda with lemon juice also cures hiccup, and hot barley water with ghee gives relief. A decoction of myrobalan is of much use, as also long-pepper, sugar, Emblica myrobalan, and ginger with honey. The fried flesh of wild pigeons, and of different birds, porcupines, deer, granhas, formed into broths with acid fruits and ghee should be used. Purgatives, with salt or sugar, and clysters are also in some cases used with advantage.

5. *Diseases of the Heart.*

Painful affections of the heart *Ridraga* (Angina pectoris?) are produced by want of attention to the calls of nature, the use of hot and dry food; the improper mixture of food; an intemperance in eating, or unusual food; which causes indigestion, and deranges the humors. The impure chyle is received into the heart, and produces this painful disease; of which there are five varieties. When produced by deranged *air* the patient feels various acute kinds of pains, sometimes it is lancinating, at other times as if the heart was cut or torn. When produced by deranged *bile* there is much pain in the heart, with thirst, heart-burning and dryness. This is succeeded by fainting, much sweating, dryness of the mouth, and smoke appears to come out of the mouth. When produced by *phlegm* the patient feels a heaviness of the heart, a discharge of mucus from the mouth and nose, loss of appetite, and a sweet taste in the mouth.

When produced by *worms* there is a lancinating, or piercing pain in the region of the heart; nausea, vomiting, belching and loss of appetite. The eyes become dark greenish, with emaciation of the body. All these diseases of the heart terminate in emaciation, languor, loss of appetite and strength, with giddiness.

Treatment. When produced by derangements of the *air*, the patient should first have his body anointed with oil, and he should take an oleaginous purgative followed by an emetic. He should next take the following mixture: Powdered long-pepper, cardamums, *Bacha*, asafœtida, saltpetre, rock-salt, dry ginger, and *Jawání*, with the juice of acid fruits and whey-wine or vinegar. He should eat good rice, with the broth of wild animals properly prepared, and occasionally use oleaginous glysters.

When *bile* is deranged the patient should be treated as in bilious fever, and all the decoctions and mixtures recommended in this disease are to be used. When produced by deranged *phlegm,* take an emetic with a decoction of *nimb* leaves and *bacha;* with the mixture recommended above for derangements of the air. He should also take a purgative of *Tribrit* with ghee.

When produced by *worms,* the patient should eat meats prepared with ghee and rice, for three days; and then he should take purgatives of salt, and a decoction of aromatic plants. He should afterwards take wine with powdered *Biranga.* By this means the worms will come out of the heart. He should next eat *Biranga* powder (the best anthelmintic medicine), with barley for food.

Class VI.
Diseases of the Abdomen.

---

1. *Dyspepsia, (Agni Mándya.)*

This disease is supposed to be produced by derangements of the internal fire. It has four varieties.

1st. When there is too little fire, it is called *Manda Agní;* when food is not digested, or only imperfectly. In this form, the diseases of phlegm are often present.

2nd. When the fire is too strong, as when bile is deranged, it is called *Tikhna Agní.* In this case, little or even large quantities of food are digested; and the diseases of bile are liable to occur.

3rd. When the air is deranged the food is sometimes digested and sometimes not; from fire being sometimes in the natural state, and at other times it is deranged. In this case the disease is called *Bishama Agní,* when other diseases of air are present.

4th. *Bhasma Agní, (Bulimia,)* when pungent, sour and dry food are taken for some time; phlegm is diminished, and air is much increased; the internal fire, with the deranged air, absorbs the liquid part of the body, and the food when taken is soon digested, or reduced to ashes, and the person is not satisfied. This disease is accompanied with great thirst, dry cough, fainting, giddiness, burning of the body and emaciation, with severe constipation, and much perspiration.

When there is no increase or diminution of the air, bile, and phlegm, in the same person; the fire remains in the natural state, and is called *Sama Agní.* This is not a disease, but is the most favourable state of digestion, and is the condition in which food is properly digested; when not taken in too small, or too large quantities. The divisions of the digestive organs into the parts in which the food are received, *Amasia,* (stomach;) *Agniaria,* (the duodenum;) and in which the digested food is removed *Pakasía,* (the small intestines,) is probably from the known structure of the intestines of the inferior animals.

This disease is produced by drinking much water, and eating at unusual hours, when very little food is taken, and the calls of nature are resisted; when the person is sleepy or is in a passion, or is afraid, grieved, or fatigued at the time of eating; and when he dislikes the food during the time of eating. It is also produced, when the person sleeps during the day, instead of at night, or is irregular in the time of sleeping, and when at the usual time of dinner, little is eaten. By such causes the food is not digested in the proper manner. When phlegm is deranged the food tastes sweet, and is indigested; when bile, the taste is sour, and the food in the stomach produces eructations; and air when deranged causes the partially digested food to be dried up, with pain in the stomach.

2. *Ajírna,* (*Indigestion.*)

This disease is divided into three varieties, *A'ma Ajírna, Bistabdha Ajírna,* and *Bidagdha Ajírna.* When digestion is good, the food is properly prepared for the use of the body, the eructations are free and without taste, and the dejections are natural; the body is light and elastic, and the person is inclined to exertion, he has a good appetite and the food is tasty, and is accompanied with thirst.

When digestion is imperfect the person's temper becomes bad, he is subject to anger, is fearful, and becomes covetous. The food of persons with a bad and hasty temper is not properly digested. When indigestion occurs, there is a disinclination to exertion, with giddiness; the body is heavy, the colour of the skin bad, and there is no passage of air; such a person does not like his food, his understanding is impaired, and his bowels are either constipated or there are copious dejections.

The unfavourable symptoms of this disease are fainting, delirium, vomiting, a copious discharge of saliva from the mouth, with languor, and giddiness.

A'ma Ajírna. In this disease the body feels heavy, with a flow of saliva and phlegm from the nose. The eyelids swell, and there are eructations of the substances eaten, some time before.

In *Bistabdha Ajírna,* the air is deranged, and produces severe pain in the stomach, with flatulency. The stomach swells, there are no dejections, no air escapes, and the person remains stupid, with his understanding impaired, and pain over the body.

In *Bidagdha Ajírna,* the bile is deranged, the person has sour eructations, complains of thirst, is giddy and often dozes. He compain in the abdomen, has a free perspiration over the body, which feels hot.

When there is want of digestion, although the individual thinks the appetite good and eats, still it does not nourish the body, but acts as a poison in destroying the person. When the food is not taken in the usual quantities, digestion is not performed, and is often followed by disease. When a person eats like an animal, without consideration, he will be affected with indigestion, which is the cause of other diseases, as cholera, drum-belly, and constipation.

Treatment. As indigestion, dispepsia, and costiveness, are considered as only varieties of the same disease, the same plan of cure is to be followed in these cases.

In dispepsia, myrobalan, dry ginger, and sugar are to be taken internally ; rock-salt and myrobalan ; dry ginger with sugar ; the powder of long-pepper and myrobalan, or the juice of the pomegranate. In the morning, to clear the bowels the patient should take the following mixture : mix equal parts of

Dry ginger,
Black and long pepper,
The seeds of *Danti,* (Croton polyandrum,) the
Root of *Tribrit,* (Convolvulus turpethum,) and the
Root of *Chitra,* (Plumbago root, *rizia,*)

and take with a little sugar. This powder produces appetite and cures costiveness, pain (*súl*), enlargement of the spleen and Jaundice.

In indigestion the following mixture is recommended : Take of Asafœtida, black pepper, long-pepper, and dry ginger, equal parts ; make this into a paste with water, and rub it over the abdomen (*Charaka*). The decoction of coriander seed and ginger is recommended, as also a mixture of powdered myrobalan, long-pepper, and rock-salt in whey.

In the variety of this disease which is named *Áma-jirna* emetics are given, such as a decoction of *Bacha,* Orris root (Acorus calamus), rock-salt, each half a *tolá* in hot water. This will be repeated four or five times until the person vomits : or he may take as a diuretic the infusion of coriander seeds with a little ginger.

Bidagdha-jirna. Fasting is also recommended, and cold water to drink (*Sushruta*).

In *Bistabdha-jirna* warm applications are to be made externally to the abdomen. In other cases of despepsia take of

Black pepper,
Long-pepper,

Ginger,
Ajamodá, (Ligusticum ajwaen,)
Rock-salt,
Jirait, (Cumin seed,)
Krishna-jiraka, (Nigella Indica or Sativa,) and
Hingu, (Asafœtida,)

of each equal parts. Mix and reduce them to powder; dose two scruples. Small quantities of wine and honey mixed with water may also be administered.

In despepsia, should the patient have sour eructations, with heartburn, dried grapes *(kismis)* with myrobalan and honey, are to be given in the form of an electuary.

In *Bhasmágni (Bulimia)* the treatment should consist in taking purgatives frequently followed by heavy, indigestable, and oily food; unleavened cakes of rice, ghee, and sugar; the flesh of amphibious animals, as the buffalo, tortoise, &c. Fish is also recommended, mutton prepared with cocoanuts, &c., barley with wax-flower and water, ghee and sugar; oily fruits, as walnuts, almonds, &c., so as to weaken the digestive powers which will cure the disease.

3. *A'lasaka,* (drum-belly.) The abdomen in this disease becomes enlarged and tight, with a rumbling noise, and the air passes upwards, followed by a constipation of fæces and air; with great thirst, eructations, and pain in the stomach.

4. *Bilambika,* or constipation, is somewhat different from drum-belly, as there is no swelling nor tightness of the abdomen; nor is the indigested food either rejected by vomiting nor by stool; but is retained in the abdomen causing much pain there, and likewise producing various diseases in different parts of the body. Constipation is always difficult to cure.

5. *Bisúchika,* (Cholera.) The person first feels pain, as from indigestion, in the abdomen, followed by frequent stools and vomiting, great thirst, and pain in the abdomen, fainting, giddiness, yawning, and cramps in the legs. The colour of the body is altered, accompanied with shivering, pain in the chest, and head-ache. The unfavourable symptoms of cholera are, the lips, teeth and nails become blackish, the person insensible, with frequent vomiting. The eyes become sunken, voice feeble, and the joints loose, with great debility. Such a person may be taken out to be burnt, as he will not recover. The most fatal symptoms of cholera are, want of sleep, restlessness, shivering, no secretion of urine, and insensibility.

This is certainly the same cholera which is still so common, and fatal in this country; but as a sporadic disease. It did not then appear to have taken on that wide spreading epidemic form, which it has done so frequently since the year 1817.

The treatment of drum-belly, constipation and cholera are nearly the same. In all it is to be commenced by exhibiting a strong emetic. In cholera it is recommended to apply the actual cautery to the inner side of each ankle joint; and hot external applications to the body. In all these cases fasting is enjoined, and after the emetics, medicines for correcting and soothing the pain in the stomach are to be used, followed by purgatives. When the faintness and purging has ceased, light easily digested food is to be given when hungry; such as conjee mixed with stomachics, &c. clysters, with purgatives, such as a decoction of *Zowhori* (Convolvulus turpethum), castor oil, &c.

For internal exhibition, *Sushruta* recommends the following: Take of

Myrobalan,
Bacha, (Orris root,)
Hingu, (Asafœtida,)
Indrajab, (Wrightea antidysenterica seed,)
Gringha, (small variety of garlic of a red colour,)
Sabardala, (rock-salt,) and
Atíbisha, (Atis or Bitula.)

The powder of these is to be mixed with warm water for use. Mustard seed with sugar is likewise recommended, also *Burhok* or *Bítlaban*, or black salt.

Saindhaba, (rock-salt,)
Hingu, (Asafœtida,) with acid fruits.

These are to be mixed in water and taken two or three times a day.

The treatment of cholera must vary, and hence it is that so many different plans of treatment are recommended according to the prominent symptoms that are present.

Vomiting is to be produced by a decoction of *Bacha* and salt. When there is much vomiting it is to be stopped by the following preparation: Take thirty-two *ratis* of each of the following medicines:—

Caranja, (Galedupa arborea, Roxb.)
Nímba, (Melia azadirachta,)
Gluchi, (Minespermum glabrum,)
Arjuna, (Pentaptera Arjuna,)
Bacha, (Orris root,)

Mix them with one pint of water; boil to a quarter. This will check the vomiting. For cramps, take mustard oil, rock salt, and *Kusta*, (Costus speciosus.) Mix when warm, and rub it into the parts effected.

6. *Chardi, or Vomiting*

Deranged air, bile, and phlegm, produce this disease; as also when the three humors are deranged, or when the person takes too much fluid, or bad articles of food. When disgusting objects are seen, smelt, or eaten, it may produce this disease. In other persons it is produced by eating food too fast, or at unusual times, and by great fatigue, grief, indigestion, and worms. The state of pregnancy likewise produces vomiting.

Before vomiting occurs, the person complains of nausea, a cessation of belching, a watery and saltish discharge from the mouth, he dislikes food, becomes weak and unsteady in walking, which is followed by vomiting.

When produced by air the vomiting is frothy and scanty, much pain is felt in the back, and sides of the abdomen; great exhaustion, and vomiting occurs, with a loud noise, and an astringent taste in the mouth. When *bile* produces vomiting, the person feels faint, thirsty, the mouth is dry and the head, palate, and eyes hot. He sees indistinctly as if he was in darkness, his body turns round, and he vomits a bitter matter of a yellow, hot, green, or sour nature. When phlegm is the cause the patient is heavy and dozes, his mouth is sweet, phlegm is discharged, thick, white, and copiously mixed with mucus, and a horripilation is felt. The person has no appetite, and the fluid vomited is neither salt, sour, nor bitter. When air, bile, and phlegm are deranged, all the above symptoms are present. When produced by the sight of disagreeable objects, pregnancy or worms, the humors will be deranged, and the variety of the disease will be distinguished by their peculiar symptoms. When produced by worms, there is frequent eructations, and much pain, accompanied with the symptoms of those diseases of the chest which are produced by worms.

The unfavourable symptoms are great debility, and the matter vomited being mixed with blood and pus, or resembles the variegated colour of the peacock's tail. There is also frequent vomiting in other dangerous diseases. All the varieties of vomiting are produced by disorders of the stomach, and in the treatment fasting is always to be enjoined. When vomiting is caused by indigestable matter in the stomach, emetics and purgatives are recommended. In all the varieties, light, dry and agreeable food should be exhibited. Different decoctions are also to be used according to the derangement of the humor as recommended in the treatment of fever. The juice of lemon, mixed with the powder of long-pepper and honey, may be sucked in the mouth with advantage in vomiting. A decoction of barley with honey, or fried rice boiled in water, and made into conjee is to be used. The paste of coriander seeds mixed with salt, and the juice of acid fruits will be of use. The pulp of prunes or myrobalan, with spices, will also be of use ; as well as all articles possessed of agreeable smells. The broth of wild animals, bitter mixtures, and different kinds of agreeable food are all useful in checking vomiting.

During pregnancy the woman should be supplied with those articles of food which she wishes to eat, as the want of them will hurt the fetus, and will increase the tendency to sickness and vomiting.

7. *Dysentery, (Atísár.)*

Dysentery is produced by a variety of causes ; such as exposure to cold, eating very cold articles of food in considerable quantities, eating much ghee and oily articles, very heavy or hot substances, or very thin or dry articles of food ; eating several articles of food with contrary qualities, such as milk and fish, &c., or any kind of indigestable food, causes this disease. In other cases it is produced by the food not being properly boiled or mixed, or being eaten at improper times ; or when not properly seasoned, or in unusually small or large quantities. In some cases the disease is produced by poisons, great fear, or grief ; by unwholesome drinking water ; by much wine, and peculiar food which thus affects certain persons ; and by irregular or sudden changes in the seasons. Remaining long in the water while bathing, worms, deranged or constipated alvine, or other excretions, sometimes produce the disease. The symptoms are explained by the internal fire being diminished by morbid watery secretions, or phlegm generated in the intestines ; this is mixed with the fæces, and is carried off downwards by the air of the part. Hence the production of watery stools, &c. In some cases the fever occurs first from the derangement of air, bile, and phlegm ; in other cases the dysentery precedes the fever, and sometimes both occur together. In these cases abstinence from eating and drinking is to be observed, and such medicines are to be given as prepare the food that is in the abdomen. If dysentery is present such medicines are to be used as will dry up and stop this discharge, and the physician is to decide in each case which sort of remedies are to be given, whether they should be to cure first the fever or the diarrhœa.

There are six varieties of this disease, as when the air, bile, and phlegm are deranged, it forms so many kinds; when the three are deranged together, when produced by grief, and when caused by mucus in the abdomen. *Dhanantwari* says, there are many other varieties as the symptoms vary from time to time.

Before this disease developes itself a sharp pain is felt in the chest, umbiliacus, and anus, and in the abdomen under the false ribs, which is succeeded by want of appetite, languor, and lassitude of the body; no air passed by the anus, the patient is costive, the abdomen swelled, and every thing taken remains undigested. When air produces the disease it commences with great pain; the dejections are of a dark yellow colour, frothy, dry and frequent, and in small quantities mixed with the indigested substances, which have been eaten, pain is felt in the anus on the expulsion of air, and the urine is scanty.

2. When bile is deranged, the dejections are expelled with an effort. They have a bad smell, are hot, and of a red yellowish colour, like the water in which flesh had been steeped. In other cases they are of a blue or red colour, and are accompanied with thirst, dozing, heat of body, free perspirations, and tenesmus at the time of the evacuation. There is often in such cases inflammation of the rectum with violent fever.

3. When phlegm is deranged, the person dozes, the dejections are white, thick, and constipated, mixed with phlegm. He has no appetite, complains of languor and lassitude with dozing, and has frequent calls to stool, which are passed without any noise.

4. When the above three humors are deranged the dejections are of different colours. The patient is very thirsty with languor, dejection of mind, and drowsiness. This kind of dysentery is fatal when children and old people are attacked; and in all cases it is difficult to cure, and will cause much vexation to the physician. The symptoms will vary according as one or other of the above forms predominate. The cause of the disease will likewise vary the symptoms.

5. When grief produces dysentery, the person has the internal fire of *pakasia* deranged by the watery vapours, which are formed by grief, and passing into *pakasia* mixes with the fire, and deranges the bright blood of the part. This blood is mixed with the dejections, often becomes putrid, and is expelled with them. In other cases it is discharged by itself. Sometimes it has a bad smell, in other cases it has not. The cure is tedious, and physicians are vexed by its obstinacy. If the dejections are frequent, the cure will be very difficult.

6. The sixth form is when it is produced by mucus, which deranges the stomach and is discharged frequently of various colours.

There are also two forms of dysentery, one being acute *(Ámaapáka)* or crude, and the other chronic *(Pákátísár)* or mature.

Acute Dysentery, (Ámaraktátísár.)

This form is known by the dejections sinking in water, and being very fœtid. In the *páka* variety the opposite symptoms to the above are most prominent, and the abdomen does not feel heavy.

The unfavourable symptoms are a stiffness of the body, dejections of a dark bluish colour, like the ripe rose-apple ; in other cases the colour of the dejections is like that of the lime, of ghee, or of oil, of tallow or marrow ; in other cases they are like milk or curds ; or like water in which flesh had been washed ; or black, blue, or yellow ; or like the colour of these three mixed together in different proportions ; or like the water of Madar. In other cases they are very thin, of a fœtid smell, and cold ; or of the colour of peacock's feathers, or that of the rainbow, or dry and hot. Sometimes the dejections are consistent, or like the brain, or like the refuse of well washed and beaten bark (fibrous), or its decoction, and are evacuated in large quantities. When the sick person is thirsty and hot, breathes through the nose, has hiccough, and pain in the side, and skin, with loss of memory, dosing and stupor, the disease will be fatal. Such a person has no inclination to do any thing, and remains stupid and complains of pain in the anus, like that of a ripe boil. He speaks incoherently and becomes insensible, with an involuntary discharge from the anus : such persons will not live. When the person is very much reduced in flesh, is cold and the abdomen distended, with pain in the anus : such a person should not be attended by the practitioner, as the disease is incurable.

The physician should be able to distinguish the symptoms of *Áma*, or acute, from those of chronic dysentery. Without this he will not be able to treat the disease properly.

In the acute form the person should abstain from food, and very light medicines should be administered to improve the dejections. If there is much pain and flatulency, he should take an emetic of salt, long-pepper, and hot water. After vomiting, very light food, of a farinacious kind, is to be given. The physician should be careful in the acute stage not to stop the stools by astringents, or the like, as it will produce *Gulma*, anasarca, dispepsia, piles, and drum-belly. When the stools are frequent, and very scanty, he may take myrobalan *(haritakí)*. If the watery stools are copious, emetics, and the following medicines are to be administered. A specimen of these will only be given, as so very numerous receipts of this kind are given in the Hindu MSS. Take equal parts of

Haritakí, (Myrobalan,)
Atibisa, (Atis or Batula,)
Hingu, (Asafœtida,)
Soubor chullon, (rock-salt,)
Bacha, (Orris root, Acorus calamus,)

powder, mix, and give half a *tolá* or more, according to the age of the patient, for a dose, with a little hot water, wine, or conjee.

When deranged bile produces this disease, heating and stimulating medicines are not to be given; but he should take conjee, and agreeable bitter medicines. After some days of fasting, when he has some appetite, such bitters as

Atis, (turmerick,)
Atíbisha, (a plant *Aknudhi, B.)*
Indrajab, (the seed of Wrightea antidysenterica,)
Pata,
Rasánjana, (Sulphurate of antimony,)

are to be formed into a decoction, and given two or three times a day with honey. In cases of bloody flux, boiled rice is given for food without water. In this manner the acrimony of the disease is supposed to be absorbed by the dry rice.

When the symptoms yield to these remedies; the urine increases, and is discharged without the passage of fæces, which are discharged freely and without pain, the appetite is restored, and when there is no uneasiness in the abdomen the person will recover. When there is swelling of the hands, feet, and joints, without any secretion of urine, and the dejections are very hot, the disease is considered to be increasing in violence.

In the chronic state *(Pákátisár)*, when the stools are frequent, astringent medicines are to be given as follows. Take of

Sámangá, (Lycopodium imbricatum, a sensative plant,)
Datakipuspa, (the flowers of Grislea tomentosa,)
Manjistá, (Madar,)
Lodra, (Symplocus racemosa,)
Mustaka, (Cyperus rotundus,)
Sálmulíbesta, (a kind of kino,)
Rodhra, (a tree called *Lodh*),
Darimata, (bark or shell of the pomegranate fruit,)

mix equal parts of these medicines in powder, and give half a *tolá* two or three times a day. When there is much pain, with costiveness, and blood is passed with mucus, take milk boiled with three pints with oily purgatives, and enemas of demulcent medicines with nourishing broths.

8. *Diarrhœa, (Grihiní.)*

By the use of improper food the internal fire is weakened, which deranges the place where it is situated, between the stomach and place of the chyle. When any thing is eaten, which is not properly digested, and is frequently discharged, with or without pain, sometimes liquid, at other times consistent, sometimes it is evacuated without air, and at other times it is fœtid, it forms this disease. Before it commences the patient complains of lassitude and weakness of the body, accompanied with noise in the intestines, sour and bitter eructations, and a bad taste in the mouth. When a singing of the ears, œdema in the hands and feet, with pain in the joints, vomiting, fever, thirst, loss of appetite, and a heaviness and burning sensation of the body occurs, in old cases, the prognosis should be guarded. These symptoms are varied when either the air, bile, or phlegm, or their peculiar symptoms are present.

Treatment. The bowels are first to be cleaned by an aperient stomachic; astringent remedies are then to be taken, with wine in the morning, and butter-milk. Asafœtida, and other stomachic remedies, as ginger, are useful. The fever and other diseases which sometimes accompany it, are to be treated in the usual manner.

Another form of Diarrhœa is called *Sangraha Grihiní;* from *Sangraha,* (a collection,) and *Grihiní,* (place of internal fire;) in which there is much noise in the stomach, with laziness, weakness and lassitude. The stools are unnatural, irregular, and evacuated with noise; sometimes they are thin, and in other cases they are consistent or hard, and of a pale colour like indigested food. Some people remain ten or fifteen days, or even one month, without any fecal discharge; other patients feel well during the day, but have frequent dejections during the night. The prognosis of this form of disease is unfavourable, as it is obstinate and is cured with much difficulty. The treatment of this is the same as that of *Grihiní;* consisting of laxatives, stomachics, and astringent, light, and farinacious diet.

9. *Gulma, (Swellings in the Abdomen.)*

When air, bile, and phlegm are deranged by eating bad food, at irregular times, or by unsuitable exercise, this disease is produced, which resembles a ball in the abdomen. There are five kinds and situations of this disease: One in either side of the abdomen, one in the umbiliacus, another in the pelvis, and one between the chest and the abdomen, (scrobiculus cordis,) sometimes the swelling is fixed, and at other times it is moveable.* There are four kinds of this disease in the male, three by the derangement of air, bile, and phlegm, another by the morbid mixture of the three, and the fifth kind is peculiar to females from the retention of the menses.

Gulma is ushered in by much belching, costiveness, loss of appetite, difficulty of making water, fulness of the body, with flatulence, and indigestion. These symptoms are followed by others produced by the use of food and drink of a dry nature, by a kind of wine which produces roughness of the surface of the body, by improper food, or by eating it at irregular times, or eating too much, by taking unsuitable exercise, and by neglecting the calls of nature, such as sneezing, and dejections, grief, accidents, bruises, or by too great evacuations or fasting. The symptoms of *Gulma,* produced by air, are its being situated in the abdomen, in the umbiliacus, or sides, and its moving about. It is sometimes small, and at other times large; sometimes round, at other times long; sometimes the pain is slight, at other times severe, with constipation, dryness of the throat and mouth; the skin of the body having a dark yellow colour, and fever commencing with chilliness. The pain in the breast and sides of the abdomen, shoulders, or head are considerable, particularly after the food is digested, but the person feels better immediately after eating. Astringent, dry, bitter, or pungent things increase the complaint.

Bile. When the disease is produced by eating sour, bitter, hot, or other things of the same kind; by living on dry food; by anger; by drinking much wine, remaining much in the sun, or near the fire; by collections of indigested food, or diseased blood in the abdomen, the bile is deranged producing the *Pitta Gulma* with the following symptoms. The disease commences with fever, thirst, and a red colour of the mouth and skin. When digestion is going on, there is much pain, and perspiration, with a severe burning sensation in the pit of the stomach, which is tender on being touched, or it is followed by a swelling in the stomach, which is painful like a boil.

Phlegm is deranged by cold, or by eating indigestable or oleaginous articles of food; particularly when the person does not take exercise, eats too much, and sleeps too long during the day. When *phlegm* is thus deranged it produces coldness and languor

* Under the term *Gulma* are arranged very different diseases: as tumors of the pylorus, partial enlargements of the liver, and diseases of the large intestines.

of the body, with low fever, nausea, cough, no appetite, and heaviness of the body, without much pain. The ball gradually becomes harder, and larger.

When air, bile, and phlegm are deranged, and are produced by the causes given above, there will be severe pain, great heat of body, and the *Gulma* or swelling feels hard like a stone, and is large, and quickly produces the heat of the body ;—so severe is this form of the complaint, that the person is in great distress. His body becomes thin, with a bad colour, and he has no appetite, nor strength. Such a disease is incurable.

There is a kind of *Gulma* so like pregnancy that it may deceive physicians, unless they observe the precaution of not giving medicine until after the tenth month, (the supposed time of utero-gestation).*

The unfavourable symptoms of *Gulma* are its enlarging so as to fill the abdomen ; and the increase being rapid, and the swelling being surrounded by vessels, with much pain in the breast, as well as in the part. When the swelling is of the figure of a turtle, when there is much debility, loss of appetite, nausea, cough, vomiting, restlessness, fever, thirst, coma, and the discharge of mucus from the mouth and nose, without either taste or smell, such a person will not recover.

When a person with *Gulma* has fever, asthma, vomiting, diarrhœa, and swelling of the breast, umbiliacus, with swelling of the hand or feet, the disease will be fatal.

When after asthma, cough, thirst, with no appetite, much pain, and the swelling has suddenly disappeared with much weakness,

* My Pandit related an instructive case in point. A young woman became pregnant, and for the uncomfortable sensations attending that state consulted a physician, who after trying various remedies, without effect, one of which was thrusting a red hot iron into the tumor, which is frequently done for spleen, and sometimes with good effect by raising its activity : but in the present case the woman escaped. The physician finding that the disease did not yield to his treatment declared the case to be one of *Gulma,* for which nothing could be done, and that it would increase, and she would die with much pain, and violent shrinking. As this frightened very much the other females the patient was removed to a distant room, and in that state of anxiety passed some months, until parturition commenced. That was considered as the approach of death, and not to defile the house she was put out into the compound upon a mat, and her female friends deserted her. In this state she was delivered of a female child to the astonishment of all, and to the disgrace of the medical man.

the person will soon die. Such cases are in some of the Hindu MSS. said to be cured by the use of a few medicines, many of which have very little effect on the system, and consequently on the disease.

Treatment. When air is deranged the application of unctious substances to the surface of the body are to be used ; but particularly over the tumor, after which oily purgatives are to be used, such as castor-oil, and oily clysters.

When bile produces *Gulma* unctious remedies are to be used externally, and he should take internally *Kákaládí** prepared with ghee, followed by purgatives mixed with sugar.

When the bowels are constipated, milk with ginger is to be given ; and the application to the abdomen of an earthen pot filled with warm water will be useful.

Phlegm. In this form, ghee prepared with a decoction of *Pipuládi,* a mixture composed of long-pepper, and other heating medicines. These are to be taken for some time internally, followed by strong purgatives and enemas. When air, bile, and phlegm, are diseased at the same time, the class of symptoms that appear most prominent will decide which of the above forms of treatment is to be preferred. When the disease is produced by retention of the menses, as sometimes occurs in women soon after delivery, eating improper food, or after abortion, or during the flow of the menses air is deranged, which prevents the flow of the menses, and produces *Gulma.* The symptoms of this form are the same as that produced by diseased bile, and at the same time the swelling moves about like a ball of clay, with the symptoms of pregnancy. When a round swelling is felt in the abdomen of a woman, the same as in utero-gestation, and it is so painful that the part cannot be touched, you are not to use remedies for the cure of this disease for ten months, and then you may prescribe medicines for it. The treatment of this variety is the same as that for derangements of the three humors in other parts of the body, combined with those for *Gulma* produced by bile with amenagoge medicines, such as potassa prepared from the *Palása* tree (Butea frondosa). This is to be mixed with ghee and taken internally, so as to separate and discharge the coagulated blood, which is supposed to be pent up, and produce the disease. Injections into the vagina of the female, with ghee prepared with long-pepper, black-pepper, and other hot medicines, are also recommended.

* A medicinal mixture of an antibilious nature. It is principally composed of a medicine said to be brought from Nepal.

10. *Sul, Colic, (Gastroperiodynia.)*

This disease is called *Sul,* from the pain resembling that produced by piercing the abdomen with the deadly *Trisula* or three-pointed instrument in the hands of *Shiva,* the destroying power of the Triad, and it is said to be sometimes so incurable that even *Shiva* himself cannot remove it. It frequently happens that the individual, in despair of being cured, commits suicide, as the only means left of relieving himself, and of propitiating the anger of the deity. Such fancies have a pernicious effect upon the progress of medical knowledge, for instead of endeavouring to discover the cause and nature of the disease, and the means of alleviating the sufferings of the afflicted, the Hindu practitioner finds a ready excuse for his indifference and ignorance in what he declares to be the will of God.

There are eight varieties of *Sul,* produced by derangement of air, bile, and phlegm ; by two being deranged together, by the three being deranged together, and the last form is by indigestion. In all these forms, however, air is more or less deranged.

1. The causes of Air Colic *(Báyu Sul)* are violent exercise, as fighting, riding, frequent intercourse with women, watching at night, drinking too much cold water, eating peas (especially *Kaláí, Mudga, Araki),* dry food, as dry flesh, vegetables, and fish, overeating, or eating too often ; injuries, and bitter or astringent food. When rice is eaten, and other grain that have vegetated, or an improper mixture of food is taken, as milk and flesh, &c., or when the calls of nature are not attended to, and the semen, urine, air, fæces are constipated ; or by grief, fasting, much and loud laughing or speaking, they produce *Sul* by deranging the air. When air is so deranged the accession of pain occurs at intervals when the person drinks cold water on an empty stomach, when the food has been digested, towards the evening in the rainy season, when the sky is overcast, and during the winter months.

The pain is in the chest, sides of the abdomen, back, in the joining of the lumbar vertebræ with the os coccygis, and in the pelvic region. It is accompanied with difficulty in breathing, rigidity of the body, and scanty evacuations. It is diminished by the application of hot external medicines, frictions, or shampooing over the part with oleaginous applications, and drinking hot liquids. The pain in *air Sul* is first to be checked by hot applications, as bruised til-seed made into a poultice, and applied hot to the part, the external application of hot rice and milk is recommended, or flesh boiled, and applied hot to the pained part. For internal use take equal parts of powdered

Biranga, (a vermifuge seed like black-pepper,)
Sigrí, (Silvius singio,)
Kampila, (a purgative root like rhubarb,)
Pateá, (yellow myrobalan,)
Tribrít, (Convolvulus turpethum,)
Amblabítasa, (Rumex vincarius,)
Surussah, (Ophiorrhiza mangos,)
Ashwakarna, (Shorea robusta,)
Souborchsiloh, (an impure soda,)

one *tolá* is a dose, and may be taken with wine. This will at once relieve the pain. The following is another mixture. Take of,

Pritíka, (Nigella Indica,)
Ajjaghi, (Cumin seed,)
Chobiká, (Orris root, Piper chavya,)
Jawání, (Ligusticum ajwaen,)
Marich, (black-pepper,)
Pipuli, (long-pepper,)
Sunti, (dry ginger,)
Chitraka, (Plumbago zeylanica,)

powder, and take it with warm water, wine, or hot conjee; or with the juice of the lemon, a decoction of prunes, or with asafœtida, or sugar.

The Diet in this disease should be milk and oleaginous substances, and soup made of the flesh of wild birds, and of burrowing animals. Wine-whey is also of use with butter-milk, curdled-milk, black-salt, and vinegar, with diaphoretics and purgatives.

2. When the disease is produced by fasting the person may take hot milk, light rice puddings, or animal broths with ghee. When deranged bile produces this disease, it is caused by eating nitre or heating salts of the same kind, hot food like white mustard-seed, pepper, or the like; different kinds of wines; roasted articles or oils, or shoots of the young bamboo, or oil cake, sour or bitter articles; great anger, remaining near the fire, exposure to the sun, great fatigue, excess in venery, or any thing that is very heating is to be carefully avoided. These different causes derange bile, and produce that form of *Sul* which is felt in the umbiliacus. In this case it produces thirst, his senses are dull, body hot, with great grief, and severe pain in the umbiliacus. He perspires much, and he is giddy and sometimes faints, with dryness of the mouth, is eager to remain in a cold situation, and to take cold articles of food. Accessions of pain occur at noon and midnight, during great heat of the weather, and at the beginning of the rains. The pain is diminished during the

cold hours of the day, when the body is cool; and when cold or bitter things are taken, especially when they feel grateful they mitigate the symptoms.

In the treatment mild vomits are to be used, and then drink cold water, and every thing cooling, while warm articles are avoided. Cooling things are to be applied to the pained part, as stone, silver, copper, or vessels filled with cold water. He should use purgatives and barley, rice, milk, ghee, the juice of the flesh of wild animals, birds and aqueous plants; and medicines that diminish bile, such as the juice of

Parasaka, an acid fruit, (Xylocarpus granatum,)
Mirdiká, (grapes,)
Kharjura, (the fruit of Phœnix Sylvestris.)

3. When deranged phlegm produces *Sul*, it is caused by eating the flesh of the rhinoceros or buffalo, fish or any kind of food obtained from water, whey, milk, or butter-milk; or sugarcandy, rice cakes, or sesamum-seed, oil, rice, and other articles of food which are of a cooling or heavy nature, as *Máskalái*. All these articles increase phlegm, and thus may produce *Sul*. In these cases the patient complains of nausea, cough, langour, and want of appetite, phlegm proceeds from his nose and mouth, the pit of the stomach is cold, and his body is very heavy with head-ache. In such cases after eating great pain occurs, especially at sun-rise, and during the spring or dew months. (*Sishira*.)

The cure of *Sul* produced by phlegm is to commence by exhibiting an emetic so as to remove from the stomach what he has eaten. For this purpose, long-pepper, boiled in water may be used, and apply hot and dry remedies to the part. A hot regimen is to be followed; such as the use of long-pepper, and dry ginger, with the following mixture. Take equal parts of the root of the

Gokra, (Ruellia longifolia,)
Maricha, (black-pepper,)
Pipula, (long-pepper,)
Sunti, (dry ginger,)
Bacha, (Orris root,)
Pátá, (Aknuda, a plant,)
Katrahiní, (black Helibore,)
Chitraka, (Plumbago zeylanica,)

mix together in water, which is to be boiled until reduced to a quarter. This is given internally with nitre.

This last decoction will be found of great use in that kind of *Sul* which is produced by derangements of air, phlegm, and bile. It will cure it, as wind disperses clouds. In all forms of the disease castor-oil, wine, whey, milk or lemon juice, will be of use. There are also different remedies, recommended according to the situation of the pain, whether it be in the scrobiculus cordis, bladder, or region of the heart.

4. When air, bile, and phlegm are deranged together the symptoms of the three above forms are combined in one person. When so deranged in one spot a physician will know it by examining the part. This form gives much distress, like poison or thunder, and such a person should be avoided by the physician as incurable.

The treatment of this form is the same as above, varying the remedies according to the severity of the symptoms of air, bile, and phlegm.

5. When *Sul* is produced by indigestion the symptoms are the same as produced by deranged phlegm. There is a rumbling noise heard in the abdomen, nausea and vomiting, the body feels heavy and cold, as if covered with a wet cloth, and the breathing is difficult. The person can get neither appetite nor sleep, he is costive with severe pain in the abdomen, and there is a discharge of phlegm, from the nose, mouth, &c.

In this variety first use a vomit, enjoin total fasting, with such remedies as increase the internal heat or appetite. The other remedies used for *Gulma* may be given with advantage, particularly when the symptoms stated under the form produced by derangements in phlegm, appear in this variety.

In order to distinguish the different forms of *Sul* the practitioner should know that air is chiefly affected when the pain is principally confined to the pelvic region. When bile is much deranged, the pain is principally felt in the umbiliacal region ; and when phlegm is deranged it produces pain in the breast, sides of the abdomen, and in the scrobiculus cordis. When air, bile, and phlegm are deranged the pain is felt in all the above situations. When phlegm and air are deranged there is severe pain in the pelvic region, sides of the abdomen, and back. When bile and phlegm are deranged the pain is in the scrobiculus cordis, and between the chest and the umbiliacus. When air and bile are deranged there is great heat of the body, and inflammatory fever. *Sul* may be cured when it is produced by either air, bile, or phlegm, being deranged singly. When two are diseased, with difficulty ; but when all the three are deranged at the same time it is incurable. In *Sul* some other forms of disease may accompany and complicate it ; such as severe pain, thirst, fainting fits, spasm of the intestines with costiveness, the body is heavy and there is no appetite, with cough, asthma, and hiccough. Other shástras enumerate the following symptoms, severe pain in the abdomen, vomiting, fever, thirst, and the body seems to swim round. When the person becomes thin, and has no strength, he will not recover.

6. *Parinám Sul** is the variety produced during the digestion of food. When air is deranged by the usual causes it affects also bile and phlegm, and *Sul* is the consequence. After eating, when digestion has taken place, severe fever occurs. The symptoms of this

* *Parinám Sul.* This variety had not been described before 1836, (see the *Indian Journal* for March, page 114,) by European Physicians, which induced me to add the following particulars of this curious disease.

Gastroperiodynia, or periodical pain in the stomach, often commences with symptoms of indigestion and heart-burn, succeeded by a feeling of uneasiness in the scrobiculus cordis, slight at first, and occurring at irregular intervals, and these lessening gradually while the pain increases in violence. In severer cases, the paroxysm of acute pain generally occurs rather suddenly, when the stomach is empty; sometimes early in the morning, or three or four hours after dinner; increasing slowly when the digestive process is finished, and the activity of the abdominal organs has ceased.

The excruciating pain is confined to the pit of the stomach, particularly towards the right hypocondrium, although the neighbouring parts often participate, as the muscles of the loins, &c. The pain is of a cutting or gnawing nature; and during the paroxysm is intense, from which the patient generally obtains temporary relief from pressure. For this purpose he often turns upon his breast and places a hard ball in the pit of the stomach, on which he rests his body, and keeps rolling from side to side. A few days since I ordered an unfortunate person, in this position, to turn round for me to examine him; but such was the agony, that he could not remain without the soothing influence of pressure. As a substitute, he drew from under his clothes a piece of prepared bamboo, an inch in diameter, and a cubit in length, round at one end. This extremity he placed to the pit of the stomach while he rested the other on the floor; and by bending the body over it, produced such a degree of violent pressure, that at first I feared he would injure himself, and even penetrate the abdomen. He continued in this position while I gained the necessary information of his state, and then returned to his former position, commenced rolling from side to side upon the hard ball, placed in the pit of the stomach, and his low wailing proved how intense were his sufferings. This was an acute form of the disease, and until checked by remedies, it occurred daily about 4 o'clock, and he continued in dreadful agony the whole night.

These paroxysms usually occur at intervals of a day or two, and remain from two hours to as many days, with occasional intervals of ease. During these accessions the state of the pulse, although full, continues slow and natural, and there is not usually more heat of body than is occasioned by a continual movement.

variety are, when air is deranged, the abdomen swells, a gurgling noise is heard in the abdomen, the dejections and urine are constipated, with lassitude and shivering, and oleaginous and hot medicines give relief. Bile, when much deranged in this form of *Sul*, produces thirst, heat, restlessness, and copious perspirations; and when sour, pungent, or salt things are eaten the pain is increased, and when cold food is eaten they give relief. When phlegm is much deranged there is vomiting, nausea and dulness of the intellect, with pain, not severe, but remains many hours; in which case pungent or bitter things give relief. When two of these are deranged the respective symptoms are combined, and when three are

---

In the intermissions the patient feels well, and all the functions are performed as when in perfect health. The tongue is clean, but sometimes parched, appetite good, and alvine secretions healthy and regular.

I have not been able to obtain any certain evidences of the causes which produce this disease. It appears to be the effect of a combination, individually slight; but when occurring in a peculiar constitution, produces this distressing complaint. I have generally known it to occur in the young and robust male; to be aggravated by exposure to the weather, and by eating indigestable food, sleeping on the damp ground, &c. The accession seems oftener to occur when the organs are in a state of inactivity, than from causes increasing the nervous susceptibility. I have not seen it in females, although there is no reason why they should not be also effected; and I am informed that they are sometimes attacked but in a less violent degree. Persons of a nervous temperament are in general not so liable to this disease as might be supposed.

The severe pain which occurs in paroxysms, the relief obtained by pressure, and the absence of participation in the circulating system, indicates, with sufficient accuracy, the disease being of a nervous nature. But we are still unacquainted with the peculiar diseases of the large plexuses of the sympathetic nerve, situated in the scrobiculus cordis and its neighbourhood, with those of the 8th pair, &c. These nerves seem to be affected in this disease, much in the same manner as we sometimes find those of the face, arm, thigh, &c. The resemblance of paroxysms of gastroperiodynia to those of Tic-douloureux is marked, not only in the nature and severity of the pain, but in the means of relief, and the difficulty of curing both diseases. The severe paroxysms of otolgia, which so frequently occur in this country, some varieties of colic, &c. form examples of the same species, varying more from the situation, and nature of the parts affected, than from any difference in the disease itself.

The diet I have found most efficacious in gastroperiodynia is liquid farinacious food, with boiled milk, which in some cases I have seen diminish the violence of the paroxysms. In strong and plethoric persons blood should be taken from the arm; and may sometimes be repeated generally, or locally with advantage. During the paroxysms, pressure,

deranged the person will die. When such a person's flesh, strength and internal fire are much diminished the disease will be fatal.

The treatment should consist of emetics followed by bitters, purgatives, and enemas. The following powders are also recommended. Take equal parts of

Biranga, (virmifuge seed,)
Sunti, (dry ginger,)
Pipulí, (long-pepper,)
Maricha, (black-pepper,)
Dantí, (Croton polyandrum,)
Tribrit, (Convolvulus turpethum,)
Chitraka, (Plumbago zeylanica,)

make them into an electuary with sugar, and take it every morning with warm water.

Another remedy in this form of the diseases is

Sunti, (dried ginger,)
Tila, (Til-seed,) and jagry, which is made into an electuary with milk.

Annadrabáka, is another form of *Sul,* in which the pain occurs after eating, or during or after digestion. When present it is not removed by following a proper regimen, or eating good or bad food; but after vomiting bile the patient feels better, but the pain continues under all circumstances of food, &c.

This form is to be treated with fasting, and the administration of emetics. A mixture of Emblic myrobalan, yellow myrobalan, and ginger, with the mixture of iron (carbonate) is of use.

Another mixture is formed by mixing equal parts of

Biranga, (vermifuge seed,)
Musta, (Cyperus rotundus,)
Haritaki, (Myrobalan,)

---

heat, tinctures, ether, peppermint, anodynes, particularly opium, henbane and camphor, are of use in diminishing the severity of the pain: small doses of calomel and opium are also of use.

During the intervals the oxyd of zinc and bismuth, carbonate of iron, sulphate of quinine, are also in some cases of use; but it must be acknowledged that the relief is often of a temporary nature; and in some patients diminish, in effect, or in some cases seem to aggravate and prolong the succeeding paroxysms. I have found the application of moxa, blisters to the loins, and fomentations only of use temporarily; and that the probability of effecting the cure of this disease by medicine, depends on the severity and frequency of the attacks, and particularly on the length of time the disease has existed.

Ámlaki, (Emblic myrobalan,)
Bibitaka, (Beleric myrobalan,)
Gulancha, (Menispermum glabrum,)
Danti, (Croton polyandrum,)
Tribrit, (Convolvulus turpethum,)
Sunti, (dry ginger,)
Pipulí, (long-pepper,) and
Marich, (black-pepper.) These medicines are to be mixed with the powder of *Jawání,* (Ligusticum ajwaen,) and the carbonate of iron and water. The regimen in this form of the disease should consist of prepared rice in the form of conjee, and sugar and ghee with conjee.

Other *shástras* recommend promoting perspiration by hot baths, or vapour baths, by medicines to promote digestion, such as nitre, impure soda, and alum. It is also recommended to take eight *másá* of dried ginger, the root of the castor oil plant and barley, and mix them in a mortar with half a *ser* of water. This is boiled down to a quarter, and is to be tried as a dose; and it will generally relieve, or remove the pain of *Sul.*

11. *Worms, (Krimí.)*

There is an internal sort of worms, and another which appears upon the surface of the body. Others say that there are four kinds; one is external and produced by filth on the surface; others are internal and are produced by phlegm, by blood, and by the fæces. There are twenty varieties of worms, each of which has a particular name. When produced externally by filth, the insect is like a small Til-seed with many feet, and is generally found in the hair and clothes. They are called *juka* (lice). They produce small very itchy pimples, and sometimes a large boil.

When *phlegm* produces the worms internally, it is deranged by indigestable food, particularly when taken at improper times, or with much sugar, or sweetmeats, or much liquids, as vinegar or sour food, curdled milk, vegetables, and unleavened flour when taken daily and frequently. A sedentary life, and sleeping during the day predisposes to worms.

When *blood* produces worms many diseases are the consequence. In this case it is caused by improper mixtures, or by indigestable food, or certain vegetables, &c. The worms are produced in the blood.

The general symptoms of internal worms are fever, paleness, and discoloration of the surface, severe pain, or *Sul,* especially in the breast, with languor, giddiness, loss of appetite, and diarrhœa. When produced by phlegm they are usually found in the stomach *(Ámásiya)*, and resemble earth-worms, and when very large they pass from one intestine to another. Some of the worms are like rice which has begun to germinate, some are long, others are short, and very small; some are white, or like mahogany, others are copper-coloured. There are seven varieties of worms found in the stomach. 1st. *Antrada,* or the gnawing kind; 2nd. *Udarábesta,* large form; 3rd. *Rhidayada,* produces a gnawing pain in the breast; 4th. *Mahágada,* with a large tail; 5th. *Chara,* like flattened rice; 6th. *Durbakusama,* like the flower of a certain grass, and 7th. *Sugandha,* which has a pleasant smell. These seven kinds of worms produce nausea, a copious discharge of saliva, indigestion, and want of appetite; fainting, dozing, vomiting and fever; constipation of urine and fæces, and weakness, sneezing, and a discharge of mucus from the nose.

The worms in the blood have no feet, some have a round figure and red colour (red globules of the blood), and they are so small that they cannot be distinctly seen. Their names are, 1. *Káysáda:* this form eats the roots of the hair of the head which drop out. 2. *Romabidhansa:* this form eats the roots of the hair over the body. 3. *Romadipa:* this variety produces elevations at the roots of the hair. 4. *Arambara,* are like the seeds of the wild fig; these worms may produce the *(kustha),* leprosy. 5. *Saurasa,* (father,) and 6. *Mútrí,* (mother.) These two pass quickly from one relation to another, or are hereditary.

Sushruta enumerates other kinds of worms generated in the blood; as,

Nakáda, which destroys the nails.

Dantáda, which produces the caries of the teeth.

Kikísa, which always accompanies leprosy.

When worms form in the small and large intestines they are called *Parisajya,* which are produced in the fæces, and are discharged by the anus. When these worms grow and ascend in the abdomen frequent eructations occur, which have the smell of the dejections. They are large, round, thick or thin, and are sometimes of a gray colour, or of a yellow white or dark colour. There are five kinds of such worms, 1. *Kakíraka;* 2. *Makíraka;* 3. *Sausuráda,* producing much pain; 4. *Sasulákiya;* 5. *Sailika,* which licks the intestines. These worms produce diarrhœa, pain in the stomach, dryness of the fæces, constipation, weakness, roughness, and dryness of the surface of the body, which is of a dirty yellow colour. There is loss of appetite with an itchiness towards the anus.

For removing external worms, live mercury is to be rubbed with sulphur until a homogeneous black mass is produced; or the sulphurate of mercury which is to be mixed with the juice of *Datura Stramonium,* and rubbed over the part. In the present day a weak infusion of tobacco is often used.

The thirteen first kinds of internal worms are curable, but the seven last are very difficult, or are incurable. The treatment in this case is to commence with the administration of an emetic prepared with ghee and *Sarasádí,* which is a mixture formed of various stimulants and bitter remedies. Strong cathartics are then to be given with clysters. The oil of *Biranga,* made of vermifuge seeds, is to be given with salt, and with the decoction of *Biranga.* The patient should at the same time be careful to avoid such food, and other causes which promote the generation of worms. He should take of the juice or paste of the *Palása* seeds (Butea frondosa), with the decoction of the *Balanga* seeds. The juice of the leaves of *Paribadraka* (Erythrina fulgens), with honey ; or the juice of the leaves of *Patura* (Salincha B.) or the powder of *Biranga* with honey. *Biranga* powder should be mixed with the bread and used by the patient. Different preparations of iron, or the powdered root of long-pepper taken with goat's urine are of use. Tin is recommended to be rubbed upon a rough stone, and the small particles thus removed from the mass is taken in whey. The treatment in cases of insects at the roots of the hair, causing them to fall of, is the same as that for baldness. The worms in the blood are to be treated, as for Leprosy.

Patients with worms should live on food mixed with pungent and bitter food, while the following articles of food are avoided : milk, flesh, ghee, curdled-milk, vegetables with leaves, acids, sweetmeats, and cold articles of food.

12. *Retention of Discharges, (Adábarta).*

If a man wish long life he should attend to the calls of nature, while he avoids indulgence of the passions, particularly anger, pride, lust, revenge, and covetousness.

There are thirteen kinds of diseases produced by checking the efforts of nature to relieve herself. As by stopping the evacuation of air, fæces, urine, by yawning, tears, sneezing, belching, vomiting, semen, appetite, thirst and abstaining from liquids, the stopping of breath, watching, and another variety of indisposition is produced by taking bad food. When these are not indulged in, it produces the constipation which forms this class of diseases.

1. When air *(Apanna báyu)* is stopped in its passage through the anus it produces a swelling in the abdomen, severe pain, difficulty of breathing, head-ache, hiccough, cough, discharge of mucus, difficulty of diglutition and a vomiting of bile, phlegm, or fæces with constipation, and severe pain in the anus followed by a discharge of air.

2. *Dejections.* When the fæces are confined a gurgling noise is

heard in the abdomen, with pain in the anus, as if the part was cut; the dejections are confined, as air ascends, and sometimes stercoraceous vomiting occurs. It is to be treated as for *A'naha.*

3. *Urine.* When confined, there is severe pain in the pelvis, urethra, anus, scrotum, groins, navel, and sometimes in the head, when the urine is discharged in small quantities with pain. The bladder swells, and the body remains bent forward. *Sabarchala,* (impure soda,) and other such salts, wine, cardamum seeds, with wine and milk, are to be given. The juice of the fruits of *A'mlakí,* (Emblic myrobalan) with water; or the juice of the sugar-cane, and the juice of the fæces of a horse or ass are recommended; as also the seeds of cucumber with water and salt, and other diuretics.

4. When *gaping* is checked the diseases of the neck, throat, and of the head are produced; with other diseases of air, such as diseases of the eyes, nose, ears, and mouth. To remove this anoint the body with oil or ghee, previously heated.

5. When *tears* are confined they flow when the person is very happy, or very sorrowful; and when confined the head becomes heavy, and various severe eye diseases are produced. In such patients the phlegm discharged from the nose and mouth is without smell or taste. In this form anoint the body with warm oil, a pigment of a hot nature is to be applied to the border of the eyes to make them discharge the tears; such as cloves rubbed up with honey and strong errhines, such as pungent smells will also be found useful.

6. When *sneezing* is confined, diseases of the head, eyes, nose, and ears are produced. Tickle the nose with something, so as to produce sneezing, and look at the sun so as to allow his rays to fall upon the mucous membrane of the nostrils.

7. When *belching* is confined, the throat and mouth feel as if distended, and very painful; the person's speech is not intelligible, air is confined by the mouth, anus, &c., and the disease produces the diseases of air. A cheroot is to be formed of spices and ghee, which is to be smoked. Wine with soda, the juice of lemon and wine are likewise to be administered.

8. Should *vomiting* be impeded it produces leprosy, loss of appetite, jaundice, fever, great sensibility of the skin and nausea. In such cases ghee is to be externally applied and internally administered, mixed with saltpetre or salt. Emetics should also be used.

9. When *semen* is confined, the bladder, rectum, and testicles swell, and become painful. The urine is confined and is discharged in small quantities with pain, or the urine has a white deposit, and the semen is discharged involuntary. The other diseases may occur

that deranged semen produces. In this case certain diuretics and decoctions with milk are to be administered, and the person is to approach his favourite wife.

10. When the *appetite* is not gratified, it is followed by drowsiness, pain as if the part was crushed, loss of appetite, fatigue, and the eye is dim. In this disease anoint the body with warm ghee and give it in the food, with hot drinks.

11. When the *thirst* is not gratified, the mouth and throat are dry, the hearing becomes dull, and pain is felt in the breast. To remove this the person should take fresh conjee or barley water, with sugar and lemon juice.

12. When the *breathing* is difficult from being confined from the fatigue produced by severe exercise, the food appears to stick in the throat, the understanding is impaired which produces *(Gulma)*, and there is a feeling of hard lumps in the abdomen. In such cases, rest, and gruel are to be enjoined with animal broths.

13. When *sleep* is not gratified, it is followed by yawning, and pain of the body, as if it was crushed. The eyes and head feel heavy, and coma supervenes. Give milk, employ soothing language, and what promotes sleep.

The air of the stomach when dry, astringent, sour, or bitter food is eaten, produces quickly *Udábarta*, and deranges the canals of air, urine, fæces, blood, phlegm, fat, and the vessels which feed them. Air closes these canals and produces pain in the breast and pelvis, with heaviness of the body, and no appetite, with scanty evacuations.

The retention of the above discharges produces pain of the chest and abdomen, nausea, laziness, and the air, urine, and dejections are evacuated with pain. If produced by phlegm there is difficult and noisy breathing, and the phlegm is discharged from the mouth and nose. *(Coryza)*. In this case there is neither taste nor smell; and the body feels hot, with dejection of mind. The person is insensible, and complains of thirst, fever, vomiting, hiccough, and head-ache. The person is deaf, the body swims round, followed by the other symptoms produced by deranged air. The life of such a person should be considered hopeless, when there is much thirst, great weakness, and languor, severe pain in the abdomen, and stercoraceous vomiting. All kinds of *Udábarta* are to be treated as diseases of air, so as to open the closed up passages, and the body in such cases of disease should be anointed with oil and salt, and prepared ghee should be taken internally, enemas should also be used. If the disease is not cured by these medicines, hot applications are to be placed upon the abdomen, followed by oleaginous purgatives. The person should take a decoction made of *Tribrit, Pilu, Jawáni,* and the juices of acid fruits, mixed with water.

The following is also recommended. Take

Hingu, (Asafœtida,)
Kusta, (Costus speciosus,)
Batsá, (Pothos officinalis,)
Sarjiká, (impure soda,)
Biranga, (a vermifuge medicine,)

mix and form a decoction. These remedies will cure *Udábarta,* and pain. Suppositories will also promote the evacuations, glysters are also given, with the fumes of certain medicines. Other practitioners recommend, with the above plan of treatment, fasting, the hot bath, with purgatives, and hot carminatives.

13. *Unhealthy (Costiveness) Discharges, (Amaha.)*

When the fæces are not properly prepared for expulsion, but are discharged in small quantities, with pain, it forms this disease. It is accompanied with great pain in the epigastric region, thirst, a discharge of mucus from the mouth and nose, accompanied with head-ache and heaviness of the body, particularly in the chest. The person has no eructations, complains of pain in the loins and back; the urine and fæces are constipated with severe pain, and there is difficulty in breathing, fainting, and stercorous vomiting. These two last symptoms are only present when the *Pákasia* (the large intestines) are affected. The treatment is the same as in *Udábarta.*

14. *Acidity of Stomach, Vomiting of Bile, (Amlapitta.)*

This disease is produced by improper mixtures of food, by bad water, or articles that derange the bile, which is collected, and is discharged producing this disease. It is characterized by dispepsia, languor, nausea, sour and bitter eructations, and the body is heavy, with burning of the breast and throat. The person has no appetite, is thirsty, complains of syncopy, and the head turns round. A dulness of the intellect may be observed, and the fæces are various in appearance, and hot. The internal heat and pain of body diminishes, and the person sometimes vomits green, yellow, and blue matter. Sometimes it is like blood, and is very sour; sometimes it is like phlegm, or the washings of flesh, or has a mucilaginous appearance. In other cases jaundice is produced with free perspiration, and the body is of a yellow colour. When phlegm and bile are diseased, the abdomen is very hot when any thing is eaten, and if nothing is taken, the vomited matter and eructations are bitter and sour. The neck, chest, and sides are hot; there is head-ache, and the hands and feet are burning. The person has a disgust for food, is feverish, and itchy eruptions, and patches appear over the body.

If this disease be recent it may be cured with difficulty; and if old, it will often be incurable. There are three forms of the disease: when air or phlegm are deranged; when air and phlegm; or when phlegm alone is deranged, which will be distinguished by the experienced physician.

When *air* is diseased the person speaks foolishly, is affected with syncopy, and his body is languid, with slight uneasiness and pain. The room he is in appears dark;—in other cases he is still, is always forgetting, and complains of severe pain of the body.

Phlegm. In this form phlegm is always discharged from the mouth, the body feels heavy, the person is languid, has no appetite, the body is cold, and the person is lazy and vomits. The surface of the body feels as if it was rubbed with something, it is itchy, the patient looses his appetite, and he takes much sleep.

When air and phlegm are deranged in one place, the symptoms of the two above forms of disease are present.

Treatment. In this disease emetics are first to be used, followed by laxatives. When the patient has vomited, and has been purged, anoint his body with oil, and exhibit enemas. His food should be taken with bitter substances, but without any heating mixture. He should eat a preparation of barley and flour, and the powder of fried rice, with honey and milk. He should likewise take a decoction of the *Patal* leaves, ginger and coriander seeds, when there is much itching pain, and indigestion. When there is much fever and vomiting, accompanied with pain, take a decoction of the *Patal* leaves with ginger, myrobalan, and *Gulancha.* Tonics are also of great use, with carminatives.

15. *Enlargement of the Abdomen, (Udara.)*

This disease is divided into eight varieties, three of these are produced by derangements of the air, bile, and phlegm, and one by the combination of the three. The fifth is accompanied by enlargement of the spleen; the sixth is called *Baddaguda,* concretions; the seventh *Parisrábyudara,* or *Agantuka,* or accidental; and the eighth *Dakodara,* or Asitis.

This disease *(Udara)* is produced by eating bad food without an appetite; eating dry putrid food, and the improper administration of purgatives, emetics, and other active medicines by which the air, bile, and phlegm are deranged in the abdomen. The first symptoms of this disease resemble *Gulma;* followed by swelling of the abdomen. It is produced by the taking up of the fluid part of the chyle, which is conveyed by air into the surface, and produces swelling under the skin, and enlargement of the abdomen.

The disease is ushered in by weakness, unhealthy colour of the skin, languor, and want of appetite. There are no wrinkles on the abdomen, which swells, while the rest of the body is thin, and prominent veins appear over the surface of the abdomen. He has pain in the pelvis; fulness in the abdomen, with burning; the feet swell, and the person is weak and cannot walk. By degrees the body swells, the air and dejections are stopped, the body is hot, and the person complains of faintness. The forms of this disease, called *Busrabí*, and *Baddaguda* are incurable; the other forms are cured with much difficulty. In the latter stages of this disease manual assistance or operations are sometimes required for the cure of the disease.

At the commencement of the disease the person should carefully avoid heavy food, or when not properly prepared, likewise oleaginous, dry, indigestable food, and animal food, bathing, &c. He should live on barley, rice, and wheaten flour, or the like.

1. When diseased *air* produces this disease, the hands, feet, and abdomen are swelled, with pain in the sides of the abdomen, pit of the stomach, loins, and back, with pain in the joints as if they were broken. He complains of cough without expectoration, stretching and heaviness about the loins, the dejections and urine are constipated, the skin and eyes are of a dark yellow colour. The swelling is not always the same; sometimes it increases, and at other times decreases, with severe pain in, and over the abdomen. Dark coloured vessels are prominent over the abdomen, which is swelled like a leather bottle, and makes a noise like it when it is struck. The treatment in this form should consist in taking preparations of ghee, laxatives with ghee, oleaginous enemas, and the abdomen should be rubbed with hot preparations; minced meat boiled and applied warm over the pained part is recommended; or rice and milk may be applied in the same way. He should also take milk with a decoction of *Bidáríganda*, and the broth made of wild animals.

2. *Bile.* The symptoms of this variety are fever, faintness, burning, thirst, and an acid taste in the mouth; the head swings round, looseness is produced, the eyes and skin are of a yellow colour, the abdomen is of a green colour, and small yellow vessels appear upon the surface, with much perspiration; the body burns, there is a feeling as if smoke was rising in his throat, and the symptoms of bilious diseases; as well as the peculiar symptoms of this disease are quickly developed.

Treatment. Take prepared ghee, with a decoction of sweet medicinal plants, such as *Kákolí, Kírokákolí,* prepared ghee, with

Tawarhi, (Myrobalan,) *A'mlakí* (Emblic myrobalan,) and *Bibhítaka,* as a purgative. Then take a decoction of *Botah,* and other astringent plants, with sugar, honey, and ghee. Boiled rice and milk, is to be applied to the abdominal region.

3. *Phlegm (Shleshmodara)* when much deranged the person cannot work, is always sleepy, the abdomen swells, and there is no feeling in the abdomen, heaviness, sickness, no appetite, difficulty of breathing, cough, the eyes and skin are pale, abdomen cold, and the bowels are constipated; and white vessels appear upon its surface: After many days the swelling is completely formed, and is very difficult to remove. The body feels cold and hard, and the abdomen heavy.

The *treatment* of *Shleshmodara* consists in administering ghee prepared with long-pepper, and other stimulant and carminitive medicines. Enemas of cow's urine, oil, and a decoction of long and black pepper and ginger, are to be exhibited. The abdomen should be rubbed with the following mixture: take equal parts of linseed, hemp seed, and mustard seeds with the seeds of *Mulaka* (horse-raddish). These are to be formed into a plaster, and applied with other hot medicines to the part. When there is much pain, constipation and swelling of the abdomen, it proves that air is deranged; when faintness, thirst, heat, and fever are present, the bile is deranged; and when there is a sense of weight with no appetite, and hard abdomen, the phlegm is deranged.

4. The derangements of the *air, bile,* and *phlegm* are said by the moderns to be often caused by enchantment, or by the use of Philters, as of a woman to her husband, or lover. For this purpose the parings of nails, the cuttings of hair, fæces, urine, menstrual blood, &c. are used, on the absurd supposition of increasing their love towards them. Certain poisons administered by an enemy are said also to produce this disease. These causes not only derange the three humors, but also the blood. This form of disease is increased by cloudy weather, when the abdomen is swelled; and when the air is cold, it is also increased in violence, and the person becomes faint, the body yellow, the person very thin and dry, and he complains of thirst. This form of disease is called *Dakodara.*

The *treatment* of this disease is very difficult. The physician should, before commencing it, inform the friends that the disease is incurable; then he may try the effects of remedies. Administer strong purgatives repeatedly for a fortnight or a month. The root of *Aswamárika,* with *Jangá,* and *Kákádiní,* may be formed into a paste with wine, with which it is to be taken. Different forms of Nepál poison, as Aconitum, is said sometimes to be used. In other cases a sugar-cane is to be employed to irritate a poisonous snake, and when he has stung it, the sugar-cane is to be given to the patient to eat.

The general treatment of the above forms of this disease varies with the cause. Should the derangement of air, and the accumulation of fæcal matter in the abdomen produce it, laxatives are to be freely used; such as castor oil, with cow's urine and milk, or rice. These are to be exhibited for one or two months, without drinking water. The person must live entirely on camel's milk. He should take daily a dose of long-pepper, rock-salt, *ajwain*, with the oil of Croton (poliandas), milk, with the juice of fresh ginger, or myrobalan and sugar. The following medicine is also recommended. Take one thousand cloves of long-pepper, macerate it for seven days in the milk of Euphrobium. The seeds are then to be powdered, and to be taken occasionally. All forms of purgatives are useful in this disease, and many formulæ are recommended.

5. *Plihodara* (spleen). This is a swelling of the abdomen with an enlargement of the spleen. It is produced by eating indigestable food, or of a heavy nature, as also articles which produce cold; as curdled milk, and articles which increase phlegm. These substances when frequently eaten derange blood and cough, and swell the spleen. In this disease there is languor, loss of appetite, and symptoms of deranged phlegm, &c. The person becomes very weak, and the body of a yellow colour. When the liver is swelled it is called *Jakrit Udara.* In this form the air, bile, and phlegm are deranged, and the disease is severe.

For treating spleen first give ghee, then promote perspiration by employing the steam bath, give rice with curdled milk for one day. General bleeding is then recommended by opening the veins at the bend of the left arm, and while the blood flows press the spleen, so as to evacuate the bad blood. He should then take nitre with asafœtida and rock-salt; or a decoction of *Sabhánjana,* with long-pepper, rock-salt, *Chitraka,* the root of long-pepper, ginger, and nitre; eight *tolá* of each; add four seers of ghee, and four of milk; and boil; and when the watery part is dissipated, it is to be removed from the fire, strained and taken daily. Afterwards reduce to powder the long bivalve shells of the country by roasting them, and give the powder with milk. The liver is to be treated by opening the vein at the bend of the right arm, after ghee has been given, and perspiration has been promoted. The rest of the treatment is the same as in spleen and liver.

6. *Baddaguda.* This form is produced by the accumulation of indigestable matter with the food, such as hair, gravel, &c. These form balls which produce constipation, and swelling occurs be-

tween the chest and umbiliacus. The person has stercoral vomiting, as a drain is stopped by an accumulation of filth. The air, bile, and phlegm are deranged at the obstructed part, and the fæces is confined. The stools are in small quantities, and are evacuated with great pain, the umbiliacus, and breast are much swelled.

In this disease it is recommended to give ghee internally, and rub it over the abdomen, while perspiration is produced by hot baths, &c. When the remedies are of no use, and the situation of the patient desperate, an operation is recommended, which is to be performed in the following manner: Below and on the left side of the umbiliacus, and four fingers breadth from the linea alba, an incision is to be made four fingers breadth in length, and the breadth of four fingers of the gut are to be drawn out, and the substance, whether stone or hair, or a bad secretion, which was the cause of the disease is to be removed; ghee and honey is to be rubbed over the wound in the intestine, and it is then returned into the abdomen. Apply sutors, and treat the external wound as recommended in such cases. Avoid any currents of air after the operation, and carefully follow the physician's prescriptions. *(Sushruta.)*

7. *Parisrábyudara* is produced by sharp substances, such as fish bones, portions of wood, &c. being taken with the food, and wounding the canal. A watery discharge is evacuated by the anus, proceeding from the wounded surface. The abdomen increases in size under the umbiliacus with much pain and burning. It is to be treated as the last; but both are generally incurable. The other forms are cured with difficulty. Warm baths, and a milk diet are recommended.

8. Asitis, (*Jalodara*, or *Dakodara*.) When a person has taken a large quantity of prepared ghee, or has had frequent enemas, or after emetics or purgatives he drinks large quantities of cold water, they stop the absorbent vessels, and produce this disease. In this case the abdomen becomes large, the umbiliacus prominent, and appears shining as if anointed and full of water, and like it moves about, and gives a sound like a leather bag.

In all these forms of diseases there is swelling, weakness, loss of appetite, languor, and swelling of different parts of the body, constipation, burning, and great thirst. When with these symptoms water collects, the disease is incurable.

Treatment. In Asitis the abdomen is to be anointed with oil prepared with medicines to cure diseased air.—A friend is to hold the patient in a reclining posture by the arm-pits. The practitioner then introduces a trocar an inch (four fingers breath) below, and on the left side of the umbiliacus. The trocar is removed, and a tube is put in its place. The morbid fluid for 16 days is to be allowed slowly to evacuate itself; and a light bandage is to be placed round the abdomen after the operation, so that the air may not swell the abdomen; this bandage must be continued for a considerable time. For six months after this operation milk is to be freely used with rice, or the broths of wild animals, with rice; and after three months and a half the quantity of water and milk with rice may be taken; and other three months light and wholesome food. The disease will be cured in one year.

Class VII.

Diseases of the Urinary Organs and Organs of Generation.

Order I.

Diseases of the Urinary Organs.

Under this head will be considered the diseases of the urine, bladder and urethra.

Morbid secretion of urine, (Prameha.)

This disease is produced by a sedentary life, as sitting, lying down, or sleeping in the day time, using too much curdled milk, various kinds of fish, amphibious animals, or the flesh of buffaloes, new rice, or new water, such as rain or fresh river water, or food with different preparations of jagry, or whatever produces phlegm. It is also produced by the deranged phlegm of the bladder which affects the fat, flesh, or serum of the body; but particularly the region of the bladder. The bile is deranged by its peculiar causes, and in like manner the air may produce the disease, when the other humors are deranged, and convey them to the bladder.

There are twenty varieties of diseased urine; of which phlegm forms ten varieties which are curable, bile forms six varieties which are cured with great difficulty, but do not destroy life; and air forms four varieties, which are incurable. The causes of the different degrees of facility of removing these different varieties are that all the forms are accompanied with deranged phlegm, and when combined with deranged bile the cure of the disease is difficult, as those remedies which diminish bile will increase the phlegm. In like manner those remedies which decrease the air increase the phlegm therefore the cure is difficult; and on this account the disease produced by air is dangerous even from the beginning. These twenty kinds of disease are produced by derangements of air, bile, and phlegm, fat, blood, semen, serum *(Amba)*, lymph *(Basá)*, the essential parts of all the humors *(Ozzo)*, the flesh and the chyle.

This order of diseases is ushered in by the appearance of morbid secretions about the teeth, ears, nose, and eyes. The hands and feet are very hot and burning, and the surface of the skin is shining as if oil had been applied to it. This is accompanied with thirst, and a sweet taste in the mouth. The different varieties of this disease are distinguished from each other by the symptoms of deranged humors, and by the colour of the urine.

In the disease produced by phlegm, insects approach the urine; the person is languid, his body becomes fat, and there is a discharge of mucus from the nose and mouth, with dispeptic symptoms, and looseness of the skin. He is always sleepy, with cough and difficult breathing.

When the disease is produced by bile, there is a cutting pain in the scrotum, bladder, and penis, with fever, dispepsia, vomiting, heat of the body, thirst, want of sleep, and yellowness of the excretions. In some cases it is accompanied with jaundice.

When produced by diseased *air* there is pain in the chest, the patient has a desire to eat every thing, there is watching, shivering, pain and costiveness. The following are the names and characteristic symptoms of the twenty varieties of diseased urine:—

1. *Udakameha.* In this disease the urine is nearly of the natural colour, without any sediment. It is white, cold, has no smell, and is like water. For its cure use a decoction of *Páríjáta*, Erythrina fulgens.)

2. *Ekhyumeha.* The urine is like the juice of sugar-cane in colour and taste; and for the cure give a decoction of *Baijaintí.*

3. In *Sándrameha* the urine becomes thick after standing sometime, and for the cure give the patient a decoction of *Nímba.*

4. When the urine is of a white colour, is thin and pure above, and thick below, it is named *Surámeha;* and is cured by a decoction of *Chitraka.*

5. *Pishtameha.* At the time of micturition the hair over the body is erect, and the urine has a copious white powder; as if flower had been mixed with it. For the cure use a decoction of *Tamarinds.*

6. *Sukrameha.* In this variety the urine is the colour of semen, which sometimes appears mixed with it. For its cure give a decoction of *Durba, Saibala, Loba,* and *Kaseruka,* with other medicines of the like kind.

7. When the urine lets fall a hard and small deposit like sand it is called *Sikatámeha,* and is cured by giving a decoction of *Chitraka.*

8. In *Swetameha* there is a copious secretion of urine which is sweet and cold. For the cure give a decoction of *Trifalá*, formed of three varieties of myrobalan.

9. When there are frequent calls to make urine, which is discharged in small quantities, the disease is called *Shanairmeha ;* and for its cure give a decoction of *Catechu*.

10. *Lálameha*. When the urine is like mucilage, and has long adhesive fibrous matter mixed with it, the disease is named *Lálameha ;* and is cured by means of astringent decoctions.

11. In *Khármeha* the urine has the colour, taste, and smell of potassa, and is like it to the touch. Cure, use the decoction of the three varieties of myrobalan.

12. In *Nilameha* the urine is of a blue colour ; and for the cure give a decoction of the bark of the banian tree.

13. In *Kálameha* the urine is of a black colour, like ink. For the cure use astringent decoctions, with honey.

14. In *Haridrameha* the urine is bitter and of a yellow colour like tamarind water, and there is great heat in passing the urine. Cure, use a decoction of *Cassia fistula*.

15. In *Manjistameha* the urine has the smell of indigested food, and is of the colour of the water of madder. Cure, use a decoction of madder, and red sandal-wood.

16. *Raktameha*. The smell is like that of indigested food, is hot, is saltish to the taste, and is of a red colour. Cure, use a decoction of *Gulancha, Casurga, Curjura,* and the seed of the *Tindaka*.

17. *Basámeha*. The urine in this variety is of a light colour like fat, and seems as if mixed with it. It is discharged frequently. Cure, use a decoction of *Saptaparna*.

18. *Majjámeha*. The urine in this form is like the colour of marrow, and appears as if mixed with it. It is discharged frequently.

19. *Kandrameha*. The urine is astringent and sweet to the taste. It has a troubled appearance.

20. *Hastímeha*. In this disease there is an incontinence of urine, which is discharged involuntary. It appears mixed with fat.

The unfavourable symptoms of the above varieties of disease are when they are congenital ; when the seven forms of diseased air, bile, and phlegm are present ; when accompanied with a great discharge of the humors ; when accompanied with large deep-seated abcesses ; and when accompanied with *Madhumeha*, or sweet urine. These forms destroy the patient. All hereditary diseases being incurable, the congenital forms are such. All these different forms of *Prameha* if not properly treated, terminate in *Madhumeha,* or sweet urine, and they are then incurable.

The following forms of *Prameha* may be cured; when the urine is of the natural colour, is neither shining on the surface, nor white; and is of the usual taste, or is bitter and pungent. The following eruptions and abscesses may occur in the course of this disease in joints, and in vital or sensible parts; as the temples, or where there is much muscle.

1. *Sarábika;* with a central hollow, with high edges.
2. *Kachchhapíki* are hot, and are in the form of a turtle, in appearance.
3. *Jwaliní* is hot, and part appears irregular in its surface.
4. *Binatá* eruption is of a blue colour, and is accompanied with severe pain. It appears in the back or abdomen, and is accompanied with a copious secretion of urine.
5. *Alagi* is of a red and dark colour, in spots.
6. *Masuriká* is of a small figure with a central depression of a yellow colour.
7. *Sarsapika* is of a light yellow colour, and has the figure of mustard seed.
8. *Patirní* is elevated, and is surrounded with small eruptions.
9. *Bidáríká* like a bulbous root, hard, and hot.
10. *Bridadí* is a kind of abscess; and will be considered in another chapter.

These various forms of eruptions may be produced by the derangements of fat without the presence of *Prameha;* and they are not observable until they have arrived at their full size, as it does not affect the pulse, &c. When they appear about the anus, breast, head, shoulders, back, and other sensible or vital parts, and if accompanied with bad symptoms they are dangerous. When boils, are severe, and the internal heat is diminished, the physician is to give the case over as desperate. At the termination of the eruption, when there is thirst, cough, sloughing of the flesh, fainting, hiccough, delirium, slight fever, erysipelas in the temples, and the other sensible parts are very painful, so that the patient cannot be moved, the case will be fatal. Females are not liable to these diseases, as by the monthly discharge the body and humors are purified.

Treatment. There are two kinds of *Prameha;* one of which is congenital, and the other is produced by the use of bad food. In the first form the patient becomes weak, thin, and the surfaee of the body is rough. He eats much, and is always thirsty and restless. In the second kind, or that produced by bad food, the patient becomes fat, eats much, the surface of the body is smooth and oily, and he is always sitting and sleepy.

In the first form give nourishing food, and in the second light food, with occasional fasting. In both forms the following articles are to be avoided, all kind of wines, milk, especially curdled milk, oil, ghee, sugar, or sweet cakes, and acid drink. The flesh of domestic or amphibious animals are to be avoided, and the various kinds of fish. The patient is to use good old rice, barley, and flour, he should eat the different kinds of beans and peas, bitter and astringent vegetables, the flesh of wild animals without fat or ghee. The treatment should be oily purgatives, as castor oil. This is to be followed by the exhibition of emetics. If there is much pain or scalding, give him antiphlogistic remedies, with the juice of Emblic myrobalan, tamarinds, and honey. The physician should also exhibit tonics and astringents. He should drink sharbats containing honey, liquorice, and an acid fruit called *Kapitta,* with powdered black-pepper, and ashes of the dung of camels and asses. When the urine is increased much in quantity the patient should take prolonged exercise, as by walking and riding on horse-back, or on elephants. He should also drink different kinds of tinctures, particularly those with preparations of iron.

For the cure of *Basámeha,* use a decoction of the bark of *Agnimanta* or *Sinsapá,* (a tree,) *Kadrameha,* with *Katikí,* and betel-nuts.

In the cure of *Hastimeha* use a decoction made of *Tindika, Kapitta, Sírisa, Palása, Pátá, Murbá,* with honey. Another remedy is the ashes of the bones of elephants, horses, asses, and camels.

Samarogá or *Bahumutra,* is a disease only mentioned in modern books, most probably by its being classified as a variety of *Prameha.* Some manuscripts state that it is a disease peculiar to woman and is probably mistaken for Lucoreah, although generally considered to be Diabetes.*

It is produced by excessive venery, grief, much exertion, and poison. In this disease all the humors are deranged, and pass through the vessels of the urinary passages; and are discharged copiously, without pain, and pure like water. The woman becomes weak suddenly, and the discharge of urine becomes involuntary. The patient becomes uneasy with giddiness, and the mouth and palate become dry, followed by fainting and delirium. The skin is dry and rough, with great thirst.

* See *Chikitsá Ratnasangraha,* or the jewels of treatment.

The treatment consists in eating ripe plantains; in taking the fresh juice of Emblic myrobalan mixed with honey, powdered *máskalái*, liquorice, *bádám*, honey, ghee, and milk. The carbonate of iron and sulphurate of mercury is likewise recommended with honey; or the seeds of the wild fig with honey. Different other vegetable mixtures are also recommended with ghee in this disease.

a. Suppression of Urine, (Mutragháta.)

The derangements of air, bile, and phlegm in the bladder produce the thirteen forms of this disease.

Bátakundaliká. This disease is produced by eating dry articles of food, by retention of the natural discharges; by which the air is deranged in the bladder, which mixes with the urine producing pain, and they turn round in a circle, and the urine is retained, or it is discharged in drops. The person is very fearful in this disease.

Astila. When the air is deranged between the rectum and bladder it forms a large ball like a stone (prostate gland?) and produces suppression of the urine, fæces, and air; and is accompanied with swelling in the bladder and much pain. This disease is also called *Bátastíla.*

Batabasti. When an ignorant person stops the evacuation of the urine or dejections, which deranges the air stops up the neck of the bladder, and produces retention. This disease produces pain in the pelvis, and in the sides; which from is cured with much difficulty.

When a person allows the urine to flow for some time, and then stops, it produces the disease called *Mutrátíta*, or retention, when the urine is only discharged in small quantities.

When urine is retained by such causes as produced the same effect as the retention of air, which is situated near the rectum, it produces swelling of the abdomen, with much pain under the umbiliacus. This disease is called *Mutrajathara.*

When the urine stops by impediments in the urethra, near the glans penis or elsewhere; or when expelled with great force mixed with blood, sometimes with much pain, in other cases with no pain, this variety is called *Mutrasanga.*

When the body is dried up by the free use of stimulants, and dry food, and great fatigue, the air and bile are deranged in the bladder, and the urine, which becomes scanty is of a black colour, and produces severe pain and heat. This disease is called *Mutrakia.*

When there is a small hard round ball at the neck of the bladder, accompanied with much pain, it may prevent the passage of the urine, and produce the symptoms of stone, it is called *Mutragrinti.*

When at the proper time urine is not discharged, and the patient has connection with woman, the semen is discharged with the urine, sometimes before, and in other cases after the urine. This urine is of a white colour, as if mixed with chalk, and the disease is called *Mutrasukra*.

When violent exercise is taken, as in fighting, travelling, or great heat, the bile is deranged in the bladder with air, which passes mixed with urine, and produces a burning pain in the bladder, penis, and anus. The urine becomes yellow as if mixed with tamarinds, or blood; it is discharged with difficulty, and is called *Usnabáta*.

When deranged air produces this disease it is accompanied with great pain and heat, on its being discharged.

When the urine is yellow from bile, it causes in its passage a burning pain in the part, and there is much sediment.

When phlegm produces the disease the urine is white, like the powder of shells, and is of different consistence: this variety is called *Mutrakasáda*.

When the body is very dry and weak, and the fæces is collected for some time, it may be evacuated with the urine, have the smell of fæces, and pass with difficulty and much pain. This is most probably the recto-vaginal fistula, which is only described in modern books; and is called *Bierbigáta*.

---

b. Strangury, (Mútrakrichchhra.)*

This disease is produced by wrestling, or other violent kinds of exercise, hot spices, dry food, wines, excessive venery, riding on horseback very quickly; eating the flesh of the buffaloes, of the rhinoceros, &c., or other indigestable food; another cause is eating too frequently, or it may be produced by bad digestion.

There are eight forms of this disease. The derangements of air, bile and phlegm separately or combined, when they occur in the bladder, produce this and diseases in the urinary passages, when the urine is discharged with pain. This disease is also produced by injuries of the parts, by constipation of the bowels, and by calculi.

1. When the deranged air produces the disease it causes severe pain in the pelvis, in the testicles, and in the penis. The patient has a frequent desire for making water, and the urine passes in drops accompanied with pain.

2. When the bile of the part is deranged the urine is of a yellow

* From *Mutra*, urine, and *Krichra*, slow and painful.

or red colour. There is much scalding or burning pain in the passages; the urine is discharged in small quantities frequently, accompanied with heat and uneasiness.

3. When the phlegm is deranged the pelvis, bladder, urinary passages, and testicles feel heavy; they are swelled, and the urine is cold, shining like oil, and soon dries up.

4. When the air, bile, and phlegm are deranged the separate symptoms of each variety appear in the same person, and is cured with difficulty.

5. *Salajah.* When the parts are injured by external violence, the disease is accompanied with much pain, followed by other symptoms of deranged air.

6. *Sakripratikatajah,* when the bowels are very costive, from air being deranged, it is accompanied with much swelling and pain in the abdomen, with difficulty in mictirition.

7. *Asarijah* is produced by calculi, with a difficulty and pain in mictirition.

When a person runs quickly or jumps, is much fatigued, is fasting, or the part is injured, the bladder rises out of the pelvis of a round form, and large like the gravel uterus. It is accompanied with much pain and moves from side to side, and the urine is very hot, and passes in drops. If the swelling is pressed, above the pubis, the urine passes easily, and in a continued stream. When the person cannot move, it is called *Bastikundala,* and is a severe and dangerous disease.

When bile produces the disease it is incurable; when phlegm it may be cured, especially if it continues to be discharged, except in the case of "*Kundalí báta.*" When the bladder is round above pelvis, with thirst and insensibility and noisy breathing, it is incurable.

Treatment. Different kinds of diuretics, alkalis, honey, wines, fomentations and injections, &c., are recommended in this disease.

The seeds of cucumbers bruised, and taken with salt and vinegar, or wine with salt, rum with animal flesh and honey, saffron with water and honey, different sharbats with acid fruits, especially pomegranate, the fresh juice of the dung of asses with the decoction of *Abayá, Debdáru, Murba,* and *Madhuka.*

Cold water is to be given to drink with the juice of grapes, saltpetre, and other salts in water are to be used, and the body is to be anointed with oil, fomentations, and purgatives.

8. *Sarajah,* when the semen is affected by deranged humors, and carried into the passage of the urine, it is discharged with much difficulty and pain.

9. *Asarí* and *Sakará* produced by stone or gravel. They are produced by the same causes, and the symptoms of both are the same. When the stone is broken and dried up with bile and air, it is discharged through the urethra. When stone is retained in the bladder, it forms the peculiarity of the two diseases.

In *Sakará* there is shivering with severe pain in the chest and sides, loss of appetite, and fainting. This is followed by a fit of strangury, which is a severe disease, the pain being only mitigated when the urine is not discharged, and the suffering is very acute, as the gravel is passing through the urethra.

The *treatment* will vary according to the humor particularly deranged. The medicines prescribed for stone are to be given in this disease, with a preparation of ghee, oil, and fat, with a decoction of

Shadanshtrá,
Asabiet,
Kumbhí,
Apushá,
Kantikárí, (Prickly nightshade,)
Balá, (Sida cordifolia,)
Shatábarí,
Rásná, (Mimosa octandra,)
Baruna, (Capparis trifoliata,)
Girikarniká.

These are to be taken internally and used as glysters, and as injections into the urethra.

Another remedy to alleviate the pain is prepared by the juice of *Sadanstra* with jagry, and milk. A diuretic mixture called *Trinádu panchaka* made by the decoction of the root of sugar-cane, the roots of

Kusha, (species of grass,)
Kásha, (Saccharum spontaneum,)
Shara, (Saccharum Sarah,) and
Ushara, (Khuskhus.)

These are to be mixed with sugar and taken frequently.

When bile is deranged give purgatives, with the juice of sugar-cane, grapes, and milk. A decoction of *Sarasáda* or *Barnáda* prepared with oil. Barley water is to be given as drink.

When phlegm is much deranged, prepare oil with the above decoctions. When the three humors are deranged, the three kinds of medicines above stated are to be used conjointly as a mixture.

When produced by external injuries employ the usual treatment for such injuries.

In all these forms fomentations and warm bathing should be used.

c. *Urinary Calculi,* (*Ashmarí.*)

When air, bile, and phlegm are deranged it produces different forms of calculi; and another kind is produced from semen. Phlegm is the chief cause of the disease in all its different forms.

This disease is produced in those who live on hard indigestable food, and do not use evacuating remedies, by which the phlegm is deranged, and mixing with urine passes into the bladder and forms the stone.

Others suppose that the calculi are produced by collections of the impurities of the urine which sink down and form, by being dried with the internal fire, calculi in the bladder. Others suppose they are formed as hailstones are formed in the sky.

This disease is ushered in by pain in the bladder, especially in its neck, scrotum, and penis. In some cases languor and fever are present, and the urine has the smell of goat's urine. When formed the pain is in the umbiliacus, bladder, perineum, penis, particularly during mictirition. The urine does not pass in a stream, but in drops: it also stops suddenly. It is sometimes mixed with blood, in other cases it is clear or mixed with gravel. The pain is increased by walking, jumping, and riding.

Four different forms of this disease are observed. The following are the peculiarities of each form.

When produced by *air* it is always accompanied with deranged phlegm, and this forms the stone. This stops near the neck of the bladder, and suddenly impedes the flow of urine; and is accompanied with much pain. To assist the evacuation of the urine the patient presses the parts particularly the umbiliacus, penis, and anus. The colour of the calculi are black, rough, and unequal; and are surrounded with elevations like the *kadam.*

Bile. In this case the bile being mixed with deranged phlegm, become a thick mass, increases in size, passes to the neck of the bladder, and prevents the passage of the urine. In the bladder there is a burning pain, as if produced by the application of heat. The air from the anus is hot, and the stone is yellow and sometimes red, black, or greyish, and resembles the stone of the "marking-nut."

Phlegm. A person who eats much of those articles of diet which produce diseases of phlegm is liable to have this form of stone. In such cases the phlegm becomes thick, and a stone is formed in the bladder. It produces a sudden stop of the flow of the urine, with severe pain in the bladder, and the person feels as if beaten. The bladder feels heavy, and cool; and the stone is white, shining, large, like the appearance of a hen's egg.

The fourth kind of stone is produced by excesses in venery, or by the stoppage of semen which collects between the scrotum and penis. There it dries, and stops the passage of urine. This produces pain in bladder and scrotum, and a difficulty in mictirition. In such cases the scrotum sometimes swells.

The three first forms frequently attack children, and old people; by sleeping during the day, and using improper food and sweetmeats. The stone is easily extracted in the young, as the parts are small. In old people the disease is produced by derangements of air, bile, and phlegm.

Treatment. When stone is threatened, ghée and other like substances are to be used, and will prevent its formation.

Stone is a dangerous disease, being like poison, or thunder. When recent it may be cured by medicines; but when of long standing an operation is required.

In the beginning give different decoctions and preparations of medicines, which dissolve the calculi; as *Pásánbheda, Basuka, Bashera, Ashmantaka, Sotábari; Shwadashtrá, Brihatí, Kantakárí,* &c. These decoctions are most useful when air is particularly diseased.

When bile is deranged, several different decoctions are to be used. The same is observed, when the calculi is produced by deranged phlegm. In all forms of this disease diuretics are to be used. If not cured by the above, an operation is to be performed, which is difficult and dangerous. It is consequently proper that the sanction of the rájá be obtained to its performance.

The operation of *Lithotomy.*—The person should take ghee internally, for several days, with aperients. If very robust he should be reduced in strength. When the operation is to be performed; collect the necessary instruments, offer up prayers, and speak kindly and encouragingly to the patient. He is to sit on a table supported by a person behind, while his legs and arms are raised, and tied by proper bandages. The abdomen is to be well rubbed to make the stone descend. Two fingers of the left hand, well oiled, are to be introduced into the rectum, and the stone felt and brought down. Should the patent faint at this stage of the operation, it should not be proceeded in, as he will in this case die. An incision is then to be made on the left side of the perineum, a barley corn in breadth from the raphe, and carried down to the stone. The incision is to be larger in proportion to the size of the stone, and in other cases it may be made on the right side avoiding always the raphe. If there be more than one stone be careful to remove them all.

Care should be taken not to break the stone, nor to leave any fragments behind, as it will in such a case again form. These small pieces should be removed with a schoop called *Agrabakra*. During the operation the practitioner should carefully avoid the raphe, the seminal canals, the vessels of the spermatic cord, the anus, and the rectum. If the seminal canals, or the spermatic vessels are wounded, the person will become impotent. Wounds of the vagina and raphe, will produce much distressing pain.

In females the bladder is situated near the uterus, and care must therefore be taken not to thrust the knife directly forward, as it will wound the uterus, and the urine will pass through the vagina, forming a fistula.

The wounds of the bladder are always difficult to heal up.

After the stone has been removed, place the patient in a hip bath of warm water, to promote perspiration, and to prevent the accumulation of blood in the bladder. When this collection of blood takes place inject a decoction of *Kshirabriksha* (Ficus Indica) by means of a syringe. To heal the urinary passages; give sherbats, over the wound honey and ghee are to be rubbed; and remedies are to be exhibited to render the urine pure, such as barley with warm ghee twice a day for three days; after this time give sugar, rice, and milk in small quantities for ten days. Then take acid fruits, with the broth smade of the flesh of game animals for ten days, and for ten more days promote perspiration by warm fomentations with oil and ghee. The wound is to be cleaned with the decoction of the *Kshira-briksha* tree, and other astringent medicines are to be mixed and placed in the wound. Oil and turmerick is also used with much benefit. If the wound does not heal up, and the urine does not pass by the natural passages, the actual cautery is to be applied. When the urine passes by the natural passages give sweet decoctions in the form of glysters.

When the calculi produced by semen cannot be dislodged from the urethra by pressure; an incision is to be made over them, and the calculi is to be removed by the assistance of a hook.

After the operation of Lythotomy connexion with women should be avoided for a year, as also riding on horse-back, on elephants, or in carriages; avoid at the same time swimming in water, or eating indigestable articles of food.

Order II.

Diseases of the male Organs of Generation.

Diseases of the Scrotum (*Briddhi*).—There are seven varieties of swelling of the scrotum produced by air, bile, phlegm, blood, fat, urine, and by the descent of the intestine. Any of those deranged humors may produce the swelling of the scrotum, or the testicle. The bowel only causes the swelling of the scrotum. The preceding symptoms are pains in the loins, pelvic region, and penis, followed by the swelling of the scrotum.

Symptoms. When the swelling is produced by deranged *air* the scrotum is extended as a bag of air, the surface is rough, and the peculiar pain produced by air is felt in the scrotum.

When produced by *bile* the swelling is red like the red fig, has a burning sensation and is accompanied with fever. In this form suppuration soon takes place.

When caused by diseased *phlegm,* the swelling is hard, is not painful, the surface is cool, it is itchy, and is not accompanied with fever.

Produced by *blood* the swelling is surrounded with black tubercles, and is accompanied with the symptoms of bile.

Fat produces the disease which is characterized by softness, shining, itchiness, and little pain. It becomes like the fruit of the palm tree ; that is rough and tuberculated.

The form produced by *urine* (yellow serum), collected between the testicle and its external covering, moves like a bag of water.

The last form is hernia which is produced by carrying heavy weights, by fighting with strong persons, falling or jumping, and the like. By such causes air is deranged which propels the intestine downwards, it remains in the groin, and if not treated for some days it descends still lower, and produces a swelling of the scrotum. The tumor is oblong, and when pressed it passes upwards with a peculiar noise, and again descends when the pressure is removed.

Treatment. With the exception of the last form, this disease is to be treated as follows :—

In all these diseases riding on horse-back, sexual connexion, sedentary employment, and indigestable food are to be avoided. When produced by air, give the patient oleaginous food, and anoint his body. The parts are then to be fomented, and then give purgatives, especially castor-oil and milk. This treatment is to be continued for one month. The patient's diet should be broth made of wild animals, rice, and occasional glysters. If the swelling does not decrease by these means, apply poultices, and when it suppurates evacuate the pus, taking care to avoid the raphe of the scrotum. The treatment is then to be the same as that of abscesses in general.

When the disease is caused by *bile,* and if it does not suppurate, it is to be treated, as other swellings produced by bile. If it suppurates evacuate the pus, and apply honey and ghee. After this use such poultices as promote the healing action of the part.

When produced by blood apply leeches, give purgatives with honey and sugar; after which it is to be treated as swellings produced by *bile*.

When the disease is produced by diseased phlegm apply pressure with stimulants mixed with urine. If it suppurates, open it, and use such applications as will clear and heal the abscess.

In swellings when produced by *fat*, foment the part, and apply such poultices as will make the swelling be absorbed, such as *Sarosádi*.

This is to be mixed with urine, and applied hot to the part. Surround the upper part of the scrotum with a bandage, and remove the lower and walled parts, taking care to preserve the testes and the raphe. Then apply a mixture of the sulphate of iron and rock salt to the wound, over which a bandage is to be applied. When the wound is clean apply prepared oil to heal it.

Mútrabriddhi (hydrocele).—Apply the same bandage as above recommended, then at the lower part of the side of the raphe a trocar is to be introduced. Leave the canula in the wound, and when the fluid is discharged, apply a tight bandage round the scrotum.

Antrabriddhi (Hernia) is incurable, unless when it is recent and situated in the groin, when it is to be treated in the same way as when the swelling is produced by air, that is by fomentations and oleaginous purgatives. When by these means the gut has been returned into the abdomen, the groin is to be cauterized (by a half moon cautery) over the part where the tumor was situated. In diseases of the scrotum it is also recommended that the skin of the right or left great toe be divided, according as the swelling is on the right or left side, and the wound is to be cauterized. This superstition is followed from the supposed connexion with the vessels of the scrotum and of the foot, and is intended to prevent the recurrence of the disease. It is still generally followed, and rings are also worn on the great toe, for the same purpose.

Brishanakachchhú, (itchiness of the scrotum *pruzigo*.) This is a common and troublesome disease. Medical authors say that it is produced by not attending to cleanliness, by which the perspiration is accumulated, which irritates and produces an eruption on the part. This sometimes degenerate into sores. The treatment consists in cleaning the part well, and applying simple ointment prepared with wax and bruised mustard seed, and *Satrak* (a small seed like aniseed); these are mixed, strained, and applied to the part.

2nd. Diseases of the Penis. These consist of sores on the genital organs, phymosis and pharymosis, stricture of the urethra, inflammation of the penis, and impotency.

Sores on the genital Organs, (Upadangsha.)*

These diseases are supposed to be produced by mechanical injuries of the part, want of cleanliness, and washing with impure water, after sexual intercourse. It is also produced by impure connexion, excessive venery, and the stimulants sometimes employed to enlarge the penis. There are five different forms of these sores, which are distinguished from each other by their colour, and the nature of the discharge. These are:

1. *Bátika,* characterised by the black colour of the pustules (primary), by the lancinating pain, and white discharge.

2. *Paittika* is distinguished by the reduess of the pustules, by the burning pain, and bloody discharge from the part.

3. *Shleshmika.* In this form the pustules is larger, and are attended with an itching sensation. The discharge is white, and thick.

4. *Sannipátika.* This is a complicated form of the disease, in which the above symptoms appear. It is considered incurable.

5. *A'gantuka, or accidental injuries* of the organs of generation. In this description no secondary symptoms of syphilis are mentioned. The description is confined entirely to the primary sores. The unfavourable symptoms of this .oca disease is confined to the suppuration, sloughing, and destruction of the penis, and to the generation of worms in the sores. In such cases the disease was supposed to be incurable.

It is stated that these sores should be treated by an ignorant person, or should the person continue to have intercourse with women, he will die; from the sloughing of the parts, and the irritative fever which accompanies it.

Another local disease of the genitals is named *Mingubartí* (warts) and consists in excrescences near the vagina, between the scrotum and penis, or corona glandis. They appear crop after crop, and resemble a cock's comb; they are without pain, and are cured with difficulty.—(*Charaka—Sushruta.*)

The treatment of the above local diseases of the genitals is as follows:

For the cure of *Bátika* apply ghee, or some oleaginous matter to the local disease, and give the same internally, to promote perspira-

* From *upa,* near; and *dangsha,* biting.

tion. Open a vein of the penis, or apply leeches to that organ, so as to remove any unhealthy humors that may be there; and for the same purpose administer strong purgatives and emetics. For the former medicine, glysters may be substituted when the patient is weak. The parts are next to be fomented, and then apply to them poultices of flour, mixed with the powder of the castor-oil seed.

Paittika. In this variety apply fomentations of milk and water, sugar and water, or honey and water. The following poultices are then to be applied :—Take of

Gairika, (yellow earth,)
Anjana, (sulphate of antimony,)
Lukarna,
Sáríbá, (Echites frutescens,)
Jashtimadhu, (liquorice,)
Ushíra,
Kusha, (grass,)
Padmaka, (a fragrant wood,)
Sandal-wood and water-lily.

Mix these together with ghee and use it as a poultice.

Shleshmika is produced by a diseased state of the phlegm in the part, and is treated by fomenting with a decoction made of the bark of

Sála, (Sal tree,)
Ashwakarna, (a kind of Sala tree,) and
Dhaba, (Grislea tomemtosa.)

The same barks may be mixed with wine and mustard oil, and used as a poultice.

By thus employing bleeding and other antiphlogistic means, according to the nature of the case; by the use of fomentations and poultices, with the assistance of emetics and purgatives, this disease will be most easily cured. Washing the sores with astringent decoctions, will also be found of much use. Much care is required in the treatment, when accompanied with sloughing or suppuration of the parts. In this case the abscess is to be immediately opened, as soon as it is discovered; and then apply *til*, honey, and *ghee*. A fomentation of the leaves of

Karabíra, (Oleander,)
Játí, (Jasmin,) and
Arakbada, (Cassia fistula,) is then to be applied to the part. Various mixtures of powders are recommended to be applied with honey to these sores of the genitals. The following may be given as an example. Take of

Saurástra mirtiká, (a kind of earth,)
Gaerika,

Tute, (sulphate of copper,)
Pushpaka, (sulphate of zinc,)
Kasísa, (sulphate of iron,)
Saindhaba, (rock-salt.)

These, and other medicines of the same kind, with various astringent powders and decoctions, are used. When the disease is produced by a derangement of the three humors the treatment recommended for foul ulcers is to be followed. If the parts have sloughed, or gangrene has taken place, the dead part is to be separated, the actual cautery applied, and the part is to be dressed with honey and ghee.

History of Syphilis

The history of Syphilis is so peculiar, and various opinions as to its origin has produced so much discussion in Europe, that I shall here add a few remarks on the subject.

From the above account of these diseases of the genital organs, as given in the ancient Sanskrit writings, it appears that there were only five, or rather six, varieties of local sores to which they were liable. These are stated to have been produced by injuries, or other causes of irritation, such as want of cleanliness, &c.; which are quite sufficient to account for the varieties of these sores, and resemble those recorded by the Jews. They are quite different from the peculiar disease known by the name of syphilis, or the venereal disease. The history of this disease in Europe affords the explanation of these peculiarities.

The veneral disease, as it now appears in its characteristic local and general features, seems to have been unknown before the return of Columbus to Spain, after the discovery of America (1494), when the sailors introduced the disease into Spain. Astruc asserts, on the authority of Oviedo, the historian, and of many contemporary physicians, who flourished a short time after that period, that the disease was communicated to the Spaniards by the Indian women of Hispaniola, when Columbus first arrived in that country; and they, in their turn, communicated it to their country-women.

In like manner, Sapelvida, a Spaniard, who flourished towards the middle of the sixteenth century, asserts, "ex-Barbaricarum mulierum consuetudine Hispani morbum contraxerunt." In the course of a year or two afterwards (1495) Ferdinand, king of Spain, sent an army under the command of the great Gonsalva de Cordova to the assistance of the Neapolitans, at that time engaged in a war with the French. The Spaniards infected the Neapolitans, who communicated the disease to the French. As tney had not had the disease before they attributed it to the climate, and called it the "Mal de Naples." The Neapolitans, as much astonished as the French, and treating them as the hostile power, imagined that they had brought it to the country, and called it the French disease.

I regret not having had an opportunity of referring to a late work entitled "*Lettere sulla Storia de mali Venerei, di Dominico Thiene, Venezia,* 1823;" in which Mr. Prescott states "that the author has assembled all the early notices of the disease of any authority, and discussed their import with great integrity and judgment."* This classic historian supposes that this loathsome disease was not brought from America;—but his evidence does not appear to me to be conclusive; particularly when the low state of the medical profession, at the time, is considered, and the mild form in which this disgusting disease may be supposed to have appeared among the abstemious natives of America, in a fine tropical climate. Besides the active and healthy sailors of the expedition were obliged to live on farinacious food and vegetables, which would prevent the disease appearing in a virulent form so as to attract their particular notice; and explains the reason of the silence of Columbus and his son, on the subject of this loathsome disease in their correspondence. Nor can we suppose that the disease would be noticed until it began to commit ravages in its epidemic form. Before this occurred there is no description of this peculiar disease, previous to the discovery of America; nor could it be expected that such writers would trace it to its origin, until more attention was called to the nature of the disease. During such an age we can easily understand how the disease should be rapidly propagated over Europe when introduced into an army of mercinary soldiers, composed of nearly every nation of Europe, who thus conveyed the infection with them on their return to their respective homes; and explains many circumstances related of its progress in different countries. It was from the great intercourse at that time subsisting between the French and Scots that the disease first appeared in Scotland, and it was not until a year afterwards that it appeared in England. Astruc assigns another cause in the licentious manners of the age, for the rapid spreading of the venereal disease, on its first appearance in Europe. So much was this the case that Popes, Cardinals, Bishops, and the lesser dignitaries of the Church, were alike its victims. All ranks, and few ages were exempt from the disease.

* See his History of the reign of Ferdinand and Isabella, vol. iii. p. 50: London, 1838.

Soon after the appearance of the disease in Europe its ravages extended over a considerable part of Asia and Africa, as well as Europe.* This is stated by Fracastorio, who flourished at the close of the fifteenth century, was an eye witness of the extensive progress of the disease; and from his high medical reputation, and residence almost on the spot of its first appearance, and more largely engaged in the cure of it than any physician in his day, had the best opportunities of judging of the nature of the disease. He says, that the disease first appeared in central Europe and extended its ravages from France to Great Britain, where it got the name of the French disease; and still approaching towards the East, it was called, "Armaní danah;" from which country it extended to Persia, where Mír Bahaú Daula Nur Baxsh was said to have been the first who described and treated the disease. From Persia it advanced into Hindustán, where it is still known by its Persian name: Nár Fársí (النارفارسي), Persian pox; or Jumra (الجمرة), blotches; or from its peculiar symptoms A'tshak (آتشك), nocturnal fire; بادفرنگي disease of foreigners, strangers, more especially of Europeans. Soon after (A. H. 950) in the time of Timur Lang, emperor of Persia, Amír Imámdin Muhammad Shirází wrote a short treatise on the venereal disease; in which he declares it to have been of recent origin, and, with the exception of Nur Buxsh is stated to have been the first who wrote correctly on the subject.

The same evidence is afforded by the Hindu writers. We have seen that the early writers gave minute and characteristic descriptions of the usual local diseases of these organs; and what is remarkable, syphilis has not got a Sanskrit name, but is named from the Europeans, who first visited these shores. This was more readily adopted, as the presence of the disease conveyed a feeling of disgust and reproach. It is in the modern Sanskrit compilations, such as *Bhábaprakása*, where the disease is named the "*Faringí Roga*," or Portuguese disease. In this work the disease is characterized by all the symptoms of secondary syphilis, as detailed by European authors; such as cutaneous eruptions, and affections of the bones, particularly those of the nose and palate. In these modern works syphilis is divided into three varieties; one of which is characterized by the appearance of cutaneous eruptions, the second by diseases of the bones; and in the third variety both the skin and bones are affected.†

* Europam ferè omnem Asiæ verò, atque Africæ, partem non parvam occupavit:—see *de contagiosis morbis*.

John of Vigo, in 1514, first described venereal exostosis and caries.

† It is curious that *Bhábaprakása* does not speak of the primary symp-

The disease is attributed to connection with the Portuguese, whether male or female, and it was supposed that it could only be cured by the use of mercury. The same author likewise states that after the mercurial treatment has been completed, *Topchiní*, or China-root, must be administered to complete the cure.

We have thus a disease presenting characteristic appearances, and of peculiar virulence, without a Sanskrit name—not even mentioned by the ancient Hindu medical writers; and still called by the name of the people who first visited these shores from Europe. But as the disease was also introduced into Hindustán from the south-east by the Portuguese, it was called the Portuguese or European (*faringhí*) disease; and likewise from Persia in the north-west, when the disease was named the "Persian pox." It was only after the disease was introduced from the north and south of Hindustán, that an account is recorded of the characteristic disease, by modern compilers, including both the local and constitutional symptoms. Hence it would appear that this disease was introduced from America to Europe and Asia, as the small-pox and measles seem to have first appeared in Asia, from whence they spread, and committed such ravages in Africa, Europe, and America.

The following proofs may be thus adduced of the venereal disease having been brought from America:—

1st. The opinion of ancient authors who have left us minute descriptions of disease, such as *Moses, Charaka, Sushruta, Hippocrates, Celsus*, &c., not having mentioned the venereal disease. Local sores on the genitals, and even the occurrence of buboes, &c. being no proof of the presence of this disease, without its specific secondary symptoms. Any irritating cause applied to the genitals would produce local sores, and if not properly attended to would inflame the inguinal glands; as sores on the feet are often found to produce the same swellings.

2nd. The consternation into which all Europe was thrown by the rapid progress of this fearful disease. Like all new diseases, soon after its introduction into Europe, by the followers of Columbus, it spread in the most alarming manner; or like that leprosy from the east, which at one time filled the Lazar-houses of Europe with its victims. Masses, prayers, and alms, were offered up to avert the anger of offended heaven; as the superstitious notions of the age made people believe that it was a dispensation from God,

---

toms of Syphilis; probably from their not being considered as of consequence, or as having a connection with each other.

to correct the licentious, and wicked manners of the times. The severity of a new disease when it occurs in a country is seen in the visits of the small-pox, to islands, and distant countries; as occurred in the Mauritius in our day, and committed such dreadful ravages at first, and slowly appeared to wear itself out. Such was the case with Syphilis when it first appeared in Europe, compared with the mittigated symptoms of the present times. This is certainly in part owing to our following a better plan of treatment, but still more to this disease being of a less virulent nature than before.

3rd. The progress of the syphilitic disease indicates that it was first brought to Spain, from whence it spread over Europe, Africa, and Asia.

4th. The analogy of other diseases prove that new diseases may so appear, and spread as the small-pox, measles, &c. from Asia; and perhaps the croup and sweating sickness of Britain, &c.

Paribarttiká—Phymosis. This disease is produced by pressure, or external injuries, by which the prepuce is swollen by the diseased air, and covers the glans. When it remains swollen, hard, and very painful, the inflammation sometimes passes to suppuration.

Abapátiká—Pariphymosis. When much force is used during connection with a young girl, or when the prepuce is forced back with force, it remains there, and is followed with much swelling and pain.

Another variety of the above disease is called *Niruddaprakasha*, or stricture, or diminution of the urethra. In some cases this is produced by an adhesion of the prepuce to the glans, impeding the passage of the urine, which in some cases only passes in drops.

In *Phymosis* ghee is to be applied to the part with warm fomentations followed by poultices, which are to be continued for from three to five days. Ghee is again to be applied, and the skin is then to be pulled gently backwards. When in its natural position apply fomentations, administer oleaginous food, with animal broths, and ghee.

The same treatment is to be followed in Pariphymosis, only instead of backwards, pull the prepuce forward.

In *Niruddaprakasha* introduce a metalic, wooden, or gumelastic canula, after the parts have been rubbed with oil. Then the size of the canula is to be increased every third day, so as to increase the size of the passage of the urethra.

Should the prepuce adhere to the glans divide them, and heal the wound in the ordinary way.

Shúkadosha, inflammation of the penis, is a common disease in this country, from the pernicious habit of applying stimulants to enlarge the organ. There are eighteen forms of this disease, *Sarshápiká, Ashthiliká, Grathita, Kumbhiká, Aladí, Mridita, Sammúṛhapiṛaka, Abamantha, Pushkariká, Sparshaháni, Uttamá, Shatápánaka, Twakapáka, Sanitárbuda, Mángsapáka, Bidradhi, Tilakálaka, Mángsárbuda,* &c.

Sarshápiká are small pimples, like mustard seed round the penis, which are produced by the presence of a kind of insect, which is sometimes applied to the part with the intention of increasing the size of the organ.

The other forms of inflammation are produced by the application of other stimulants which cause inflammation of a chronic or acute form. Sometimes abscess and mortification of the part occur so as sometimes to destroy the penis. The other varieties are merely modifications of these inflammations, and their terminations.

Treatment. Astringent decoctions and oils are to be used, after the application of leeches, fomentations, and poultices. When matter forms it is to be evacuated, and the abscess cleaned with tonic decoctions. The ulcers are to be healed by the application of prepared oil.

When sloughing takes place it is to be treated, as when it occurs in other parts. In all these forms of disease the antiphlogistic treatment is to be employed, particularly purgatives, and the local application of astringent, and healing powders.

Order III.

Diseases of the Female Organs of Generation.

There are twenty forms of these diseases, which are produced by using bad food, or taking improper exercise. They are also caused by diseased menses, or semen. In other cases they are produced without any apparent causes.

1. *Udábertá.* When the menses are discharged with great pain, and are frothy.

2. *Bandhyá.* Difficult menstruation, Dismenorrhagæa (*nostartoboh*) where the menses are stopped, by the accumulation of unhealthy humors in the part. When the woman is barren, the disease is called *Bandhyá.*

3. *Bíplutá.* Continued pain in the genital organs.

4. *Paríplutá.* Severe pain during connection.

5. *Bátalá.* In this disease the vagina is contracted and rough, accompanied with pain. In these five diseases *air* is locally deranged,

the parts are hard and swollen, with the various seven varieties of pain produced by diseased air.

6. When the menses are discharged very hot, the disease is named *Sanítakara*. When there is an unusual discharge of a red colour from the vagina, accompanied with pain, and followed by lassitude, &c., the disease is named *Prodoroh* or *Menorrhagia*. This disease is produced by bad food, diet, or milk, or any improper mixture of food, sleeping during the day, by the use of ardent spirits, or hot food, or eating frequently without being hungry; by abortion, or frequent venery, by severe exercise particularly riding and walking, by grief, by carrying heavy weights, and by external injuries. These causes produce the disease which is accompanied with fever, and pain over the body; and after a time the patient becomes weak, is affected with giddiness, fainting, thirst, great heat, delirium, jaundice, and drowsiness. It is also accompanied with the general symptoms of diseased phlegm, air, and bile separately, or combined.

When *phlegm* is particularly deranged in this disease; the discharge is whitish, mucilaginous, and has the smell of the water in which flesh had been steeped, or of the colour of water in which straw has been immersed.

When *bile* is particularly deranged, the discharge is sudden, and is of a yellow or reddish, blue or black colour. It is hot, and the other symptoms of diseases of bile appear.

When *air* is particularly affected the discharge is of a red colour, like the washings of flesh, is frothy, is in smaller quantities than the last variety, and is accompanied with more pain.

When the three humors are deranged producing this disease, the discharge is of the colour of honey mixed with ghee, or of a yellow colour like marrow, and has a fœtid smell. In this form a cure is not to be expected, and the practioner should refuse to attend such a patient.

The unfavourable symptoms of this disease are when it has continued long, is accompanied with a copious discharge, with fever, great thirst, and heat followed by great debility. When the menses occur every month, without pain or burning, are of the natural colour, and neither too copious, nor too scanty, it is advantageous to health. When the discharge is red, like the colour of the blood of a hare, or like a decoction of lac, and does not permanently discolour cloth when it falls upon it, it is healthy.

7. *Bámíní*. When seamen is discharged with the menses.

8. *Srangsiní*. When the blood is discharged, and the parts are diseased, so that it prevents easy delivery.

9. *Patraganí.* When the infant has died, or abortion has taken place with a great discharge of blood. In all these cases bile is much diseased, and is accompanied with fever.

10. *Pittalá.* When bile is deranged, there is much heat of the part, which suppurates and is accompanied with fever. These five last diseases are the symptoms of bile.

The following are the diseases produced by deranged phlegm.

11. *Atyánandá.* When the woman has no pleasure in the embraces of her husband.

12. *Karníní.* When phlegm and blood are deranged in the vagina, small granulations form, like the grains of rice from deranged phlegm and blood.

13. *Churuná.* When the semen of the male is more copious than that of the female.

14. *Charaná.* When the male semen does not enter the uterus.

15. *Shleshmalá.* It is produced by diseased phlegm with itchiness and coldness, and the part appears as if covered with oil.

16. *Sandí.* In this variety the menses are not discharged, the breasts do not swell, and the parts are hard, and rough like a file.

17. *Palaní.* When a large man has connection with a small, and young female he injures the parts, and produces this disease.

18. *Mahatí.* When the vagina is very large.

19. *Suchíbuktra.* When the entrance is very small.

20. *Sarbalingasamutpanná.* Different varieties of pain, &c. produced by the derangement of the three humors in the part.

The five last forms of these diseases are cured with difficulty.

The *treatment* of these diseases will vary according to the humor diseased.

When the *air* is diseased apply warm fomentations such as steam baths, &c., and poultices, use also injections of oleaginous and other medicines heated, which cure diseased air. A piece of cloth soaked in oil is to be kept in the vagina.

When *bile* is deranged with much bearing down and inflammation, use cold lotions. If there is a bad smell, use the decoctions of astringent barks.

When *phlegm* is deranged take the juice of garlic every morning, with food made of rice and milk, and apply different tinctures to the part, as recommended under the head of midwifery.

In dismenorrhagæa the patient should live on nourishing food, fish, *máskalái*, sesamum seeds (*til*), curdled milk, and drink cow's urine, whey, and wine. The pubis should be well rubbed with oil and ghee, and the vagina is to be kept distended by the introduction of a roller of cloth.

The treatment of menorrhagia should resemble that of hemorrhagia, such as the application of cold and astringent medicines, avoiding venery, and living on cooling and simple food.

Kanda, (Utero Vaginal Tumors.)

These diseases are produced by the person sleeping during the day, by an angry disposition, by great fatigue, and by too much venery. They may also arise from mechanical injuries of the part. These tumors are like the fruit of the *Lakucha* tree, (a kind of Bread fruit tree, *Artocarpus lacucha*, or *Madar*.)

When *air* produces the disease the tumor is dry, and is of a dirty or yellowish colour, and has furrows on its surface.

When diseased *bile* produces the tumor it is very hot and red, and is accompanied with fever.

When *phlegm* produces the tumor it is like the colour of the Indigo flower and is very itchy.

When air, bile, and phlegm are diseased, all the separate symptoms are present. When three are so diseased in one part, it is incurable, and when produced by spirit or by phlegm, &c. it is cured with difficulty.

Treatment. For the treatment of these tumors use the flesh of shell-fish, and the pulp of tamarinds, rub them together, and apply the mixture to the tumor. A paste made with the flowers of *Gossa*, are to be applied to the part, and will be found of great use.

Dhajabhanga or *Claiba, (Impotence.)*

There are six kinds of Impotency, 1st, It may be produced by dejection of the mind, or connection with distasteful women.

2nd. By eating too dry and pungent food, as black-pepper, capsicum, &c. or too much acid, salt, or stimulating food. By such causes the secretion of semen is diminished.

3rd. Excessive venery, and eating little food.

4th. Old diseases of the organs of generation, or of injuries or diseases of the vital parts.

5th. The congenital variety; and the

6th. Variety is caused by avoiding sexual indulgences.

The fourth and fifth kinds are incurable. The other four kinds may be treated. For this purpose different kinds of nourishing food and drink are to be used : the patient is to live in a good house, indulge in good beds, in music, in the society of beautiful women, in wines, and in perfumes, as all these tend to remove sterility. The medicines to be used are as follows: Take of the powder of *Bídárí* or of *Anuloka* mixed with honey and ghee; and eat the testicles of goats roasted and prepared with salt, ghee, and long, pepper. The preparations of *máskalái* and sugar, barley, wheat are also of use. The eggs of crabs and of crocodiles, or of turtles properly prepared will be of great use. Flour prepared with ghee, and milk, and rubbed on the feet with oil, prepared with crocodile's eggs ; the flesh of rats, frogs, and the eggs of sparrows are recommended. The patient is to drink fresh milk with sugar, honey, and powder of *Swayanguptá* and *Ekuruka.*

Class VIII.

Diseases of the Rectum and Anus.

These consist of piles, stricture of the rectum, prolapsus ani, ulcers near the anus, and fistula-in-ano.

Order I.

Arsa, (Piles.)

There are six varieties of this disease according as it is produced from deranged air, bile, phlegm, the three humors deranged at the same time, diseased blood, and the last form is congenital or hereditary.

That part of the rectum called *guda* is five and a half fingers breadth in length, and like the spiral cavities in the sacred shell, used in the Hindu temples, has three spiral turns called *Prabáhiní,* which accelerates or assists in expelling its contents. The second is called *Bisarjiní,* or that which expells ; and *Sambariní,* or sphincter. Piles are usually situated in these parts, the causes producing them are as follows : The improper mixtures of food, excessive venery, the unnatural position of the body when long indulged in ; horse riding, and the want of attention to the calls of nature. By these causes the humors are deranged in the anus and produce tubercles, or piles.

When *air* is deranged it affords the following signs ; round the anus small tumors form, which are dry, slightly painful, red, and irregular like the *kadamba* fruit. The disease is accompanied with constipation, pain in the back, loins, penis, anus, and umbiliacus ; and is occasionally accompanied with pain in the breast, want of appetite, cough, and noise in breathing ; sometimes the appetite is good, at other times it is much impaired. The blood is often evacuated by a small orifice from time to time. The skin, eyes, face, mouth, teeth, and nails appear dirty and yellow with unhealthy yellowish dejections, and urine. Symptoms likewise appear like *Gulma* or spleen, or it even produces these diseases. In other cases the piles produce *Astila*, a kind of hysterical ball.

When bile is deranged the swelling has an erysipelatous appearance; at other times it has a blue, yellow, red, or black colour, with orifices in its surface, like the mouths of leeches. The blood evacuated is very thin, and there is a considerable discharge, with pain in the part, accompanied with fever, thirst, and fainting.

When phlegm is deranged the tumors are pendulous, near each other, hard, round, shining, and of a white colour, like the paps of the cow. There is no discharge, they are cold, itchy, heavy, remain stationary, and the stools are mixed with mucus, and appear like water in which flesh had been washed. In some cases the disease is accompanied with swelling of the extremities, with feverishness, loss of appetite, heaviness and pain of the head; and the skin, nails, eyes, face, urine, and fæces becomes white. In these diseases there is a great discharge of urine, the person often becomes impotent, and digestion is impaired, with vomiting. Those diseases which impair digestion, produce this disease. When the three humors are diseased, the symptoms of the three separate diseases are present.

When blood produces the disease, the pain is like that of a needle thrust into the skin, and symptoms appear like those of deranged bile. The tumors resemble the hanging roots of the banian tree, or the *kunch* seeds, small red seeds with black spots, or they are like coral. When costiveness occurs it is accompanied with a free and rapid discharge of blood, which is hot, and produces the usual effects of a great and sudden loss of blood; the person with this disease remains yellow, like the yellow frog; weak, silent, and sad; his skin is dirty, and all his senses perform their office imperfectly or they are depraved. The dejections are gray, like smoke, dry and hard, and in others they are thin, yellow, and frothy.

The last form of this disease is produced by hereditary disposition, from the taint being mixed in the semen and female blood. The tumors in this form become rough, of a white unnatural colour, with internal openings. The patient cannot eat much, his body has large veins over the surface, and his voice is low. He is impatient, is easily roused, has little appetite, is afflicted with diseases of the eyes, ears, nose, and head, and is always complaining of diseases of the stomach and intestines.

When piles are external they are easily cured, but when situated internally they are cured with difficulty, or are incurable. Tumors like those of piles sometimes form in the cavities of the ear, nose, mouth, vagina, and upon the penis.

When affecting the internal ear, they produce deafness, pain, and a fetid discharge from the organ. In the eyes they cover the eye-lids; and sometimes destroy the sight of the organ. When in the mouth, they are attached to the throat, lips, and palate, they impair the voice and taste, and produce other diseases of the mouth. When in the nostrils they produce difficult breathing, a fetid smell, a change of voice, pain in the head, and a considerable discharge from the nose.

The deranged humors produce the disease on the surface of the body when they form tumors of different sizes, which are called *Charmkíla*. When the air is deranged the disease is accompanied with throbbing; when phlegm, the color of the tumor is the colour of the skin and hard. When bile and blood are deranged, producing the disease, the tumors become black and rough. Those piles which form externally are curable, as also those in the first and second convolutions of the rectum, but in the third the disease is incurable, and also after they have existed for upwards of a year.

Treatment. There are four indications for the cure of piles. The first is by medicine, the second by the application of caustics, the third by the application of the actual cautery, and the fourth by the knife. When the disease is recent, and it is not accompanied with any bad symptoms, they may be cured by medicine. When soft and elevated with a thick base, they are to be cured by the use of caustic. When hard, rough, and large, by the actual cautery; and when the base is narrow and they are elevated and moist, they are to be removed by the knife.

The caustics are to be applied in the following manner: the patient is first to take some oleaginous and bland diet, such as rice and milk; the parts are then to be well fomented, and on a cool day, when there are no clouds in the sky, the patient is to be placed upon a table with a good light thrown upon the part. He is to be supported by two assistants holding his head and shoulders; and his loins are to be elevated with a soft cushion. The knees and legs are to be raised, and separated by a bandage passing round the knees, feet, and neck. The body is thus firmly fixed, and a little ghee rubbed upon the part. The patient is next to press downwards, so as to press out the anus. The piles are then to be dried with a piece of cloth, and the caustic fluid applied over the part by a broad pointed probe. The caustic is allowed to remain as long as is required to pronounce one hundred words, when it is to be rubbed off, and it is only when necessary that it is to be again applied.

When the piles become black, and are diminished in size by the caustic, the necessary effect has been produced. The part is then to be washed with a spirituous cooling application, whey, or water mixed with the juice of acid fruits. Dry the part, and then apply ghee mixed with the decoction of liquorice. A warm bath is then to be given, and pour tepid water over the body. He is then to be left in a room shut up, and is to live on a spare diet. When any other piles appear or when there are many, the application of the caustic is to be made every seventh day until the cure is completed. The applications are first to be made to the piles of the right side, then the left, and after that the part behind and before.

If the caustic is too freely applied the anus is destroyed, with burning fever, fainting, and discharge of blood.

When the piles are large and the person strong, they are to be removed with the knife, and the actual cautery applied. The diet is the same as after the application of cauteries. When the piles are not visible internal remedies must be used, such as myrobalan with jagry every morning. A hundred seeds of the *Myrobalan* are to be boiled in the hot urine of cows. Take them out after they have been boiled for some time, dry them, and then reduce them to powder. Such doses are to be taken as will operate on the bowels. The farina of the *Satabim* root is to be taken daily with milk. Tonic and bitter tinctures may also be used with advantage.

When the piles are painful use fomentations and poultices, with purgatives, emetics, and clysters. He should also avoid stopping the calls of nature; should avoid connexion with women, horse riding, &c.

2.—*Saníraguda, (Stricture of the Rectum.)*

This disease is produced by habitual costiveness, by which the air of the part is diseased, which diminishes the size of the rectum. The fæces are then evacuated with difficulty, and in small quantities. It is very difficult to cure.

Treatment. Apply oleaginous substances to the part, such as hog's lard and oil, prepared with a decoction of those medicines which cure air. Every third day introduce a rectum bougie,* covered with ghee, which is to be increased in size from time to time.

The food is to be of an oleaginous nature.

3.—*Gudabhrangsa, (Prolapsus Ani.)*

The rectum is prolapsed during the evacuation of the fæces in weak persons; particularly when affected with long continued diarrhœa, or much straining.

* This may be made of lac, wax, wood, or metal.

The treatment to be pursued is to foment the part, apply oleaginous substances to the prolapsed gut, and return it slowly. Then a bandage is to be applied, on which a convex piece of hard leather is to be placed over the anus, and retained there by means of a bandage tied round the loins and between the legs.. Fomentations are to be occasionally exhibited, and the body of a rat from which the intestines have been removed, is to be made warm and applied to the part effected. Milk and a decoction of *Mahá Pankamúla* are to be given. The decoction is to be strained, and exhibited internally and externally.

4.—*Ahiputana*, (*Superficial Ulcer round the Anus.*)

Eruptions sometimes form round the anus, from want of cleanliness. They become itchy, are scratched, and ulcerate, producing this disease. They often occur in children.

These ulcers are to be treated by exhibiting purgatives, and other medicines, to purify the milk of the mother. Then give a decoction of tonic medicines to the child consisting of *Patalapatra*, the three kinds of myrobalan, with prepared ghee. These are to be given internally. Locally, astringent decoctions are to be applied, and the sulphate of zinc *(Kapalatuta)* is to be sprinkled over the ulcers

5. *Bhagandara*, (*Fistula-in-Ano.*)

This disease is called *Bhagandara*, because the anus, vagina, bladder, and its surrounding parts, are affected.

It is produced by deranged air, bile, and phlegm, by their combinations, and by external injuries : thus five varieties of this disease are produced.

The symptoms of this disease are ushered in by pain in the loins, of an itching nature, and by a swelling near the anus.

1. *Satapanaka.* This variety is produced by deranged *air*, from living on bad food, when accompanied by a bad temper. The swelling usually takes place a finger breadth from the anus,—by the air deranging the flesh, and producing swelling and pain of different kinds. When not properly treated the swelling suppurates, and is perforated by many holes, through which a copious discharge of matter with air takes place. Sometimes the pain is as if the part was torn, or needles were thrust into it. Towards the termination air, urine, fæces, and semen is discharged from the opening.

2. *Utragraba* is produced by deranged *bile*, which affects the part, and produces a large red swelling resembling the shape of the neck of a camel. It produces a burning and painful sensation, like those produced by deranged bile. When neglected it suppurates,

and terminates in ulcers. The parts feel burning, as if it was burnt with fire or caustics, and it discharges a fœtid and hot fluid. If neglected in this state the air, urine, fæces, and semen are discharged.

3. *Parisrábí* is produced by diseased *phlegm*. It is characterized by a white, hard, and itchy swelling near the anus, with the peculiar pain characteristic of diseased phlegm. If not properly treated it suppurates, and passes to ulceration. This is hard, itchy, and discharges freely a mucilaginous matter, followed by a discharge of air, urine, fæces, and semen.

4. *Sambúkábarta* is produced by the combination of these three humors. It appears first in the form of a swelling, like the great toe, and is accompanied with different kinds of pains. It ulcerates, as in the other kinds, and discharges different coloured fluids.

5. *Unmárga* or the accidental form of fistula-in-ano. When an ignorant person eats the bones with fish, or animal flesh, they are carried to the rectum with the hard fæces, and should they be in a transverse direction in the gut, the bones injure the parts, and produce inflammation, and ulceration. Matter is then discharged mixed with blood. When this variety is not properly cleaned, worms form in it, and various openings are formed, and the air, fæces, urine, and semen are discharged from these openings. Sometimes an eruption forms round the anus which is not fistulous. The pain is slight in this disease, and is spontaneously cured. In fistula-in-ano there is much pain accompanied with fever, and the patient feels much inconvenience in walking, or riding, and at the time of the evacuations. He complains likewise of pains in the loins.

All the forms of fistula-in-ano are cured with difficulty, more particularly when produced by a derangement of the three humors, and by accidents, as by the gut being transfixed by bones, or the like.

Treatment. When there is only a swelling, use antiphlogistic regimen, as scanty diet, purgatives, and fomentations to the part. Cold applications, and poultices to the part are of use in some cases. Give these decoctions to diminish the swelling ; and if they are not sufficient to remove the disease, apply such medicines as promote suppuration. The swelling is then to be opened, and treated as in other swellings of the same kind. Emetics and purgatives will also be administered with advantage in this disease.

When the fistula is open, and there is an external and internal apperture, place the patient on a bed, introduce a director, and divide the flesh between the fistula and anus ; then apply caustic or the actual cautery to the wound. When several fistulæ exist, perform the operation for one, and then for another. When they communicate with each other open them all, if external, so that they be all formed into one wound. But when they do not communicate with each other, the opening is to be made separately into the gut. After the operation the actual cautery is to be applied, by means of a red hot probe.

The form called *Satapanaka* is incurable in a weak and fearful person. When the person will not submit to an operation apply fomentations and poultices, and give him tonic medicines, and apply ghee, and oil to the part. By these means the fistulous opening may be healed up.

In *Utragraba* use a similar plan of treatment as in the last case, but the actual cautery is not required. Caustic in this case is sufficient; after which apply a poultice and bandage to the part. On the third day clean the part, and apply healing medicines.

In *Parisrába* the part is to be divided as in the other forms, and apply the actual or potential cautery to the part. After which warm oil is to be applied to the part, with fomentations and poultices; aperient medicines are likewise to be given.

When a fistula-in-ano either of the internal or external kind, occurs in children, neither caustic, cautery, nor the knife, are to be employed. In this case a small bougie is to be introduced. It is composed of *Arakboda,* turmerick, and *Kula,* mixed with ghee and honey. This is to be introduced into the fistulous opening, which will by this means heal up.

In the last or accidental form of fistula, first remove the bone, and the fistulous opening being enlarged in the usual way, the actual cautery is to be applied to its surface, and the means for removing worms are to be resorted to in this disease.

The after treatment of the wounds and ulcers should resemble those recommended under the head of surgery.

For one year after the cure the patient should avoid any great excitement, as horse exercise, fatigue, connection with women, anger, and heavy indigestable food, which might produce a relapse.

Class IX.

Diseases of the Extremities.

The diseases of the upper extremities are few, and of little importance, compared to those of the lower extremities; to which the following remarks are principally confined. These diseases are *Urustambha* and *Slipada,* or swellings of the extremities, diseases of the nails, of the soles of the feet, and ulcers of the axilla, and groin.

The other diseases of the extremities have been already considered under those of *Bátabadí*.

U'rustambha (large abscess). These are produced under the fascia of the thigh by cold, hot, or very liquid or dry food, heavy oleaginous or indigestable food, or other articles of the like kind, fatigue, grief, agitation, sleeping during the day, and watching at night. By these means the air, phlegm, and fat are deranged and mixed with bile, which accumulates in the thighs, and in the external parts of the thigh-bone. The thigh then becomes senseless like a dead part, and is very painful.

This disease produces lowness of spirits, pain over the body, drowsiness, and chilliness, cold, vomiting, loss of appetite and fever. The thigh cannot be moved, and it is raised with difficulty, and as if asleep. Other practitioners call the disease *Adabáta*.

Before the accumulation of humors in the thigh, the person feels sleepy, is in low spirits, the body cold, with fever, loss of appetite and vomiting. Both legs and thighs are heavy and weak. When the pain is supposed to be rheumatic, and the part is rubbed with oleaginous medicines, the disease increases, affects the feet and prevents the person walking; and is accompanied with much pain, swelling, and inflammation, followed by insensibility, and the leg feels as if it was broken. When there is much lancinating pain, inflammation, and shivering, the patient will die. When these symptoms are absent, or the disease is recent, the patient may be cured by the practitioner, as the disease under this circumstance is not always fatal.

Treatment. Give such medicines as decrease phlegm, but which do not increase bile. Avoid oleaginous applications, give emetics and purgatives, and apply hot applications to the part. Mustard and Coringo seeds, honey, and the earth of the white-ant's nests are to be mixed together, and applied to the part. Give at the same time *Silagita, Guguli*, long-pepper, and ginger. These are to be mixed with the urine of the cow. This form may be varied with the following. Take of castor-oil and *Guguli*, mix, and take internally: or a decoction of *Dasamula* with cow's urine, which may also be used.

Shlipada, (Elephantiasis.)

The short and indistinct account of this disease in the ancient Hindu writers, seems to be intended as merely to suit the writer's own peculiar theory. Elephantiasis is so common in Bengal and is so peculiar that we should have expected something more than a short account of the leading symptoms. In the *Mádhab Nidán* it is merely stated that the patient's groin first swells, and become very painful, with fever. The swelling then slowly descends to the foot, producing this disease. In other MSS. it is stated that the same disease may occur in the hands, ears, eye-lids, nose, lips, and penis. When it occurs in the groin, and descends to the leg and foot, or when situated in the hand it is produced by bad flesh and fat; and the parts affected become hard and rough.

When air produces this disease the swelling is of a black colour, rough, dry, with cracks and small sores. This form is very painful,—and occurs suddenly, with much fever.

When produced by diseased bile it is of a yellowish colour, hot, soft, and accompanied with fever.

When produced by diseased phlegm, the skin is shining, of a white or grey colour, the part is very heavy, hard, fixed to one place, and has the appearance of a large white-ant's hill, of an irregular sharp-pointed appearance. This form is difficult to cure after it has been present a year, when very large, when it discharges continually, is itchy, and when all the above symptoms are present, as this indicates that air, bile, and phlegm are diseased.

Elephantiasis is most frequent in those countries where there is much stagnant water, and in cold damp situations, such as Rungpore, Furridpore, &c.

In the above description the marked accessions and remissions are not mentioned, but it is stated that the damp and cold situations produce this disease, that it attacks different parts of the body, and that it is incurable, after it has remained upwards of a year, or is very large. It is also observed that it is incurable, when the skin is much affected, as indicated by the continual discharge, the itchy or painful nature of the swelling, and its discolouration.

Treatment. When *air* is deranged in the part oleaginous substances are to be applied to the part to promote perspiration. Four fingers breadth above the ankle joint a vein is to be opened, and some blood is to be removed from the part. If the person be strong, give purgatives and enemas, which promote urine. Give castor-oil in cow's urine for a month, then take rice and milk, with the infusion of dry-ginger. The actual cautery may also be applied round the leg near its middle.

When *bile* produces the disease open a vein below the ankle joint, and use antiphlogistic and other medicines to cure diseased bile. The treatment followed in erysipelas should also be used.

In *phlegm* open a vein of the great toe, give astringent decoctions with honey, such as myrobalan with cow's urine; and rub the swelled part with a mixture of

Kotako, (Michelia Chumpaca,)
Amirta, (Menispermum glabrum,)
Biranga, (Verbesina prostrata,)
Chitraka, (Plumbago zeylanica,)
Sunti, (dry ginger,)
Dári, (Laurus cinnamomum,)

mixed with the urine of a cow.

Give mustard oil internally, and use the juice of the clear *Patikaringo*. Impure potassa obtained from the ashes of the following drugs is likewise recommended; such as

Kákúdani, (Ficus oppositifolia,)
Kákigungá, (Leea hirta,)
Birhutti, (egg-plant,)
Kantikáriká, (Ruellea longifolia,)
Kadamba-puspa, (a plant like *Kadamba*,)
Mundaru, (Asclepius gigantea,)
Lamba, (a bitter gourd,)
Sokonosá, (Cucumis sativus.)

This when taken internally cures elephantiasis and scrofulous tumors, and improves the appetite.

Fasting is to be enjoined for the cure of elephantiasis, and medicines are to be rubbed over the part; as *Dhaturá* root, castor oil plant root, *Inchur* root, *Sajiná* bark, and mustard seed. Mix them with water, or *Sajiná* juice, and rub them over the part; which will cure even old cases. It thus appears that perspiration, the local discharge of blood, and purges, are the remedies recommended for this disease.

Slight diseases of the Extremities.

Painful swellings in the axilla are produced by bile, and phlegm. Deep seated swellings, which produce much heat, inflammation, and fever, like fire, kill after seven or twelve days, or after a fortnight. They are called *Agnirohíní*.

When the nails are affected with inflammation round the edges it is called *Chipya*. It is produced by derangements of the bile, air, injuries, &c. The part which is connected to the flesh, especially at its angles swell, become very painful, and then ulcerate, particularly at its angles, when it is called *Upanaka*. When the nails become dry, rough, and discoloured, the disease is called *Kunakh* or *Kulina*.

When the sole of the foot is injured by some external cause, as by thorns, or the like, it produces much pain, and is called *Darí*. When the swelling is hard, indolent, and like the seed of plumbs, accompanied with much pain, and a considerable discharge, it is called *Kadara.* When the space between the toes ulcerate *(Rhagas)* the disease is called *Alasa.* The other diseases of the leg are described under *Búdobadí.*

Sometimes ulcers form near the axilla or groin, which become hard, red, and sinuous; in such cases the deep seated parts are so affected that when opened they discharge frothy matter like a mixture of honey and ghee. The part then becomes dry, irregular, and discharges fœtid matter of different colours with blood. Sometimes the hemorrhage is sudden and great. This disease is called *Sharkarárbuda, (Sarkara,* a piece of earthen pot, and *Arbuda,* tumor.) This is probably an aneurismal tumor.

CLASS X.

Poisons and their Antidotes, (Panata.)

The origin of poisons is explained in the following manner. Soon after the creation of the world, *Bramha* was displeased at the violence of *Kaitaba,* one of the demons *(Asura),* and in his anger poison was generated and destroyed *Kaitaba.* The poison increased so much that the *debtás* were afraid that it would destroy the whole animated creation. They prayed to *Bramha* to relieve them, and petitioned that he would distribute the poison over the animal, vegetable, and mineral kingdoms. This was done; and when the poison is introduced into the living body it is not digested, and produces languor,* and deranges all the humors of the body.

It is necessary for the practitioner to have a knowledge of the symptoms of the different poisons, and their antidotes. As the enemies of the Rájá, bad women, and ungrateful servants sometimes mix poison with food. On this account the cook should be of a good family, virtuous, faithful, and not covetous, not subjèct to anger, pride, or laziness. He should also be cleanly, and skilful in his business. The practitioner should have like qualities with an intimate knowledge of poisons; and should examine the food to be eaten by a Rájá in the cooking-room. This should be large, airy, light, and surrounded with faithful servants, and no one should be allowed to enter unless he is first examined. In the *Mitákshara* shástra there are copious directions regarding the manner of detecting a person who gives poison: He does not answer questions, or they are evasive answers; he speaks nonsense, rubs the great toe along the ground, and shivers; his face is discoloured; he rubs the roots of the hair with his fingers; and he tries by every means to leave the house. The food

* Hence the name *Bisak.*

which is suspected should be first given to certain animals, and if they die, it is to be avoided. The authority the bráhmans assumed, and the confidence they inspired, has no doubt often had the best effect, in making the wicked shrink from perpetrating deeds, which would be detected and exposed by them.

The long account which is given of these poisons, and the means of preventing their bad effects seems to prove the frequency with which they were employed with bad intentions, at a very early period.

All poisons have the following qualities: they are drying, heating, and stimulating; their effects quickly extend over all the body; they destroy very quickly, are not digested, and from the rapidity with which they produce bad symptoms it is difficult to use remedies with sufficient quickness. The following stages of the effects of poisons are observed. 1st. The tongue becomes black and rigid, the person faints, and breathes with difficulty.

2nd. Shivering, perspiration, heat, and pain in the stomach, and chest.

3rd. Severe pain in the stomach, the eye changes its colour, becomes yellow and swells, and when the poison has extended to the intestines pain of the part, hiccough, coughing, and a peculiar noise is heard in the intestines.

4th. Heaviness of the head.

5th. Discharge of saliva from the mouth; change of colour of the skin, and pain in the joints and belly.

6th. Insensibility and purging.

7th. Rigidity and death.

Vegetable poisons (*Dushibisha*) when dried by the fire, by the air, or by the sun, may be given in solution, or in any other way in which their effects are less powerful. In this case the poison does not produce immediate death, but remains in the system for a long time; and the first effect is looseness, fœtid smell of the mouth, great thirst, fainting, vomiting, and paralysis of the tongue. These are followed when taken into the stomach by diseases of phlegm and air, and in the intestines, by diseases of the bile and air. The person's hair falls off, and he becomes like a bird without feathers. When mixed with the humors of the body as chyle, blood, &c., the poison produces diseases of the humors, as leprosy, and various other kinds of symptoms, as languor, weakness of the joints, and pain over the body; swelling of the legs and face, dropsy, and in other cases vomiting and diarrhœa, intermittent fever, discoloration of the body, madness, impotency, and other like diseases. All these symptoms are aggravated in cloudy and damp weather.

Such effects may be removed by proper treatment, and a year after the person has taken the poison he will either be cured, or get worse. When weak, and the patient does not observe his diet, the poison will destroy him.

Poisons are usually arranged into two classes, the first consisting of vegetable and mineral poisons, are named *Stábarah;* and the second animal poisons, *Jangamah.* They are not used internally, as medicines.

I. *Vegetable, and Mineral Poisons.*

The general symptoms produced by vegetable poisons are fever, hiccough, grinding of the teeth, suffocation, foaming at the mouth, vomiting, want of appetite, difficulty of breathing and fainting.

The *Mineral poisons* produce drowsiness, languor, burning of the body, indigestion, horripilation, swelling, and dysentery. The dejections of a person who has taken poison are of a black colour, large, and are discharged with wind.

Vegetable poisons are divided into nine varieties, which are derived from the roots, leaves, fruits, flowers, bark, milky juice, gum, and pith of plants.

1.—The *Roots* of the following plants are poisonous :—and when eaten they produce pain over the body, delerium, and stupidity.

Klitaka, (Olibanum,)
Asamása, (Andropogon muricatum,)
Gunja, (Abrus precatorius,)
Sugandá, (Alpinia galanga,)
Gargaraká, (Cissus glauca,)
Karagáta,
Bidyuchchikhá,
Bijayá, (Cyperus difformis.)

2.—The *Leaves* of the following vegetables produce gaping, shivering, and difficulty in breathing.

Bisaputriká, (Vangueria,)
Alumbá, (Arum campanulatum,)
Abadáruka, (Sideroxylon spinosum,)
Karamba, (Dalbergia arborea,)
Mahá Karamba, (Antirrhinum cymbalaria,)

3.—The following poisonous *Fruits* cause a loss of appetite, heat of the body, and a swelling of the testicles.

Kamudatí, (Nelumbium speciosum,)
Bínáká,
Karamba, (Dalbergia arborea,)
Mahá Karamba, (Antirrhinum cymbalaria,)
Karakataka, (Cleome viscosa,)

Ranaka,
Kadataka,
Charmara, (Viola suffruticosa,)
Ebajandá,
Sarpagata, (Hibiscus populneus,)
Nandana, (Cedrela Tuna,)
Sarapáka, (Nelumbium speciosum.)

4.—The following poisonous *Flowers* when eaten produce vomiting, swelling of the abdomen, and difficulty in breathing.

Betra, (Chenopodium album,)
Kadamba, (Sinapis dichotoma,)
Ballija, (Ocymum,)
Karamba, (Dalbergia arborea,)
Mahá Karamba, (Antirrhinum cymbalaria.)

5, 6, 7.—The following poisonous *Bark, Pith,* and *Gums,* produce a bad smell in the mouth, a roughness of the body, head-ache, and a discharge of saliva from the mouth.

Antra Pásaka, (Æschynomene grandiflora,)
Kutanía, (Solanum Jacquini,)
Sauríaka, (Tetranthera quadrifolia,)
Karagáta,
Karamba, (Dalbergia arborea,)
Nandana, (Cedrela Tuna,)
Baerátaka, (Solanum melongena.)

8.—The following poisonous *Milky Juices* produce foaming from the mouth, looseness, and a swelling, and heaviness of the tongue.

Kamadugna, (Carpopogon neveum,)
Stnahu, (Euphorbia antiquorum,)
Jálakírjah,

9.—The poisonous *Bulbous roots* are:

Kálakuta, (Arum colocasia,)
Batsanábha, (Sida cordifolia,)
Sarshapa, (Panicum colonum,)
Kapálaka, (Cucumis utilatissimus,)
Kardamaka,
Baerátaka, (Solamum melongena,)
Mustaka, (Pistacea lentiscus,)
Sringíbísa, (Betala,)
Prapanduríka, (a small herbaceous plant,)
Múlaka, (tamarind,)
Halahala, (Valisneria octandra,)
Mahábisha, (a speices of lily,)
Karkataka, (Cleome viscosa.)

The *Mineral poisons* are,

Phenáshmabhasma, (white oxide of arsenic,)
Harítála, (yellow sulphurate of arsenic : *Sushruta.)*

Other authors have added the following poisons :

Tuta, (sulphurate of copper.)
Tezpatra,
Deámaká, (white oxide of arsenic.)

There are others of the same kind.

These poisons when administered to a person, produce pain in the chest and body, fainting, shivering, followed by a burning and swelling of the body, but particularly of the throat. These symptoms are succeeded by diarrhœa, languor, coma, and insensibility. When these symptoms are present, the disease will be fatal.

Antidotes for Vegetable and Mineral Poisons.

In the first stage of the effects of these poisons, give cold water to drink, with an emetic. In the second stage, give an emetic with a preparation called *Agada*. This medicine is prepared with ghee, and the following vegetable decoctions :—

Madaka, (Bassia latifolia,)
Tajara, (Amaranthus,)
Kusta, (Costus speciosus,)
Badradára, (Phrynium dichotomum,)
Haranu, (Trophis aspera.)
Pannája,
Allá,
Albáluk,
Nágapuspa, (Bauhinia anguina,)
Utpala, (Nymphœa cærulea,)
Sítiá, (Lycopodium phlegmaria,)
Balanga, (Ocymum,)
Chandana, (Sirium myrtifolium.)

Mix this with honey and ghee. Soon after a purgative is to be given. In the third stage give *Agada* internally as an errhine, and collyrium.

In the fourth stage give *Agada*, and ghee.

In the fifth stage give *Agada* with honey, and a decoction of liquorice.

The sixth stage is to be treated as a case of Dysentery.

In the seventh, errhines of *Agada* alone, are to be used.

In all the stages the antiphlogistic treatment is to be followed, with ghee and honey. Conjee water is also to be given, mixed with a decoction of

Kakátukí, (Diospyros tomentosa,)
Agníka, (Premna integrifolia,)
Pátá, (Sida lanceolaria,)
Surgíbalí, (Cleome pentaphylla,)
Amertá, (Menispermum cordifolium,)
Abayeá,
Surísa, (Sinapis dichotoma,)
Kíníhí, (Achyranthes aspera,)
Sála, (Shorea robusta,)
Haridrá, (Curcuma longa,)
Dár Haridrá, (Curcuma zanthorrhizon,)
Punanabbá, (Trianthema monogynia,)
Huranu,
Tríkatí, (Monetia barleroides)
Sáriba, (Periploca Indica,) and
Ballá, (Pavonia odorata.)

Poisons introduced into a wound, as by a poisoned arrow. The part quickly swells, blood flows, and from time to time pus is evacuated. The wound becomes of a black colour, and dirty round it, with a bad smell and sloughing. The person is very thirsty, faintish, with fever, and the body becomes very hot. The same symptoms will be produced when poison is placed over a sore.

II. *Animal Poisons.*

Serpents. Poison is found in all parts of the serpent, but when they are irritated the poison collects in the hood like teeth, when they snap with the head erect, they lodge the poison in the wound; but when the head is turned upside down they do not convey the poison into the wound. The poison is very acid and hot, and for preventing its effects, every thing cooling should be employed.

There are some serpents (*Dibya* or heavenly) which poison the air by their breathing, and by their sight. Others are called *Bhauma,* which live in holes in the ground, and the poison is in their teeth.

Sushruta does not mention the symptoms, and cure of the first kind; as they kill by their breathing and sight, and the method of preventing their effects is not known. The *Básuki, Takhyak,* &c. belong to the first kind of serpents. It is this class, that are supposed to support the world on their heads, and when angry may destroy the whole world. Of the second class, their names, the symptoms which their bites produce, and their antidotes are as follows:

There are eighty kinds of *Bhauma,* serpents, which are again divided into five classes.

1. *Dabíkara,* or hooded snakes.
2. *Mandalá,* with figures of round arches on their bodies.
3. *Rajalámanta,* with longitudinal lines.
4. *Nírbísa,* without poison.
5. *Quíranja,* or mixed class; which combine the peculiarities of several of the others.

Certain animals have poison in their teeth and nails; such as dogs, monkeys, cats, snub-nosed aligators, frogs, a kind of fish called *páka mucha,* guanas, a shell-fish *(sambuka),* and lizards.

Others have poisonous urine and fæces, as

Chipita,
Phíchataka,
Kasháyabásika,
Sarsapabásika,
Totaka, and
Kaundilyaka.

Musíka or rats have poisonous semen. Spiders *(Luta)* have poisonous saliva, urine, and fæces; and their bites, and scratches are poisonous.

Brischika (centipede), *Bissambara, Rajíbámacha* (a fish), *Uchírangá* and *Samudra Brischika* have poisonous stings.

The *Chitrasira, Sarabakurdí, Satadaruka, Animadaka,* and *Sarikamukha,* convey poison by breathing, by biting, by urine, and by fæces. The bones of animals killed by poisonous arrows, and the like; the bones of serpents, and of the fish called *Baratí,* produce poisonous effects when eaten.

Makkíka, a kind of flea, *Kanaba,* and *Jaliká* (a kind of leech), are poisonous by biting.

The fishes called *Sákulí* and *Raktarájí,* have poisonous bile.

General Symptoms.—There are some kinds of serpents that only produce diseases of air, others of bile, and a third kind of phlegm; accordingly diseases of air are produced by serpents of the *Baghís* (*Darbíkara*), or hooded kind, the diseases of bile by those of the *Mandalá* kind, and the derangement of phlegm is produced by those of the *Rajalá* kind.

The *Baghí* leaves a black colour in the wound, with the symptoms of various air diseases. They are known by being hooded. The following symptoms are present. The skin, eyes, nails, teeth, urine, and fæces, and the part which is bitten, become black, with roughness of the body and heaviness of the head; pain in the joints, weakness in the loins, back, and neck; gaping, shivering, alteration of voice, languor, hiccough, thirst, foaming and sluggishness of the circulation; and the secretions, and all the external passages are closed.

The bites of the *Mandala* serpent produce in the part a yellow colour. It swells, is painful, and soft; accompanied with the following symptoms: thirst, stupidity, fainting, fever; blood is discharged from the mouth and anus, and gangrene occurs in the bitten part. These serpents are shining, and are marked with different circles over the body.

The *Rajíla* serpent produces a swelling, a glistering grey-colour of the part, and the blood is thick, accompanied with the various symptoms of diseased phlegm. They are distinguished by the longitudinal lines along their bodies.

There is a fourth kind of serpents called *Nirbísa,* or serpents without poison.

Should a serpent bite a person under the sacred *pipul* tree, near a temple, where bodies are burnt, on a holy hill, on a white-ants nest, during the two hours in the evening and morning when the sun is disappearing, where four roads meet, towards the south of the house, or if the person is bit on his birth-day, in the temples, or in vital parts of the body, he will not recover.

The bites are also dangerous when the food in the stomach is not digested, when the body is labouring under a bilious disease, when the person is fatigued and languid from heat, when the person is affected with a discharge from the urethra; in pregnant women, in old, weak, sickly, or hungry persons; and during rainy and cloudy days. In these cases practitioners must be careful in undertaking the treatment of such patients, as they will be rarely cured. This will also be the case when no blood follows cutting the part, and when the person is senseless so that no weals are produced by the strokes of a whip, or horripilation after throwing cold water on the body. The following symptoms are likewise unfavorable: when the tongue is black, the hair falls off, the nose and mouth become changed in their shape, the voice is altered, and the bitten part becomes black and red, or tetanus supervenes; when thick mucus proceeds from the mouth, or when the blood is discharged from the mouth and anus, and there are the wounds of four teeth.

The hooded snakes are quickly fatal in their effects.

When after being bitten the person is insensible with other bad symptoms, as a stoppage of the throat, the body becoming blue, and the feet and hands immoveable, the disease will be fatal.

These poisons first derange the blood, producing a blackness of the part, and a feeling as if ants are moving upon the surface of the body.

2. The poison affects the flesh, and produces a blackness and swelling of different parts of the body.

3. It next affects the fat.
4. It enters the viscera and organs.
5. The bones.
6. The marrow and lastly semen, which is followed by death.

Treatment of Snake bites. When the extremities are bitten immediately apply a tight bandage above the bitten part. This may be a piece of cloth, a piece of leather, the flexible bark of a tree, or the like; so as to prevent the poison entering into the system. When a bandage cannot be so applied the bitten part is to be cut out. In all cases cutting out the part, sucking the wound with a horn, or burning the part is highly proper. When the mouth is used for sucking place a piece of bladder over it first, and then suck. Different prayers *(mantras)* are to be used as the bandage is applied; but a scientific man should not rely on *mantras*, as other means should be used, as antidotes, &c. to prevent the effects of the poison. When the poison has reached the head, the person should be bled; and cold water prepared with *Chandana* (Sirium myrtifolium, a fragrant wood), and *Usíra* (Andropogon muricatum, a cooling root), is to be used for bathing, and internally the different antidotes are to be given mixed with honey. If these antidotes are not at hand, give the black earth of ants nests, or *Sirisa* (Mimosa Siris), and *Karbudára* (black helibore); and avoid spirits or wines. Fluids that cause vomiting are of use, as the poison is thus removed from the system. If these means do not succeed, then bleed the person, and give *Azída* with honey and ghee. The errhines and collyria are likewise of use, when made of different antidotes. In the fourth stage give emetics, followed by barley corn for food. In the fifth and sixth stages use an antiphlogistic treatment, and in the seventh give strong errhines, as ammonia, &c.

The above treatment is applicable to the other, as well as to the hooded-snake bites; but when the class of *Rájíla* serpents have inflicted the bite, bleed, and then give the antidotes as above mentioned. When the treatment is not successful, and the person is insensible, make a crucial incision on the crown of the head, and apply to it a piece of recent flesh of an animal; then exhibit errhines, make a loud noise to rouse the person, and when his senses return give him a strong purgative. The antidotes should be continued for some time after the symptoms have disappeared, otherwise the violent symptoms will be liable to recur.

The following are varieties of *Azída*, or mixtures of antidotes for the cures of poisons, particularly of snakes. Take of

Trivrit, (Convolvulus turpethum,)
Bishalá, (Aconitum ferox,)

Madaka, (Bassia latifolia,)
Haridrá, (Curcuma longa,)
Dára Haridrá, (Zanthorrhizon,)
Raktá, (Nymphœa odorata,)
Arjúna, (Terminalia alata,)

The five salts, with long-pepper, black-pepper, and ginger powder, are to be mixed with honey, and kept in a close vessel. They are to be given internally in water, and used at the same time as a collyrium, and errhine. This is considered as the most efficacious antidote known.

The following is an antidote for animal and vegetable poison:—Take of

Bíranga, (Verbesina prostrata,)
Pátá, (Sida lanceolaria,)
Trifolá, (the varieties of myrobalan,)
Ajamodá,
Hingu, (Asafœtida,)
Chakrá, (Citrus decumanus,)

Mix with black-pepper, long-pepper, dry ginger, and the different kinds of salt. Reduce them to a powder, mix them well with honey, and keep them in the horn of a cow. This is to be shut with a piece of *pith,* and keep it so for a month. It may be used as an antidote for animal, vegetable, and mineral poisons. It is called *Azíta,* or never failing antidote.

Different other varieties of these antidotes are given in *Sushruta,* &c. but these two are considered the most efficacious.

When animals are affected by animal poisons, their bodies become swollen, they are sluggish, and saliva proceeds from their mouths, with pain in the chest. In the third stage there is pain in the head they cannot support: and

4th. The body shivers, they become insensible and die.

Birds when affected with poison first become sluggish, senseless, and die.

Poisons do not affect cats, nor the mongoose.

Poisonous rats. The symptoms of different kinds of these poisons is given in the medical *shástras.* When they discharge their semen upon any part of the body, the blood is affected, and produces different glandular swellings, blotches, and eruptions. In other cases erysipelas accompanied with pain, fever and fainting, followed by debility, loss of appetite, difficult breathing, and vomiting. In these cases *Sirisa,* (Mimosa Siris,) and *Kusta,* (Strychnos Nux Vomica,) are to be taken internally, with impure potassa made of the wood *Palása.* In these cases bleeding is recommended with purgatives and emetics. The parts first touched by the poison are to be burned or scarified, and over the part a mixture of *Sirisa* (Mimosa Siris), *Rajani* (Cleome corocana), *Kusta,* (Strychnos Nux Vomica), *Kunkuma* (Crocus sativus), and *Amrita* (Menispermum cordifolium), is to be applied.

The Bites of Mad Dogs.

When a dog, a jackal, a fox, a wolf, a bear, or a tiger become mad they foam at the mouth, which remains open, their tails hang down, they do not hear or see well, and saliva flows from their mouths. In such a state they snap and bite each other. The part that is bitten becomes senseless, blood flows from the wound which becomes black, and the other appearances are observed, as when wounded with a poisoned arrow. The person bitten makes the same kind of noise and movements, as that of the animal which has bitten him. When such a person sees the shape of the animal which has bitten him either in water, or in a glass, it is an unfavourable symptom. It is also unfavourable when the person is afraid of water, and dreads either seeing or hearing it. This is called *Jalatrása* or hydrophobia, the fear of water. When the person dreams of the rabid animal, it is unfavourable. Towards the termination of the disease the person is convulsed, becomes insensible, powerless, and dies.

Treatment. In all cases the first part of the treatment should be to scarify the part, and squeeze out the blood, after which the part is to be burnt by means of hot ghee. Then apply to the wounded part *Azida,* or a mixture of antidotes, and give old ghee internally. Errhines are also to be given with the milk of the *Arka* plant, (Calotropis gigantea.) Apply also the *Sitá, Punarnabá,* (Trianthema monogynia,) *Dhatura,* (Datura metel,) or the flesh of animals; and *Til* oil, jagry, milk of *Rupiká* mixed and applied to the wound. By such means the poison may be destroyed soon after the infliction of the wounds. In other cases take two *tolás* of the following root—

Sharapunkhá, (Trophis aspera,)
Dhatura, (Datura metel.)

Let one *tolá* be mixed with flour of rice and water, and wrap up in the leaves of stramonium. Roast it into cakes, and give it to the patient. The quantity is not stated. After taking this medicine other bad symptoms may occur, which may however disappear without any other remedies. During the treatment the patient should be kept in a cool situation, without any water. When the symptoms disappear the person should then bathe, and on the third and fifth days the above cakes are to be administered in half the dose given at first. He is then to take rice and milk. It is recommended in these cases to act powerfully on the system by strong medicines, before the poison has produced its constitutional effects. After the infliction of the wound, and before it has produced any constitutional effects, the free use of water in bathing is recommended, and the bowels are to be afterwards opened by purgatives and emetics, followed by errhines to clear the passages.

The Poison of Insects.

These poisons are divided into four classes, one of which derange the air, another the bile, a third the phlegm, and a fourth, or a combination of the three former symptoms.

There are 18 insects which derange air; as a kind of cricket *(Urchingará)*, the centipide *(Satabáhu)*, &c.

2nd. There are 24 of the second class which derange bile, as the wasp *(Barati)*, the bee *(Bhramara)*, &c. This class produce great heat and pain in the part wounded.

3rd. There are 13 of this variety, which derange phlegm; such as the bug (*Kutuba*), and other like insects.

4th. There are 12 varieties of this class of insects, the bites of which are very dangerous, as they affect the three humors, such as *Tunginása, Bihilaka*, &c.

The bites of venomous insects thus produce a derangement of the air, bile, and phlegm of the body, and the wounds are inflamed, brown, red, yellow, or black, according to circumstances. They are sometimes followed by fever, diarrhœa, vomiting, thirst, or a burning sensation over the body. Sometimes there is a shivering, the glands proximate swell, and patches of eruptions or erysepelas appear over the body.

Different kinds of flies, gnats, mosquetos, ants, &c., produce a painful itchiness, and swelling of the part bitten.

Scorpions. There are three varieties of these bites, according as they are mild, strong, and very strong. Those which are generated in dunghills are not so poisonous as those generated in bricks, and dry places. Those generated in the putrid carcases of serpents, and other venomous animals, have the most violent poisons. There are twelve kinds of the first class, three of the second, and fifteen of the third, or dangerous kind. The symptoms resemble those produced by the bites of serpents. The weak kinds produce pain, swelling, followed by shivering and fever, with perspiration, and stiffness of the body. The second class produce swelling of the tongue, so as to prevent swallowing, fainting, and much pain.

The third, or most dangerous class, produce delirium, fever, burning of the body, a discharge of black blood from the nose, and other parts of the body. In this case the person soon dies.

Treatment. In mild cases apply oil (*Chakartaila*); warm water prepared with *Bidári*, (Gmelina Asiatica,) and other sedative vegetables. Apply to the part a poultice made of the antidotes, the powder of turmeric, salt, long and black pepper, dry-ginger, and *Sirisa*, (Mimosa Siris.) It is also recommended to apply the juice of the lemon, cow's urine, with the leaves of *Sirisa*; or apply cow-dung after it has been heated. Give internally honey with ghee, or milk with sugar, or cold water with sugar, and different kinds of sherbats.

Spiders. It is stated that *Bishwámitra* made *Bashistha* angry on some occasion, and the perspiration which fell from his head fell in drops upon the grass, and in it the spiders were generated. These spiders are therefore called *Lutá*, from being generated in grass intended for the cow. There are sixteen varieties, eight are cured with difficulty, and eight are incurable. The names of the first eight are given, and they produce head-ache, itchiness, pain, and swelling of the part, followed by hot fever and diarrhœa, with derangement of phlegm and air. The eight other varieties produce sloughing of the part, discharge of blood, fever, burning, looseness, and diseases of the three humors. The general appearance of these eruptions over the body, are in the form of blotches or swellings. Some of them are large, others are soft or red, and others black. They pass from one part of the body to another. The first day after the bite there is no change of colour in the part, which feels itchy. The second day the part swells, and the third the characteristic symptoms of the poison develope themselves. The constitution is affected on the fourth day, and on the fifth and sixth all the severe symptoms appear. On the seventh day the person dies, when the poison is strong. If the poison remains in the upper part of the stomach it produces diseases of phlegm and air; and if in the stomach, the diseases of air and bile, when the hair falls off. Cloudy, windy, and cold weather increase the violence of the poison. These poisons produce drowsiness, languor, and pain in different parts of the body, and indigestion. Blotches appear over the body, the person loses flesh, his hands and feet swell, followed by faintness, vomiting, diarrhœa, sonorous breathing, thirst, fever, spasm, and swelling of the abdomen *(Anáha)* with delirium. Each variety is treated in a particular manner according to the symptoms. It is, however, unnecessary to descend to these particulars. The part should be cut out, and the actual cautery should be applied to the wound. The part is then to be rubbed with honey, and salt, or *Azída*. The person is also to have purgatives, and emetics administered to him; and should there be much swelling, apply leeches. In all the varieties of spider-bites apply *Azída* to the part.

The red lizard produces a black tinge and grey colour, or mottled colour over the body. This is accompanied with delirium and diarrhœa.

Frogs if seized by a serpent and escape, and bite a person, the person's hair stands on end, severe pain is felt over the body, and the part is insensible. The part swells, and small pimples appear on the part, with vomiting and drowsiness.

Fish poison produces great heat, swelling, and severe pain.

Leeches when poisonous produce an itchiness, and swelling of the part, with fever and fainting.

When poisons .have been taken and the person gets well, it is known by his feeling well, the different fluids are healthy, his appetite, urine, dejections are of the natural colour, the body has the natural appearance, as also the senses and mind, and they act properly.

Emetics for Poison. Drink goat's milk, after the poison has been taken, until the person vomits; this is to be repeated until it does not produce this effect, when no more poison is present. Black coloured poison is never to be used as medicine.

Weak Poisons, (*Apabísha.*) There are seven varieties of these poisons.

Vegetable Poisons.

Hemp, (Gánjá or *Grinjá.)* The extract of hemp combined with opium is employed by the Hindus, for enabling them to commit fearless actions. It throws them into a state of ferocious madness, when no crime stops, and no danger terrifies. The fanatics whom the old man of the mountain intoxicated in this manner (*Hechíki*), to prepare them to commit assassinations.* A mixture of tobacco and the extract of hemp, *(Gánjá pitu)* acts as a poison of a very strong kind. For preventing these effects, ghee, the juice of the sugar-cane, raisins, sugar, water and honey are recommended; after sour articles have been given to produce vomiting. The symptoms it produces are fever, insensibility, thirst, swelling of the abdomen, difficulty of breathing, cough, dryness of the mouth, &c. The mouth is to be washed with sweet, sour, and bitter substances, which will improve the senses, and its effects on the heart; and the bad particles of the poison which get into the brain will be discharged. For doing this more effectually, as is supposed, incisions are sometimes made into the crown of the head, with the fanciful intention of discharging the pernicious smoke. During the cure hot articles of food are avoided, and light food and ghee, and the like is proper.

* J. Hammer Mem: de l'Orient.

Dhatura, (Datura metel,)
Amrita, (Aconitum,)
Aiphena, (Opium,)
Karabíra root, (Nirium odorum,)
Arka, (Calotropis gigantea,)
Lánguli, (Gloriosa superba.)

All these poisons are purified by being boiled in hot milk, or in water mixed with cow-dung for half an hour ; and the kernel of the seed is generally used internally, mixed with other stimulating medicines. Thus *Jaypal* (Croton seeds), when it has been so boiled, is mixed with pepper, vermilion, and other medicines. This mixture is given in small doses in the beginning of fever. Datura is prepared in this same way, mixed with other medicines and used as a narcotic and stimulant. Euphorbium *(Síhunda),* and the root of the Abrus precatorius, Oleander (*Karabíra*), Helibore *(Kata ki),* and the different varieties of aconitum are prepared by reducing the roots to small pieces, soaking them in cow's urine, and three days before it is to be used removing it from the liquid ; dry it in a strong heat, and administer it at first in doses the size of a mustard seed, increasing it for seven days, and then diminish the dose. A leprous person may take one *gunja,* which is about the weight of one *rati,* or one and a half grains. When this poison has been administered in too large doses give goat's milk, which will produce vomiting, and thus remove the poison from the stomach. The dried bile of fish, of goats, buffaloes, wild boars, and peacocks are used, and are administered as stimulating medicines. These five varieties of bile are much employed as stimulants. They are purified by being macerated in the juice of lemon. (These different poisons with Croton seeds are the chief ingredients in the celebrated " *bis bari*" or poisonous pills.)

Nux Vomica (*Kusta, Kupilu*) is prepared by being steeped for three days in conjee-water. It is then mixed with mustard oil and other medicines, and is used by the moderns as a powerful internal medicine in small doses, and as an external application for the cure of leprosy.

Bitumen (*Silájatu*), *Petrolium* (*Boomutylum*), are got in hills in which gold and silver are found. It has the smell of cow's urine, and is bitter, salt, and cold. It is usually mixed with different other medicines, is supposed to have an alterative effect, and may be advantageously used in the cure of all diseases.

The most common manner in which it is employed is as an external application in rheumatic complaints, and in cases of epilepsy, hysteria, and palsy. See Celsus, lib. 3, cap. 5.

Poisons should be taken internally in the quantity of a mustard seed for the first day, and increase it for seven days, adding the same quantity each day. For the next seven days a quantity equal to a mustard seed, is to be given less each day. The third week a quantity equal to a barley-corn in size is to be administered, and increase one each day for seven days; and the fourth week each day one less is to be given for seven days. No more is to be given unless in cases of leprosy when the size of a *rati* is to be given. Poison is to be taken with milk, it is not to be given to very hot-tempered persons, to those with deranged bile, to eunuchs, or to patients with bloody-sputa. When the person has a great appetite, or is very thirsty; when greatly fatigued, when any of the humors *(dhátu)* are weakened during pregnancy; in the house of a rájá, or when there is a violent quarrel with the patient and another person, poisons must not be used in the treatment of diseases.

The mineral poisons may likewise be used in a diluted form as medicines. Such as the

Rasa-carpura, (corrosive sublimate,)
Gadanta, (yellow orpiment,)
Tuta, (sulphate of copper, &c.)

The last poison is prepared as a medicine in the following manner. Mix it with half its weight of sulphur, expose it to heat for two hours. It may then be used in medicine, and it will neither produce vomiting nor giddiness. The other poisons when prepared so as to diminish their power, may be employed with advantage in the cure of many diseases.

The *weak poisons*, such as

A'kunda, (Asclepias gigantea,)
Segdutra, (Euphorbia,)
Bislánguli, (Nama zeylanica,)
Karabíra, (Cleome pentaphylla,)
Gusinga, (Rondeletia cinerea,)
Dephena, (saliva of serpents,)
Noki, (Pontedera vaginalis,)

and other sweet smelling drugs. These are divided according to their colour and form, as like animals, ears, &c. They are mixed with cow's litter, honey, and conjee; are boiled, or made into a powder. They are to be washed in pure water, and dried in the sun.

None of the above poisons should be given to a person under ten, or above eighty years of age. The teachers should take a dose, so as to remove the fears and doubts of the pupils.

Spirits are a kind of poison which, when taken in moderate quantities, and with food, produce good effects, being heating, pungent, subtile, light, placid, and drying. They act quickly, and increase semen. When in large quantities these qualities act unfavourably on the humors, and instead of strengthening the body they will destroy it. Spirits, like medicine, when taken in a proper manner, restore appetite and strength to the body. When taken with butter and rice, flesh, or other food, they increase the person's life beyond the period written at the individual's birth, by strengthening, and increasing the person's health. When drank in large quantities it increases so much the internal heat, that it deranges the humors, and the person becomes mad. His sense becomes deranged, and whatever he fancies to do he will not desist from; as singing, telling secrets, speaking nonsense, &c. When spirits are not drank according to rule, it produces different effects. There are three stages of drunkenness. In the first stage the person feels very happy, and strong. The energy of his body is increased, as also the acuteness of the senses, memory, appetite, and sleep. The person can apply to abstruse books, can play on instruments, and sing better than usual.

2nd. After these symptoms, the mind is obscured and memory deficient, the person speaks and works badly, and the person becomes like a fool. At his work his mind is not quiet, he is always lazy, sleepy, and is like a drunkard.

3rd. Then he goes after women, or persons that are respected; his father, mother, &c.; unnatural articles are eaten, and the person speaks every thing, and takes no care of his body or goods.

4th. He becomes quite foolish, and falls to the earth like a piece of broken wood. He can do nothing, knows nothing, and lives like a dead man. If a good man, he can no longer perform good actions.

When cooling substances are eaten, or such food as does not increase phlegm, as oleaginous substances, the person will not become so easily drunk. Habit diminishes the susceptibility very much, but becomes liable to the attacks of the most fatal diseases, with severe pain. He also becomes passionate, fearful, thirsty, and melancholy. His body becomes covered with sores, &c. is constipated, and he is fond of eating sour things. In weak persons the body becomes hot, and the habit so bad as to produce various diseases.

When nothing is eaten with the spirit, he soon becomes drunk, accompanied with the diseases produced by great grief. When the person is very angry, and drinks spirit; as also when very fearful, severe diseases are produced; when very thirsty, or when there is great grief, or when he is very hungry and spirits alone are taken. When violent exercise, as fencing, &c. is taken, or when fatigued with walking, spirits are very bad; as also when the stomach, urine, &c. are constipated, or when very sour things have been taken, or what has been eaten is not digested, spirits will produce dangerous diseases. When the person is weak, when the body is very hot from the sun, &c. When the air is deranged, different substances of a heating nature may be given with the spirit and salt. Spirits with emetics, are also used; avoiding sour articles. All these produce severe diseases of various kinds. Such as *Pánátya, Parammada, Pánárjírna* and *Pánárbibhrama*, in which the body is hot and heavy, has no taste, and there is much cough, no appetite, with a constipated state of the dejections and urine. In *Pánárjirna* the body is hot, head-ache, thirst, pain in the joints, swelling of the abdomen, sour belching, &c.

When air is diseased by spirits, there is pain in the limbs, and the mind is deranged, hiccough, noisy breathing, head-ache, and severe pain in the side, such a person has no sleep, becoming delirious. When bile is deranged, thirst, heat of the body, fever, sweating, and *meha* are produced. When urine is deranged, *Atisár* (diarrhœa), *Abaran* (no memory), and the skin becomes of a green colour. In such cases phlegm is vomited, the person has no appetite, with nausea, and dozing. He has cold fits, and the body is heavy.

When the three are deranged, they produce all the symptoms of the separate diseases, with one named *Pánátya*. The secondary effects of ardent spirits are *Parammada* with deranged phlegm, which is discharged from the body, and the mouth. The body feels heavy, and the mouth has a bad taste with constipation, dozing, no appetite, thirst, head-ache, and the joints are pained.

Pánárjirna, or Indigestion, is a consequence of the free use of spirits. The stomach swells, with much vomiting, the body is hot, he complains of head-ache, the spirit is not digested, and *Ajirna*, in all its forms are produced.

Pánárbibhrama. Symptoms of deranged bile; with pain of the chest and body, vomiting, fever, head-ache, and cough; muaus is discharged from the mouth and nose; the trachea feels like smoke to the person, and the body hot. In such cases none of the usual food, especially of rice and articles from which spirits are produced, is to be given. When a person in this disease appears as if drunk he will die of it. When the mouth of such a person is twisted or otherwise unnatural, the body is cold, but is supposed by the person to be hot, the mouth the colour of oil, the tongue, lips, teeth, of a dark colour, or blue, and eyes yellow or red, hiccough, or fever, vomiting, or shivering, pain in the sides, cough, forgetfulness, he will not recover.

Dáha (Inflammation), spirits producing heat, derange the blood, and bile of the skin and produce this disease. The medicines that cure bile when deranged, cure this disease. The following varieties are described:

1. The first variety affects the skin.

2. This variety affects the blood; producing a wrinkled and dry state and copper colour of the skin with thirst. The smell of the body and mouth resembles that of blood, and the body is hot, like that produced by fever.

3. When bile is deranged it is like the fever which this produces when deranged: and the varieties are the same.

4. This resembles the last. The thirst is not gratified from the person's foolishness, the heat of the internal and external surface of the body is increased. The throat, palate and lips are dry, and the tongue is thrust out of the mouth with shivering of the body.

5. When much blood is collected in the abdomen, great heat is produced.

6. When much of the elements are discharged from the body, a form of this disease is produced. When *dáha* occurs the person swoons, is thirsty, mucus is discharged from the nose and throat, and he cannot work. In other cases when severe, and a physician does not see the patient, he dies.

7. Sensible parts when wounded or bruised produce a kind of this disease, which is not cured, as blows on the temples. In all the above forms when the interior of the body is hot, and the exterior is cold, the disease is always dangerous.

Class XI.

Small diseases are arranged under the following heads.—(Locales.)

1. *Ajagalliká.*—Small tuberculous eruptions of the form of peas. It occurs in children.

2. *Jabaprakhia* are hard fleshy eruptions, like the grains of barley. They are produced by diseased phlegm and air.

3. *Andálaji.*—Round elevated pimples containing matter, produced by diseased phlegm and air.

4. *Bibritá.*—An eruption like the ripe fig with inflammation.

5. *Kachhapiká.*—Five or six tumors of the shape of turtles; produced by diseased phlegm and air.

6. *Balmiká,* are tumors in the soles of the feet or palms of the hand, or in a joint, or in the neck, axilla, and other parts. They increase by degrees, like the hills of white ants; and are surrounded with painful and itchy ulcers, and accompanied with a discharge.

7. *Indrabriddhá.*—Tumors surrounded by small eruptions, like the inside of a water-lily.